THE
PHILOSOPHY
BOOK

THE PHILOSOPHY BOOK

FROM THE VEDAS TO THE NEW ATHEISTS, 250 MILESTONES IN THE HISTORY OF PHILOSOPHY

Gregory Bassham

STERLING
New York

STERLING
New York

An Imprint of Sterling Publishing Co., Inc.
1166 Avenue of the Americas
New York, NY 10036

ISBN 978-1-4549-1847-9

Distributed in Canada by Sterling Publishing Co., Inc.
c/o Canadian Manda Group, 664 Annette Street
Toronto, Ontario, Canada M6S 2C8
Distributed in the United Kingdom by GMC Distribution Services
Castle Place, 166 High Street, Lewes, East Sussex, England BN7 1XU
Distributed in Australia by Capricorn Link (Australia) Pty. Ltd.
P.O. Box 704, Windsor, NSW 2756, Australia

For information about custom editions, special sales, and premium and corporate purchases,
please contact Sterling Special Sales at 800-805-5489 or specialsales@sterlingpublishing.com.

Manufactured in China

2 4 6 8 10 9 7 5 3 1

www.sterlingpublishing.com

Image Credits: see page 523

Contents

Introduction

Philosophy has a long and exciting history. In some ways, however, it is an unusual history. In fields such as science, mathematics, medicine, and engineering, the major milestones can generally be viewed as unequivocal advances: stones are added to an ever-more-impressive edifice of knowledge. In philosophy, the milestones are more like insightful and thought-provoking comments in a Great Conversation. In this Conversation, one finds many fascinating insights and much food for thought, but not much—it must be admitted—in the way of indisputable knowledge or agreement. To some, like controversial American editor and satirist H. L. Mencken (1880–1956), this is a sign of failure. "Philosophy," said Mencken, "consists largely of one philosopher arguing that all the others are jackasses. He usually proves it, and I should add that he also usually proves that he is one himself." There is some truth in this remark, for philosophy is, in large part, a story of vaulting ambitions and humbled reckonings. Philosophers have sought answers; what they have found are mostly questions. This in itself is highly instructive. As Socrates (c. 469–399 BCE) vividly reminds us, a conversation that ends inconclusively can still be very much worth having. In philosophy, success is not measured in terms of clear-cut "advances" that can be added to a growing body of knowledge. Its successes lie largely in the questions themselves, and in the rich and vibrant conversations those questions can provoke as they become increasingly sophisticated and complex.

In brief, there is a special relationship between philosophy and its milestones. In philosophy, the milestones are not like buoys in a receding wake, never again to be seen as philosophers bravely sail on into uncharted new waters. Rather, the milestones are significant contributions to an ongoing conversation. In that discussion, great thinkers like Plato (c. 428–c. 348 BCE), Aristotle (384–322), Immanuel Kant (1724–1804), and David Hume (1711–1776) are not simply mute figures in a philosophical mausoleum; they are living voices in a fascinating dialogue that extends far into the past and will continue, one hopes, well into the future.

The Nature and Scope of Philosophy

What is philosophy? What are its proper tasks? These are themselves philosophical questions, open to debate. In early Greek philosophy, there was no clear distinction between philosophy and science. Philosophy was simply "the love of wisdom," and it encompassed any field in which significant insights into the human condition and our world were believed to be found. Over time, the scope of philosophy progressively narrowed, culminating in the ultraminimalist view of some twentieth-century linguistic philosophers that philosophers are glorified lexicographers and concept analyzers, with no role to play other than as parsers and elucidators of language. Most contemporary philosophers adopt a view somewhere in the middle between these very broad and very narrow conceptions of the proper scope of philosophy.

Though philosophers often deal with issues that may seem quite technical and hairsplitting, at its core philosophy still deals with the big questions of life that exceed the ken of the physical and social sciences: Why am I here? Does life have meaning? Does God exist? Is there life after death? Can I know what true reality is? How should I live? What should my goals and values be? What is a good society? Philosophy remains most electric and vital when it remains in close contact with these big existential questions.

The Value of Philosophy

If philosophy is not, as I have suggested, a path to definite knowledge and assured ultimate truth, wherein lies its value? Its chief benefit is in the way it disciplines, enlarges, and humbles the human mind.

Philosophy disciplines the mind by introducing it to a regimen and a thought world in which standards of reasoning, argumentative rigor, clarity of expression, critical scrutiny, and logical coherence are much higher than they are in ordinary life. By means of this regimen, our powers of thinking, reasoning, and effective expression are greatly augmented, and we develop defenses against the nonsense and illogic that bombards us from the media, on the Internet, and in our daily lives.

Philosophy also enlarges the mind by expanding our intellectual horizons and exposing us to visions of reality and of the good life that we may never have thought without it. In philosophy we encounter (to adapt nineteenth-century British poet Matthew Arnold's phrase) "the best that has been thought and said" about questions of meaning, value, and the urgent existential questions of life. As we grapple with life's mysteries, reading the great thinkers of the past can be of immense value. As American philosopher Tom Morris (b. 1952) has noted, these thinkers are like "native guides" who have thoroughly and skillfully explored territories that are all new to us. In studying the great philosophers, we can also achieve a better understanding of the important ideas and intellectual traditions that have shaped our world today.

Finally, philosophy humbles the mind by bringing home the depth, intricacy, and difficulty of the great questions. In many ways, the story of philosophy is a narrative of humbled ambitions. Time and again, great thinkers have claimed to discover ultimate truth, only to be shot down in flames. The lesson to be drawn from this is not that philosophy is a waste of time (Mencken's view), but that philosophy is tough sledding and rarely can produce definitive answers beyond dispute. Realizing this is itself an important kind of wisdom.

Chronology and Principles of Selection

The "milestones" in this volume are significant ideas, events, and works in the history of philosophy. I have arranged these in chronological order, providing precise dates whenever possible, and approximate dates when precision is impossible. Since this is a book written for general readers, I have included some works (e.g., the *Vedas* [c. 1500 BCE], Ecclesiastes [c. 300 BCE], and Sigmund Freud's *The Future of an Illusion* [1927]) that are only broadly philosophical, and I have omitted some twentieth-century thinkers (e.g., Michael Dummett, Alfred Tarski, and David Lewis) who are of interest chiefly to professional philosophers. By training, I am an analytic philosopher; not surprisingly, therefore, I have omitted some important European philosophers of the twentieth and twenty-first centuries (e.g., Jacques Lacan, Gilles Deleuze, Paul Ricœur, and Julia Kristeva) that an editor with continental proclivities would likely have included. I have endeavored to be inclusive in featuring a good number of Indian, Chinese, Islamic, and women philosophers, though doubtless I could have included many more. For these omissions and others I can only apologize and plead ignorance; no one can hope to be knowledgeable on every major philosopher, and I thought it the better part of valor to focus on those thinkers I know. Finally, readers will note that I have included entries not only on individual philosophers, ideas, and works, but also on major events that have powerfully shaped the course of philosophy (e.g., the birth of Christianity, the Renaissance, and the growth of modern science). I thought this important because no adequate understanding of philosophy can be achieved by focusing on isolated thinkers and individual achievements. Philosophy is embedded in streams of social and political life, and it both shapes and is shaped by larger cultural forces. I hope I have conveyed some sense of this rich and complex interaction.

Acknowledgments

I am grateful to all the professors who have taught me the history of philosophy, most especially Ken Merrill, Tom Boyd, J. N. Mohanty, Stewart Umphrey, R. T. Wallis, Paul Brown, Stephen Wykstra, John Robinson, Phil Quinn, Alfred Freddoso, and Neil Delaney. My colleagues Bernard Prusak and Bill Irwin have provided helpful feedback on their areas of expertise. I am grateful to them, and to my wife, Mia, without whose love and support this book could not have been written. At Sterling Publishing, for their courtesy and skill, I am most grateful to project editor Barbara Berger, acquiring editor Melanie Madden, photo editor Linda Liang, prepress designer Rich Hazelton, and jacket designer and director Elizabeth Lindy. Special thanks also go Katherine Furman and Ashley Prine of Tandem Books.

The Vedas

It is impossible to pinpoint when philosophy first began. Most histories of philosophy written by Westerners begin with the ancient Greeks. As American philosopher-historian Will Durant remarked, Hindus and Chinese "smile at our provincialism." More than two thousand years before the earliest glimmerings of philosophical thought in Greece, the Egyptian statesman Ptahhotep was writing golden pearls of wisdom to his son. But as good a place as any to begin a chronology of philosophy is with the ancient Hindu scriptures, the Vedas, which were composed roughly from 1500 BCE to 500 BCE.

The Vedas are a large collection of texts consisting mostly of hymns, prayers, chants, and ceremonial instructions. Many different approaches to religion are found in the Vedas, including polytheism (many gods exist), monotheism (only one god exists), monism (there is one absolute reality), and even agnosticism (it is impossible to know whether any gods exist). The most philosophical parts of the Vedas are the Upanishads, which were written about 800–400 BCE. There you find many traditional themes of Hindu philosophy discussed in depth, including reincarnation, karma, the idea that the world as we experience it through the senses is illusion (*maya*), liberation of the soul (*moksha*), the transcendental self (Ātman), and absolute Reality (Brahman).

Although it took many centuries for the idea to come into clear focus, the central concept of the Upanishads is that Ātman is Brahman, and Brahman is Ātman. Ātman is our ultimate, transcendental self—our deeper or truer self. It is permanent, unchanging, and the ultimate source of all knowledge and consciousness. Brahman is absolute, transcendent Reality, ungraspable by words or the rational mind, but knowable through direct experience. The most staggering insight of the later Vedic philosophers is *tat tvam asi* (thou art that): you, at your deepest core, are identical with Brahman. This is a form of monism, the belief that all reality is one. Later Hindu philosophers, such as Shankara (c. 788–c. 820) and Ramanuja (trad. c. 1017–1137, alt. c. 1077– c. 1157) , developed this idea with great subtlety and sophistication.

SEE ALSO Reincarnation (c. 540 BCE), No-Self (*Anatta*) (c. 525 BCE), The Bhagavad Gita (c. 400 BCE)

The sacred river of India, the Ganges, at sunrise; the creation of the Upanishads began during the late Bronze Age in the heart of northern India, bounded by the Ganges to the east and the Indus River to the west.

Birth of Western Philosophy

Thales (c. 625–c. 545 BCE), **Anaximander** (c. 610–c. 546 BCE),
Anaximenes (fl. c. 545 BCE)

Socrates said that "philosophy begins in wonder." In Western civilization, philosophy began when a group of Greek sages in the Aegean seaport of Miletus sought to satisfy their sense of wonder by asking new kinds of questions. Instead of relying on mythology and supernatural forces to explain nature, these thinkers began to use reason and observation. This marked the beginning of science as well as philosophy.

Thales has traditionally been regarded as the first Western philosopher. He was one of the Seven Wise Men of Greece and was reputed to have studied in Egypt, where he learned geometry. Some early sources claimed he successfully predicted eclipses. One anecdote relates how Thales was mocked by a servant girl for falling into a well while stargazing; perhaps to demonstrate that he was no absentminded professor, it is also said he was the first to show that there are 365 days in a year.

Thales asked whether there is some basic "stuff" out of which everything is made, and concluded that there is. Everything is made of water, he claimed. Why he believed this is unclear. Perhaps he was impressed by the fact that water can be a solid, a liquid, or a gas. Aristotle speculates that Thales was struck by the linkage between water and life, noting that seeds, for example, always contain moisture. Whatever the reasons, what is important is the kind of explanation Thales was looking for. Here, for the first time in recorded history, someone was trying to explain the natural world entirely in terms of natural phenomena.

Thales inspired others to seek similar explanations. His follower, Anaximander, suggested that the fundamental stuff is not water, but an indeterminate substance he called the *apeiron*, Greek for "boundless" or "indefinite." Not long after Anaximander, another philosopher from Miletus named Anaximenes—apparently impressed by the fact that air can become more or less dense—speculated that everything is some form of air. From such seemingly unpromising beginnings, the Western philosophical quest began.

SEE ALSO Anthropomorphization (c. 530 BCE), Atoms and the Void (c. 420 BCE)

A nineteenth-century engraving of Thales of Miletus, considered by many to be the first Western philosopher.

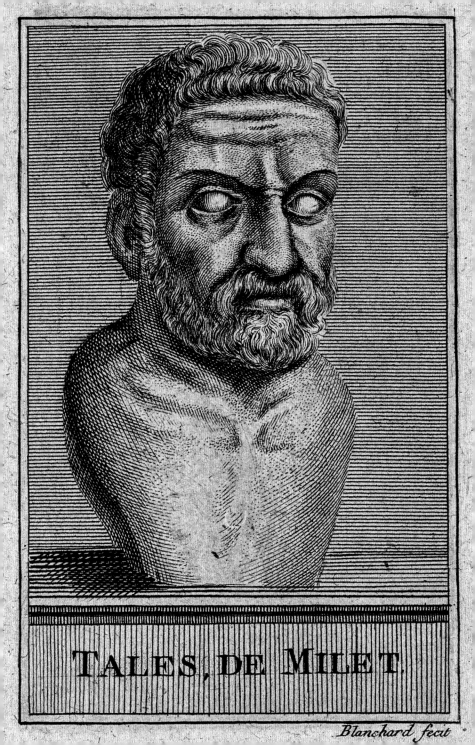

TALES, DE MILET.

The Dao

Laozi (fl. c. 550 BCE)

Chinese civilization has been shaped by three major traditions: Confucianism,
Buddhism, and Daoism. The oldest of these may be Daoism, but it is difficult to sa
because the origins of Daoism are shrouded in mystery and legend.

According to Chinese tradition, Daoism was founded by the sage Laozi aroun
550 BCE. Laozi is the reputed author of the classic Daoist text the *Dao De Jing* (C
of the Way and Power), a short book full of memorable aphorisms and profound say
but not easy to understand. There is a point to this ambiguity, however, for Daoists
believe that life itself is inherently mysterious. Ultimate Reality, they claim, canno
grasped by words or concepts; it can only be felt in the pulse in moments of tranqu

The central concept of Daoism is that of the *Dao* ("the Way"). The Dao mean
at once, the way of ultimate Reality, the way of the universe, and the way that hum
should order their lives. It is the ineffable and transcendent ground of all existence
yet it is also immanent; it orders and flows through all things. To live well is to live
harmony with the Dao, and this means to live simply, naturally, and contentedly in
way attuned to the rhythms and harmonies of nature.

In many ways, Daoism is the direct opposite of Confucianism, which is the mo
influential tradition of Chinese wisdom. The strong emphasis Confucianists place
on book learning, active government, and elaborate ritual are all rejected by Daois
They favor a natural, spontaneous approach to life. This idea is captured in the Da
concept of *wu wei*, or "effortless doing." Wu wei literally means "inaction" or "non-
doing," but it is not a recipe for do-nothing passivity. Rather, it is a counsel for letti
things happen naturally and without meddlesome interference or unnecessary con
Daoists believe that people often mess things up when they try to "fix things" by pa
too many laws or by trying to micromanage people's lives. In most cases, they claim
more can be accomplished by means of a less activist, more yielding approach.

SEE ALSO Confucian Ethics (c. 500 BCE), Cynicism (c. 400 BCE)

A monumental statue of revered Daoism founder Laozi at Mount Qingyuan in the city of Quanzhou, on
coast of southeast China.

Reincarnation

Pythagoras (c. 570–c. 490 BCE)

We have little definite information about Pythagoras. He left no writings and many legends sprang up about him after his death. It is certain, however, that he had a huge impact on Western civilization. What we do know is that Pythagoras was born in Samos, a small island off the coast of what is now Turkey, very close to Miletus. In midlife he moved to Croton, a major Greek colony on the coast of southern Italy. There he established a quasi-monastic community, open to women and men, which was dedicated to both religious and intellectual pursuits. One of the few surviving quotations attributed to Pythagoras is that "friends have all things in common."

So far as we can tell, Pythagoras was one of the first Western thinkers to believe in metempsychosis, or reincarnation. Though the evidence is uncertain, he seems to have held that the body is the soul's "tomb," that the soul is weighed down and polluted by the impurities of the body, and that the soul is fated to be reborn again and again into human and animal bodies until it finally shakes itself free from the wheel of rebirth by living a pure and religious life.

Pythagoras is famous, of course, for proving the Pythagorean theorem in geometry. Like Plato, he believed that mathematics elevates the mind and helps it to focus on what is eternal and divine. He also taught that mathematics is crucial for understanding the physical world, for nature is an organized harmony that (as Galileo would later say) is written in the language of mathematics. It was claimed that he also coined the term *philosophy* ("love of wisdom") to designate the rigorous intellectual work that was necessary to purify the soul and raise it to the level of divinity.

Pythagoras is also important because of his influence on Plato. Plato's beliefs in a separation of mind and body, in reincarnation, in the immortality of the soul, in the corrupting influences of the body, and in the role of philosophy and mathematics in living the best kind of human life and achieving spiritual fruition are all strongly Pythagorean. Plato is unquestionably one of the most important thinkers in Western civilization, and therefore, indirectly, so too is Pythagoras.

SEE ALSO The Vedas (c. 1500 BCE), Ahimsa (c. 540 BCE), No-Self (*Anatta*) (c. 525 BCE), Mind-Body Dualism (c. 380 BCE)

Pythagoras, likely the earliest Western thinker to believe in reincarnation and, legendarily, one of the earliest proponents of the round-earth theory, is shown resting his hand on a globe in this vintage engraving.

PYTHAGORAS.

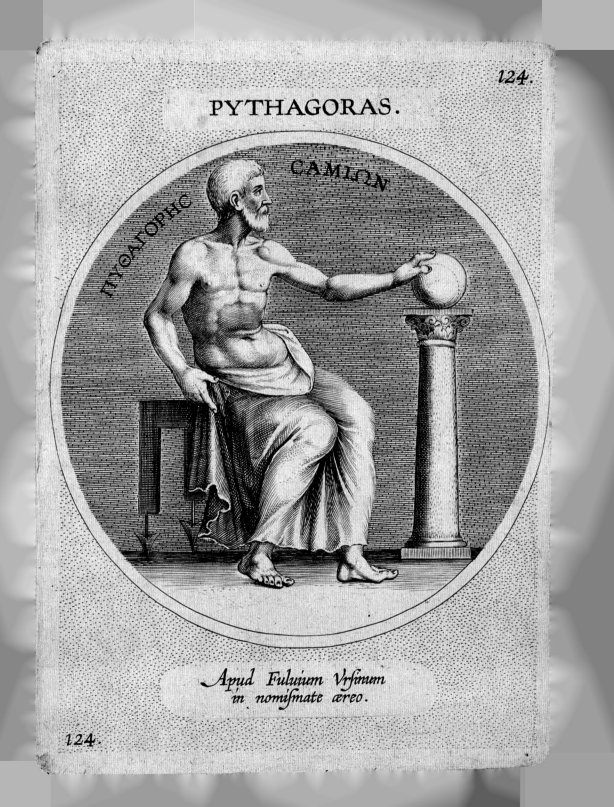

ΠΥΘΑΓΟΡΗC   CAMIΩN

Apud Fuluium Vrsinum
in nomismate æreo.

Ahimsa

Nataputta Vardhamana (Mahavira) (c. 599–c. 527 BCE)

The sixth century BCE was an exciting time to live in India. The Hindu Upanishads were being written around this period, and two major religions emerged as reactions to the orthodox schools of Hinduism. One was Buddhism; the other was Jainism, which was founded by Nataputta Vardhamana, known as Mahavira ("Great Hero" in Sanskrit), sometime in the middle of the sixth century BCE, though some scholars think it was a few decades later.

According to Jain sources, Mahavira was born in 599 BCE in northeastern India, not far from present-day Nepal. Following a privileged upbringing as part of a royal family, Mahavira decided at the age of thirty to renounce the world and seek enlightenment. Few have ever done so with greater determination. For over twelve years he wandered naked all over India, practicing extreme bodily austerities and carefully avoiding all harm to other creatures. Finally, in his early forties, he achieved complete enlightenment and release (*moksha*). For the next thirty years he taught others the path to liberation that he had discovered. He ended his own life, at age seventy-two, by voluntary self-starvation.

Like Hindus and Buddhists, Jains believe in karma and reincarnation. The ultimate goal of life, they hold, is to liberate the soul from karma and rebirth. The way they seek to do this is by practicing asceticism (self-denial, nonattachment) and trying to avoid all injury to other life forms. Jain monks pursue this path in a particularly rigorous way, taking five vows that include celibacy, complete nonpossessiveness, noninjury or nonviolence (*ahimsa*), truthfulness, and refusing to take anything that isn't given to them. Lay Jains are allowed to marry and pursue a more moderate (but still extremely disciplined) lifestyle of renunciation.

Jains believe that all living things have souls, and they take great care to avoid any unnecessary killing or harm. Mahavira himself reportedly used a broom to gently sweep the ground in front of his feet, lest he should tread on any tiny creatures. This idea of ahimsa greatly influenced many Indian schools of philosophy.

SEE ALSO The Vedas (c. 1500 BCE), Reincarnation (c. 540 BCE)

A miniature painting depicting Mahavira, founder of the Jain religion, from a c. 1503 manuscript of the Kalpa Sūtra, *a sacred Jain text.*

Anthropomorphization

Xenophanes (c. 570–c. 470 BCE)

Homer (fl. c. ninth or eighth century BCE) was more than a poet to the ancient Greeks. He was a revered moral and religious sage. It therefore must have created quite a stir when Xenophanes, a traveling philosopher-poet, attacked him with both guns blazing.

Xenophanes accused Homer of maligning the gods by casting them in human shape and endowing them with moral failings, such as theft and adultery. He noted that humans anthropomorphize the gods, imagining that they "are born and have clothes and voices and shapes like their own," but Xenophanes believed this is simply a human conceit. For "if oxen, horses, and lions had hands or could paint with their hands and fashion works as men do, horses would paint horse-like images of gods and oxen oxen-like ones, and each would fashion bodies like his own."

Xenophanes was born around 570 BCE in Colophon, a city about fifty miles north of Miletus in Asia Minor. When the Medes conquered Colophon in 546 BCE, Xenophanes was expelled and fled west. He spent the rest of his long life as a wandering bard, primarily in Italy and Sicily, reciting his own poems as well as others'. Perhaps it was during his travels that it dawned on him how humans everywhere seemed to shape the gods in their own image. As he wryly noted, "the Ethiopians consider the gods flat-nosed and black; the Thracians blue-eyed and red-haired."

In truth, Xenophanes believed "there is one god, among gods and men the greatest, not at all like mortals in body or mind." Some scholars believe that Xenophanes identified god with the world, viewing the entire cosmos as a living, conscious, and divine being. If so, he would be the first Western philosopher to embrace a form of pantheism.

Refreshingly, Xenophanes was modest about his philosophical and religious musings. He wrote, "Certain truth no man has seen, nor will there ever be a man who knows about the gods and about everything of which I speak; for even if he should fully succeed in saying what is true, even so he himself does not *know* it, but in all things there is opinion."

SEE ALSO Birth of Western Philosophy (c. 585 BCE)

In ancient Greece, the gods were usually depicted in idealized human form—a fallacy according to Xenophanes—such as in this c. 400 BCE votive frieze known as the Relief of the Gods *from the Sanctuary of Artemis at Brauron, in southeastern Greece. From left to right are Zeus, Leto, and their children Apollo and Artemis.*

The Four Noble Truths

Siddhārtha Gautama (Buddha) (c. 560–c. 380 BCE)

The foundation of Buddhism is veiled in clouds of myth and uncertainty. What we do know is that Buddhism was founded by Siddhārtha Gautama, who lived and taught in southern Nepal and northern India sometime around the sixth or fifth century BCE. Born the son of a wealthy king, Siddhārtha lived a life of luxury before becoming discontented in his late twenties and deciding to leave home to seek his enlightenment. For six years he practiced meditation and severe bodily austerities but did not find the answers he was looking for. Finally, he sat under a fig tree one day and resolved not to get up until he had achieved enlightenment. At dawn, the Great Awakening occurred and he became Buddha ("the enlightened one"). He gathered a community of disciples and spent the next forty-five years teaching the liberating path he had discovered.

What was this secret to inner peace that Buddha discovered? It is encapsulated in his "Four Noble Truths": life is suffering, the cause of suffering is selfish craving (*tanha*), suffering can be overcome, and the way to overcome suffering is by following the Eightfold Path (right views, right aspiration, right livelihood, and other beliefs and practices that signal a serious commitment to the Buddhist lifestyle and path of liberation).

Though Buddhism has become encrusted with speculative doctrine, Buddha himself always maintained a "noble silence" about metaphysical issues. One of his disciples commented, "Whether the world is eternal or not eternal, whether the world is finite or not, whether the soul is the same as the body or whether the soul is one thing and the body another . . . the Lord does not explain to me." What Buddha taught was a practical therapy for rooting out the persistent causes of unhappiness and discontent. He recognized that people live in chains forged by their own hands. We suffer because we are self-centered and thirst after empty pleasures and things we cannot have. Once we liberate ourselves from all clutching desires, we are free, Buddha said, to "cultivate love without measure toward all beings."

SEE ALSO The Vedas (c. 1500 BCE), No-Self (*Anatta*) (c. 525 BCE), Stoicism (c. 300 BCE)

Buddha is said to have reached enlightenment under a fig tree (a sacred tree whose name in Sanskrit is "Bodhi," or enlightenment, *tree) in Bodh Gaya, India, the most sacred city in Buddhism. The Great Buddha statue of Bodh Gaya is shown here; completed in 1989, it stands 80 feet (25 meters) tall.*

No-Self (*Anatta*)

Siddhārtha Gautama (Buddha) (c. 560–c. 380 BCE)

In Buddha's time, like today, Hinduism was the major religion of India. Buddha agreed with some Hindu teachings, including the doctrines of karma and reincarnation, but rejected others. Among these was the Hindu idea, found in the Upanishads, of a permanent soul or self (Ātman) that is ultimately identical with the absolute Reality (Brahman). By contrast, Buddha taught that there is no soul or self in the sense of a self-identical ego, a substance that endures over time. This idea of no-self (*anatta*) is a central teaching of Buddhism, one of the three so-called "marks of existence," or dharma seals.

Buddha believed that what people call a soul or self is really only a temporary bundle or aggregation of mental and physical features (*skandhas*). These include body, perception, feelings, consciousness, and instincts or predispositions (some of which are subconscious). These five constantly changing features more or less hang together as an integrated unit while we are alive, but they do not constitute a "thing" or an "entity," and at death they dissolve or disperse. There is no soul, or "me," that survives death. This raises an obvious problem for Buddha's belief in karma and reincarnation. For if there is no enduring soul or self, what is it that gets reincarnated into another form and is the bearer of karma? Buddha's answer was that a kind of karma-laden psychic structure carries over into the next life, yet this is not a soul or self but simply an information-bearing packet of habits, predispositions, and so forth that survives death and forms the basis for a person's next incarnation.

Buddha's denial of a permanent self is related to another key teaching of Buddhism: impermanence (*anicca*). Buddha taught that reality is an ever-changing phantasmagoria, a flux in which nothing is permanent. Everything is constantly changing, so that nothing remains literally "itself" or "the same" from one moment to the next. This is part of why Buddha denied the existence of a permanent self. As he saw it, change is such a fundamental feature of empirical reality that each of us is literally a different person each second of our lives.

SEE ALSO The Vedas (c. 1500 BCE), The Four Noble Truths (c. 525 BCE), *A Treatise of Human Nature* (1739)

In Tibetan Buddhism, the concept of impermanence—a key teaching of Buddhism—is symbolized by sand mandalas: complex, sacred diagrams symbolizing the cosmos. They are painstakingly created by monks with grains of colored sand, and then ceremonially disassembled and poured into nearby bodies of water to carry their blessings.

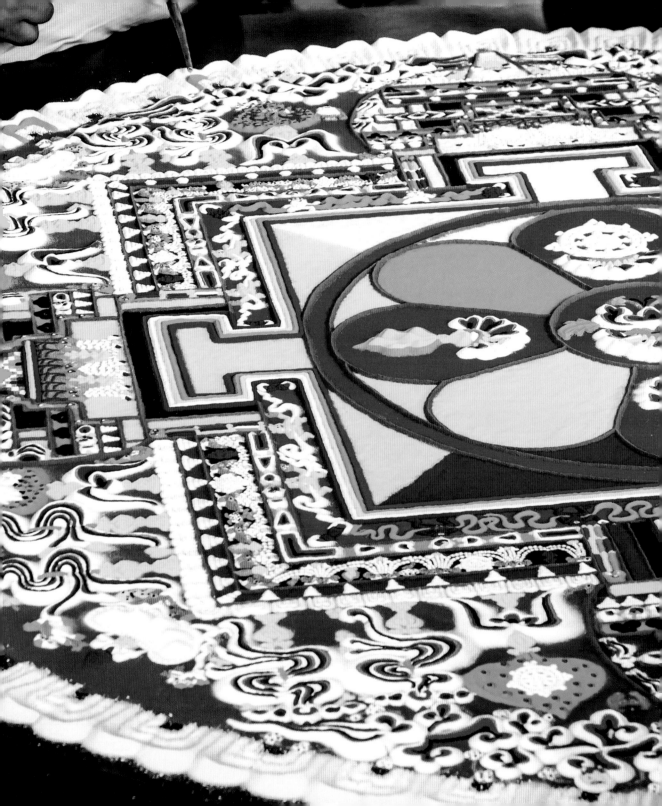

Confucian Ethics

Kong Qiu (Confucius) (551–479 BCE)

Without question, Confucius is one of the most influential philosophers in human history. For more than two millennia, he has molded the Chinese mind and way of life.

"Confucius" is a latinized form of Kong Fuzi ("Master Kong"); his real name was Kong Qiu. He was born in the mid sixth century BCE near present-day Qufu, in south-central China, and grew up poor following the early death of his father. After holding a series of menial jobs, he opened a school and became a teacher during what was a turbulent period in Chinese history, filled with constant warfare and social disorder. Throughout his long career as a teacher and public servant, Confucius sought to restore peace, good governance, and a strong social fabric to China. He believed that the key to any healthy society lies in building strong families, educated leaders, and ethical individuals. Most of his teaching focused on these themes.

Confucius looked back to an earlier period of Chinese history, the era of the so-called Sage-Kings, that he believed provided a model of a good society. This was a period when rulers led by example and displayed *ren* (benevolence, love) toward their subjects. It was also a time when people displayed both *li* (proper manners and ceremonial behavior) and *xiao* (respect for one's parents, elders, and ancestors).

The stress Confucius laid on proper ritual and ceremony may be puzzling to Westerners. Why have elaborate rules about how many times one should bow, how tea should be served, how long one should mourn the death of a parent, and so forth? Confucius believed that such rules help to order our minds, calm our passions, and show proper respect to one another. They are outward symbols of inner harmonies and proprieties.

Confucius's greatest contribution to Chinese culture may lie in the field of education. Largely because of his influence, China and other Eastern cultures have historically placed great importance on educational achievement, learning, and respect for teachers. Many Asian nations, including China, South Korea, and Singapore, observe "Teachers' Day" as a national holiday. In Taiwan, Teachers' Day falls on September 28, Confucius's presumed birthday.

SEE ALSO Reciprocity (c. 500 BCE), Revival of Confucianism (c. 1180)

A statue of Confucius at Beijing's Guozijian, or Imperial Academy, which was founded in 1306 and closed in 1905.

Reciprocity

Kong Qiu (Confucius) (551–479 BCE)

Confucius was a humanist in the sense that he focused mainly on practical human concerns and said very little about spiritual matters or the ultimate nature of reality. The core of his teaching deals with questions of ethics and politics. With respect to ethics, Confucius was a thinker far ahead of his time. One example of this is his doctrine of reciprocity (*shu*).

It is said that one day Confucius's disciple Tse-kung asked, "Is there one single word that can serve as a principle of conduct for life?" Confucius replied, "Perhaps the word 'reciprocity' will do. Do not do unto others what you do not want others to do unto you." This is one of the earliest formulations of what is now called the Golden Rule. Most religions have some form or another of the rule. Jesus offers perhaps the most familiar version: "Always treat others as you would like to be treated" (Matthew 7:12). Confucius expressed essentially the same insight five centuries earlier, though he phrased the rule negatively ("Do *not* do unto others"), whereas Jesus stated it positively.

The Golden Rule may or may not be the most fundamental rule of morality, but it certainly captures something very basic about the moral life. It rules out any kind of irrational special pleading of the form "It's OK for me to do X, but not for anybody else to do it." It also impels us to empathize with others, to see and feel things from their point of view. This capacity for empathy is critical to human moral response.

Some critics reject the Golden Rule because they think it invites people to impose their own tastes and desires on other people. That, however, is a misunderstanding. What the rule really requires is that we try to imagine what it would be like to be in another person's shoes and then to act in accordance with that person's legitimate desires and needs. Thus understood, the Golden Rule does not compel us to satisfy desires that are, say, harmful or immoral, but only those that are reasonable and legitimate. This, of course, requires judgment, which we might get wrong. But that is true of many basic moral norms.

SEE ALSO Confucian Ethics (c. 500 BCE), Revival of Confucianism (c. 1180)

This Chinese stamp from 1989, commemorating the 2,540th anniversary of Confucius's birth, shows the great philosopher instructing his disciples.

Change Is Constant

Heraclitus (fl. c. 500 BCE)

Heraclitus is the most quotable of the pre-Socratic philosophers. From the 130 or so fragments of his writings that have survived, a vivid personality shines through: proud, passionate, contemptuous of the common herd, yet moved by a deep religious impulse to find unity in difference and order in apparent disorder. Like the Chinese sage Laozi, Heraclitus wrote in pithy, enigmatic aphorisms. For this reason, he was known in antiquity as Heraclitus the Obscure.

Heraclitus taught that all things are in flux. "Change alone is unchanging," he declared. Though some things appear to be permanent and unchanging, a closer look reveals that "nothing stands but for [time's] scythe to mow." "You cannot step twice into the same river; for fresh waters are ever flowing in upon you." "The sun is new every day."

Another way in which Heraclitus reminds one of Laozi is in his doctrine of the "unity of opposites." Both in nature and in human affairs, harmonies flow from the strife and tension of opposites. In the interplay of light and darkness, summer and winter, male and female lie the creative tensions that give meaning and richness to existence. "From things that differ comes the fairest attunement."

Heraclitus offered his own take on the much-debated issue of whether there is some fundamental "stuff" out of which everything is made. His answer was fire. In ever-living fire, constantly renewing itself and transmuting all things into itself, he saw the essential pattern of the world.

The deepest source of life's goodness and harmony, Heraclitus believed, lies in what he called the "Logos" (the Greek word *logos* means "word" or "reason"), the divine word or universal reason. The Logos was not a personal god, but a fiery divine force or process ordering all things for the best through creative strife. "To God all things are beautiful and good and just; but men suppose some things to be just and others unjust."

Heraclitus's doctrine of the Logos, or universal reason, was picked up by the Stoics and contributed significantly to their teaching. It also was taken up, and given a fundamentally new interpretation, in the famous opening words of the Gospel of John: "In the beginning was the Word [*Logos*], and the Word was with God, and the Word was God."

SEE ALSO The Dao (c. 550 BCE), Change Is Illusory (c. 470 BCE), Epictetian Stoicism (c. 125)

Heraclitus, known as the Obscure or the Weeping Philosopher, in a painting by Dutch artist Hendrick ter Brugghen from 1628.

The Book of Job

Nineteenth-century Scottish historian Thomas Carlyle thought the biblical book of Job, which deals with the perennial problem of life's injustice, was "one of the grandest things ever written with a pen." It was axiomatic in Hebrew theology that God rewarded the good and punished the wicked, yet there was no belief in heaven or hell at the time Job was written. It follows, then, that God's perfect justice must prevail on earth. Yet is it not obvious, as soberly noted in Psalm 73:12, that it is the "ungodly, who prosper in the world"? The book of Job wrestles with this problem without finding an intellectual solution. Job does, however, find something even more important.

The book of Job is framed around an ancient folktale. In God's heavenly court, Satan suggests that Job is pious and upright only because God has blessed him with good fortune. As a test, God permits Satan to inflict upon Job a slew of calamities. His children, servants, and animals are killed, and he is afflicted with terrible boils. Three friends of Job come to comfort him but without success. They try to convince Job that he must have committed some great sin to deserve such grievous punishment. Job, however, holds firm and insists on his own innocence and the greatness of God. Finally, God himself appears and speaks to Job out of a whirlwind. What does Job know about God and his ways? Where was Job when God laid the foundation of the earth and "all the sons of God shouted for joy"? (Job 38:7). Job admits that he has uttered what he did not understand and repents "in dust and ashes." God then restores Job to prosperity, blesses him with ten new children, and Job dies an old man, "full of days."

In the end, Job offers no philosophical solution to the mystery of suffering. Indeed, it seems to suggest that no such solution can be found. But by the conclusion of the book Job has received something far more important than intellectual understanding: personal communion with God. In this way, "patient Job" is presented as a model of the person of faith.

SEE ALSO Ecclesiastes (c. 300 BCE), Soul-Making Theodicy (1966)

Job is tormented by demons in this seventh-century engraving by Lucas Vorsterman after Peter Paul Rubens.

Change Is Illusory

Parmenides (fl. c. 470 BCE)

Parmenides is a giant among the pre-Socratic philosophers. Plato called him "venerable and awful" and praised his "glorious depth of mind." Parmenides has been characterized as the world's first metaphysician, and he was the first to offer a sustained deductive argument for a philosophical conclusion. His thought marks a watershed in Greek philosophy and largely reset its agenda.

Other than that he was a native of Elea in southern Italy, little is known about Parmenides. According to Plato, late in life Parmenides traveled to Athens, where he matched wits with the young Socrates. Like several pre-Socratic philosophers, he wrote in verse. Only about 150 lines have survived.

Parmenides defended the startling idea that change is an illusion. Although our senses indicate that things change, logic tells us that change and motion are impossible. Whatever is real must be eternal, uncreated, and unchanging. The very idea of change, Parmenides argues, is contradictory. Change implies transformation from "what is" (for example, a green leaf in summer) into "what is not" (such as an orange leaf in autumn). But "what is not" is nothing, and nothing is a complete lack of existence, a void. Thus, change is impossible because there is no "nothing" into which something could change. For similar reasons, being ("what is") must be eternal. If being comes into existence, it must arise from either being or nonbeing. It cannot arise from nonbeing because nonbeing is nothing, and nothing can come from nothing. Nor can it arise from being, because then it would already exist rather than come into existence. Despite what our senses tell us, therefore, reality must be static. All that exists is "the One": eternal, uncreated, unchanging Being.

Parmenides's astonishing claims were controversial: Many later philosophers tried to answer him in one way or another. Others became fervent disciples and sought to elaborate his cryptic arguments. Plato offered a famous compromise, suggesting that Parmenides was wrong in thinking that change is impossible but right that nothing changes at the highest level of reality (the so-called "Realm of Being"). But perhaps most importantly, Parmenides set an example of closely reasoned logical argumentation that profoundly influenced Western philosophy.

SEE ALSO Change Is Constant (c. 500 BCE), The World of the Forms (c. 380 BCE)

A rare fragment of Plato's Parmenides on parchment, written by a scribe in the third or fourth century.

Mind Organizes Nature

Anaxagoras (c. 500–c. 428 BCE)

Anaxagoras came from Clazomenae, a coastal town north of Ephesus in Asia Minor. In midlife he moved to Athens, where he taught for many years, thus becoming the first in a long line of distinguished philosophers to make Athens their home. He wrote a book titled *On Nature*, which so shocked religious conservatives that he was tried and convicted of impiety. Saved by his friend Pericles, he fled to Lampsacus in northern Asia Minor, where he opened a school and died an honored citizen. Among his happier legacies was a month-long holiday in which the students of Lampsacus were let off school.

Anaxagoras believed that all things are composed of tiny particles or "seeds." These particles come in an indefinite number of kinds, and everything that exists contains some of each element. So, for example, water contains elements of fire, earth, and every other sort of element. What we call a thing is based on which element predominates in that thing. Thus, we call something "fire" because it is made up mostly of fire particles.

Anaxagoras also taught that the universe originated from a primeval chaos. What caused the universe to become organized was Mind (*nous*), a corporeal substance composed of the finest and purest of material elements that, unlike other things, is mixed with nothing. Mind produces a rotation that separates out the elements, creating objects such as stars and planets. All living things contain and are ruled by Mind, which has "complete understanding of things" and "the greatest power," and is henceforth conscious and intelligent, and presumably divine.

Plato and Aristotle considered Anaxagoras's theory of Mind to be a great philosophical advance. They complained, however, that Anaxagoras makes very little use of Mind, resorting to mechanical explanations whenever he can and invoking Mind only as an original source of motion. Nevertheless Anaxagoras deserves great credit for distinguishing mind from matter, for groping toward a concept of a purely immaterial substance, and for introducing the idea of Mind as a source of nature's apparent "design."

SEE ALSO Survival of the Fittest (c. 450 BCE), The World of the Forms (c. 380 BCE), Hume's *Dialogues* (1779)

Plato, Anaxagoras, and Democritus debate the mysteries of the universe (although Plato was born later than the other two philosophers) in this miniature painting from an early illuminated manuscript.

platon.   Auaragoras   moriu

460 BCE

Around 470 BCE, Parmenides astonished educated Greeks by arguing that reality is completely static. There is a conflict, he claimed, between logic and our senses. Our senses tell us that things move and change, but reason forces us to conclude that the very ideas of motion and change are self-contradictory. Since our senses can deceive us, we should trust our reason and conclude that reality consists of a single eternal, unchangeable, indestructible sphere that Parmenides calls the One.

As outlandish as this view seems, it attracted some brilliant defenders. One was Zeno of Elea, who accompanied Parmenides on a visit to Athens in 450 BCE. Zeno formulated a whole slew of arguments to show that Parmenides was right. Some arguments were designed to show that a plurality of objects is impossible, while others attacked the concept of empty space or the reliability of the senses. The most famous were various "paradoxes of motion," which sought to prove that motion is an illusion. One of the best-known paradoxes is known as The Dichotomy, or The Race Course.

It goes like this: A swift runner could never complete a short race. Why? Because to win a race one must get to the finish line. To get to the finish line, one must first travel half the distance to the line, then three-quarters of the distance, then five-sixths, etc. Any finite distance can be divided into an infinite number of segments. That means that no runner could reach the finish line without passing through an infinite number of points in a finite amount of time. But that is impossible, Zeno argued, so no runner could ever finish a race.

Philosophers and mathematicians continue to debate Zeno's paradoxes today. In the big picture, what is more important than the paradoxes themselves is the manner in which Zeno argued for them. Aristotle stated that Zeno invented the art of "dialectic." By this he meant the type of argument strategy that was Socrates's stock-in-trade, namely, bringing out hidden contradictions or absurdities in a person's initial assertion. If Socrates did learn this technique from Zeno, then Zeno's contribution to Western philosophy was huge.

SEE ALSO Change Is Illusory (c. 470 BCE)

Survival of the Fittest

Empedocles (c. 490–430 BCE)

Early Greek philosophers often combined science and religion in ways that strike us as strange. The philosopher-poet Empedocles offers a prime example. He was born in Acragas (modern-day Agrigento), a Greek colony in Sicily. For a time he studied with the Pythagoreans, taking to heart their beliefs in reincarnation and vegetarianism. According to legend, Empedocles declared himself to be a god who had been condemned to a series of earthly rebirths as punishment for some celestial crime. It is said that he ended his life by leaping into the crater of Mount Etna to prove his immortality.

It is the scientific side of Empedocles's thought that is of more lasting significance. He was an eclectic thinker who sought to synthesize a number of conflicting views of his predecessors. For example, he agreed with Parmenides that reality must be eternal, material, and in some sense unchanging. At the same time, the reality of change is too obvious to be denied. His solution was to distinguish two levels of reality. At the micro-level there are four elements—earth, air, fire, and water—that are eternal and indestructible. These mix to form larger objects—trees, clouds, horses, and so forth—that undergo constant change. This doctrine of the four basic elements survived until the birth of modern science.

Empedocles also sought to explain natural phenomena in terms of two fundamental forces that he called Love and Hate. Love is a force of attraction that binds things together, while Hate is a force of repulsion that breaks them apart. For all eternity, these two powers wax and wane in endlessly repeating cosmic cycles.

To explain the origin of living creatures, Empedocles proposed a theory of evolution. Random mixing of the four elements produced bone, flesh, etc., which united to form primitive organisms. Because of the haphazard way these organisms were formed, most were oddly shaped and quickly died out. Through a slow process of natural selection and survival of the fittest, the better-adapted animals (including us humans) are here today. In recognition of his prescient theory, Empedocles earned a shout-out in Charles Darwin's *Origin of Species*.

SEE ALSO Change Is Illusory (c. 470 BCE), Mind Organizes Nature (c. 460 BCE), Darwin's *Origin of Species* (1859)

The philosopher-poet Empedocles—who supposedly declared himself to be a god—looks to the heavens in an early-sixteenth-century French engraving.

EMPEDOCLES PHILOSOFVS.

Protagoras and Relativism

Protagoras (c. 490 BCE–c. 420 BCE)

Protagoras was the first and greatest of the ancient Greek Sophists, a group of wandering teachers—or what we today might call life coaches—who traveled from city to city, offering to teach the art of personal success for a handsome fee. Protagoras practiced this profession for forty years and became rich and famous in the process.

In that period of Greek history, the path to power and success was effective public speaking. Protagoras was a master at giving speeches, and he claimed to be able to teach anyone "how to make the weaker argument the stronger." He had shocking ideas about many things, including religion. According to one source, Athens expelled him for writing a book in which he declared: "As to the gods, I have no means of knowing either that they exist or that they do not exist."

Protagoras was apparently the first Western philosopher to teach a radical form of relativism. He famously pronounced that "man is the measure of all things." What he meant by this is not completely clear, but most scholars believe he embraced an extreme form of subjectivism that rejects any notion of objective truth and instead leaves truth entirely up to the individual. Whatever seems true to a particular person *is* true for that person, and there are no belief-independent "facts" that could prove such a person wrong. As Protagoras's critics quickly pointed out, this implies that all beliefs are true, including the belief that all beliefs are *not* true. Protagoras stuck by his guns, but also asserted that even though all beliefs are true, it does not follow that they are equally useful. In particular, he taught there will always be a need for skilled teachers such as himself to teach the quickest and most advantageous ways to achieve worldly success.

Protagoras's radical relativism was seen as a threat to morals, religion, and civilization itself by many of his contemporaries. Great thinkers like Plato and Aristotle attempted to refute him by developing sophisticated theories of knowing and truth. Ultimately, Protagoras's most important legacy may be the great conversation he sparked.

SEE ALSO The Sophists (c. 450 BCE), Truth Is Subjectivity (1846)

In this eighteenth-century engraving, Protagoras (standing), the first and greatest of the Sophists, lectures the younger philosopher Democritus, kneeling at left.

c. 450 BCE

The Sophists

The Sophists were a group of wandering teachers who professed to teach how to achieve power and success in life, particularly through the art of public speaking. Protagoras was the first and greatest of them, but there were other well-known Sophists, including Gorgias of Leontini (c. 483–c. 376 BCE), Hippias of Elis (c. 485–c. 415 BCE), Prodicus of Ceos (c. 465–c. 395 BCE), and Thrasymachus of Chalcedon (c. 459–c. 400 BCE).

The Sophists were deeply polarizing figures in their day. Many were clearly brilliant men. Some made important contributions to grammar, rhetoric, dialectic, and other fields. Unquestionably they filled an important need, teaching people how to make an effective speech when speechmaking was the path to public success in democratic societies such as Athens. Perhaps most importantly, they contributed to the intellectual ferment of the golden age of Athens by challenging conventional ideas and fueling their era's passion for close reasoning.

At the same time, many Greeks regarded the Sophists as money-grubbing charlatans and threats to traditional morality and religion. Some, like Protagoras, taught a thoroughgoing relativism that rejected any form of objective truth or absolute values. Others, like Thrasymachus, taught that "might makes right" and that ethics is for saps. Prodicus argued that the gods were personifications of the sun, moon, and other natural objects, and was widely considered to be an atheist. Many Greeks were offended by the hair-splitting "sophisms" that Sophists sometimes offered to demonstrate their skill in reasoning. Gorgias published a book, now lost, in which he claimed to prove that nothing exists; that if anything exists it cannot be known; that if anything were known it could not be communicated from one person to another.

Socrates, Plato, and Aristotle were all deeply opposed to the Sophists and portrayed them in highly unflattering terms. Plato is by far our most important source of information about the Sophists, and he saw them as mortal threats to the ideals of objective knowledge, truth, and the values he held dear. Were his fears exaggerated? Was his portrayal of the Sophists overly negative? These continue to be issues of lively scholarly debate today.

SEE ALSO Protagoras and Relativism (c. 450 BCE), The Trial and Death of Socrates (399 BCE)

The Sophists touted the art of public speaking, or rhetoric. Here, German illustrator Georg Pencz personifies rhetoric in an engraving, c. 1550.

Ladder of Love

Diotima of Mantinea (fl. c. 450 BCE?)

In Plato's dialogue the *Symposium*, Socrates says he was taught "the philosophy of Love" by a woman, Diotima of Mantinea. Scholars debate whether Diotima really existed, but she might have. Although women generally had very low status in ancient Greece, many Greek philosophers were more broad-minded. Women and men were treated as equals in the schools of Pythagoras, Epicurus, and Aristippus, and Plato shocked his contemporaries by proposing that women should receive the same education and opportunities as men. Whether real or fictional, Diotima is credited with teaching one of the most sublime views of love in Western thought.

Diotima tells Socrates that there are lesser and greater mysteries of love. The lesser mysteries are that love is a desire for beauty and for the permanent possession of the good. Love is a divinely implanted impulse that subconsciously impels people to pursue immortality through having children, creating enduring works of art, and making lasting contributions to society.

The greater mystery is that love is a ladder. We begin by loving a single beautiful individual and conceiving fair thoughts about that person. Next we observe that attractive bodies are everywhere and that all physical beauty is the same, and so we become lovers of all beautiful bodies. As we mature, we come to see that beauty of soul is more worthy of love than beauty of body. Casting our gaze still wider, we perceive that good laws and institutions have a higher kind of loveliness than any form of personal beauty. But love of laws and institutions is still love of particular things. We must cast our gaze still wider to "the vast sea of beauty," so that we perceive the high beauty inherent in all knowledge and science, being inspired thereby to "create many fair and noble thoughts and notions in the boundless love of wisdom." Fortified by these thoughts, we catch a glimpse at last of beauty itself—perfect, eternal, and changeless; the source of all lesser beauties; and the ultimate object of all forms of love and desire. Love for beauty itself, Socrates says, is the highest and truest form of love; and those who strive for the noblest things in life "will not easily find a helper better than love."

SEE ALSO Universal Love (c. 420 BCE), The World of the Forms (c. 380 BCE)

Venus, the goddess of love, gazes at her beautiful reflection in a mirror held by Cupid, in a painting by Peter Paul Rubens titled Venus and Cupid, *c. 1606–1611. Diotima of Mantinea tells Socrates that there are lesser and greater mysteries of love and that we must cast our gaze to "the vast sea of beauty."*

Know Thyself

Socrates (c. 469–399 BCE)

Socrates is an iconic figure in Western civilization. It is remarkable what an impact this scruffy sidewalk philosopher had, both in his own time and through the centuries.

Socrates was born in Athens around 470 or 469 BCE. His father, Sophroniscus, was a stonemason or sculptor, and apparently was fairly well-to-do. As a young man, Socrates became convinced that the gods had commanded him to become a kind of philosophical missionary to his fellow Athenians. Except for periods in his forties when he served as a soldier in the Athenian army during the Peloponnesian War with Sparta, he spent his entire adult life in the streets of Athens, buttonholing anyone who would talk with him, exposing their shoddy and often inconsistent thinking, and encouraging them to join him on a quest for true wisdom and goodness. Since few people like to be shown up in public, Socrates naturally made plenty of enemies. In 399 BCE, a few years after democracy was restored in Athens following a brutal dictatorship, Socrates was put on trial for corrupting the youth and introducing strange gods into the city. He was convicted by a jury of five hundred fellow citizens and sentenced to die by drinking poison (hemlock). In prison, he spent his last days gaily discussing philosophy with his friends, refused an offer to escape, and met his death calmly and cheerfully.

One of Socrates's most constant watchwords was to "know thyself." As he went about talking philosophy on the streets of Athens, he became convinced that most people are overconfident in their beliefs. They think they know much more than they do. By being honest with ourselves and leading what Socrates called "an examined life," we can come to recognize our true condition: ignorance. Most people, Socrates taught, are in the grip of not only false beliefs but false values as well. We chase things like wealth, fame, status, and pleasure, when what really matters is wisdom and virtue. Only those who make a sincere effort to know themselves can recognize their true condition and be motivated to seek the wisdom they lack.

SEE ALSO The Trial and Death of Socrates (399 BCE), Socratic Dialogues (c. 399 BCE)

A nineteenth-century statue of Socrates by Greek sculptor Leonidas Drosis, in front of the Academy of Athens.

Atoms and the Void

Leucippus (fl. c. 440 BCE), **Democritus** (c. 460–c. 370 BCE)

The most influential philosophy of nature developed by the early Greek philosophers was atomism. The theory was first put forward by Leucippus, believed to be a native of Miletus, of whom we know very little. It was his student, Democritus of Abdera, Thrace, who really developed the theory.

Democritus was a prolific author, writing more than sixty books. (Unfortunately, none survive.) Among these were works on ethics, making him one of the first Western philosophers to think systematically about moral issues. Democritus believed that contentment was the goal of life. To achieve lasting happiness and freedom from disturbance (*ataraxia*), we should live a life of moderation and balance, cultivate our minds, and free ourselves from fear and superstition. Because of the stress he laid on "good cheer," Democritus was known to the ancients as "the laughing philosopher."

Democritus also taught that nothing exists except atoms and empty, limitless space, or void. Atoms (from the Greek *atomos*, or "uncuttable") were seen as tiny indestructible particles that come in an endless variety of shapes. Atoms are eternal and exist in infinite numbers. For all eternity, atoms have swirled in ceaseless motion, combining with other atoms of similar size and shape, and innumerable worlds were created and destroyed before the current one arose. There is no purpose or design in nature; the universe is a blind, deterministic process in which necessity rules over all. Humans and other animals originally arose from primeval mud and water. Humans have souls, made up of especially fine atoms, but there is no life after death; all life and thought are purely material phenomena.

The atomism of Leucippus and Democritus might have fizzled out like most other pre-Socratic philosophies of nature except that it was embraced not long after Democritus's death by Epicurus, who did much to popularize the theory. In Roman times, it got another boost in Lucretius's classic poem *On the Nature of Things*. As historian Will Durant remarked in summing up Democritus's achievement, Democritus "formulated for science its most famous hypothesis, and gave to philosophy a system which, denounced by every other, has survived them all, and reappears in every generation."

SEE ALSO Epicureanism (c. 300 BCE), *On the Nature of Things* (c. 55 BCE)

In 1628, Hendrick ter Brugghen created this painting of Democritus, the Laughing Philosopher, as a companion piece to his portrait of weeping Heraclitus (see page 32). Democritus stressed being of good cheer, an optimistic viewpoint in light of his belief that nothing exists except atoms and empty space.

Universal Love

Mozi (Mo-tzu) (fl. c. 420 BCE)

Mozi ("Master Mo") was an important critic of Confucianism who lived sometime around the end of the fifth century BCE. Very little is known about him. Since he was always defending the poor and criticizing the wealthy, he may have come from a lower-class family. According to one account, he studied with Confucianists but came to reject many of their characteristic teachings. Instead, he founded his own school, the Mohist school, and gathered round him a loyal band of pupils who were highly skilled at fighting and formed a kind of Robin Hood–force that protected the weak from the strong.

Mozi believed in a utilitarian approach to values. The ultimate test of an act or government policy is whether it benefits everyone. Many of the things Confucianists praised, such as elaborate and costly ceremonies, music, and in-depth study of the Chinese classics, Mozi condemned because they wasted time and money and did not benefit the common people.

Mozi is best known for his doctrine of universal love. He rejected Confucius's teachings that a peaceful and well-ordered society must be one in which social hierarchies are respected, and where our first loyalties must be to our parents, elders, rulers, and betters. Mozi believed that loyalties of this sort are a major source of conflict and often lead to indifference to the plight of the less fortunate. He taught that we should love and respect everyone equally. He wrote: "What is the way of universal love and mutual benefit? It is to regard other people's countries as one's own. Regard other people's families as one's own. Regard others as one's self."

Mozi believed that the gods practice universal love and so should we. To his mind, most of the bad things people do to each other are caused by selfishness, partiality, and lack of concern. The radical cure he proposed was akin to the type of universal, unselfish love (*agape* in Greek) preached by Jesus. Only when such love fills the world, Mozi believed, will the strong stop oppressing the weak, will the hungry be fed, and will peace reign.

SEE ALSO Confucian Ethics (c. 500 BCE), Reciprocity (c. 500 BCE), Ladder of Love (c. 450 BCE)

Mozi is shown on this detail of a stamp issued in China in 2000, as part of a series of six commemorative stamps honoring great Chinese ancient thinkers.

中国邮政 CHINA

古代思想家 孟子 南魯 80分

Cynicism

Antisthenes (c. 445–c. 365 BCE), Diogenes of Sinope (c. 412–323 BCE)

Some of Socrates's disciples admired him less for his teachings than for his example. One of these was Antisthenes, the founder of a philosophy known as Cynicism. He was a well-to-do Athenian who became one of Socrates's closest disciples. What Antisthenes admired most about Socrates was his moral independence, his disdain for money, fashion, and reputation, and the priority he placed on "improvement of the soul" over all else. After Socrates's death, Antisthenes opened a free school where he took such values and pushed them in a direction Socrates would not have approved. What Antisthenes taught is that civilization itself is bad and corrupting, that we should abandon government, marriage, and conventional morality and get back to a radically simpler and more natural way of living.

Antisthenes's pupil, Diogenes of Sinope, took his master's teaching to an extreme, prompting Plato to call him "Socrates gone mad." Diogenes lived on the street as a beggar, and relieved himself and had sex in public. Though he had no money or possessions, he claimed to be rich because he was satisfied with what he had. Seeing a child drink with his hands, Diogenes threw away his cup, saying "A child has beaten me in plainness of living." As an old man living in a barrel in Corinth, it is said that Diogenes was approached by Alexander the Great. "Ask of me any favor you choose," said Alexander. "Stand out of the light," replied Diogenes. "If I were not Alexander," said the young prince, "I would be Diogenes."

For understandable reasons, Cynicism was never a very popular philosophy in ancient times. However, some of its key teachings were embraced by the Stoics. These included an emphasis on minimizing desires, avoiding excessive attachments, and regarding virtue as the sole good and sufficient in itself for happiness. An austere brand of Stoicism, taught by Epictetus around the first century CE, was heavily influenced by Cynicism. Today, Cynicism is enjoying a modest revival as growing numbers of people look to simplify their lives either to escape the rat race or to live in a more earth-friendly way. Few, however, take it to the countercultural extremes of Diogenes.

SEE ALSO The Trial and Death of Socrates (399 BCE), Epictetian Stoicism (c. 125), *Walden* (1854)

Diogenes of Sinope was a radical proponent of Cynicism. He is said to have lived in a barrel and, upon being approached by Alexander the Great, admonished the mighty king to stand out of his light—a scene depicted here in a miniature painting from a fifteenth-century theological manuscript.

Cyrenaic Hedonism

Aristippus (c. 435–356 BCE)

Socrates had a number of disciples who went on to become famous philosophers in their own right. Certainly the most surprising was Aristippus, who was born in Cyrene, an ancient city in North Africa known for its wealth. While attending the Olympic Games, he heard about Socrates and immediately went to Athens to become his pupil. For several years he was among Socrates's closest disciples. Sometime after Socrates's death, Aristippus returned to Cyrene to open a school of philosophy, where he taught what came to be known as "Cyrenaic hedonism."

Socrates believed that everyone innately desires to be happy, and that happiness (properly understood) is the greatest good. Aristippus latched on to this view and took it in a direction Socrates would have totally rejected. Aristippus taught that pleasure is the natural goal of life and that each person should pursue as much pleasure as possible. Later hedonists, such as Epicurus and John Stuart Mill, would agree with Aristippus that pleasure is the ultimate good; however, they believed that intellectual pleasures are often preferable to bodily ones and that short-term pleasures should often be avoided in order to maximize pleasure over the long run. Aristippus would have rejected such refinements. He believed that the keenest pleasures are physical and that it is foolish to postpone short-term pleasures for the sake of uncertain future ones.

Aristippus practiced what he preached. Charging a hefty fee for his teaching, he spent lavishly on fine food, expensive clothing, and female companionship. When one of his mistresses told him she was with child and that he was the father, he replied, "You can no more tell that it was I, than you could tell, after going through a thicket, which thorn had scratched you."

Aristippus had a daughter, Arete, who also became a philosopher and succeeded him as head of the Cyrenaic school. Reputedly, she wrote forty books, so she may well have differed with her father about the superiority of bodily pleasures to intellectual ones.

SEE ALSO The Trial and Death of Socrates (399 BCE), Epicureanism (c. 300 BCE), Utilitarianism (1789)

Aristippus would have approved of this bacchanalian scene. This mid-seventeenth-century engraving, featuring an inebriated, sleeping Pan, is by Franciscus van den Wyngaerde after Peter Paul Rubens.

The Bhagavad Gita

The *Bhagavad Gita* ("Song of God") is one of the most-loved works of Indian literature. This poem, written in dialogue form, is part of the great Hindu epic the *Mahabharata*. Countless people of all faiths have found in it wisdom and inspiration.

The book consists of a series of exchanges between Prince Arjuna and his charioteer, Krishna, who is the avatar, or earthly embodiment, of the god Vishnu. Arjuna is about to begin a great and just battle when he notices many friends, relatives, and former teachers in the opposing army. He hesitates, wondering whether even righteous victory and a great kingdom should be sought at such a price. Krishna reminds him that as a Kshatriya, a member of the warrior caste, he has a duty to be strong, brave, and responsible. Selfless performance of one's duties is the glue that keeps society stable and well ordered. It is also, Krishna tells him, a way of serving God and attaining liberation from worldly burdens.

Krishna goes on to describe three paths (*yogas*) to enlightenment and freedom. One, *jnana* yoga, is the way of knowledge, which pursues liberation through mystical understanding of absolute Reality (Brahman). The second, *bhakti* yoga, is the way of loving devotion to God. The third, *karma* yoga, is the way of action or selfless duty fulfillment without attachment or worries about the fruits of one's deeds. Krishna reminds Arjuna that even though performing our duties may seem trivial or pointless in the grand scheme of things, it is a way of worshiping God and working off and avoiding bad karma.

One measure of the popularity of the *Bhagavad Gita* is the large number of commentaries that have been written on it by major Indian thinkers, including Shankara, Ramanuja, Sri Aurobindo, and Sarvepalli Radhakrishnan. Gandhi said of it, "When doubts haunt me, when disappointments stare me in the face, and I see not one ray of hope on the horizon, I turn to *Bhagavad Gita* and find a verse to comfort me; and I immediately begin to smile in the midst of overwhelming sorrow. Those who meditate on the *Gita* will derive fresh joy and new meanings from it every day."

SEE ALSO The Vedas (c. 1500 BCE), Monism (810), Qualified Dualism (1135)

Krishna preaches to the legendary prince Arjuna, in a Kashmiri miniature, c. 1875.

The Trial and Death of Socrates

Socrates (c. 469–399 BCE), **Plato** (c. 428–c. 348 BCE)

After winning its long war with Athens in 404 BCE, Sparta overthrew the Athenian democracy and imposed a puppet government of thirty pro-Spartan oligarchs known as the Thirty Tyrants. One of the leading members of the Thirty, Critias, was an associate of Socrates and a relative of Plato. Following an eight-month reign of terror, the Thirty were overthrown and the democracy was restored. As a former teacher of Critias and a well-known critic of democracy, Socrates was not popular with the new democratic leaders in Athens, and in 399 BCE he was brought to trial on charges of impiety and corrupting the young.

Plato's account of Socrates's trial in the *Apology* (c. 390 BCE) is one of the great masterpieces of Western literature and philosophy. In Plato's account, Socrates skillfully rebuts the two charges against him but in the end flat-out refuses to do what the leaders of the Athenian democracy clearly wanted him to do, namely to stop practicing philosophy. "Men of Athens," he said to the jury, "I honor and love you; but I shall obey God rather than you." As Socrates saw it, his service to the gods was a great blessing to the people of Athens, and he preferred death to abandoning his divine mission. Remarking that "no evil can happen to a good man, either in life or after death," he refused to plead with the jury or to bewail his fate. Instead, he spoke calmly about death, saying that "there is great reason to hope that death is a good." As Socrates saw it, death was like either an eternal dreamless sleep or a journey to a blessed realm in which he could converse happily with the gods and Greek heroes of old. His final words to the jury were "The hour of departure has arrived, and we go our ways—I to die, and you to live. Which is better God only knows."

Following his death, his disciple Plato memorialized him saying, "Of all the men of his time whom I have known, he was the wisest and justest and best."

SEE ALSO Know Thyself (c. 430 BCE), Socratic Dialogues (c. 399 BCE)

Socrates addresses his grieving disciples before drinking the cup of hemlock in an engraving by French artist Jean-François Pierre Peyron, 1790.

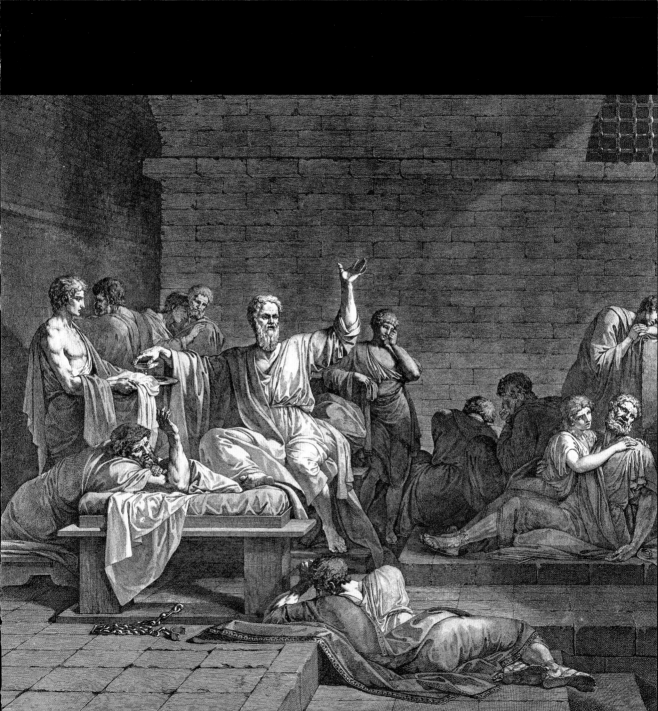

Socratic Dialogues

Plato (c. 428–c. 348 BCE)

After Socrates's death, a number of his disciples, including Aeschines, Antisthenes, and Aristippus, wrote books in dialogue form celebrating his memory. Books of this sort, which Aristotle called Socratic *logoi* (conversations), became something of a literary genre in fourth-century Greece. By far the greatest writer of Socratic *logoi* was Plato.

Plato was a wealthy Athenian aristocrat who originally planned to enter politics but decided instead to devote his life to philosophy after meeting Socrates and witnessing the political troubles of his day. After Socrates's execution, Plato traveled widely and probably began writing what are termed the "early dialogues," including such well-known works as *Apology*, *Crito*, and *Euthyphro*. The main character in those dialogues is Socrates, who emerges as an unforgettable personality: homely in body but concealing a mind and character of the finest gold. The Socrates of these early dialogues is merely a humble seeker of wisdom; he claims to know nothing except his own ignorance. By means of his famous Socratic (or "elenctic") method of question-and-answer, he punctures false claims to knowledge, pursuing a deeper understanding of moral concepts and what it means to live a good human life. Invariably, these early dialogues end inconclusively, with valuable insights gained but no final conclusions reached. The only rock-solid convictions that emerge in these conversations are the critical importance of leading an "examined life" and caring more about the "greatest improvement of the soul" than about such things as money, status, or fame.

In Plato's later writings, a quite different Socrates emerges. Instead of being an unassuming seeker of knowledge who claims to know nothing, Socrates confidently lays out grand theories of ethics, politics, knowledge, the soul, the afterlife, and the ultimate nature of Reality. This shift is part of what scholars call the "Socratic problem": the difficulty in determining what the real Socrates was like given the limited and sometimes conflicting sources of information we possess. The general view among scholars is that in Plato's later dialogues, he is actually espousing his own developing philosophical ideas, but there is no certain way of disentangling Socrates's views from Plato's.

SEE ALSO Know Thyself (c. 430 BCE), The Trial and Death of Socrates (399 BCE)

The Athenian nobleman and general Alcibiades (c. 450–404 BCE) as a young man being advised by his teacher Socrates; Plato wrote one or possibly two dialogues featuring discourse between Alcibiades and Socrates. This painting is by François-André Vincent of France, 1776.

Plato Founds the Academy

Plato (c. 428–c. 348 BCE)

According to several ancient sources, when Plato was about forty, he visited Sicily, offended the tyrant of Syracuse, Dionysius I, and was sold into slavery. He was ransomed, and soon afterward Plato's friends used surplus funds raised for his ransom to purchase a pleasant grove of trees with gardens, a gymnasium, and other buildings outside the walls of Athens. Because the grove was said to be sacred to a legendary hero supposedly buried there named Academus, it was called the Academy. Though earlier schools of higher education had existed, including the Pythagorean school in southern Italy and Isocrates's school of rhetoric in Athens, Plato's Academy rightly deserves to be called the first university because of the breadth of subjects that were taught there.

The primary purpose of the Academy was to train rulers, lawmakers, and political advisors who would fan out over the Greek world to improve the quality of government. Like Socrates, Plato charged no fees for his teaching. Students and faculty lived a communal life, with meals taken in dining commons. The school was open to both women and men. The chief subjects were mathematics and philosophy (especially political theory), though other subjects, such as science, music, literature, history, and law, were also probably taught. The principal method of instruction was no doubt Socratic discussion, though we know from Aristotle that Plato also gave lectures, including a public lecture "On the Good" that included so much high-powered math and astronomy that many in the audience walked out shaking their heads.

Remarkably, the Academy existed as a center of intellectual life in Greece for over nine hundred years. It underwent many changes throughout this long period. Beginning around 266 BCE, under the leadership of Arcesilaus and later of Carneades, the Academy adopted a strongly skeptical orientation. This persisted until 86 BCE, when the original Academy seems to have been largely destroyed by the Roman general Sulla. Platonists continued to teach in Athens throughout the Roman era but probably not at the site of the original Academy. Around 437 CE, the Academy was revitalized under the leadership of the Neoplatonist Proclus. In 529 CE, the Byzantine emperor Justinian closed all the pagan schools, including the Academy.

SEE ALSO Aristotle Enrolls in the Academy (c. 367 BCE), Carneades on Justice (155 BCE), Justinian Closes the Academy (529)

A group of philosophers converse at Plato's Academy (Plato is believed to be second from the left) in this first-century Roman mosaic from a villa at Pompeii.

The World of the Forms

Plato (c. 428–c. 348 BCE)

Probably Plato's best-known idea is his theory of forms, sometimes called the theory of ideas. The rough idea is this: The most real things that exist are not physical things like cats and trees that we perceive through the senses. Rather, the most real things are eternal, unchanging "essences" or "patterns" that can only be perceived through the mind. These eternal essences or patterns are what Plato calls forms.

Why did he believe that they exist? One reason is our knowledge of math. We know what triangles are. We can define "triangle" and can prove all sorts of things about the essential properties of triangles. But have we ever perceived a real triangle through the senses? No, all physical triangles, if examined closely, would be seen to lack perfectly straight lines or some other essential feature of triangles. If we know something, there must be something we know. Knowledge, that is, must have objects. But our knowledge of triangles is not of physical triangles, which are imperfect and perishable. Therefore there must exist some eternal, perfect, super-sensible triangle. This perfect triangle is what Plato calls the form of a triangle.

Plato believed that anytime we use a general word like "cat" there must be some shared form—in this case, universal catness—that makes all particular cats *cats*. Moreover, all true knowledge is of forms, not of individual things that we can perceive through the senses. Individual things are constantly changing and thus have different properties at different times. A leaf, for example, might be green today and orange tomorrow. For Plato, this meant that there is a sense in which the leaf both "is" and "is not," and so is not fully real. True knowledge must be infallible and have for its object something that is fully real. All true knowledge, therefore, is knowledge of the forms.

As Plato himself came to realize, there are many problems with the theory of forms. But even in his late writings he continued to affirm that something like the theory of forms must be true. Only in this way, he believed, can we provide adequate foundations for knowledge and even objective morality.

SEE ALSO Plato Founds the Academy (c. 386 BCE), Mind-Body Dualism (c. 380 BCE), Matter and Form (c. 330 BCE)

According to Plato's theory of forms, the most real things that exist aren't physical things, like cats, that we perceive through the senses, but rather unchanging "essences" or "patterns" that can only be perceived through the mind; there must be some shared form—in this case, universal catness—that makes all particular cats cats.

Plato's *Republic*

Plato (c. 428–c. 348 BCE)

In his masterwork the *Republic*, Plato sketches the world's first utopia, or ideal society. In Plato's day, Greece was divided into a constellation of relatively small city-states. Dictatorships, clashes between rich and poor, and civil unrest were commonplace. In Plato's view, the two major causes of bad government were self-interestedness (rulers who pursued personal gain at the expense of the common good) and incompetence (rulers who lacked the wisdom to govern well). In the *Republic*, Plato offers a radical solution to both of these root causes of poor government.

As Plato saw it, a good and well-ordered society would be a bit like a successful and well-coached sports team. Everybody would work together under effective leadership, each doing what he or she does best, to make the community as good as it can possibly be. To achieve this kind of team-oriented social cohesion, Plato proposed an elaborate system of testing and education. All citizens, both male and female, would go through a lengthy system of public education. The goals of the educational process would be threefold: (a) to create a citizen-body that is well educated and committed to the common good, (b) to determine what social role each citizen would be best at, and (c) to select "philosopher-rulers" who are both wise and public-spirited.

To ensure that only the smartest and most experienced people became rulers, Plato proposed that each prospective ruler undergo a rigorous process of testing and education lasting fifty years. This would guarantee that rulers would be wise and competent. The harder challenge, Plato believed, is to prevent rulers from abusing their power for personal gain. To achieve this, Plato's philosopher-rulers would be required to live Spartan, austere lives. They would not be permitted to possess money or to own personal property or even to have a family life. Instead, they would live in military-type barracks, eat simple meals together, and mate only with state-approved partners in order to produce the best possible offspring.

Very little of this sounds "utopian" to most contemporary readers. But Plato believed that bad government is a huge and chronic source of human misery. Only a radical fix, he was convinced, could solve such deep-seated problems.

SEE ALSO *Utopia* (1516)

A modern photomontage of the Parthenon in Athens, which was built from 447 to 432 BCE (a few years before the birth of Plato) at the apex of Athenian rule; today it remains an iconic symbol of ancient Greece and the birth of Western civilization.

Mind-Body Dualism

Plato (c. 428–c. 348 BCE)

One of Plato's most important ideas involves his distinction between mind and body—what philosophers call mind-body dualism. Probably due to the influence of Pythagoreanism and an Eastern-inspired Greek religious movement known as Orphism, Plato believed that human beings are composed of two radically different parts: a physical body and a nonphysical soul. For Plato, the union of body and soul is not a happy one. The soul is immortal and existed before the body. Perhaps for some primeval sin, the soul is temporarily imprisoned in the body, where it is constantly hindered and weighed down by the body's distractions and appetites. A wise person takes little interest in food, drink, sex, or bodily pleasures; her goal is to free the soul from the corruptions of the body and focus on higher, nobler, and more lasting things. When we die, our souls leave our bodies and go off to some kind of afterlife, and many souls will later be reincarnated in another body, human or otherwise. Only those who have purified their souls through philosophy will enjoy a "blessed" afterlife. For this reason, philosophy is a preparation for death, and the true philosopher "is always pursuing death and dying."

In Plato's magnificent dialogue the *Phaedo*, he presents a number of arguments to try to prove the immortality of the soul. One is the argument from simplicity. Briefly, it goes like this: Things do not just vanish or cease to exist. The only way something can be destroyed is by breaking it apart into its component parts—for example, by smashing it with a hammer, burning it, or blowing it up. But the soul is not a physical object. It has no parts. Therefore, the soul cannot be destroyed. By its very nature, it is immortal.

Plato's dualistic view of mind and body had a profound influence on Western civilization. Largely due to Plato, belief in the immortality of a spiritual soul entered into Jewish, Christian, and Islamic thought and became a widely held view. Today, most philosophers reject dualism, though it continues to have many articulate defenders.

SEE ALSO Reincarnation (c. 540 BCE), *Meditations on First Philosophy* (1641)

A detail of a statue of Plato in front of the Academy of Athens, sculpted by nineteenth-century Greek artist Leonidas Drosis.

Aristotle Enrolls in the Academy

Aristotle (384–322 BCE)

Plato and Aristotle are unquestionably two of the greatest philosophers of all time. Although Aristotle studied with Plato for twenty years and clearly revered him, they were very different types of thinkers. Whereas Plato emphasized abstract thinking, such as math, and tended to focus on otherworldly concerns, Aristotle's thoughts were practical, empirical, and scientific. The fact that two such outstanding geniuses with such different personalities were master and pupil for so many years is truly amazing.

Aristotle was born in Stagira, a Macedonian seaside town in northern Greece. His father was personal physician to the king of Macedon. Around age seventeen, Aristotle traveled south to enroll in Plato's Academy in Athens. Plato was about sixty years old at the time and immersed in the dense and highly technical speculations that are reflected in his later dialogues. Although all of Aristotle's early writings are lost, we know from various sources that as a youth his thinking was deeply imbued with Platonism. Like Plato, he wrote engaging and finely crafted dialogues. Also like Plato, he sharply distinguished soul from body, affirmed the preexistence of the soul, and offered proofs of the soul's immortality. Over time, however, Aristotle's views began to diverge from Plato's. When Plato died at the ripe age of eighty or eighty-one, Aristotle might have expected to succeed him as head of the Academy. Instead, Speusippus, Plato's nephew, was chosen. Aristotle then left Athens, traveled widely, and served as tutor to the young Alexander the Great. In 334 BCE, Aristotle returned to Athens, where he founded his own school, the Lyceum. He died at age sixty-two at the height of his career.

Despite his later differences from Plato, Aristotle was always conscious of the debt he owed to his great teacher. In Plato's Academy, Aristotle was part of a close-knit community of scholars and truth-seekers where, as Plato said in one his letters, the deepest insights arose "only out of much converse" and "a life lived together." In such a community, exciting ideas flow from mind to mind like "a light kindled from a leaping flame." Perhaps Plato was thinking of some of his talks with the young doctor's son from remote Macedonia.

SEE ALSO Plato Founds the Academy (c. 386 BCE), *Nicomachean Ethics* (c. 330 BCE)

The two greatest philosophers in history, Plato and Aristotle, stand at the center of this detail from the masterpiece titled The School of Athens, *a fresco painted by Raphael in the Apostolic Palace at the Vatican, 1509–1511.*

Hellenization Begins

From 334 to 323 BCE, Alexander the Great conquered Persia, Egypt, Babylonia, and lands as far east as northwestern India. This was the beginning of Hellenization, the spread of Greek culture into non-Greek parts of the world. The Greek language was spoken from the shores of the Mediterranean to the mountains of Afghanistan. Greek art, customs, and ideas spread throughout the Near East. The effect on philosophy was profound.

Alexander founded more than twenty eponymous cities—including the great Alexandria, in Egypt—some of which became major centers of philosophical activity. Many of the most important philosophers of late antiquity were not native Greeks, such as Plotinus (c. 204–270 CE), from Egypt; Porphyry (c. 234–c. 305), from Tyre; and Proclus (c. 410–485), from Constantinople. Because of Hellenization, Greek philosophical ideas entered deeply into the theology of early Christian thinkers such as Saints Justin Martyr (c. 100–c. 165), Clement of Alexandria (c. 150–c. 215), and Gregory of Nyssa (c. 335–c. 395); and Origen (c. 185–c. 253). Following the Muslim conquest of Syria and Egypt, Greek philosophical texts were translated into Arabic by scholars in the famous House of Wisdom in Baghdad, and fueled the rise of Christian Scholasticism when they were later translated into Latin.

Another important effect of Hellenization was that copies of the works of Plato, Aristotle, and other Greek philosophers were preserved in libraries throughout the Near East, increasing the chances they would survive into modern times. Most of the earliest Latin translations of Aristotle's works from the original Greek were made by William of Moerbeke (c. 1215–c. 1286), who obtained his copies in or near Constantinople. Practically none of the writings of Plato were available in Western Europe until Greek manuscripts of his dialogues were brought from Constantinople to Italy in the fourteenth and fifteenth centuries.

The spread of Greek ideas and culture to the East is symbolized by the copy of Homer's *Iliad* that Alexander the Great carried from Macedonia to the Indus River Delta; it is said that he slept with it under his pillow. The book was given to him by his tutor, Aristotle, and included Aristotle's personal annotations.

SEE ALSO Platonism and Christianity (c. 150), Neoplatonism (c. 250), Islamic Philosophy Begins (c. 840)

The heroic Alexander the Great in battle; a detail from the Alexander Mosaic, c. 100 BCE, *from the House of the Faun in Pompeii.*

The Invention of Logic

Aristotle (384–322 BCE)

Aristotle was a towering genius who made immense contributions to many fields of knowledge. But perhaps his greatest and most lasting achievement was laying the foundations of logic.

Logic is the study of the methods and principles used to distinguish good reasoning from bad reasoning. Aristotle wrote a series of works on logic, collectively known as the *Organon* or "tool" of thought. As Aristotle himself noted, very little systematic work had been done on logic before his time. He had to create the science pretty much from scratch.

Logic involves the evaluation of arguments, that is, claims defended with evidence. The simplest arguments are composed of just two statements. For instance, from the statement "No dogs are cats," it logically follows that "No cats are dogs." In Aristotle's logic, this is known as an "immediate inference." But Aristotle mostly focuses on a certain type of three-step deductive argument he calls a *syllogism*. For example, from the two statements "All kangaroos are marsupials" and "All marsupials are mammals," we can logically infer that "All kangaroos are mammals." One of Aristotle's great achievements was to work out the logic of syllogistic reasoning and discover rules for distinguishing good ("valid") syllogisms from bad ones. He also was the first to use letters in logic (A, B, C, etc.), making it possible for logic to be a general science.

All sound thought, Aristotle noted, rests on the principle of contradiction, which states that no statement can be both true and false. Good thinking is consistent thinking. Aristotle worked out the logic of consistent thinking, noting that there are different kinds of inconsistency. The most obvious is contradiction, which occurs when a person asserts a claim and also its direct denial (e.g., "God exists" and "God does not exist"). With contradictions, one statement must be true and the other false. Another kind of inconsistency involves "contraries." This occurs when two statements cannot both be true but can both be false (e.g., "All Democrats are blonde" and "No Democrats are blonde").

Aristotle's was not the last word in logic. Modern logicians have improved on what he did, but he certainly got logic off to a fantastic start.

SEE ALSO *A System of Logic* (1843), The New Logic (1879), The Rise of Informal Logic (c. 1971)

In this allegorical engraving from c. 1680, a woman representing wisdom bestows to Aristotle a key to the sacred house of knowledge and reason.

Distinguo à brutis, RATIONIS Sacra recludens

The Earth-Centered Universe

Aristotle (384–322 BCE)

Throughout the Middle Ages and up until roughly the middle of the seventeenth century, a certain model of the universe dominated the intellectual imaginations of educated Europeans. It was an earth-centered model, and its main source was Aristotle.

Aristotle's basic world picture is this: The universe is divided into two parts: Nature and Sky. Nature consists of the earth and the atmosphere that surrounds the earth, which Aristotle believed extends all the way up to the orbit of the moon. The earth is at the center of the universe, and everything above the moon is part of Sky. Nature and Sky are two totally different realms. Things in Nature are made up of the four elements (earth, air, fire, and water), which each have their own natural motions (e.g., earth naturally moves downward). Nature is the realm of mutability, impermanence, birth, decay, and death. Things in Sky, such as planets and stars, are made up of a special kind of heavenly matter called *aether* or *quintessence*, which is perfect, eternal, and changeless. Aether naturally moves in circles, which is how Aristotle explained the observed motions of the sun, moon, planets, and stars.

Aristotle did not believe that the stars and other celestial objects moved through empty space. Instead, he said, they are embedded in concentric crystalline spheres (also made of aether) that revolve at various speeds around the earth. Each celestial object is inhabited by an immaterial divine being that Aristotle called an "Intelligence." The outermost sphere is that of the fixed stars, which is set in eternal motion by God, the chief Unmoved Mover. The universe is eternal and was not created by God, but God is the ultimate cause of why things happen in nature as they do.

For centuries, this earth-centered view, suitably modified to fit with Christian teachings, provided a comforting and flattering picture of humanity and our place in the cosmos. When it finally broke down with the rise of modern science, a spiritual and existential crisis resulted. Some believe it is a crisis that we are still wrestling with today.

SEE ALSO The Birth of Modern Science (1543)

Aristotle believed that celestial objects were embedded in concentric crystalline spheres (made of a special cosmic substance called aether*) that revolved at various speeds around the earth. Here, a Ptolemaic astronomical map called* The Figure of the World, *c. 1650, shows the planets, sun, and moon revolving around the earth. On the outer ring is the heavenly "Place of the Blessed Souls."*

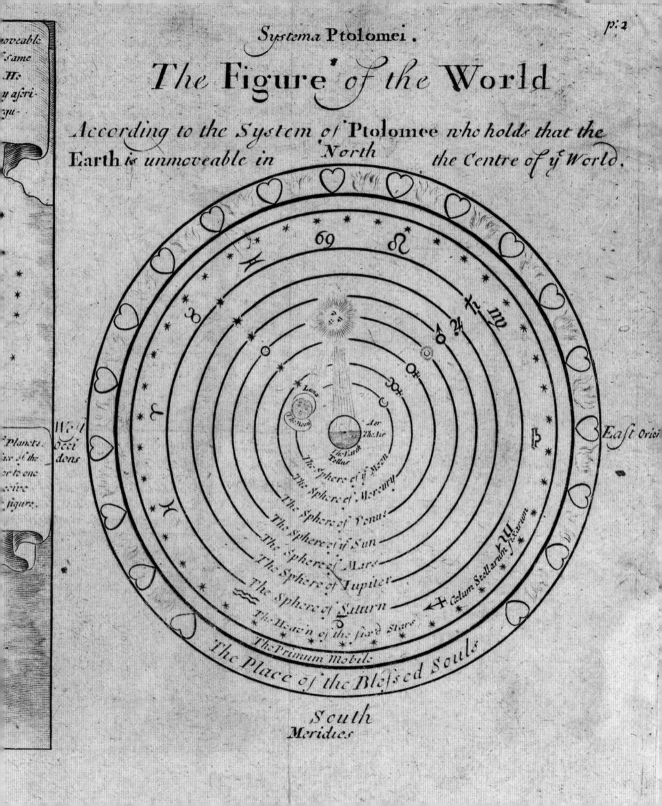

Systema Ptolomei.

The Figure of the World

According to the System of Ptolomee who holds that the
Earth is unmoveable in the Centre of ỵ World.

North

West
Occidens

East
Oriens

The Sphere of ỵ Moon
The Sphere of Mercury
The Sphere of Venus
The Sphere of ỵ Sun
The Sphere of Mars
The Sphere of Jupiter
The Sphere of Saturn
The Heaven of the fixed Stars
The Primum Mobile
The Place of the Blessed Souls

Cælum Stellarum firmarum

South
Meridies

Matter and Form

Aristotle (384–322 BCE)

Aristotle rejected Plato's pivotal doctrine, the theory of forms. It clearly pained him to do so. Though he revered Plato, he said to his students that as philosophers we must "honor truth above our friends."

Aristotle did not deny the existence of forms, but he disagreed with Plato's view that forms exist in some timeless realm, completely separate from matter. Rather, he theorized that forms are built *into* things in the material world. A brass sphere, for example, is composed of both matter (the brass) and form (its spherical shape). For Aristotle, it made no sense to talk of shape existing separately from matter. Any shape must be the shape of some material object or another.

More generally, Aristotle believed that all things in nature are composed of two mentally distinguishable parts: matter and form. This is how he explained change. In any physical change where one and the same thing continues to exist (e.g., an apple changing from green to red), there must be something that changes (the form) and something that undergoes the change (the matter or material substrate). Some forms are "accidental," meaning that they do not change the nature or essence of a thing (the same apple, for example, can be green one week and red the next). But other forms are "substantial," meaning they determine the very "essence" of a thing. A tiger, for example, is a tiger because it has a tiger-soul, which is what makes it a tiger, rather than, say, an antelope or an azalea bush. The same is true of human beings, Aristotle believed. Humans are not just souls temporarily hanging out in a certain human body, as Plato held. Rather, human beings are essentially *composite* creatures, made up of both a human body and a human soul. This is why Aristotle did not believe in any personal survival after death. Even if your soul could leave your body at death (which Aristotle doubted), it would only be your soul that survived, not *you*. Christian Aristotelians in the Middle Ages, like Thomas Aquinas (1225–1274), would later struggle to square this composite view of the human person with Christian teachings about the immortality of the soul and the resurrection of the body.

SEE ALSO The World of the Forms (c. 380 BCE), The Four Causes (c. 330 BCE)

According to Aristotle, in any physical change where one and the same thing continues to exist, such as an apple changing from green to red, there must be something that changes (the form) and something that undergoes the change (the matter or material substrate).

c. 330 BCE

The Four Causes

Aristotle (384–322 BCE)

Both in science and in ordinary life we often wonder why things exist and why they are the sorts of things that they are. To help address this enigma, Aristotle developed an interesting theory called the Four Causes. It works best with man-made things, so let's consider a simple example: a hand-carved wooden paperweight in the shape of a bullfrog. Aristotle says there are four key explanatory questions we can ask of such an object. First, what is it made of? In this case, the answer is wood, and that is what Aristotle calls the "material cause" of the paperweight. The wood is a "cause" of the paperweight because without it the paperweight would not exist.

A second question to ask is: Who made it? Suppose a well-known woodcarver made the paperweight in his shop. Aristotle would then say that the woodcarver is the "efficient cause" of the paperweight. It was through his carving skills that the paperweight was fashioned into the likeness of a bullfrog.

A third question is: What is it that is being made? Answer: a paperweight in the shape of a bullfrog. This is what Aristotle calls the "formal cause" of the paperweight (though forms need not be limited to shapes). The paperweight has the form (shape) of a bullfrog and not, say, of a raccoon or of the Eiffel Tower. Without the formal cause the paperweight wouldn't be what it is—a paperweight that looks like a bullfrog.

The final question is: Why was it made? Meaning, what purpose does it serve? Answer: so someone can use it as a paperweight. This is what Aristotle calls the paperweight's "final cause." Things like paperweights are made for a reason. Knowing why things were made can help us understand why they exist and what they are used for.

Aristotle's doctrine of the Four Causes works reasonably well with human productions. But he also applies it to things in nature, and there you run into problems. What is the final cause (purpose) of a mosquito or of a rainbow? In modern science, such questions are regarded as unhelpful and other sorts of explanations are sought that lend themselves to scientific investigation.

SEE ALSO Matter and Form (c. 330 BCE), The Birth of Modern Science (1543)

What is the final cause or purpose of a rainbow? It is one of many enigmas in the world that is problematic to answer by applying Aristotle's Four Causes theory.

Nicomachean Ethics

Aristotle (384–322 BCE)

Except for the Bible, no book has influenced Western thinking about morality and the good life more than Aristotle's *Nicomachean Ethics*. Yet Aristotle's book is not what we would expect from a work with "ethics" in its title.

The book's main focus is what it means to live a flourishing and successful life. Aristotle believed that everything in nature has a *telos*, a natural end or goal. The telos of a living thing is to fulfill its nature by realizing its potentialities. The telos of a lion, for example, is to be a great specimen of lionhood, living a great leonine life. In like fashion, the natural goal and ultimate good of a human being is to be a great person living a great human life. This is what Aristotle calls *eudaimonia*, a word that is often translated as "happiness" but really means something closer to "flourishing" or even "the ideal life." But what does it mean, exactly, to "flourish" as a human being?

Two things must be considered, Aristotle says: the quality of the human being, and the quality of the life he or she is leading. To be an outstanding human being is to be a flourishing specimen of humanity, to possess excellence (*arete*) of mind, body, and character. To live an outstanding life is to live a life that is both rich in excellent activities and fortunate in what Aristotle calls "external goods" (good birth, many friends, ample wealth, good health, and so forth). An outstanding person who lives an outstanding life right up to the point of his or her death has achieved the human telos and is, in Aristotle's robust, objective sense, "happy."

At the end of the *Nicomachean Ethics*, Aristotle adds an important wrinkle to this account. He argues that the highest form of human excellence is *intellectual* excellence and, more specifically, theoretical contemplation (*theoria*). By spending as much time as possible thinking about the noblest things in the universe, we imitate the gods and their supremely blessed lives. Not surprisingly, then, Aristotle thinks that the happiest life is the life of the philosopher—a view that many of my students see as a tad overzealous.

SEE ALSO The Revival of Virtue Ethics (1981)

In the Nicomachean Ethics, *Aristotle said that to be an outstanding human being is to possess excellence of mind, body, and character, and he commended the great Athenian leader Pericles (c. 495–429 BCE), shown here in a photomontage: "Pericles and men like Pericles are held to be prudent, because they can see what is good, not only for themselves, but also for mankind in general."*

Maybe Life Is a Dream

Zhuang Zhou (Zhuangzi) (c. 369–286 BCE)

Next to Laozi, Zhuangzi ("Master Zhuang") is the most important figure in Chinese Daoism. We know little about him other than what we can infer from scattered references in a collection of writings called the *Zhuangzi*. His real name was Zhuang Zhou, and reportedly he was a minor official in the town of Meng, in central China, but he seems to have spent most of his life as a teacher and recluse.

Zhuangzi is delightful to read because he writes in a playful, fanciful, paradoxical, and sometimes humorous way. Often he speaks in parables that take the form of minidialogues, sometimes with human participants but frequently with animals, mythical creatures, or even personified forces of nature such as the wind. There are recurrent themes of skepticism, relativism, and nature-mysticism in his thought. Generally, he tried to free people from the illusions that flow from analytical thinking and purely human-centered perspectives. We think we possess objective knowledge and have carved up reality into the correct categories of "this" and "that." In reality, Zhuangzi taught, all knowing is relative and all apparent opposites are unified in what he called the "equality of things" in the all-embracing Dao.

One of the stories he told to illustrate the limitations of human knowledge is called "Three in the Morning." A zookeeper told a group of monkeys that they would receive three acorns in the morning and four in the evening. They were upset, so he said they could have four acorns in the morning and three in the evening. This made them happy. The monkeys were bent out of shape, Zuangzi says, because they thought that something was different when it was really the same. Moral: we humans do the same.

One day Zhuangzi dreamed he was a butterfly. When he awoke, he realized that he was only dreaming. But then it occurred to him that he really did not know if he was a human who dreamed he was a butterfly or a butterfly that was now dreaming he was a human. Is it possible, he wondered, that everything we call life is part of some "great dream"?

SEE ALSO The Dao (c. 550 BCE), Huineng and the *Platform Sutra* (c. 700), Monism (810)

Zhuangzi Dreaming of a Butterfly, *mid-sixteenth century, an ink on silk drawing by Lu Zhi.*

Ecclesiastes

The book of Ecclesiastes is one of the shortest books in the Hebrew Bible and also one of the most perplexing. Its central themes—the futility of human striving, the injustice of life, and the oblivion of the grave—run counter to the usual biblical orthodoxies. For this reason, American rabbi and best-selling author Harold Kushner has labeled Ecclesiastes "the most dangerous book in the Bible."

Ecclesiastes is purportedly written by "the son of David, king in Jerusalem" (1:1), that is, King Solomon, but the language indicates a date closer to the fourth or third century BCE. The principal writer is apparently an elderly man reflecting back on what he largely sees as a life spent in empty pursuits. He tells us that he tried many paths to happiness—pleasure, wisdom, riches, toil—and found none of them fulfilling. Life is an endless round of repetitive and often futile strivings that ultimately comes to nothing. We are told that God punishes the wicked and rewards the good, but what do we in fact see? "[T]he race is not to the swift, nor the battle to the strong, neither yet bread to the wise . . . but time and chance happeneth to them all" (9:11).

Nor can we look for consolation in an afterlife, since all share the same fate; "as is the good, so is the sinner" (9:2), and "the dead know not any thing, neither have they any more a reward, for the memory of them is forgotten" (9:5). Despite the usual biblical pieties, this is simply humanity's lot. The Ecclesiastes's resigned conclusion is that we should eat our "bread with joy" and drink our "wine with a merry heart" (9:7), for such fleeting joys are gifts of God and genuine goods, notwithstanding their ultimate "vanity."

Despite calling Ecclesiastes the most dangerous book in the Bible, Kushner believes that its deepest message is positive: that we should not seek some big answer to life's mysteries but rather "learn to find meaning and purpose in the transitory, in the joys that fade." Whatever one's final take on the book, it is a rich and beautiful reflection on the human condition.

SEE ALSO The Book of Job (c. 500 BCE), Existential Defiance (1942), Atheistic Existentialism (1946)

Vanitas still lifes *(this one from 1646 is by Pieter Symonsz Potter) were a popular seventeenth-century Dutch genre. Latin for "vanity," they symbolized the impermanence of our earthbound existence and the need to repent our vain insistence on earthly pleasures and pursuits. In Ecclesiastes, though, the resigned conclusion is that we might as well our drink our "wine with a merry heart" since life is endlessly futile and amounts to nothing.*

Epicureanism

Epicurus (341–270 BCE)

Epicurus was what we today call a hedonist. Hedonists believe that pleasure is the sole intrinsic good, or that pleasure is the proper goal of life. In ancient times, there were two major schools of hedonism. One was Cyrenaic hedonism, founded by Socrates's disciple Aristippus. The other was Epicurean hedonism, founded by Epicurus. Aristippus's version was pretty crude, emphasizing instant gratification of bodily appetites. Epicurus's version was more refined, stressing pleasures of the mind over pleasures of the body and recognizing that a continuous attitude of "going for the gusto" can sometimes land one in a boatload of trouble.

Epicurus was born in Samos, on what is now the west coast of Turkey, in 341 BCE. At eighteen he came to Athens and studied philosophy with Platonists, Aristotelians, and Democritean atomists. Eventually, he opened his own school in Athens, called the Garden. Remarkably, his school was open to women as well as to men, and to people of all social classes, including slaves and prostitutes. Epicurus taught in the Garden for over thirty-five years. He was revered by his pupils and wrote some three hundred works. Unfortunately, only a few short writings survive.

With a few minor modifications, Epicurus accepted the atomism of Democritus. Everything, he believed, is made of atoms. There is no divine providence, no afterlife, and no gods that can be moved by prayer or sacrifice. All that matters, therefore, is making the most of this life. Our goal should be to live as pleasantly as possible, but this requires thoughtfulness and self-discipline. Smart people recognize that long-term pleasures outweigh short-term pleasures, and that pleasures differ in quality as well as quantity. As Epicurus saw it, the best pleasures are those of mental tranquility (*ataraxia*), friendship, freedom from pain, and intellectual interests that excite and engage our minds. By all accounts, Epicurus led a restrained, even austere, life as far as bodily pleasures go, living a secluded existence with his friends and students, and eating and drinking sparingly. For him, philosophy was above all a form of therapy. "Vain is the word of a philosopher which does not heal any suffering of man," he wrote.

SEE ALSO Cyrenaic Hedonism (c. 400 BCE), *On the Nature of Things* (c. 55 BCE), Utilitarianism (1789)

An 1813 stipple engraving of a bust of Epicurus, by Belgian artist Antoine Cardon.

Stoicism

Zeno of Citium (c. 334–c. 262 BCE)

One of the most influential philosophical schools of ancient times was Stoicism. The founder of Stoicism was Zeno, who was born in Citium on the island of Cyprus and came to Athens as a young man. There, partly as a result of reading Plato's *Apology*, he decided to devote his life to philosophy. After studying with many Athenian philosophers, including the Cynic Crates, he opened his own school. Because Zeno taught from a colonnaded porch, or stoa, his school was called Stoicism.

Since only fragments of Zeno's writings have survived, it is difficult to separate his teachings from those of later Stoics, although it's likely that the main tenets of Stoic doctrine go back to him. These doctrines include: that everything is made of matter; that the world is wisely and providentially governed by God (the fiery and all-pervasive divine Logos, as Heraclitus taught); that everything happens for the best and is fated to happen as it does; that all persons contain a "spark" of the divine Logos and so are all co-equal children of God and of the cosmos; and that moral goodness is sufficient for happiness, and the only thing that is categorically "good."

Zeno's most important teaching deals with the idea of inner strength and mental tranquility. What Zeno particularly admired about Socrates was the way he always stood strong and upright no matter what life threw at him. "Nothing bad can happen to a good man," Socrates had said. Zeno took this literally and pressed it to its ultimate conclusion. If a person is truly good and virtuous, then things like death, pain, sickness, or imprisonment are not really "bad" (though Zeno does concede that they are "dispreferred"). It follows that we should approach life's hard knocks without fear, disappointment, or regret, but instead with fortitude, acceptance, and equanimity. We should stand like a rock, firm and unmoved, through all the storms of life. As English poet William E. Henley put it in his poem "Invictus" (1888): "It matters not how strait the gate, / How charged with punishments the scroll, / I am the master of my fate: / I am the captain of my soul."

SEE ALSO Change Is Constant (c. 500 BCE), The Death of Seneca (65), Epictetian Stoicism (c. 125), The Philosopher-King (180)

The Stoic Zeno of Citium is depicted holding a book in this 1672 print by Spanish printmaker Jusepe de Ribera after a painting by Dutch artist Bernard Vaillant.

Innate Goodness

Mencius (Mengzi) (c. 372–c. 289 BCE)

The two most important Chinese philosophers are Confucius and his devoted disciple and interpreter, Mencius. Often referred to as the "Second Sage" of Confucianism, Mencius is best known for his teaching that human nature is good and his deep understanding of moral psychology.

In China, Mencius is known as Mengzi ("Master Meng"). Born as Meng Ke in the state of Zou in northeastern China, Mencius was raised by a widowed mother who sacrificed greatly so that her son could receive a good education. Trained in Confucianist philosophy by followers of Confucius's grandson, Zisi, Mencius became a famous scholar by the age of forty and spent many years as a public intellectual working for political reform and defending Confucianism against hostile critics, such as the Mohists and the Daoists. After his death, Mencius's disciples published his writings and discourses in a work known simply as *Mengzi*. For centuries it has ranked with the major works of Confucius himself, among the so-called "classics of Confucianism."

In Western philosophy and religion, there has been a long-running debate between those who think that human beings are naturally good (e.g., Jean-Jacques Rousseau, 1712–1778, and William Wordsworth, 1770–1850) and those who think that human nature is fundamentally evil or corrupt (e.g., John Calvin [1509–1564] and Thomas Hobbes [1588–1679]). A similar debate occurred in Chinese philosophy. Mencius believed strongly that people are innately good. All of us, he taught, are born with certain positive emotional predispositions, such as compassion and shame, which incline us to be good. These good emotions, if properly cultivated, can blossom into stable moral virtues, such as wisdom and propriety. According to Mencius, the two most important virtues are benevolence (*ren*) and righteousness (*yi*). Because all human beings are innately good, all are fundamentally equal and all possess great potential. Given the right education and the right environment, anyone can preserve or recover their original goodness. "The great man," Mencius said, "is he who does not lose his child's-heart."

SEE ALSO Confucian Ethics (c. 500 BCE), Revival of Confucianism (c. 1180), *Emile* and Natural Education (1762)

According to Mencius, anyone can preserve or recover the original, innate goodness they were born with, their "child's-heart."

Carneades on Justice

Carneades (c. 214–c. 129 BCE)

Less than a century after Plato's death, the school Plato founded, the Academy, took an unexpected turn. When Arcesilaus (c. 315–c. 240 BCE) became head of the Academy, the school embraced a robust form of skepticism that later came to be called Academic Skepticism. Arcesilaus attacked all forms of "dogmatism," including Stoicism and virtually the entire philosophy of Plato. The Academic Skeptics looked beyond Plato to Socrates, and his claim to know almost nothing.

Although Arcesilaus left no writings, he appears to have taught not only that we have no knowledge but also that we should suspend judgment and form few, if any, firmly held beliefs. He was a master at arguing pro or con for any thesis as a way of demonstrating the limits of human understanding.

Arcesilaus's skeptical turn marked the beginning of the so-called Middle Academy. Roughly a century later, the Academy adopted a more moderate from of skepticism under the leadership of a brilliant new head, Carneades. Carneades agreed with Arcesilaus that we cannot know anything, but he did not support wholesale suspension of belief. Instead, he argued that some beliefs are more probable than others and that we should act upon those beliefs that appear to be most credible. Carneades's school became known as the New Academy.

In 155 BCE, Carneades was sent by Athens on a political embassy to Rome. He was joined by two other notable Athenian philosophers: Critolaus (an Aristotelian) and Diogenes of Babylon (a Stoic). During his visit, Carneades put on a virtuoso display of his argumentative prowess before the Roman Senate. One day he gave an awesomely compelling speech in favor of justice, and the next day an equally compelling speech against it. The Romans were not amused and sent Carneades packing.

As we know from the writings of Cicero, who studied philosophy in Athens in 79–78 BCE, skepticism continued to dominate the Academy for many years after Carneades's death. Unfortunately, Cicero was unable to study on the grounds of the original Academy, for it had largely been destroyed by the Roman general Sulla in 86 BCE.

SEE ALSO Plato Founds the Academy (c. 386 BCE), *Outlines of Pyrrhonism* (c. 200), Revival of Classical Skepticism (1580)

Arcesilaus and Carneades are featured on a page from Philosophica Omnia, *a collection of Cicero's works published in London in 1810, edited by one Johann August Goerenz.*

M. T. CICERONIS

ACADEMICA

EX SCRIPTIS RECENS COLLATIS EDITISQVE

LIBRIS CASTIGATIVS ET EXPLICATIVS

EDIDIT

IO. AVG. GOERENZ.

ARCESILAS et CARNEADES.

LIPSIAE, CIƆIƆCCCX

IN LIBRARIA WEIDMANNIA.

On the Nature of Things

Lucretius (c. 99–c. 55 BCE)

Lucretius is generally considered to be the greatest of philosophical poets. It is both surprising and regrettable, therefore, that we know so little about him.

Titus Lucretius Carus won renown for one work: the classic book-length poem *De rerum natura* (*On the Nature of Things*), left unfinished at his early death in the mid-first century. It is believed that he was a Roman aristocrat and was well educated, being thoroughly at home in both Greek and Latin literature. Given his intimate familiarity with country life, it seems likely that he owned a villa outside Rome. He was a passionate disciple of the Greek philosopher Epicurus (340–270 BCE). Other than these facts, we know practically nothing about Lucretius other than what we can conjecture from his poem.

The poem has an unlikely theme: how Epicurus's teaching that nothing exists except "atoms and the void" can banish fear and superstition, lead to inner tranquility, and explain the workings of the universe. An intense hostility to popular religion pervades the work. Like an early Richard Dawkins (b. 1941), he enumerates the evils religion has produced (bloody sacrifices, pointless hopes and fears, dread of divine punishment, and so forth). To Lucretius, Epicurus was a torchbearer of light and reason to a world mired in darkness and fear.

As Martin Ferguson Smith remarks in the introduction to his 1969 translation of *De rerum natura*, the work "is one of the world's greatest poems not because it is merely artistic, but because it is also full of passion, fervor, and emotion: the poet . . . puts all his heart and soul, as well as all his intellectual power, into his writing, and that is largely why the work still grips our attention, still throbs with life and excitement." Of course, many readers from Lucretius's day to ours have not shared his sense of the liberating effects of atomism as a worldview. Some find his picture of the universe as a blind collocation of atoms depressing, offering little basis for meaning or optimism. Whatever one's take on these ultimate issues, all readers can agree that Lucretius is a supreme poet.

SEE ALSO Atoms and the Void (c. 420 BCE), Epicureanism (c. 300 BCE)

On this title page of a 1725 edition of De rerum natura (On the Nature of Things) *engraved by Dutch printmaker Jan Wandelaar, the Roman goddess Diana kneels before the personification of poetry on a pedestal; she is flanked by Minerva and Hercules. Two putti in the lower left corner hold a portrait of Lucretius.*

DE

NATURA

RERUM

LUGDUNI BATAVORUM,
Apud
JANSSONIOS VANDER AA,
Bibliopolas.

Universal Moral Law

Marcus Tullius Cicero (106–43 BCE)

Cicero is best known as an orator and Latin stylist, but he is also an important figure in philosophy. He was not an original thinker; his importance lies as a translator and transmitter of Greek philosophical ideas. One of the most significant Greek ideas he passed along is the Stoic notion of universal moral law.

Marcus Tullius Cicero was born in Arpinum, in south-central Italy, to a well-to-do family. He received a superb education, learning Greek at an early age and later studying philosophy and rhetoric in Athens and Rhodes. Cicero spent most of his career in public life, as both a lawyer and a statesman. Toward the end of his life, however, he found time to write philosophy. He was an eclectic, drawing freely from Platonic, Stoic, and Aristotelian sources. On most matters, he was a skeptic, agreeing with the Platonist Carneades that certainty is impossible and that we must make due with probable opinions. In ethics, though, Cicero agreed mostly with the Stoics. While he rejected some of the more extreme Stoic doctrines, he agreed with their ideas about divine providence, the universal fellowship of mankind, fundamental equality, and virtue as the most important object of human striving. He also concurred with their view of what they called "natural law." The Stoics distinguished human law, which changes, varies from place to place, and is often unjust, from a perfect and eternal law that emanates from the Logos (Cosmic Reason, or God). Cicero describes this higher law in a classic passage from his *De re publica* (*On the Republic*, 51 BCE) that greatly influenced later Western thinking on law:

> True law is right reason in agreement with nature; it is of universal application, unchanging and everlasting; . . . We cannot be freed from its obligations by senate or people, and we need not look outside ourselves for an expounder or interpreter of it. . . . [O]ne eternal and unchangeable law will be valid for all nations and all times, and there will be one master and ruler, that is, God, over us all, for He is the author of this law, its promulgator, and its enforcing judge.

SEE ALSO Carneades on Justice (155 BCE), The Death of Seneca (65), Epictetian Stoicism (c. 125), The Philosopher-King (180)

An early-twentieth-century statue of Cicero graces the front of the Palace of Justice in Rome, Italy.

The Christian Era Begins

Jesus of Nazareth (c. 4 BCE–c. 30 CE)

Sir Anthony Kenny, author of *A New History of Western Philosophy* (2007), has aptly stated that for "the long-term development of philosophy the most important event in the first century of the Roman Empire was the career of Jesus of Nazareth." How one assesses the impact of Christianity on Western philosophy depends heavily on one's general attitudes toward philosophy and Christianity, but most scholars would agree that Christianity had two major effects on philosophy.

First, it dramatically reduced general interest in philosophy. In ancient times there were flourishing schools of philosophy in every major city, and the works of Plato, Aristotle, Epictetus, and other philosophers were widely read for the wisdom they could provide on life's fundamental questions. This changed after Christianity became the official religion of the Roman Empire in the fourth century. Schools of philosophy petered out or were shut down, and many works by classic philosophers were lost or no longer read. A clear example of the lack of interest in philosophy is evident in the distinctly lackluster history of Byzantine philosophy. For over 1,100 years, the works of Plato and Aristotle lay moldering in the libraries of Constantinople. Aside from some of the logical and scientific works of Aristotle, they were virtually ignored. Apparently it was believed that the writings of pagan philosophers were either dangerous or useless in light of the true and definitive wisdom of the Christian revelation.

The second major effect Christianity had on philosophy was to change its agenda. When Christianity became the dominant religion, philosophical speculation that was opposed to Christian teachings was generally discouraged or suppressed. Philosophy came to be seen as a "handmaid" to theology. Its primary role was to support and to systematize Christian doctrine. Thus there was significant interest throughout the Middle Ages in philosophical "proofs" of God's existence, His perfect nature, and the immortality of the soul. It was not until the seventeenth century that philosophy began to break free of its subordinate role to theology and to pursue a different and wider array of questions.

SEE ALSO Platonism and Christianity (c. 150), The Great Medieval Synthesis (c. 1265)

The Basilica of Sant'Apollinare in Classe, a Roman harbor town near Ravenna, Italy, is an iconic Byzantine church that dates to the sixth century. The apse mosaic, shown here, is a symbolic depiction of the transfiguration of Christ. Saint Apollinaris, a legendary bishop of Ravenna, stands in prayer below an enormous gold cross that represents Christ (his face is at the center of the cross), while the sheep symbolize the apostles.

Buddhism Comes to China

Buddhism originated in India, but within a millennium had spread to many parts of East and Southeast Asia. Exactly when Buddhism first came to China is unclear. Scholars debate whether the earliest Buddhist missionaries to China arrived by boat or came overland along the Silk Road. According to one account, Buddhism was introduced to China around 65 CE by the Han emperor Ming, who had a dream about a golden Buddha flying through his room and sent a delegation to India to learn about Buddhism. According to the story, the delegates returned with two Indian Buddhist missionaries and a number of Buddhist sacred writings. From the emperor's court, the new religion slowly began to spread throughout China.

At first, Buddhism grew slowly in China. Chinese rulers tended to be hostile to foreign influences, and monkish ideals of celibacy and asceticism were alien to the practical-minded and family-oriented Chinese. However, when Chinese translations of Buddhist texts started to circulate in the fourth century, the religion began to spread. A number of schools of Buddhist thought arose, and monasteries were built throughout the land. Most of the schools belonged to the Mahayana branch of Buddhism. Unlike the stricter Theravada tradition of Buddhism, Mahayana Buddhists rely upon scriptures that appeared later in the Buddhist canon and generally pursue salvation through prayer and devotion to various supernatural beings, rather than through the arduous spiritual discipline recommended in the earliest Buddhist texts. Three of the most popular schools of Chinese Buddhism were the Pure Land school, the Chan (Meditation) school, and the Tiantai (Lotus) school. Of these, Chan (or Zen, to use the more familiar Japanese term) Buddhism has had the greatest impact on Western thought. Unlike many strands of Mahayana Buddhism, Chan stresses enlightenment through direct spiritual insight rather than salvation through devotion to supernatural beings.

Though Confucianism has always been the dominant philosophical or wisdom tradition in China, Buddhism has profoundly shaped Chinese culture. Many of the deepest works of Chinese philosophy have emerged from the Buddhist tradition.

SEE ALSO The Four Noble Truths (c. 525 BCE), Origins of Chan/Zen Buddhism (c. 520), Huineng and the *Platform Sutra* (c. 700)

The courtyard of the White Horse Temple in the ancient city of Luoyang, Henan Province, in east-central China. Built in 68 under Emperor Ming, it is one of the first Buddhist temples established in China.

The Death of Seneca

Lucius Annaeus Seneca (c. 4 BCE–65 CE)

Together with Epictetus and Marcus Aurelius, Lucius Annaeus Seneca is one of the most widely read and quoted of the Stoic philosophers. Though he did not always live up to his high ideals, he died in a manner befitting the rugged Stoics of old.

Seneca was born into a wealthy and literary family in Spain but came to Rome at an early age. There he studied Stoicism under Attalus and became a lawyer, writer, and public official. In 41 CE, Seneca was suspected of wrongdoing by the emperor Claudius and exiled for eight years to the island of Corsica. There he consoled himself by writing tragedies and bemoaning his fate in a decidedly un-stoical way. In 49, Seneca was recalled from exile and became tutor and later an advisor to the future emperor Nero. For several years, he took a leading role in ruling the Roman Empire, all the while amassing a huge fortune by taking advantage of his official position. As Nero's crimes mounted, Seneca felt tainted and sought to retire from public life. From 62 to 65, he lived quietly in his southern Italian villas, devoting himself to philosophy and donating most of his fortune to help rebuild Rome after the fire of 64. In 65, he was suspected by Nero of participating in an assassination plot and was ordered to commit suicide. He received the message with calm composure. He and his wife Paulina embraced and then each slit their wrists. Seneca also drank hemlock, apparently resolved to die as Socrates did. He died sitting in a warm bath. At Nero's orders, his wife's wrists were bandaged, and she survived him by a few years.

Seneca was a brilliant writer who expressed many classic Stoic teachings in golden apothegms. He wrote eloquently on the themes of serene acceptance of one's fate, virtue as the sole good, and the value of adversities in building inner strength. Each of us, he urged, should ask ourselves three questions before we retire to bed: "What bad habit have you cured today? What fault have you resisted? In what way are you better?"

SEE ALSO Universal Moral Law (51 BCE), Epictetian Stoicism (c. 125), The Philosopher-King (180)

The suicide of Seneca depicted in a colored engraving by the French engraver Simon Ravenet after Italian painter Luca Giordano, 1768.

Epictetian Stoicism

Epictetus (c. 55–135 CE)

By a curious twist, the thinker who taught ancient Greeks and Romans the deepest truths about human freedom was born a slave. That man was the Stoic philosopher Epictetus.

Epictetus was born in Hierapolis, in what is today Turkey. As a slave, Epictetus was passed from one owner to another, until he eventually wound up in Rome. There he became the property of Epaphroditus, a powerful official in the court of the Roman emperor Nero. Eventually, Epictetus was freed and rose to become a well-known philosopher in Rome. Around age forty, he was expelled from Rome by the emperor, Domitian—along with other philosophers—and settled in Nicopolis, a city in western Greece. There he opened a school of Stoic philosophy and lived a simple life with few possessions.

One of Epictetus's pupils, Arrian, wrote down the master's words and published them in two books, known today as the *Discourses* and the *Manual* (or *Enchiridion*). Both books are highly readable, full of simple, powerful sayings, bluff talk, and wry humor.

Epictetus taught a stern, demanding form of Stoicism that harkened back to the heroic days of Socrates and early Greek Stoicism. For Epictetus, philosophy was not something you "studied," but a total commitment to an arduous but deeply liberating and fulfilling way of life.

Epictetus's key idea was the importance of "acceptance." Like all Stoics, he believed that the universe was wisely governed by a kind of all-pervading cosmic reason or divine intelligence that the Stoics called Logos. Whatever happens in life must ultimately be "for the best." It follows that we should not grumble or complain when "bad" things happen in our lives, for all things eventually work for good in ways we cannot understand.

Hard knocks and adversities are inevitable in life, Epictetus taught. Most of the things people chase after—money, power, fame, a happy family life—are partly matters of luck and not fully within our control. The secret to happiness is to focus on the few things in life you can fully control: your own attitudes, judgments, and reactions. Make up your mind to think positive thoughts, and nothing can force you to think negative ones.

SEE ALSO Universal Moral Law (51 BCE), The Death of Seneca (65), The Philosopher-King (180)

A portrait of Epictetus, from the frontispiece of Epictetus's Enchiridion, *translated by Edward Ivie and printed in Oxford in 1715. Epictetus, who was said to have a disabled leg, is depicted with a crutch.*

Δ8λος Επίκτητος γυόμηυ, ή σῶμ' ανάπηρος,
Καὶ πευίlω Ιρος, ή φίλος ἀθανάτοις.

Platonism and Christianity

Justin Martyr (100–165), **Clement of Alexandria** (c. 150–c. 215),
Origen (c. 185–c. 254), **Eusebius of Caesarea** (c. 265–c. 340),
Gregory of Nyssa (c. 335–c. 395)

During the first few centuries of the Common Era, it was uncertain as to whether Christianity and philosophy would be enemies, allies, or ships passing in the night. Saint Paul exhorted the Colossians to "beware lest any man spoil you through philosophy and vain deceit" (Col. 2:8). Paul did not view the Gospel as the true philosophy; he claimed to preach nothing but Christ crucified, and thanked God that He had "made foolish the wisdom of this world" (I Cor. 1:20). Yet less than a century after Paul's death, serious efforts were being made to bring pagan philosophy into the service of Christianity.

Partly, this was a matter of necessity. Pagan critics used philosophical arguments to attack Christianity, and such attacks could be thwarted only by similar philosophical firepower. As time went on, Christian thinkers also found it useful to draw upon philosophy to deepen and clarify Christian truths and to develop a comprehensive Christian worldview. A number of important Christian thinkers in the Latin West resisted the attempt to harmonize faith and philosophy, most notably the Carthaginian Tertullian (c. 155–c. 240), who asked rhetorically, "What indeed has Athens to do with Jerusalem?" and exclaimed, "it [Christ's incarnation] is by all means to be believed, because it is absurd." This view was strongly rejected by a number of influential Greek-speaking Christians, including Saints Justin Martyr, Clement of Alexandria, and Gregory of Nyssa; and theologians Origen and Eusebius of Caesarea. They saw pagan philosophy (especially Platonism) both as a preparation for Christianity and as an invaluable arsenal and toolkit for its defense and development. In Latin Christendom as well, St. Augustine (354–430 CE)—by far the most important Christian thinker in late antiquity—praised Platonism for its essential congruity with Christian truth and drew upon its resources in developing key aspects of his theology, including his view of human knowledge and his response to the problem of why God allows evil. Certain strands of Protestant thought would later challenge this view of a harmonious relationship between faith and reason, but it has remained the dominant outlook in Christian thought.

SEE ALSO The Christian Era Begins (c. 30 CE), *The City of God* (426), Revival of Christian Philosophy (1984)

The Christian thinker Tertullian of Carthage, shown here in a 1689 engraving by Dutch printmakers Zacharias Chatelain and Jan Luyken, asked what "has Athens to do with Jerusalem?"

The Philosopher-King

Marcus Aurelius (121–180)

Marcus Aurelius, emperor of Rome from 161 to 180 CE, may have come closer than anyone to fulfilling Plato's dream of a philosopher who became king. Marcus was born into a wealthy, politically connected family in Rome. His father died when he was a small child, and he was brought up by his grandfather. Marcus was given a first-class education, which included a solid grounding in Greek and numerous philosophy tutors. At age eleven, under the influence of a Stoic tutor, Marcus determined to live as a philosopher, donning the coarse woolen cloak that philosophers typically wore and sleeping on the floor. At age sixteen, Marcus was adopted by the then emperor-elect, Antoninus Pius. When Antoninus died in 161, Marcus succeeded him as emperor. Though he hated war and was always in poor health, Marcus spent much of his reign away from Rome, protecting the empire's northern borders. Once, when visiting Athens, he walked the streets in a philosopher's cloak, unguarded, attending lectures by distinguished philosophers and participating in discussions, speaking fluent Greek. When he departed, he founded chairs for each of the four major philosophical schools in Athens (Platonic, Aristotelian, Stoic, and Epicurean). At age fifty-eight, after a Roman victory over northern tribes (likely near present-day Vienna), Marcus felt death approaching. He retired to his tent, refused all food and drink for six days, and died on his own terms.

After his death, a notebook was discovered in Marcus's tent, written in Greek, titled "Thoughts to Myself," standardly translated with the title *Meditations*. In these pages, we find the authentic voice of Socrates and Epictetus, written by a man who possessed absolute power but chose instead to play the role of a dutiful servant. Here, on the banks of the Danube, Marcus meditated on the Stoic themes he'd learned in his youth: the vanity of fame, the importance of duty, the brevity of human existence, the pointlessness of fear of death, and acceptance of one's fate as part of God's wise governance of the universe. In Marcus, we find one of the very few exceptions to the maxim that "power corrupts, and absolute power corrupts absolutely."

SEE ALSO Universal Moral Law (51 BCE), The Death of Seneca (65), Epictetian Stoicism (c. 125)

This equestrian statue of Emperor Marcus Aurelius on Capitoline Hill in Rome is a copy of the original, which was created c. 176 and moved inside the Palazzo dei Conservatori Museum in the 1980s for preservation.

Outlines of Pyrrhonism

Pyrrho of Elis (c. 360–c. 270 BCE), **Sextus Empiricus** (fl. c. 200)

There were two major forms of skepticism in ancient Greece and Rome. One was Academic Skepticism, founded by Arcesilaus around 270 BCE and centered in Plato's Academy. The other was Pyrrhonian Skepticism, founded by Pyrrho of Elis.

Little is known about Pyrrho. Reputedly, he accompanied Alexander the Great on his conquest of the East. While in India, he encountered a group of "naked wise men" (yogis). Apparently they made an impression, because when Pyrrho returned to Greece he set up a school devoted to the pursuit of mental tranquility (*ataraxia*) through skeptical suspension of belief. The people of his hometown, Elis, were so impressed that they made him high priest, erected a statue in his honor, and exempted philosophers from taxation.

By good fortune, a clear picture of Pyrrhonian Skepticism was preserved in a treatise by an obscure Greek physician, Sextus Empiricus: *Outlines of Pyrrhonism*. What emerges is an elaborate form of skepticism even more radical than the Academic Skepticism of Arcesilaus and Carneades.

According to Sextus's text, philosophy is both a disease and a cure. It is a disease because it leads to unhappiness and arrogant dogmatism. Philosophy promises wisdom and consoling answers, but it can provide only endless questions. The solution is to adopt a kind of meta-philosophy—namely Skepticism—that recognizes that ignorance is simply the human condition and that is content with this inescapable reality. The core of skepticism, Sextus taught, lies in the ability to construct equally forceful arguments for or against any thesis. A wide variety of argumentative strategies, called *modes* or *tropes*, are laid out to assist in this balancing process. Unlike the Academic Skeptics, who generally recognized that some beliefs are more probable than others, the Pyrrhonian Skeptics held that no belief is more plausible than any other. For this reason, probability cannot be the guide of life. Instead, we should follow our natural feelings and the laws and customs of our community.

Pyrrhonian Skepticism seems to have pretty much died out in the ancient world not long after Sextus's lifetime. In the sixteenth century, however, Sextus's writings were rediscovered, sparking a renewed interest in ancient Greek Skepticism.

SEE ALSO Carneades on Justice (155 BCE), Revival of Classical Skepticism (1580)

The opening page from a c. sixteenth-century edition of Adversus Mathematicos (Against the Mathematicians *or* Professors), *a series of eleven books written by Sextus Empiricus expounding the theories of Pyrrhonian Skepticism.*

SEXTI EMPIRICI
ADVERSVS MATHE-
MATICOS.

GENTIANO HERVETO AVRE-
LIO INTERPRETE.

IN CONTRADICENDO iis qui profitentur di-
sciplinas, idem videtur esse animus Epicureorum
& Pyrrhoneorū, non est autem eadem affectio.
Nam Epicurei quidē contradicunt, vtpote quòd
ad perfectionem sapientiæ nihil conferant disci-
plinæ:vel vt nonnulli coniiciunt, quòd hunc exi-
stiment esse prætextum suæ inscitiæ. In multis enim Epicurus argui-
tur indoctus, & nec in cōmuni quidem sermone purus. Fortasse autem etiam propterea quòd malè vellet Platoni & Aristoteli,& simi-
libus qui multarum disciplinarum erāt cognitione prediti. Est etiam
satis verisimile, quòd id fecerit propter inimicitias quæ ei intercedebant cum Nausiphane Pyrrhonis auditore.Multos enim apud se ha-
bebat adolescentes, & disciplinarum valde erat studiosus, maximè
autem Rhetoricæ. Cùm ergo Epicurus eius fuisset discipulus, vt vi-
deretur esse non ab alio quàm à seipso edoctus, suóque ingenio &
industria extitisse Philosophus, omnino ibat inficias, eiúsque famam
& existimationé delere contendebat,& in reprehendēdis in sectan-
dísque disciplinis,in quibus ille gloriabatur,multùm versabatur. Di-
cit quidem certè in epistola quam scripsit ad Philosophos qui erant
Mitylenæ: Existimo autem gemebundos illos opinaturos me esse
Pulmonis discipulum,qui eum audierim cum quibusdam crapula la-
borantibus & temulentis adolescentibus, pulmonem nunc vocans
Nausiphanem, vt qui nullo sit sensu præditus . Et rursus progressus,

*Epicurus in-
doctus.*

*Nausiphani
cum Epicuro
intercedebant
inimicitiæ.*

*Nausiphanes
cur pulmo di-
ctus.*

20

25

30

35

a   cùm

Neoplatonism

Plotinus (c. 205–270)

Plotinus is the greatest Greek philosopher of the Common Era. He founded a school of philosophy, Neoplatonism, which was a major influence on both late-classical pagan philosophy and early-Christian thought. By means of thinkers such as St. Augustine, Boethius (480–524), and Pseudo-Dionysius (fl. c. 500), Neoplatonism entered deeply into the fabric of medieval philosophy and theology.

Plotinus was born in Egypt and educated in Alexandria, where he studied for eleven years under the distinguished pagan philosopher Ammonius Saccas. Following an abortive attempt to travel to Mesopotamia to study with Persian and Indian philosophers, Plotinus settled in Rome. There he opened a highly successful school and wrote a series of fifty-four tracts that were later edited by his pupil Porphyry into six books, each with nine sections, and titled *Enneads* (*Nines*). Faithful to his mystical, spirit-centered philosophy, Plotinus was a celibate vegetarian who ate sparingly, meditated frequently, and took little interest in worldly matters. "He was ashamed," Porphyry said, "that his soul had a body."

Plotinus's Neoplatonism was basically a fusion of a souped-up, theologized Platonism with dabs of Aristotelianism, Stoicism, and other ancient philosophies mixed in. Taking hints from Plato's writings, Plotinus crafted an elaborate theological superstructure that viewed the physical universe as the result of a series of emanations from the ultimate Reality, which he called *the One*—an eternal, unchanging, immaterial, unknowable, and absolutely unitary Reality. From the One emanates another divine principle, Mind (*nous*), the source of the eternal Platonic Forms. From Mind emanates Soul, which gives rise to time, individual souls, and the physical world. Like Plato, Plotinus believed that the body is the prison of the soul. The purpose of life is to return to the One by living a life of wisdom, virtue, and self-denial. For most people salvation will be a process that requires many additional reincarnations. Good and holy souls, however, will permanently merge with the One, thereby losing all personal identity. As Plotinus lay dying, his last words were: "Now I shall endeavor to make that which is divine in me rise up to that which is divine in the universe."

SEE ALSO The Last Great Greek Philosopher (c. 460), The Way of Negation (c. 500), Eriugena's Christian Neoplatonism (c. 865).

A Roman marble bust of a philosopher believed to be Plotinus, created c. 350.

The Problem of Universals

Porphyry (c. 234–c. 305)

How should we think about terms or concepts that have general applications, like "red," "tiger," or "number"? This is what philosophers call the problem of universals. The first philosopher who squarely posed the problem of universals was the Neoplatonist Porphyry.

Porphyry's real name was Malchus ("King"), but he was called Porphyry ("Clad in Purple") because he came from the Phoenician city of Tyre, which was famous for its purple dyes. Porphyry studied in Plato's Academy in Athens and then in Rome under the greatest philosopher of his time, Plotinus, founder of Neoplatonism. Porphyry became a dedicated Neoplatonist, wrote a biography of Plotinus, and edited Plotinus's major work, the *Enneads*. Porphyry was also a great admirer of Aristotle and wrote an introduction to Aristotle's logic called *Isagoge* (*Introduction*) that was translated two centuries later into Latin by the Roman philosopher Boethius and served as a standard textbook for a thousand years. It was in the first paragraph of the *Isagoge* that Porphyry framed the problem of universals in a way that became canonical for subsequent discussions.

He asked: Do universals exist outside the mind, or are they merely concepts? If they exist outside the mind, are they material or immaterial? If they are immaterial, do they exist in physical objects, or are they separate from them? Porphyry posed these questions but did not answer them, saying they were too difficult to be tackled in an introductory text like the *Isagoge*. But many later philosophers offered answers to these questions, and the debate continues to this day.

Plato believed that universals, or "Forms," exist outside the mind, are incorporeal, and exist separately from physical objects. Many Christian philosophers, including St. Augustine and Pseudo-Dionysius, relocated Plato's Forms into the mind of God. But other philosophers favored different solutions. So-called nominalists, such as George Berkeley (1685–1753) and John Stuart Mill (1806–1873), deny that universals or general concepts exist. According to Mill, "there is nothing general except names." Other philosophers ("ultrarealists") fully supported the reality of universals, claiming they were substances that exist outside the mind. Most philosophers ("moderate realists" or "conceptualists") have argued for positions somewhere in between.

SEE ALSO The World of the Forms (c. 380 BCE), The Birth of Scholasticism (1121), Conceptualism (c. 1320)

An illustration of Porphyry from Les vrais pourtraits et vies des hommes illustres grecz, latins et payens *(The True Portraits and Lives of Illustrious Greek, Latin, and Pagan Men), published in 1584 by French Franciscan explorer and cosmographer André Thévet.*

PORPHIRE SOPHISTE.
Chap. 37.

OUR ce que traictant cy deuāt les mœurs
& vertuz de ce grand docteur Origene, i'ay
cité comme tesmoignage valable, l'opinion
qu'auoit de luy Porphire Philosophe Ty-
rien, ioinct que parmy mes autres recher-
ches est tombé entre mes mains son pour-
traict naturel, que i'ay recouuert d'vn Grec
estant en la ville de Retimo, située en l'Isle
de Crete, il ne m'a semblé impertinent vous le representer, & traicter
superficielement de luy, non pour le loüer, ains affin de mōstrer que

Augustine's Conversion

Augustine of Hippo (354–430)

Augustine's *Confessions* (c. 400) is one of the enduring and unique masterpieces of Western literature and religion. Part confession, part spiritual autobiography, it is cast in the form of an extended prayer, addressed entirely to God but meant to be overheard by us, his readers. It tells a remarkable story about a remarkable man.

Aurelius Augustinus was born in the Roman colony of Thagaste, in what is now eastern Algeria. His mother, Monica, was a devout Christian, but his father, Patricius, was a pagan. A precocious boy, Augustine rose to become a prominent teacher of rhetoric attached to the imperial court in Milan. As a young man, Augustine struggled with both his sexuality (he long kept a mistress and had a son out of wedlock) and his beliefs. For many years, Augustine was an adherent of Manichaeism, a Persian religion centered on a dualistic mythology in which the cosmos is locked in a battle between good (a spiritual world) and evil (a corrupt material world). When Augustine moved from Africa to Italy, he abandoned Manichaeism, switching first to a form of Skepticism and later to Neoplatonism. Largely through the influence of the bishop of Milan, St. Ambrose, Augustine converted to Christianity. The climactic moment of final conversion is vividly recounted in the *Confessions*. In the summer of 386, as he lay weeping in an agony of indecision under a fig tree in a garden in Milan, Augustine thought he heard children chanting *tolle, lege* ("pick up and read"). He rose, opened a copy of Paul's *Letter to the Romans*, and read the first passage he saw: "Put ye on the Lord Jesus Christ, and make not provision for the flesh, to fulfil the lusts thereof." The following Easter, Augustine and his fifteen-year-old son, Adeodatus, walked naked into the baptismal pool at Milan cathedral and were clothed in white by St. Ambrose when they emerged.

Shortly thereafter, Augustine returned to North Africa, where he later became bishop of Hippo and a prolific writer. Gifted with both a powerful mind and a brilliant literary style, Augustine created a synthesis of Christian thought that made him (in St. Jerome's words) "the second founder of the Christian faith."

SEE ALSO *The City of God* (426)

Saint Augustine of Hippo (far left) is depicted holding the heart of Jesus in a hand-colored German woodcut from c. 1450.

Death of Hypatia

Hypatia (c. 350–415)

Hypatia of Alexandria was one of the most accomplished thinkers of ancient times—a philosopher, a mathematician, and an astronomer—and is likely the earliest female scientist whose life was historically recorded. Her father, Theon, is reported to have been a professor at the famous Alexandrian Museum and a distinguished mathematician who edited Euclid's *Elements*. After publishing a number of works on astronomy and mathematics, Hypatia turned to philosophy. Sometime around 400 CE she was appointed to the chair of philosophy at the Museum and became head of Alexandria's Platonist school of philosophy. According to the Christian historian Socrates of Constantinople, Hypatia drew large audiences and "far surpassed all the philosophers of her time." Reputed to be a great beauty, Hypatia was said to have been virtuous, resisting all suitors.

As a prominent pagan and female intellectual, Hypatia attracted the ire of fanatical Alexandrian Christians, led by their intolerant bishop, Cyril. Hypatia was a friend and ally of Orestes, the prefect of Alexandria. When tensions boiled over between Cyril and Orestes during Lent in 415, a lynch mob of Cyril's supporters pulled Hypatia from her carriage, dragged her into Cyril's home church, the Caesareum, stripped her naked, murdered her with bricks, scraped the flesh from her bones with oyster-shells, and (in eighteenth-century British historian Edward Gibbon's lurid account) cast her "quivering limbs" to the flames. "After this," British philosopher Bertrand Russell (1872–1970) remarked, "Alexandria was no longer troubled by philosophers." Cyril was declared a saint and a doctor of the Church.

Russell exaggerated when he said that Hypatia's murder rid Alexandria of philosophers. In fact, a long line of distinguished philosophers later studied or taught at Alexandria in the fifth and sixth centuries, including Proclus, Ammonius Hermiae, Simplicius of Cilicia, and John Philoponus. It is true, though, that after Hypatia's death Athens replaced Alexandria as the philosophical capital of the world. Until Justinian closed the schools of Athens in 529, pagans were relatively free to teach philosophy in Athens. And it was pagans who were then most interested in philosophy.

SEE ALSO The Last Great Greek Philosopher (c. 460), Justinian Closes the Academy (529)

An engraving by Jan Luyken, 1701, of Hypatia of Alexandria being dragged from her carriage by a mob of supporters of the Christian bishop Cyril.

The City of God

Augustine of Hippo (354–430)

The City of God is the most important book of the most important Christian thinker from beginnings of the Christian era to the high Middle Ages. A sprawling treatise of 1,100 pages that was written in snatches over a period of thirteen years, it is primarily a work of theology but also had a profound influence on the course of philosophy. The first part of *The City of God* seeks to rebut pagan charges that Christians are to blame for the sack of Rome in 410 by the Goths. As the book gathers steam, it morphs into a vast cosmic drama of creation, fall, revelation, incarnation, and eternal destiny. The sweeping (and sometimes gloomy) tapestry Augustine wove dominated the imagination of Western Christendom until the Age of Reason.

As Augustine saw it, secular divisions of class and nationality are trivial compared to the one classification that really matters: whether one belongs to "God's People." Since the creation, he argued, God's rational creatures, both angels and human beings, have been divided into two warring cities: the City of God, composed of those few destined to eternal salvation; and the City of Man, made up of the vast multitudes of the damned.

Theologically, *The City of God* is a work of towering importance both for its synoptic vision of salvation history and for its powerful fusion of philosophical and biblical resources to flesh out key Christian doctrines such as creation, original sin, grace, resurrection, and heaven and hell. Philosophically, the work is important both because it showed how philosophy could be of value in constructing a comprehensive Christian worldview and because it provided the general framework within which virtually all philosophical reflection about politics was done in the Christian West for over a millennium.

Augustine died in 430, worn out by his vast labors. His city, Hippo, had been under siege for several months by the Vandals and would soon be overrun. As he lay dying, he reportedly found solace in the words of Plotinus: "How can a man be taken seriously if he attaches importance to the collapse of wood and stones, or to the death—God help us—of mortal creatures?"

SEE ALSO Augustine's Conversion (386)

Saint Augustine is shown in an alabaster relief, c. 1500, holding a walled city (likely Hippo) in his right hand.

The Last Great Greek Philosopher

Proclus (412–485)

Platonism was the only Greek philosophical tradition that continued to produce high-quality work in late antiquity. The dominant form of Platonism during this period was Neoplatonism, which had been founded by Plotinus around 250. Next to Plotinus, Proclus is widely considered the greatest Greek philosopher of the Common Era.

Proclus was born in Constantinople into a well-to-do family who sent him to Alexandria to study law. Instead, he fell in love with philosophy, supposedly learning all of Aristotle's logical works by heart. When he was eighteen, Proclus moved to Athens to study in the revived Academy, and seven years later became the head scholarch. For nearly fifty years he worked indefatigably to restore the Academy to its ancient luster. To fully devote himself to the philosophical life, he never married and ate a sparing vegetarian diet. Proclus was a prolific writer, supposedly averaging seven hundred lines a day. Although most of his writings are lost, several important works have survived, including the *Elements of Theology* and *Platonic Theology*. An unapologetic pagan who prayed to the sun three times a day, Proclus had to keep a low profile in predominantly Christian fifth-century Athens. Not long after Proclus's death, Emperor Justinian closed the Academy, as it was a prominent pagan stronghold.

Proclus believed quite literally that Plato had been divinely inspired. Proclus's basic goal was to take the best of Greek philosophy (including Aristotle's logic and physics) and fuse it into an overarching Platonic framework. But Proclus's Plato was the mystical Plato of Plotinus, which focused on the one true Reality, the "One" that lies beyond thought and all possible description. Like Plotinus, Proclus taught that the physical world comes into existence through a process of emanation from the One. Proclus, however, probably following earlier Neoplatonic philosophers, greatly complicated Plotinus's account by adding an elaborate system of triads and mediating *henads* (divine beings). The ultimate goal of life, Proclus taught, was self-perfection and union with the One. To achieve this, he recommended not only a life of virtue and philosophical contemplation, but also the practice of certain rituals (*theurgy*) that he believed the gods had revealed to assist in our divinization.

SEE ALSO Plato Founds the Academy (c. 386 BCE), Neoplatonism (c. 250), The Recovery of Platonism (1468)

A page from Proclus's c. fifteenth-century codex, Theologia Platonica (Platonic Theology).

☩ Πρόκλου πλατωνικοῦ διαδόχου, εἰς τὴν
Πλάτωνος θεολογίαν :—

Ὁ σεσοφισμένος ἐναδιαδεῖξαι τῆς πραγματείας σκοπ. μεθ᾽ ἀφ᾽ ἡμῖ-
τῆς τελετῆς τοῦ Πλάτωνος, ὁ ὁ διάδοχος διαδεξάμενος
τὴν φιλοσοφίαν :   ἴσως οὗτος εὐλόγως, εὖ τί περ καὶ
εἰ τίνι περ ἄγμα τα ἄ· ὁ ἐν θεῖ· τ᾽ ἂν παῖδα δὴ τὸν δίκεα βελτίων τε
σκ ἀπ᾽ :   ἴσως ἢ τὴν Πλάτωνα θεολ᾽ . καὶ πόθεν ἄρχεται κ
μεθ ἐστὶν ἀγαθόν τις πρὸς θεοσεων· ὁ κ τὴν ἀγαθὴ ἡμῖν διὰ δυνάμιν
ἐν δ᾽ ἐπα διαφόρων τ᾽ .   ὑπὸ θεολογίκοι, καθὼς ἐστιν ἡ πᾶσα
Πλάτωνι διάθεσις τῆς περὶ θεὸς διδασκαλία :—
τίνες τ᾽ ἐστὶν οἱ διὰ λόγοι, ἀφ᾽ ὧν ἂν εὐλήπτη ἡ περὶ τὴν Πλάτωνος
θεολογίαν. καὶ τί ἐστιν ἡ τάξις θεῶν, ἕκαστος τούτων ἡ κ ἀφ᾽ ὧν ἡ ἐστι
ταυτησὶς, περὶ τὴν σκ Πλάτωνα διὰ λόγοι ναι λέγει σιν ἡ τὰς πλ θεὶ ἡ μῖ
ᾧ θ ἐ λό πῇ· ὧδε μή δικ ἡ καὶ καθ᾽ ἃ τε με μὴ σικ εἶν ἀ εἶ μα λ᾽ οὐσι
νο εἰς τῆς προ εἰ ρημένης ἀ πάντων σεως, ἵς τ᾽ ἐν ἀ τὸν ἡ μῖ νὶ διὲν
αὐ δ᾽ ρος αθ, τὴν ὅλην περὶ Πλάτωνος τε περὶ θεῶν ἀλή θειαν :—
Κ θε οις ἡ περ διαφόρων περὶ τοῦ περ ἡ μῖ νὶ δυ δὸ θε οῦ. καὶ ἰ διὰ περ
ταῦτ περ σα τας ἀ πάντων σε ως :—   ἡ τι λογία, περὶ τ᾽ ἀπ᾽ λογικ
εἰ τ᾽ τοῦ περ ἡ μῖ νὶ δι᾽ ἃ τ᾽ πόν τας· ἐπ᾽ τ᾽ ἐν αὐ τῶ τ᾽ πράγματ᾽ ἂν· δὶ ἐν δι᾽ ἐ
ἐπ᾽ ἡ γρη κα σικ ελκ ἂν ὑπὸ τὶ θε αἱ λό σε οσ᾽   ἵνα ἐκ τ᾽ γρ θε οῦ
οἱ τε κεῖ εν ἐν τοῖς οὐ σί ναι κ ξω νι ἐν α ἰ τα σὰς ὑπὸ θε ᾶς σ᾽ ἡ π ἡ μῖ νὶ ᾶ γ
λέον τω· κ᾽ εἰ ἵνα περὶ ᾶ ᾶ τε ἐν ὁ διὰ λε γει σιν ἐκ τῆς σαῦ τ᾽ ἡ περ
κ᾽ ᾶ ἕ λε εν νο σ᾽ εἶ μα ἡ πλ᾽ ἀ δό σε ως :   —— σ᾽ ὁ δὲ ἐ ξ᾽ πλ᾽
τ᾽ σε τα ἐν τῆς ἀλη θι ᾶ ὑπο θε ᾶ ως σου με περ ᾶ σ᾽ ᾶ κ᾽ ᾶ τ᾽ ᾶ πῶ
κ᾽ τὰς θε ᾶς τὰξ ᾶς ᾶ εἰ τῆς διαιρέσεως :—
κ ο πὸ ᾶ τ᾽ ἡ ν᾽ ὑπο θε᾽ σε ων τ᾽ ἡν περ᾽ δ ᾶ λὶ ᾶ σ᾽ α εἶ τὸν ᾶ σίν ᾶ δεν ᾶ
ἐ τῆς ν᾽ περε᾽ τ᾽ ᾶ πρά᾽ γ μα τα σ᾽ ᾶμ᾽ φω νί ᾶν δῆ κ ν᾽ ὑν᾽ τ᾽   ἵνα σ᾽
κοι νω νὸς κ᾽ ᾶ μό να σ᾽ περὶ θε ᾶ ν᾽ ὁ Πλά τω ν ᾶ κ νό μιι ν᾽ πλ᾽ ᾶ δὶ
ρ᾽ ω ι᾽ . εἰ σ᾽ ὑπε ρο᾽ ξε ως θε ᾶν᾽ . κ ᾶ π᾽ π᾽ ᾶ νὸ ι᾽ ᾶ ᾶ π᾽ ᾶ ρα π᾽ ᾶ τ᾽ ᾶ τ ᾶ θρό ι᾽

The Dark Ages Begin

The so-called Dark Ages in Europe (the roughly six-hundred-year period from the fall of the Roman Empire to the latter half of the eleventh century) mark the low ebb of philosophy in the West. In the fifth century, the Roman Empire was battered and eventually overwhelmed by a series of barbarian invasions from the North. In 410, Rome was sacked by the Visigoths under Alaric I, then pillaged again in 455 by Gaiseric and the Vandals. On September 4, 476, the last Roman Emperor, Romulus, was deposed by the Gothic general Odoacer, effectively putting an end to the Western Roman Empire. During the centuries that followed, the light of civilization was virtually extinguished in Europe. Governments collapsed, cities decayed, schools and libraries were destroyed, and violence and lawlessness reigned. What small vestiges of classical learning that remained were preserved in monasteries. Few in the old Western empire could read Greek, and those who could were usually more interested in reading theology than philosophy. As a result, there were virtually no notable Western philosophers in Europe from the death of Boethius in 524 to the publication of Anselm of Canterbury's *Monologion* (1076) and *Proslogion* (1078).

The one partial exception to this bleak picture was Ireland. When Northern Europe was being overrun by barbarians, a number of scholars fled to Ireland, where they founded schools and monasteries. There, protected by the sea—notwithstanding the Vikings—communities of classical learning endured for centuries. Both Greek and Roman classics were studied and taught in their original languages. In the sixth and seventh centuries, learned Irish monks fanned out over Scotland, England, Gaul, and Germany, founding monasteries and schools, building libraries, and spreading Christianity. Heiric of Auxerre, head of St. Germanus monastery in Gaul, remarked that "almost all of Ireland . . . is flocking to our shores with a troop of philosophers." By far the greatest of these was John Scotus Eriugena (c. 810–c. 877), who astonished his contemporaries with his mastery of Greek and his subtle Christian Neoplatonism. "It was in the Dark Ages," as historian Will Durant wrote, "that the Irish spirit shone with its strongest light."

SEE ALSO Justinian Closes the Academy (529), Eriugena's Christian Neoplatonism (c. 865)

The Glendalough monastic settlement in County Wicklow, Ireland—founded in the sixth century by Saint Kevin—was one of the many medieval Irish monasteries where Greek and Roman classics were studied. The Glendalough round tower, which stands in front of a cemetery amid the ruins of the settlement, dates from between the tenth and twelfth centuries.

The Way of Negation

Pseudo-Dionysius (fl. c. 500)

Sometime around 500, a series of works appeared purporting to be written by Dionysius the Areopagite, an Athenian converted by Paul (Acts 17:34) who is said to have been the first bishop of Athens. Throughout the Middle Ages, the works were considered to be authentic by most Christian thinkers, but in modern times it was discovered that the works must be spurious because they drew heavily upon the writings of the Neoplatonist Proclus (d. 485) and were possibly written by one of Proclus's students—Pseudo-Dionysius (a name coined by two nineteenth-century German scholars). Because the authorship had been wrongly attributed to an important bishop, an influential dose of Neoplatonic thought had entered into Christian theology. One example of this is Pseudo-Dionysius's distinction (borrowed from Proclus) between "affirmative theology" and "negative theology." Pseudo-Dionysius claimed there are two ways of knowing God, neither of which is fully adequate. The "affirmative way" consists of attributing to God those positive features of created beings that are compatible with God's spiritual nature. Thus, we say that God is "wise," "good," and so forth. Yet these descriptions are inadequate because no human concepts apply literally to God's transcendent and ineffable nature. It would be better, Pseudo-Dionysius says, to call Him "supergood" or "superwise."

Further, because of the limitations of human understanding, it was better to approach God by means of the negative way: denying of God any of the qualities we attribute to creatures. We start with qualities that are furthest removed from His infinite perfection. Thus, we deny that God is "drunken" or "hateful." Slowly we work our way toward less misleading descriptors, like "jealous" or "changeable." At the highest stage we deny of God even such qualities as goodness, being, understanding, and truthfulness. Here we enter a mystical "darkness of unknowing" in which all "cognitive apprehensions" are shut out and we are united with God "superintellectually."

Pseudo-Dionysius's ideas of negation had a huge impact on the way medieval thinkers talked about God, particularly in the Christian mystical tradition. Today there continue to be religious thinkers who deny that any descriptions, positive or negative, can literally be applied to God.

SEE ALSO The Last Great Greek Philosopher (c. 460), Mystical Theology (c. 1300)

A detail of the famous mosaic of Christ at the Hagia Sophia, Istanbul, Turkey, from the late thirteenth century.

Origins of Chan/Zen Buddhism

Bodhidharma (fl. c. 550)

Westerners have long been fascinated by Zen Buddhism, the Japanese version of what is known in China as Chan Buddhism. In some ways, Chan/Zen is a fusion of Daoist and Buddhist ideas. According to Chinese tradition, the founder of Chan Buddhism was an Indian (or possibly Persian) missionary named Bodhidharma who came to China around 520 CE. In Chinese art, Bodhidharma is invariably depicted as a heavy-set, scowling, bearded monk. According to one story, Emperor Wu, a devoted Buddhist who gave generously to Buddhist causes, requested an interview with Bodhidharma shortly after the latter arrived in China. Wu asked Bodhidharma how much karmic merit flowed from his gifts. The dour monk replied, "No merit at all!" He went on to explain that no merit derives from reading or meditation or good works; all that matters is direct insight into the "empty" unitary character of Reality. Spurned by the shocked emperor, Bodhidharma traveled north to the Shaolin temple on Mt. Shaoshi, where he is said to have spent nine years meditating with his face to a wall. More than six centuries after Bodhidharma's death, Chan Buddhism was introduced to Japan by a Japanese Buddhist, Master Eisai (1141–1215), who had studied it in China.

Zen Buddhists believe that all persons have a pure Buddha-nature. The trick, they claim, is to realize it. Everything in Zen is geared toward achieving a higher state of consciousness, a sudden flash of insight into the nondual, unitary nature of ultimate Reality. The trouble is that words and concepts get in the way. For this reason, Zen masters use a variety of techniques designed to break the grip of reason and logic on students' minds. These include *koans* (brief, often illogical sayings such as "What is the sound of one hand clapping?"), *mondos* (puzzling question-and-answer sessions), and *haikus* (short poems aimed at overcoming "I" and "not-I" dualities). Occasionally a Zen teacher will respond to a conventional-minded question by whacking a student or tossing them bodily out of a room. The Zen ideal of a mystical, unitive state of consciousness has had a profound impact on many aspects of Chinese and Japanese culture, including martial arts, painting, architecture, gardening, and tea ceremonies.

SEE ALSO Buddhism Comes to China (c. 65), Huineng and the *Platform Sutra* (c. 700)

A relief of Bodhidharma at Shaolin Temple on Mt. Shaoshi, in Henan Province, China.

The Consolations of Philosophy

Boethius (c. 480–524)

Anicius Boethius was the last great Roman philosopher, and arguably the most important philosopher in the Christian West between St. Augustine (354–430) and St. Anselm (c. 1033–1109). Born into a powerful Roman family with a long Christian lineage, Boethius received a classical education and became a prolific author, writing a number of important works on logic, music, arithmetic, and theology, in addition to many commentaries and translations. Fluent in Greek, Boethius set himself the task of translating the complete works of Plato and Aristotle into Latin. Had he succeeded, the whole course of Western civilization might well have been altered. Unfortunately, Boethius became entangled in politics, rose to high office, and was suspected by the Gothic emperor Theodoric of plotting his downfall. Boethius managed to translate only the logical works of Aristotle before he was imprisoned, tortured, and executed. Soon, virtually all knowledge of Plato and Aristotle—except for the logical writings Boethius translated—became lost to the West as Western Europe slipped into the chaos of the Dark Ages.

During his imprisonment, Boethius wrote his most famous book, *The Consolation of Philosophy*; it has always puzzled scholars, because although Boethius was a devout Christian there isn't a trace of Christianity in the book. Instead, Boethius turned to the Greek philosophers he loved for wisdom and comfort in his final days.

Edward Gibbon described the *Consolations* as a "golden volume," and so it is to all who love the lucid and serene spirit of the ancient Greek philosophers. Written as a dialogue between Boethius and his "nurse," Philosophy, it is the story of a man's healing journey from sorrow and depression to acceptance and recovered understanding. Its central theme is that happiness does not lie in riches, fame, or power, but in wisdom and virtue, and that perfect happiness consists in life forever with God, who is the absolute and all-sufficient good that satisfies the yearnings of the human heart.

Boethius's *Consolations* was one of the most popular books of the Middle Ages. Through it and his translations of and commentaries on Aristotle's logical works, a living echo of ancient Greek wisdom survived the collapse of classical civilization.

SEE ALSO *Nicomachean Ethics* (c. 330 BCE), *The City of God* (426)

A miniature illuminated by the Coëtivy Master from a c. 1460 French edition of Boethius's Consolations of Philosophy; *the top image depicts Philosophy consoling Boethius and Lady Fortune turning the wheel of fate, while the bottom image shows Philosophy instructing Boethius on the role of God.*

Justinian Closes the Academy

Simplicius of Cilicia (c. 490–c. 560), **Damascius** (c. 480–c. 550)

In 529, the Byzantine emperor Justinian closed the philosophical schools of Athens, thereby ending a glorious tradition of education that stretched back nearly a thousand years. The Athenian schools, particularly the Platonic Academy, were notorious vestiges of paganism in an increasingly intolerant Christian world. One of the last heads of the Academy, Proclus, openly worshipped pagan deities and published a book attacking the Christian doctrine of creation. With the closing of Plato's Academy, Bertrand Russell sonorously declared, "the Dark Ages descended upon Europe."

Yet they did not descend everywhere. The exiled philosophers from Plato's Academy continued to write philosophy long after their school was closed. And in the East, flourishing schools of philosophy continued to exist in Alexandria and other major cities. According to one account, in 531, seven philosophers from the Academy, including Damascius, the last head, and Simplicius, the most brilliant scholar in the bunch, traveled to Persia to seek refuge at the court of King Khosrow I. The Platonists, trained in the ascetic teachings of Proclus, were shocked at the polygamy and licentiousness practiced at the Persian court and requested permission to return to the Greek world. The following year, Khosrow made a treaty with Justinian that guaranteed the Platonists safe conduct back to the West and allowed them to practice their pagan rites. Exactly where they settled is unclear, though some have suggested it was in the Assyrian city of Harran, where they formed a school of Platonism that endured until the Arab conquest.

Some of the extensive writings of Damascius and Simplicius survive. Damascius focused mainly on writing commentaries on Plato's dialogues; Simplicius concentrated largely on Aristotle, producing some of the most insightful commentaries ever written. Simplicius also wrote a delightful commentary on Epictetus's the *Enchiridion*, which also survives. The purpose of the *Enchiridion*, Simplicius informs us, is "to set our souls as free, as when their Great Father and Creator first gave them to us; to disengage them from all those slavish fears, and confounding troubles, and other corruptions of human nature, which are wont to subdue and tyrannize over them." In these words we hear the last echoes of a dying tradition.

SEE ALSO The Last Great Greek Philosopher (c. 460), The Dark Ages Begin (476)

A Byzantine c. sixth-century mosaic of Emperor Justinian in the Basilica of Sant'Apollinare in Classe, near Ravenna, Italy.

The Rise and Spread of Islam

Muhammad (c. 570–632)

For five centuries, from 700 to 1200, Islam was the world leader in most civilized arts, including philosophy. The story of the rise and spread of Islam during this period is one of the great dramas of human history.

Muhammad, the founder of Islam, is considered by Muslims as the last and most important of the prophets. He was born in Mecca, in what is now Saudi Arabia. Orphaned at an early age, Muhammad grew up to become a successful merchant. Around the age of forty he began to have religious visions in which the archangel Gabriel communicated the words of Allah (God) to Muhammad, and these divine messages would become the Islamic holy book the Qur'an. Proclaiming himself to be the prophet of Allah, Muhammad slowly won converts. In 622 he fled to Medina to escape persecution. By the time of his death in 632, Muhammad had succeeded in uniting the fractious Arabian tribes under the banner of Islam. Less than a century after his death, military conquests had created a great Islamic empire stretching from Spain to India.

Under the patronage of wise rulers, magnificent libraries were created in cities such as Baghdad, Cairo, Aleppo, Toledo, and Palermo. These contained many works of Greek philosophy translated into Arabic. Instead of rejecting these works, Muslim philosophers tried to synthesize them into an overarching structure of Islamic wisdom. Drawing heavily on Aristotelian philosophy, Islamic philosophers from the ninth to twelfth centuries such as al-Kindī al-Fārābī, Ibn Sina (Avicenna), and Ibn-Rushd (Averroës) created great philosophical systems that were far in advance of anything that existed in the West or Byzantium. This tradition petered out by the thirteenth century, largely because of the hammer-blows Islam suffered during the Crusades, the Christian reconquest of Spain, and the Mongol invasions.

In terms of Western philosophy, Islam is important as a conduit of Greek philosophy and a stimulant to the growth of medieval Scholasticism. When Christian thinkers, largely through Islamic sources, encountered Aristotle's works in the early thirteenth century, an intellectual crisis resulted. From that crisis arose the sophisticated philosophical systems of Aquinas and the High Scholastics, and ultimately the birth of modern science and philosophy.

SEE ALSO Islamic Philosophy Begins (c. 840), Aristotelian Revival in the West (c. 1130)

Interior view of the Mosque-Cathedral of Córdoba in Spain. Now a cathedral, it served as a mosque from 784 to 1236, during which time the exiled Umayyad prince Abd al-Rahman and his descendants built, expanded, and embellished the structure, including the famous arched colonnaded prayer hall seen here.

Huineng and the *Platform Sutra*

Huineng (638–713)

Chan Buddhism (or Zen Buddhism as it is known in Japan) was founded by the Indian sage Bodhidharma around 520 CE. But the most important figure in shaping the Chan tradition in China was the homegrown philosopher Huineng.

According to the traditional account, which may be partly legend, Huineng was a poor and illiterate woodcutter in southern China who achieved instantaneous enlightenment when he heard someone reading verses from the *Diamond Sutra*. Determined to become a monk, Huineng traveled to the East Mountain monastery where he hoped to study with Hongren (601–674), the famous fifth patriarch of Chan Buddhism. At first, Hongren was unimpressed with the illiterate "barbarian" from the south and assigned him to kitchen duty for several months. One day, however, Huineng secretly entered a dharma verse contest and so impressed Hongren with his deep spiritual insight that he was immediately appointed as Hongren's successor. Huineng went on to become one of the most famous teachers in China and an enduring model of a Chan sage.

After his death, Huineng's main teachings were collected in a work called the *Platform Sutra of the Sixth Patriarch*. In that work, Huineng rejects the method of gradual enlightenment favored by Shenxiu (c. 607–706), the leader of the northern school of Chan Buddhism. Shenxiu believed that everyone is born with a pure and mirror-like original Buddha-nature, and that enlightenment is best achieved through a long process of sitting meditation in which one attempts to "wipe the dust" of illusion from the surface of one's undefiled original mind. Huineng believed that this dust-wiping approach was based on a false dualism. The mind is not a "thing" that "we" must polish to free it from impurities. As the *Diamond Sutra* taught, all phenomenal reality is *shunya* ("empty," "void"). Enlightenment does not require a long period of meditation, reading, and spiritual discipline. Awakening can come suddenly, as it had to Huineng himself. All that is required is that we quiet the rational, verbalizing mind and allow our Buddha-nature to perceive in a blinding flash the Oneness at the heart of true reality.

SEE ALSO The Vedas (c. 1500 BCE), Origins of Chan/Zen Buddhism (c. 520), Monism (c. 810)

A c. 1940 photograph of Nanhua Temple, the Chan Buddhist monastery in the Guangdong province of southeastern China where Huineng lived and taught.

Monism

Shankara (c. 788–c. 820)

During the Dark Ages in Europe, philosophy flourished in India. Some of India's greatest thinkers lived during this period, including Shankara, the founder of Advaita Vedanta Hinduism.

Little is known for certain about Shankara, though legends abound. Supposedly he was a Brahmin born in the village of Kalady, in southwestern India. As a youth, Shankara dedicated himself to a studious and ascetic life. He traveled widely around India, founding monasteries, engaging in debates with other Indian philosophers, and encouraging religious reform. His major writings include commentaries on the Bhagavad Gita, the principal Upanishads, and the *Brahma Sutras*. He died at the young age of thirty-two, while traveling in the foothills of the Himalayas.

Advaita Vedanta is a form of Hinduism that asserts the absolute oneness of ultimate reality, a view known as monism. ("Advaita" means "not-two.") Shankara believed that the world we perceive through the senses is *maya*, or illusion. It is an appearance of Brahman, the one true reality, which is pure consciousness and pure bliss. In fact, Shankara argues, terms like "consciousness" and "bliss" are not adequate descriptions of Brahman, because Brahman is so unitary and simple that it has no attributes whatsoever. No human concepts apply to it at all. The goal of human existence is liberation (*moksha*), which occurs when we realize that our highest and deepest self (Ātman) is identical with Brahman, the ultimate reality. No amount of prayer, meditation, good works, or religious devotion can result in liberation. We must replace ignorance (*avidyā*) with wisdom (*vidya*) by realizing the oneness of all reality.

Later exponents of Vedanta, such as Ramanuja (d. 1037), objected that Shankara's Advaita approach was overly intellectualized and gave too little importance to devotion (*bhakti*) as a path to liberation. They also questioned Shankara's claim that Brahman has no properties. If, as Shankara claims, Brahman has no parts, doesn't it have the property of lacking parts? And what about negative properties like "not being a horse"? Doesn't that property literally apply to Brahman? These are the sorts of debates that continue today in Indian philosophy between supporters and critics of Advaita Vedanta.

SEE ALSO The Vedas (c. 1500 BCE), The Bhagavad Gita (c. 400 BCE), Qualified Dualism (c. 1135)

A statue of Shankara and his disciples adorns a shrine at a temple dedicated to him in his birthplace, the town of Kalady in Kerala, India.

Islamic Philosophy Begins

Abū Yūsuf al-Kindī (c. 800–c. 870), **Abū Naṣr al-Fārābī** (c. 872–c. 950)

During the Dark Ages, when philosophy was practically extinct in Western Europe and barely flickering in the Byzantine Empire, there was a remarkable efflorescence of philosophy in the Islamic world. The center of this philosophical activity was Baghdad, where, around 820, the Abbasid caliph al-Ma'mūn established the famous House of Wisdom. There, al-Ma'mūn employed a corps of translators (many of them Christians) who translated numerous Greek philosophical texts into Arabic. Al-Ma'mūn's translators were big fans of Aristotle. As a consequence, almost the entire corpus of Aristotle was translated, together with many Hellenistic commentaries on Aristotle, plus several works of Plato and some Neoplatonic writings that were falsely ascribed to Aristotle. What emerged was a brand of Islamic Aristotelianism strongly tinged with Neoplatonism.

The first significant scholar to absorb these newly translated works was the Basra-born Abū Yūsuf al-Kindī. He was primarily a scientist and mathematician but is also widely regarded as the father of Islamic philosophy. It was al-Kindī who convinced the Islamic world of the essential compatibility of Greek philosophy and Islamic theology. Though most of his works are lost, we know that he developed an elaborate account of how God created the world with a beginning in time (not eternity) by a process of emanation. Al-Kindī also worked out an account of knowing that gives a crucial role to divine illumination of the human intellect.

An even more important early Islamic philosopher was Abū Naṣr al-Fārābī, who was born in remote Turkestan (in modern Kazakhstan) but spent most of his life in Baghdad. Primarily a logician, al-Fārābī wrote extensive commentaries on the works of Aristotle that were highly prized in the Islamic world. He developed proofs of God's existence that later influenced major Christian thinkers such as Aquinas (d. 1274). Like al-Kindī, al-Fārābī didn't believe that humans could think without divine assistance. Following up on some obscure passages of Aristotle, al-Fārābī theorized the existence of a divine "Active Intellect," separate from the human mind, which makes human thinking possible. This idea, which was further developed by later Islamic thinkers, created a stir when it was introduced into the Christian West in the thirteenth century.

SEE ALSO Ibn Sīnā's Islamic Aristotelianism (c. 1015), *The Incoherence of the Philosophers* (c. 1093), The Commentator (c. 1185)

Abū Naṣr al-Fārābī depicted on a 1993 coin from Kazakhstan.

Eriugena's Christian Neoplatonism

John Scotus Eriugena (c. 810–c. 877)

In the ninth century, Western Europe was pretty much an intellectual wasteland. This makes the bold and original philosophical system of John Scotus Eriugena all the more remarkable. As historian of philosophy Frederick Copleston (1907–1994) remarked, Eriugena's philosophy "stands out like a lofty rock in the midst of a plain."

Eriugena was born in Ireland. He must have studied at an Irish monastery, because somehow he managed to acquire a thorough mastery of Greek. Around 845 he crossed over to France to teach in the court school of King Charles the Bald. Charles commissioned him to translate several of the works of Pseudo-Dionysius into Latin. Eriugena's own major work, *On the Division of Nature*, was probably composed around 865.

Eriugena's system is a fusion of Christianity and Neoplatonism. He defines "Nature" as the totality of all that is and all that is not. Nature thus includes God. He divides Nature into four categories: (1) that which creates and is not created (i.e., God); (2) that which creates and is created (the Platonic Forms, which subsist eternally in the mind of God and the Logos, the Son); (3) that which is created and does not create (i.e., the world of particular things, which in Platonic terms are said to "participate" in the Forms); and (4) that which neither creates nor is created (God as the final end, to which all things return).

Eriugena's Neoplatonism, derived mostly from Pseudo-Dionysius, sometimes led him to speak in pantheistic terms. For example, he taught that creation was an eternal process of emanation from God and that God is "in" all things as their substance or essence. Like some of the Greek Church Fathers, he believed that the soul preexists the body and that everyone will eventually be saved. At the end of time, all corporeal things, including resurrected human bodies, will be spiritualized and return to their source, God. Scholars debate whether Eriugena was an actual pantheist or not. In 1225, his teachings were formally condemned, and Pope Honorius III ordered that all copies of *On the Division of Nature* be burned. Fortunately, a few survived.

SEE ALSO Neoplatonism (c. 250), The Dark Ages Begin (476), The Way of Negation (c. 500)

Title page of a 1681 Oxford edition of De divisione naturae (On the Division of Nature), *by John Scotus Eriugena.*

JOANNIS SCOTI ERIGENÆ

DE

Divifione Naturæ

LIBRI QUINQUE,

DIV DESIDERATI.

ACCEDIT

APPENDIX EX AMBIGUIS

S MAXIMI

GRÆCE & LATINE.

OXONII,

E THEATRO SHELDONIANO,

Anno MDCLXXXI.

Ibn Sīnā's Islamic Aristotelianism

Ibn Sīnā (Avicenna) (c. 980–1037)

Ibn Sīnā, known to the Christian West as Avicenna, was the greatest Western philosopher over the thousand-year period from Plotinus in the third century to Aquinas in the thirteenth. Portions of his major philosophical work, *The Book of Healing*, were translated into Latin around 1150 and powerfully influenced key Christian thinkers such as Aquinas and Duns Scotus (c. 1266–1308).

Ibn Sīnā was born near Bukhara, in the northeastern part of the Persian Empire, in what is today Uzbekistan. An intensely bookish and largely self-taught lad, Ibn Sīnā acquired an astonishing range of learning by the age of eighteen. Despite a busy life as a doctor and a public official, he managed to write over one hundred works, including five encyclopedias. His major medical work, *The Canon of Medicine*, was a standard medical textbook in Western universities until the sixteenth century. Though a devout Muslim, Ibn Sīnā was primarily a philosopher and taught a number of ideas (such as the eternity of the world and the denial of bodily resurrection) that seemed to clash with orthodox Islamic theology. In his work *The Incoherence of the Philosophers* (c. 1093), the conservative Islamic theologian al-Ghazālī (c. 1058–1111) attacked Ibn Sīnā's philosophy, greatly diminishing its influence in the Muslim world.

Ibn Sīnā's worldview was basically a fusion of Aristotelianism, Neoplatonism, and Islamic doctrine. His God is the personal God of Islamic theology, but He acts in some ways like Plotinus's transcendent One. The physical world "emanates" from God in an eternal and necessitated process that is completely deterministic. From God flows ten immaterial "Intelligences" that create and govern the cosmos. It is the tenth Intelligence, the Active Intellect or "Giver of Forms," that creates human souls and infuses forms into material objects. The highest part of the human soul, the intellect, is constantly tuning in to the radiations of the Active Intellect. Only in this way can the human mind grasp general concepts and universal principles. Medieval Christian thinkers largely rejected Ibn Sīnā's Neoplatonic cosmology. But his proofs of God's existence and of the immortality of the soul, as well as such fundamental metaphysical distinctions as essence/existence and necessary being/possible being, were widely influential.

SEE ALSO Islamic Philosophy Begins (c. 840), *The Incoherence of the Philosophers* (c. 1093), The Commentator (c. 1185)

A detailed illustration of the human skeletal system is shown in a 1632 Persian edition of Avicenna's Canon of Medicine, *originally published in 1025.*

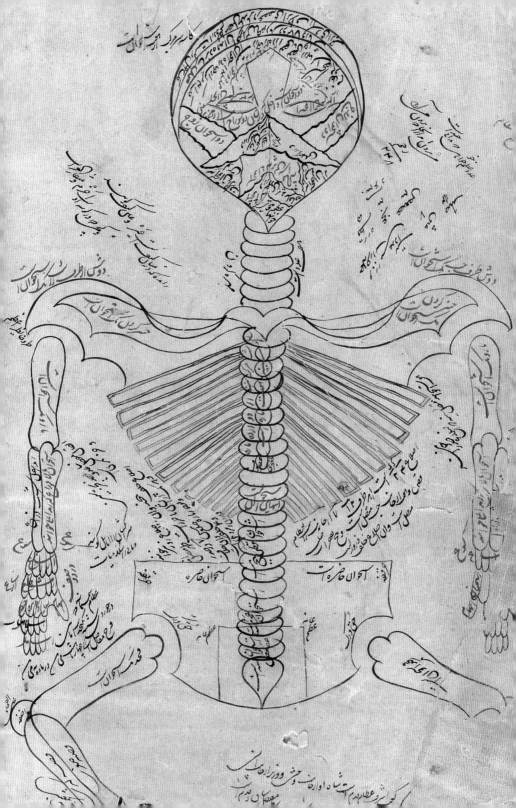

The Ontological Argument

Anselm of Canterbury (c. 1033–1109)

Anselm is widely considered the most important Christian philosopher and theologian of the eleventh century. He was born to a noble family in Aosta, a beautiful town in the foothills of the Italian Alps. In his mid-twenties he became a Benedictine monk in the monastery of Bec in western France. In 1093, he became the archbishop of Canterbury, where he clashed frequently with English kings and spent much of his tenure in exile. He is buried in Canterbury Cathedral and was later canonized.

In his work the *Monologion* (1076), Anselm drew on premises drawn from Christian Platonism to offer a densely argued proof of God's existence and His chief attributes. In the *Proslogion* (1077–1078), he offers a much shorter proof, his now-celebrated ontological argument for God's existence. The argument is often included in introductory philosophy texts and has produced an enormous secondary literature. Although most philosophers today reject the argument as unsound, many great philosophers have defended it.

There is a good deal of controversy about how exactly the argument should be construed, but the gist of it is this: God, by definition, is the greatest conceivable being. If God were merely an idea in our heads, He would not be the greatest conceivable being because then we could imagine a greater being—namely one that exists in reality as well as in our heads. Therefore God, the most perfect conceivable being, actually exists.

In the ongoing debate over the soundness of the ontological argument, some have questioned whether Anselm is entitled to assume that existence is a "great-making property," or that we know by definition that God is the most perfect possible being, or that God is even a possible being. Shortly after Anselm published his argument, a French monk named Gaunilo contended that Anselm's reasoning must be faulty because if it worked we could prove the existence of all kinds of things that we know do not exist, such as the most perfect conceivable island. Whether the argument is ultimately successful or not, it is a wonderful argument to think about, because it touches on so many deep questions of language and metaphysics.

SEE ALSO The Five Ways (c. 1265)

The visage of St. Anselm of Canterbury (on the third stained glass window from the left) overlooks the interior of the Canterbury Cathedral in Kent, England, where he served as archbishop from 1093 to 1109.

The Incoherence of the Philosophers

Abū Ḥāmid al-Ghazālī (c. 1058–1111)

When Aristotle's writings were reintroduced into Western Europe in the twelfth and thirteenth centuries, many Christian thinkers were concerned that this might compromise the truths of faith. A similar backlash occurred earlier in Islamic thought. The attempt by ninth- and tenth-century philosophers like al-Fārābī and Ibn Sīnā (Avicenna) to create a fusion of Islamic theology and Aristotelian philosophy met a worthy opponent in the Sunni theologian and Sufi mystic Abū Ḥāmid al-Ghazālī. While al-Ghazālī didn't reject Aristotle's philosophy completely, he argued that Islamic Aristotelians like Ibn Sīnā had failed to demonstrate many of their key conclusions and in some cases had lapsed into unbelief.

Al-Ghazālī was born near Tus, in what is now northeastern Iran. After establishing a reputation as a brilliant scholar, in 1091 he was appointed to teach law and theology at a famous school in Baghdad. There he wrote his celebrated book, *The Incoherence of the Philosophers* (c. 1093), attacking the Muslim philosophers. In the book, Al-Ghazālī takes twenty theses defended by the philosophers (many of which he accepts) and argues that none are successfully proved, thereby showing the limits of unaided human reason. He focuses, in particular, on three claims he believes are in direct conflict with Islamic teaching: the eternity of the world, the denial of bodily resurrection, and the claim that God knows only universals, not particulars. He blasts the "idiots" who taught these things, claiming they are heretics who have "renounced the Faith altogether."

One of the most acute criticisms offered by al-Ghazālī involves the idea of causal necessity. Anticipating arguments similar to the ones Scottish philosopher David Hume (1711–1776) would make, al-Ghazālī denies that causes necessitate their effects. The fact, for example, that wool always burns when exposed to fire does not prove that the fire caused the wool to burn. "Observation only proves that one occurs together with the other, but it does not prove that one occurs through [the agency] of the other." To assert that causes necessitate their effects is to deny God's infinite power, removing any possibility that God could perform a miracle to suspend causal laws. In fact, al-Ghazālī believed, God is the sole cause of everything in nature.

SEE ALSO Islamic Philosophy Begins (c. 840), Ibn Sīnā's Islamic Aristotelianism (c. 1015)

In The Incoherence of the Philosophers, *al-Ghazālī criticizes causal necessity, noting that "observation only proves that"* cotton wool burns when exposed to fire, "but it does not prove that one occurs through [the agency] of the other."

The Birth of Scholasticism

Peter Abelard (1079–1142)

In medieval universities there was a method of teaching and learning known today as "Scholasticism." It was a way of trying to arrive at rationally defensible conclusions by weighing opposing arguments and resolving apparent contradictions, guided by both reason and authority. In c. 1150, French theologian Peter Lombard wrote a widely utilized theology textbook called *The Book of Sentences* that illustrates the method. An important influence on Lombard was Peter Abelard's c. 1121 *Sic et Non* (*Yes and No*), in which Abelard collected opposing texts from the Bible and fathers of the Church so that students could sharpen their wits and learn to think independently. "The first key to wisdom," Abelard told his students, "is assiduous and frequent questioning."

Abelard was born in a Breton village and studied logic and theology in Paris under some of the leading scholars of his day. Handsome, vain, and combative, he challenged his teachers and founded his own highly successful school. Sometime around 1117 he fell in love with Héloïse, the sixteen-year-old niece of Fulbert, the canon of Notre Dame Cathedral. Fulbert was not amused when Héloïse secretly bore Abelard a child and married him (in that order). One night a band of thugs hired by Fulbert broke into Abelard's room and castrated him. Abelard withdrew to the Abbey of St. Denis, where he compiled *Sic and Non* and a work on the Trinity that was condemned at the Council of Soissons (1121). After a disastrous stint as abbot of St. Gildas monastery in Brittany, he resumed teaching in Paris, but his rationalistic approach to theology offended Cistercian cleric Bernard of Clairvaux, who had several of Abelard's teachings condemned at the Council of Sens (1141). Sentenced to perpetual silence by Pope Innocent II, Abelard retired to Cluny Abbey and died the following year.

Besides contributing to the Scholastic method, Abelard did important work in logic, in ethics, and on the problem of universals, where he defended a version of conceptualism, or moderate realism. In this view, there are no universal things, but there are general words and concepts (e.g., *animal* or *fruit*) that can be applied to many different individual things and are rooted in real similarities between things.

SEE ALSO The Problem of Universals (c. 285), Philosophers Join Academia (c. 1220), Conceptualism (c. 1320)

This c. nineteenth-century stipple engraving depicts Héloïse receiving the veil of nunhood from Abelard; she entered the convent at Argenteuil, outside Paris, after Abelard's castration.

Aristotelian Revival in the West

Gerard of Cremona (c. 1114–1187), **Michael Scot** (c. 1175–c. 1235), **William of Moerbeke** (c. 1215–c. 1286)

Prior to the middle of the twelfth century, Christian scholars in the West knew little about the philosophy or science of Aristotle. The philosophical elements of their Christian worldview were drawn mainly from Augustine, whose thought was strongly tinged with Neoplatonism. Then, in the twelfth and thirteenth centuries, the entire corpus of Aristotle's work was translated into Latin and became available in the West. What resulted was one of the greatest intellectual revolutions in Western civilization.

The story of how Aristotle's works were recovered is fascinating. The immediate catalyst was conquest. In 1091, the Normans conquered Sicily from the Arabs. There they found, in the libraries of Palermo, Arabic translations of Aristotle's works as well as some important Muslim commentaries on Aristotle. Several of these works were translated around 1220 by Michael Scot, an Oxford- and Paris-trained Scottish theologian who taught himself Arabic. Another important center for translations from the Arabic was the Spanish city of Toledo. Toledo was captured from the Muslims by Christian forces in 1085. Archbishop Raymond of Toledo set up a school of translators, led by Gerard of Cremona and Dominicus Gundissalinus, to translate a number of works of Aristotle and the great Muslim metaphysician Ibn Sīnā (Avicenna) into Latin. Finally, translations from the original Greek of Aristotle were made by James of Venice (fl. c. 1135) and (more important) William of Moerbeke (from c. 1260 to 1280), who obtained copies of Aristotle's works in or near Constantinople, which had been conquered by Latin crusaders in 1204 and was ruled by them until 1261.

In Aristotle, Christian scholars found a thinker who was simply too brilliant to ignore. Despite the fact that church authorities banned the teaching of many of Aristotle's works early in the thirteenth century, virtually all of his writings were being taught at the University of Paris by mid-century. For the next several centuries the works of Aristotle formed the core of liberal arts education at every European university. His thought dominated Western philosophy until it was challenged by thinkers such as Francis Bacon, René Descartes, and Thomas Hobbes in the seventeenth century.

SEE ALSO The Dark Ages Begin (476), Islamic Philosophy Begins (c. 840), Ibn Sīnā's Islamic Aristotelianism (c. 1015)

This page from a fourteenth-century book replicates Gerard of Cremona's translation of a "tree of species" diagram from an eleventh-century Islamic manuscript.

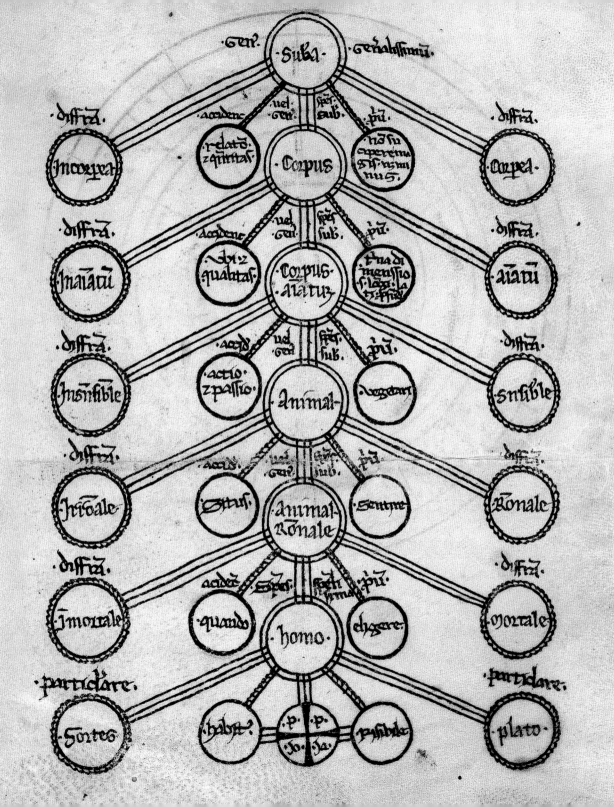

Qualified Dualism

Ramanuja (trad. c. 1017–1137, alt. c. 1077– c. 1157)

Like Western philosophy, Indian philosophy is marked by great diversity. In the ninth century, Shankara defended a strict form of monism known as Advaita Vedanta. According to Shankara, nothing exists except Brahman, the ultimate Reality, which is so transcendent and unified that it has no properties and cannot be grasped by any human concepts. Three centuries later this view came under powerful attack by one of India's greatest philosophers, Ramanuja.

Born into a Brahmin family in South India, Ramanuja married early but later left his wife to live as an ascetic. Like Shankara, he spent much of his life traveling around India, debating with other philosophers and fostering religious reform and devotion. His two most important philosophical works are his commentary on the *Brahma Sutras* of Badarayana (fl. fifth century BCE) and a commentary on the Upanishads titled *Vedartha Sangraha*.

Ramanuja founded a school of Hindu philosophy known as "qualified dualism." He argued that there is no basis in either reason or the Hindu scriptures for Shankara's strict monism. The scriptures describe ultimate reality as both one and many. To make sense of these seemingly discordant passages, Ramanuja claimed that the physical universe is God's body. Ultimate reality is one because everything that exists is either God or a mode of God, but it is also differentiated because physical objects and human bodies and souls really exist and are not mere appearances or illusions. Thus, when the scriptures famously proclaim *tat tvam asi* ("that thou art"), this does not mean that humans are literally identical with ultimate reality (Brahman). It means that we are part of Brahman in intimate union with Brahman itself, which is the cause, controller, and animating soul of the universe. Arguing that the idea of a qualityless being is simply incoherent, Ramanuja claims that God is infinitely perfect. In other words, Ramanuja is a theist rather than a monist. What the scriptures call Brahman is actually Vishnu, a personal Hindu deity. Liberation (*moksha*) can best be achieved by devotion to Vishnu, though Ramanuja concedes that other methods also have value.

SEE ALSO The Vedas (c. 1500 BCE), Monism (c. 810)

An illustration of Ramanuja in prayer from Hutchinson's Story of the Nations, 1934, *a world history by English book–publisher Walter Hutchinson.*

Revival of Confucianism

Zhu Xi (1130–1200)

During the Song Dynasty (960–1279) in China, a powerful revival of Confucianism occurred that goes by the name of Neo-Confucianism. The most important figure in that revival was Zhu Xi (or Chu Hsi), whom many scholars consider the second most important Chinese philosopher next to Confucius himself.

Zhu Xi was born in Fujian province in southeastern China and educated mostly at home by his father, a local sheriff. From an early age Zhu Xi loved the Confucianist classics. At age nineteen he passed the imperial civil service examination and served in a variety of governmental posts. His real love, though, was teaching and learning. A highly disciplined scholar, Zhu Xi wrote prolifically on a wide range of topics. For many centuries the commentaries he wrote on the Confucianist classics were widely accepted as authoritative. As a result of his influence, the so-called *Four Books*—*Analects*, *Mencius*, *Great Learning*, and *Doctrine of the Mean*—became the central texts of the Confucianist school and the basis for Chinese civil service examinations for nearly six hundred years.

Greatly influenced by an earlier Neo-Confucianist scholar, Cheng Yi (1033–1107), Zhu Xi worked out a comprehensive system of thought that incorporated key insights from Buddhism and Daoism and established a metaphysical foundation for Confucianist thought. His central idea was that everything in reality is composed of two interrelated elements: material substance (*qi*) and law, or rational principle, (*li*). Li is an immaterial, eternal, good, and unchangeable principle that inheres in all things and gives them their essence, or form. Qi is the ever-changing material stuff of reality and may or may not be good. As Confucius and his disciple Mencius taught, humans are innately good. There is a fundamental harmony between humans and nature, because the human mind is essentially one with the "Great Ultimate" (li) of the universe. By devotion to self-cultivation, particularly through moral discipline and a love of learning, humans can substantially recover the original goodness that a "turbid" material nature may have impaired. In these ways, the optimistic humanism and intellectualism of the Confucianist tradition were deepened and preserved in the Neo-Confucianist revival.

SEE ALSO Confucian Ethics (c. 500 BCE), Innate Goodness (c. 300 BCE)

A statue of Zhu Xi at a temple in the Wuyi Mountains, in the Fujian province of China.

The Commentator

Ibn Rushd (Averroës) (1126–1198)

Ibn Rushd, known to the West as Averroës, was held in extraordinary regard by medieval Christian philosophers and theologians. In *The Divine Comedy*, Dante gave him an honored place in limbo beside Aristotle. So admired were his voluminous commentaries on Aristotle, that Christian thinkers from Albertus Magnus (c. 1200–1280) to Francisco Suárez (1548–1617) referred to him simply as "the Commentator."

Ibn Rushd was born in Córdoba, in the Muslim part of Spain. Like his father, Ibn Rushd grew up to become a judge, and he served for many years as personal physician to the caliph of Marrakesh in Morocco. But Ibn Rushd's great love was the philosophy of Aristotle, which he believed was gifted to us by divine providence "so that we might know all that can be known." He wrote some thirty-eight commentaries on Aristotle's works in three different sizes: short, intermediate, and long. His long commentaries became the models for Aquinas's own brilliant commentaries on Aristotle.

Ibn Rushd set himself two important tasks: recover the authentic Aristotle by stripping away the Neoplatonic add-ons that had been superimposed by al-Fārābī, Ibn Sīnā (Avicenna), and other tenth- and eleventh-century Islamic Aristotelians, and refute al-Ghazālī's attack on philosophy in *The Incoherence of the Philosophers* (c. 1093). His response to al-Ghazālī, titled *The Incoherence of "The Incoherence,"* was a full-scale defense of the power of human reason—and of Aristotle's philosophy in particular— to discover fundamental truths about reality that harmonize with revealed religious doctrine (properly understood). His attempt to recover the authentic Aristotle resulted in a reading that posed a huge problem for Christian thinkers. Using Aristotelian premises, Ibn Rushd affirmed the eternity of the world, denied the literal resurrection of the body, and taught that all humans share the same superhuman intellect, seemingly throwing in doubt the possibility of individual life after death. Some Christian thinkers, led by Siger of Brabant (c. 1240–1284), were enthusiastic followers of Ibn Rushd, provoking a rebuke by Church authorities, notably in a condemnation by Bishop Étienne Tempier of Paris in 1277. But most of them followed Aquinas in denying that Aristotle's teachings were as opposed to Christian doctrine as Ibn Rushd's interpretations implied.

SEE ALSO Matter and Form (c. 330 BCE), Ibn Sīnā's Islamic Aristotelianism (c. 1015), *The Incoherence of the Philosophers* (c. 1093)

Ibn Rushd, or Averroës, is portrayed in this lithograph by P. R. Vigneron, 1825.

Vigneron

The Guide for the Perplexed

Moses ben Maimon (Maimonides) (1135–1204)

Moses ben Maimon, known as Maimonides in the West, was the most important Jewish philosopher of the Middle Ages. A great admirer of Aristotle, Maimonides sought to show that there is no fundamental conflict between faith and reason. His major philosophical work, *The Guide for the Perplexed* (c. 1190), was translated into Latin and strongly influenced Thomas Aquinas and other Christian medieval philosophers.

Maimonides was born in Córdoba, Spain, and educated at home by his father, a noted scholar. Forced to flee Córdoba in 1148 because of persecution of the Jews under the newly installed Almohad caliphate, it is believed Maimonides's family wandered around Spain for several years. Around 1159, they moved to North Africa, where for many years they acted outwardly as converted Muslims. Maimonides eventually settled in Cairo, where he became the personal physician to the sultan, a leading authority on Jewish religious law, and the head of the Jewish community. He is buried in Tiberias on the Sea of Galilee.

In *The Guide for the Perplexed*, Maimonides seeks to reconcile Greek philosophy and Jewish teaching by arguing against literalistic approaches to scripture. The Bible, he argues, was meant to be understood by simple, unlettered folk and thus often uses language that should be read metaphorically or allegorically. In general, Maimonides urged his readers to respect the limits of human reason. Though God's existence can be proved by rational arguments derived from Aristotle, we can know little about God's nature without the aid of revelation. In this regard Maimonides was a strong proponent of negative theology, which seeks to describe God in terms of what He is *not*, rather than by means of any categorical positive affirmation. Maimonides also denied that we can prove by reason the creation of the world in time (a line of argument that influenced Aquinas) or the inherent immortality of the soul. In fact, Maimonides seems to have been skeptical of any kind of personal immortality or bodily resurrection. This and his allegorical approach to scripture made him a controversial figure in his own day. It was several centuries before his authority became firmly established.

SEE ALSO The Way of Negation (c. 500), The Five Ways (c. 1265)

The 1986 Israeli new shekel banknotes featured a color engraving of Maimonides, the greatest Jewish thinker of the Middle Ages, who is still revered today.

Philosophers Join Academia

When we think of a philosopher, an image may come to mind of a scruffy professor in a tweed coat lecturing about "deep stuff" and occasionally writing cheery words like *death* and *despair* on the board. While philosophers have always talked about deep stuff, they haven't always been professors. That development began in the twelfth and thirteenth centuries when the first universities were founded.

The earliest Western universities (including Bologna, 1088; Salamanca, c. 1094; Oxford, c. 1096; Paris, c. 1150; Cambridge, c. 1209; and Padua, 1222) offered bachelor of arts degrees that normally took between four and a half to seven years to complete. The curriculum was organized around the seven traditional liberal arts: grammar (languages, especially Latin), rhetoric (effective speaking and writing), dialectic (logic and reasoning), arithmetic, geometry, astronomy, and music. By the middle of the thirteenth century, the writings of Aristotle formed the backbone of the curriculum. Many of the early universities also offered advanced degrees in theology, and most of the great "philosophers" of the Middle Ages were actually professors of theology.

To earn a doctorate and become a *magister* at a medieval university normally required fifteen years or more of advanced study. Students frequently began college at age thirteen or fourteen; the minimum age to receive a doctorate in theology was thirty-four. This long period of study was rigorous and involved frequent disputations, or public debates, to hone students' powers of reasoning and argumentation. As a consequence, both the quantity and the quality of philosophical thought greatly improved during this period. The first-rate philosophy produced by thirteenth-century Christian thinkers Thomas Aquinas, St. Bonaventure, and Duns Scotus could not have been achieved outside of a university setting.

There was also a downside to philosophers becoming university professors. As standards become professionalized, it often becomes more difficult to do original work. Ways of doing philosophy can become ossified due to pressures to work within approved channels. Thus, by the 1500s and up to the mid-1600s, there was relatively little top-quality philosophy being produced in academia. During this time it was nonacademics, such as Machiavelli, Francis Bacon, Descartes, Thomas Hobbes, and Baruch Spinoza, who pointed the way to the future.

SEE ALSO The Birth of Scholasticism (1121), The Silver Age of Scholasticism (c. 1525)

The Bodleian Library at Oxford—comprised of five buildings, including the iconic Radcliffe Camera building (built 1749) shown here—is one of the oldest libraries in Europe; its original collection dates back to the fourteenth century.

The Universal Doctor

Albertus Magnus (c. 1200–1280)

Albertus already had a pretty great name—Count von Bollstadt—but his later admirers gave him a better one, St. Albert the Great (Magnus). (His other title, the Universal Doctor, is rather impressive, too.) G. K. Chesterton (1874–1936) called him "the founder of modern science." That is a slight exaggeration, but his scientific learning was so vast that many people in his lifetime considered him to be a wizard and a magician. Even more important than his contribution to science was his effective advocacy for the value of philosophy and a Christianized Aristotelianism.

Albertus was born sometime around 1200 in what is now Bavaria, Germany. He went to college in Italy, at the newly founded University of Padua; it was there that he encountered the writings of Aristotle and joined the Dominican order. In 1245, Albertus received a doctorate in theology at Paris. Thereafter, he taught for many years in Paris and Cologne. Among his students was Thomas Aquinas. So shy and taciturn was Aquinas in those days that his fellow students called him Dumb Ox. Albertus, recognizing Aquinas's greatness, rebuked the students, saying, "You call him Dumb Ox; I tell you this Dumb Ox shall bellow so loud that his bellowings will fill the world." From 1254 on, Albertus spent much of his time in church service, serving for two years as bishop of Ratisbon (modern Regensburg) and traveling for two years preaching a crusade. In 1277, the elderly Albertus journeyed from Cologne to Paris to defend his most famous student, Thomas Aquinas (who had died from an illness in 1274), against accusations that he had allowed his zeal for Aristotle to compromise Christian truth.

Albertus was a prolific writer of vast learning who wrote dozens of books on logic, science, and theology. He realized that Aristotle and his Muslim commentators were too important to ignore, and he worked tirelessly to convince his contemporaries that philosophy was an indispensable ally of faith and that Aristotle's philosophy (properly pruned) was fundamentally right. Albertus's Aristotle was largely the Neoplatonized Aristotle of the Arabs. It was left to his disciple, Aquinas, to recover and popularize a more authentic Aristotle.

SEE ALSO Aristotelian Revival in the West (c. 1130), The Great Medieval Synthesis (c. 1265)

Albertus Magnus teaching, in a fifteenth-century woodcut.

A Franciscan Approach to Philosophy

Giovanni di Fidanza (Bonaventure) (c. 1217–1274)

In the thirteenth century, a number of mendicant religious orders were founded; members dedicated themselves to a life of service through preaching and poverty. The greatest of these were the Dominicans and the Franciscans. Both orders produced brilliant philosophers and theologians: most notably the Dominicans Albertus Magnus and Thomas Aquinas, and the Franciscans Bonaventure, John Duns Scotus (c. 1266–1308), and William of Ockham (c. 1285–1347). While agreeing on most things, there were clear differences in the ways the orders tended to approach philosophy. Broadly speaking, the Dominicans were enthusiastic fans of Aristotle and the Franciscans were not. The Franciscans were not deeply hostile to Aristotle—positive references to him abound in their writings—but in general they were more conservative and preferred the views of Augustine and other fathers of the Church. A good example of this is found in the philosophy of St. Bonaventure.

Giovanni di Fidanza, universally known as Bonaventure, was born in central Italy. After studying at the University of Paris, where he joined the Franciscans, he became a professor of theology there before he was appointed minister general of his order in 1257. In 1273, he was named cardinal of Albano, Italy.

Bonaventure agreed with his friend and Paris colleague Thomas Aquinas about most major issues of philosophy: both believed it possible to prove the existence of God, to demonstrate His infinite perfection, and to prove the immortality of the soul and the power of the human mind to know right from wrong by means of universal natural law. Unlike Aquinas, however, Bonaventure followed Augustine in stressing the need for divine assistance (illumination) in forming general concepts and achieving certain knowledge. He also followed Augustine in giving a central place in his metaphysics to Platonic Forms in the mind of God (exemplarism). In general, he gave a larger role than Aquinas did to grace, divine visibility, and activity in God's creation. This is evident in Bonaventure's masterpiece of mystical theology, *The Mind's Road to God* (1259), where he describes a series of steps by which God's presence in the world may be discerned and the soul may mount up, as by a ladder, to mystical communion with God.

SEE ALSO The Great Medieval Synthesis (c. 1265), Attack on the Medieval Synthesis (c. 1300)

A portrait of St. Bonaventure, c. 1490, attributed to Italian painter Girolamo da Treviso the Elder. Bonaventure was canonized in 1482.

The Great Medieval Synthesis

Thomas Aquinas (c. 1225–1274)

Thomas Aquinas is widely recognized as the greatest Christian philosopher and theologian of the Middle Ages. His greatest achievement was to fuse the philosophy of Aristotle with Christian doctrine in a vast synthesis of impressive power and scope. For over seven hundred years, Aquinas has been a leading figure in Roman Catholic thought and education, and he has been a major influence on Western thought generally, particularly in the fields of ethics and law.

Aquinas was born in Roccasecca, in southern Italy, in 1225. After studying at the University of Naples, he joined the Dominican order and devoted the remainder of his life to teaching, preaching, and writing. Blessed with a clear mind and a near-photographic memory, Aquinas wrote prodigiously on a wide range of philosophical and theological topics. The two most important sources of his philosophical work are *Summa contra gentiles* and *Summa theologica*. Aquinas stopped writing following a vision in late 1273, saying that compared to the things that had been revealed to him, all that he had written "appears to be as so much straw." He died in 1274 as he was traveling to the Council of Lyons and was declared a saint in 1323.

Like his famous teacher, Albertus Magnus, Aquinas was a huge fan of Aristotle. However, harmonizing Aristotle with Christian teaching wasn't easy. Aristotle was a pagan who taught that the universe was not created, that there is no personal survival after death, and that God is unaware of the world's existence. By virtue of some judicious pruning, Aquinas was able to show that substantial portions of Aristotle's thought could be integrated into a Christian framework.

The Christian-Aristotelian synthesis Aquinas created depended on the strength of the philosophical foundations Aquinas built for his theological superstructure. Aquinas had great confidence in the power of reason to grasp fundamental moral truths and to prove the existence of God, His perfect nature, and the immortality of the soul. Following Aquinas's death, Christian thinkers such as John Duns Scotus (d. 1308) and William of Ockham (d. 1347) began to attack some or all of these philosophical underpinnings, raising doubts in many people's minds about the viability of Aquinas's synthesis.

SEE ALSO Matter and Form (c. 330 BCE), Attack on the Medieval Synthesis (c. 1300), The Silver Age of Scholasticism (c. 1525), Neo-Thomism (c. 1920)

Transfiguration of St. Thomas Aquinas, c. 1590, by Flemish engraver Adriaen Collaert. The banner on top reads "Bene de me scripsisti Thoma" (You have written well of me, Thomas), referring to a vision Aquinas legendarily had of Christ speaking to him from the Cross.

BENE DE ME SCRIPSISTI THOMA.

DOCTOR ANGELICVS

ECCE PLVS QVAM SALOMON HIC. Luc. 11.

SVMMA D. T.

Omnes sitientes

Venite ad aquas. Isa. 55.

PRIMA PARS

SECVNDA PARS

TERTIA PARS

ECCE FONS PARVVS CREVIT IN FLVVIVM. Ester 10.

The Five Ways

Thomas Aquinas (c. 1225–1274)

Thomas Aquinas is perhaps best known for his five arguments for God's existence, the so-called Five Ways, outlined in his masterwork, *Summa theologica* (written 1265–1274). Indeed, these are among the most famous arguments in the entire history of philosophy.

The first three arguments share a similar pattern. The argument from motion claims that there must be an ultimate cause of motion—an unmoved mover—to explain why anything is in motion now. The argument from causation asserts that there must be a first cause to explain why there are chains of causes and effects. And the argument from necessity claims that there must be a necessary being to explain the existence of dependent beings—that is, things whose existence is explained by the causal activity of other beings.

The Fourth Way, the argument from degree, argues that there must be a perfect being that possesses maximal goodness and reality to explain why there are things that possess lesser amounts of goodness and reality. The Fifth Way is a version of the traditional argument from design (based on evidence of divine design in the natural world). It claims that an intelligent designer must exist to account for why things that lack awareness and intelligence (such as plants) often behave in seemingly intelligent and goal-directed ways.

Many scholars believe that the Third Way, the argument from necessity, may be the strongest of the bunch. Aquinas assumes that everything that exists must have a sufficient reason why it exists. In other words, there cannot be any brute facts—things that exist but have absolutely no reason why they exist. If there is no necessary being and the universe consists entirely of dependent beings, it seems that there'd be no sufficient reason why the universe exists; its existence would be simply a brute fact. It's plausible to suppose that the only way everything could have an explanation is if God explains Himself (He is a self-existent, self-explanatory being) and the existence of the universe. Perhaps the weakest point in this argument is Aquinas's assumption that there cannot be any brute facts. Do we know this for a fact? Many critics of Aquinas's Five Ways would say no.

SEE ALSO Ibn Sīnā's Islamic Aristotelianism (c. 1015), The Ontological Argument (1078)

An Italian hand-colored woodcut, c. 1450. The bottom panel shows Aquinas holding a beaming book, symbolizing his role as a divinely inspired writer; on top, Aquinas (right) kneels before Christ on the crucifix, receiving the word of God.

Natural Law

Thomas Aquinas (c. 1225–1274)

One of Thomas Aquinas's most enduring legacies is the theory of ethics he developed. Aquinas taught that all normal, adult human beings grasp certain basic moral truths. Aquinas calls these basic, universally knowable ethical principles "natural law."

The idea of natural law goes back to the ancient Greeks, particularly to the Stoics, who taught that there is a higher law than the moral and legal codes created by human beings. This higher law emanates from God, is binding at all times and places, and is self-evident to all who have full use of their reason. The Stoics called this higher law *natural law* because it is rooted in basic facts about human nature (e.g., that children require a lengthy period of care and education) and also because people come to know it by nature and do not need to be taught it. Aquinas took over this Stoic idea of natural law, combined it with a largely Aristotelian account of the virtues, and developed it into a full-blown theory of ethics.

Aquinas distinguishes four kinds of law. Eternal law is God's providential governance of the entire universe. Human law consists of all the enacted rules in human legal systems. Divine law is comprised of all God's commands that can be known only through revelation. Finally, the natural law is that set of basic moral principles, rooted in human nature and divine ordinance, which can be known by the natural light of reason.

Aquinas's account of natural law became standard in Catholic moral teaching and was widely accepted by non-Catholic ethicists prior to about 1800. When the U.S. Declaration of Independence speaks of "self-evident" moral truths and "Laws of Nature and of Nature's God," it is echoing this natural-law tradition. Many people now question whether moral norms can reliably be read off from appeals to "human nature" or what is "natural," as some natural law theorists appear to do. In modern liberal societies, many acts that were once widely condemned as "unnatural" (e.g., use of contraceptives and artificial insemination) aren't generally viewed as unethical. Nevertheless, natural law theory is still a fairly widely accepted approach to ethics today.

SEE ALSO Universal Moral Law (51 BCE), Law and Morality Are Separate (1832), Legal Positivism (1961)

The U.S. Declaration of Independence of July 4, 1776; its phrases such as "self-evident" and "Laws of Nature and of Nature's God" echo Aquinas's natural-law tradition.

IN CONGRESS, JULY 4, 1776.

The unanimous Declaration of the thirteen united States of America.

When in the Course of human events, it becomes necessary for one people to dissolve the political bands which have connected them with another, and to assume among the powers of the earth, the separate and equal station to which the Laws of Nature and of Nature's God entitle them, a decent respect to the opinions of mankind requires that they should declare the causes which impel them to the separation.

We hold these truths to be self-evident, that all men are created equal, that they are endowed by their Creator with certain unalienable Rights, that among these are Life, Liberty and the pursuit of Happiness.—That to secure these rights, Governments are instituted among Men, deriving their just powers from the consent of the governed,—That whenever any Form of Government becomes destructive of these ends, it is the Right of the People to alter or to abolish it, and to institute new Government, laying its foundation on such principles and organizing its powers in such form, as to them shall seem most likely to effect their Safety and Happiness. Prudence, indeed, will dictate that Governments long established should not be changed for light and transient causes; and accordingly all experience hath shewn, that mankind are more disposed to suffer, while evils are sufferable, than to right themselves by abolishing the forms to which they are accustomed. But when a long train of abuses and usurpations, pursuing invariably the same Object evinces a design to reduce them under absolute Despotism, it is their right, it is their duty, to throw off such Government, and to provide new Guards for their future security.—Such has been the patient sufferance of these Colonies; and such is now the necessity which constrains them to alter their former Systems of Government. The history of the present King of Great Britain is a history of repeated injuries and usurpations, all having in direct object the establishment of an absolute Tyranny over these States. To prove this, let Facts be submitted to a candid world.

He has refused his Assent to Laws, the most wholesome and necessary for the public good.

He has forbidden his Governors to pass Laws of immediate and pressing importance, unless suspended in their operation till his Assent should be obtained; and when so suspended, he has utterly neglected to attend to them.

He has refused to pass other Laws for the accommodation of large districts of people, unless those people would relinquish the right of Representation in the Legislature, a right inestimable to them and formidable to tyrants only.

He has called together legislative bodies at places unusual, uncomfortable, and distant from the depository of their public Records, for the sole purpose of fatiguing them into compliance with his measures.

He has dissolved Representative Houses repeatedly, for opposing with manly firmness his invasions on the rights of the people.

He has refused for a long time, after such dissolutions, to cause others to be elected; whereby the Legislative powers, incapable of Annihilation, have returned to the People at large for their exercise; the State remaining in the mean time exposed to all the dangers of invasion from without, and convulsions within.

He has endeavoured to prevent the population of these States; for that purpose obstructing the Laws for Naturalization of Foreigners; refusing to pass others to encourage their migrations hither, and raising the conditions of new Appropriations of Lands.

He has obstructed the Administration of Justice, by refusing his Assent to Laws for establishing Judiciary powers.

He has made Judges dependent on his Will alone, for the tenure of their offices, and the amount and payment of their salaries.

He has erected a multitude of New Offices, and sent hither swarms of Officers to harrass our people, and eat out their substance.

He has kept among us, in times of peace, Standing Armies without the Consent of our legislatures.

He has affected to render the Military independent of and superior to the Civil power.

He has combined with others to subject us to a jurisdiction foreign to our constitution, and unacknowledged by our laws; giving his Assent to their Acts of pretended Legislation:

For Quartering large bodies of armed troops among us:

For protecting them, by a mock Trial, from punishment for any Murders which they should commit on the Inhabitants of these States:

For cutting off our Trade with all parts of the world:

For imposing Taxes on us without our Consent:

For depriving us in many cases, of the benefits of Trial by jury:

For transporting us beyond Seas to be tried for pretended offences:

For abolishing the free System of English Laws in a neighbouring Province, establishing therein an Arbitrary government, and enlarging its Boundaries so as to render it at once an example and fit instrument for introducing the same absolute rule into these Colonies:

For taking away our Charters, abolishing our most valuable Laws, and altering fundamentally the Forms of our Governments:

For suspending our own Legislatures, and declaring themselves invested with power to legislate for us in all cases whatsoever.

He has abdicated Government here, by declaring us out of his Protection and waging War against us.

He has plundered our seas, ravaged our Coasts, burnt our towns, and destroyed the lives of our people.

He is at this time transporting large Armies of foreign Mercenaries to compleat the works of death, desolation and tyranny, already begun with circumstances of Cruelty & perfidy scarcely paralleled in the most barbarous ages, and totally unworthy the Head of a civilized nation.

He has constrained our fellow Citizens taken Captive on the high Seas to bear Arms against their country, to become the executioners of their friends and Brethren, or to fall themselves by their Hands.

He has excited domestic insurrections amongst us, and has endeavoured to bring on the inhabitants of our frontiers, the merciless Indian Savages, whose known rule of warfare, is an undistinguished destruction of all ages, sexes and conditions.

In every stage of these Oppressions We have Petitioned for Redress in the most humble terms: Our repeated Petitions have been answered only by repeated injury. A Prince, whose character is thus marked by every act which may define a Tyrant, is unfit to be the ruler of a free people.

Nor have We been wanting in attentions to our British brethren. We have warned them from time to time of attempts by their legislature to extend an unwarrantable jurisdiction over us. We have reminded them of the circumstances of our emigration and settlement here. We have appealed to their native justice and magnanimity, and we have conjured them by the ties of our common kindred to disavow these usurpations, which, would inevitably interrupt our connections and correspondence. They too have been deaf to the voice of justice and of consanguinity. We must, therefore, acquiesce in the necessity, which denounces our Separation, and hold them, as we hold the rest of mankind, Enemies in War, in Peace Friends.

We, therefore, the Representatives of the united States of America, in General Congress, Assembled, appealing to the Supreme Judge of the world for the rectitude of our intentions, do, in the Name, and by Authority of the good People of these Colonies, solemnly publish and declare, That these United Colonies are, and of Right ought to be Free and Independent States; that they are Absolved from all Allegiance to the British Crown, and that all political connection between them and the State of Great Britain, is and ought to be totally dissolved; and that as Free and Independent States, they have full Power to levy War, conclude Peace, contract Alliances, establish Commerce, and to do all other Acts and Things which Independent States may of right do.—And for the support of this Declaration, with a firm reliance on the protection of divine Providence, we mutually pledge to each other our Lives, our Fortunes and our sacred Honor.

Button Gwinnett
Lyman Hall
Geo Walton.

Wm Hooper
Joseph Hewes,
John Penn

Edward Rutledge.
Thos Heyward Junr.
Thomas Lynch Junr.
Arthur Middleton

John Hancock

Samuel Chase
Wm Paca
Thos Stone
Charles Carroll of Carrollton

George Wythe
Richard Henry Lee
Th Jefferson
Benja Harrison
Thos Nelson jr.
Francis Lightfoot Lee
Carter Braxton

Robt morris
Benjamin Rush
Benja Franklin
John Morton
Geo Clymer
Jas Smith.
Geo Taylor
James Wilson
Geo. Ross
Caesar Rodney
Geo Read
Tho M:Kean

Wm Floyd
Phil. Livingston
Frans Lewis
Lewis Morris

Richd Stockton
Jno Witherspoon
Fras Hopkinson
John Hart
Abra Clark

Josiah Bartlett
Wm Whipple
Saml Adams
John Adams
Robt Treat Paine
Elbridge Gerry
Step Hopkins
William Ellery
Roger Sherman
Samel Huntington
Wm Williams
Oliver Wolcott
Matthew Thornton

Attack on the Medieval Synthesis

John Duns Scotus (c. 1266–1308)

Though the Middle Ages is often called the Age of Faith, great Christian Aristotelians like Albertus Magnus and Thomas Aquinas possessed a remarkable confidence in the power of human reason. Both men believed that unaided human reason could prove the existence of God, demonstrate God's omnipotence and other traditional attributes, prove the immortality of the soul and its final end of eternal beatitude with God, and achieve secure knowledge of objective and immutable moral truths. All of this came under attack in the fourteenth century. The first salvos in that assault were fired by the great Franciscan thinker John Duns Scotus.

Little is known about Scotus's life. He was probably born in Duns, Scotland, and entered the Franciscan order at an early age. He studied at Oxford and Paris, becoming regent master of theology in Paris in 1306. He died at the young age of forty-two and is buried in the Franciscan church in Cologne. Historian of philosophy Anthony Kenny (b. 1931) has described Scotus as "one of the sharpest minds ever to have engaged in philosophy," but he is not an easy philosopher to read. His arguments are often complex and riddled with technicalities, and his writing was crabbed and inelegant. Yet those with the patience to study him will encounter a mind of rare power.

Scotus had a more modest view of the power of human reason than Aquinas did. Scotus believed that God's existence could be demonstrated, but he rejected all of Aquinas's purported proofs. Scotus also denied that all of God's traditional attributes could be proven by reason, and he claimed that only probable arguments could be given for the immortality of the soul. Moreover, Scotus held that many of the so-called "immutable" truths of morality that Aquinas identified are actually contingent and dependent upon the will of God. In general, then, reason and revelation do not coincide nearly as much as Aquinas believed. Many important Christian truths can be known only because God has chosen to reveal them, not because we can prove them by rational arguments. In this way Scotus was a stepping-stone between the optimistic rationalism of Aquinas and the deep skeptical challenges of William of Ockham (d. c. 1347).

SEE ALSO The Great Medieval Synthesis (c. 1265), Ockham's Razor (c. 1320)

An illustration of John Duns Scotus from Les vrais pourtraits et vies des hommes illustres . . . *(The True Portraits and Lives of Illustrious . . . Men), 1584, by André Thévet.*

JEAN DVNS DICT SCOTVS.
Chap. 72.

CHOSE aucune ne peut estre plus perni-
cieuse en la republique Chrestienne, ny plus
dommageable à l'Eglise, que ceux qui fei-
gnans de vouloir proffiter, machinent l'occasion de nuire, se voilent du manteau de ve-
rité, afin qu'ilz demolissent (si faire ce peut)
ce qui est bié asseuré & edifié. Or entre telz
ennemis simulez, encores nuisent plus ceux,
qui promettans escrire fidelement & de bonne foy, les histoires &
choses memorables auenuës és siecles passez, auec les vies des peres

Mystical Theology

Johannes (Meister) Eckhart (c. 1260–c. 1328)

There was a remarkable flowering of mysticism in fourteenth-century Europe. Weary of the technicalities and abstract theorizing of late scholastic philosophy, mystics such as Johannes Tauler (c. 1300–1361), Heinrich Suso (c. 1295–1366), Jan van Ruysbroeck (c. 1293–1381), and St. Catherine of Siena (1347–1380) sought a deeper and more intimate communion with God. The greatest of these mystics was the German theologian Meister Eckhart.

Johannes Eckhart was born in Hochheim in Thuringia (central Germany). After joining the Dominicans in his youth, Eckhart studied theology at Erfurt, Cologne, and Paris, earning a master of sacred theology in 1302. He was a master of theology twice at Paris (an unusual honor), teaching alongside his brilliant Franciscan colleague John Duns Scotus (d. 1308). A gifted administrator as well as an outstanding academic, Eckhart served in many important posts in the Dominican order, including provincial of Saxony and vicar general of Bohemia. He was a popular preacher, frequently giving homilies in his native German. His major work, the *Opus tripartitum*, was left unfinished at his death. In the mid-1320s, Eckhart's daring mystical theology came under attack and he spent his last years responding to charges of heresy. A year after his death, twenty-six of Eckhart's pronouncements were condemned either as heretical or as "evil-sounding, rash, and suspect of heresy" by Pope John XXII. Modern scholars have generally defended his orthodoxy.

Eckhart has been accused of pantheism: the view, roughly, that God is everything and everything is God. It is easy to find isolated passages in his writings that support this reading, but Eckhart was usually careful to follow up every pantheistic "zinger" with an orthodox explanation. For example, Eckhart said, "Outside God there is nothing." This sounds pantheistic, except Eckhart quickly explained that he meant that creatures are totally dependent on God for their existence, which is standard Christian doctrine. Eckhart often used bold and even shocking language in his homilies to shake people up and encourage a deeper and more fervent Christian piety. Despite the papal condemnation, Eckhart's message resonated with his contemporaries and led to a great efflorescence of mystical piety.

SEE ALSO Monism (c. 810), *Ethics* (1677)

The main door of the thirteenth-century Predigerkirche (Preacher's Church); Meister Eckhart served there as prior, when it was part of a Dominican monastery before the Reformation.

Ockham's Razor

William of Ockham (c. 1285–c. 1347)

William of Ockham was the most influential philosopher of the fourteenth century. Curiously, however, the idea for which he is most famous, the principle of theoretical simplicity known as *Ockham's razor*, was never endorsed by him in the way it is usually formulated.

Ockham was born in the village of Ockham, not far from London. After joining the Franciscan order in his teens, he studied at Oxford and was on the verge of becoming a regent master when his career was cut short by an accusation of heresy. Ockham spent four years at the papal court in Avignon trying to clear his name, but was finally forced to flee when he and the head of the Franciscan order, Michael of Cesena, butted heads with Pope John XXII on the issue of evangelical poverty. Both Franciscans were excommunicated, and spent the rest of their lives in Munich under the protection of Emperor Louis IV of Bavaria, who was at war with the pope.

Though he was a great admirer of Aristotle, Ockham's central aim was to free Christianity from what he saw as the corrupting influences of Greek philosophy. Ockham denied that God's existence or infinite perfection could be proved by reason. He also denied that reason can demonstrate the soul's immortality or the existence of free will. Moreover, he completely rejected Aquinas's natural-law approach to ethics, arguing instead that morality depends entirely upon the will or the commands of God. These views are consistent with Ockham's overriding concern to widen the gap between theology and philosophy and to protect the omnipotence and freedom of God from any human-concocted notions that might limit them.

One of the tools Ockham uses to achieve these ends is the principle popularly known as Ockham's razor. The standard formulation of the principle—that "entities are not to be multiplied beyond necessity"—is not found in Ockham's works. He *did* say that "plurality is not to be posited without necessity," which amounts to much the same thing. The core idea is that, all other things being equal, simpler theories and explanations are to be preferred. Understood in this sense, Ockham's razor is a widely accepted methodological principle in both philosophy and science.

SEE ALSO Conceptualism (c. 1320), The Reformation Begins (1517)

William of Ockham, depicted in a stained-glass window at All Saints' Church, in Ockham, Surrey, parts of which date back to the twelfth century.

Entities should not be needlessly multiplied

Pater Ockham

WILLIAM of OCCAM c.1285-1349

Doctor Invincibilis

Conceptualism

William of Ockham (c. 1285–c. 1347)

By the early 1300s, most Christian medieval philosophers had agreed on a general approach to the classic problem of universals. The view they adopted is what today is called *moderate realism*. Moderate realists believe that universals (e.g., species and properties) exist outside the human mind but aren't free-floating entities like Plato's Forms. Rather, universals exist "inside" things such as minds and physical objects. Aquinas, for example, who was a moderate realist, believed that universals exist in the mind of God as general patterns of individual things that exist in the world. Aquinas also believed that universals exist in individuals that share a common nature. For example, Peter and Paul share the universal form of "humanity"; what makes them different persons is simply the fact that they're made up of different hunks of matter. At many points, Aquinas's philosophy presupposes the objective existence of universals.

Ockham flatly denies that anything universal exists outside the mind. His view is sometimes incorrectly called *nominalism*, but nominalists believe that universals are simply names or signs. In Ockham's view, called *conceptualism*, universals aren't linguistic entities (words) but general concepts, like the idea of blue or horse, which apply to many different particulars. Ockham believed that we note similarities between things and then form general concepts by a process of abstraction. Nothing universal exists outside the mind. Indeed, Ockham argues that the very idea of an objectively existent universal is self-contradictory. If it exists, then it's a particular something with particular qualities and so isn't a universal.

Ockham's conceptualism was widely adopted in the two centuries following his death. This "modern way," as it was called, was a direct challenge to the "old way" of thinkers like Aquinas and Scotus, since so much of their philosophies depended on their realist commitments. Moreover, Ockham's nearly total rejection of traditional proofs of the existence of God, free will, and an afterlife seemed to many critics to leave Christian faith without much in the way of rational support. Some believed that it was a short step from Ockham to the rejection of Christianity altogether.

SEE ALSO The Problem of Universals (c. 285), Ockham's Razor (c. 1320)

Saint Peter and Saint Paul, c. 1590–1600, by El Greco. Peter and Paul share the universal form of "humanity"; according to Aquinas, what makes them different persons is the fact that they're made up of different hunks of matter.

The Defender of Peace

Marsilius of Padua (c. 1280–c. 1343)

During the Middle Ages, there were constant conflicts between church and state. Papal power grew during the thirteenth century, and in 1302, Pope Boniface VIII issued a bull declaring that the pope, as vicar of Christ, possessed complete authority over secular and religious affairs. Efforts by the papacy to enforce this claim caused havoc in many parts of Europe, particularly in northern Italy. This unhappy situation provoked one of the boldest and most revolutionary works of political theory ever written, Marsilius of Padua's *The Defender of Peace*.

Marsilius was born in Padua, in northern Italy, and educated at the University of Padua and the University of Paris, where he later served as rector. Drawing heavily on Aristotle's recently translated *Politics*, Marsilius totally rejected claims of papal supremacy and argued that the church should be wholly subject, in both secular and spiritual matters, to the people and their elected representatives. Denounced by the pope as a "son of perdition," Marsilius fled to Germany, where he was given refuge by Emperor Louis IV of Bavaria. In 1327, Louis conquered Italy, deposed the pope, and appointed Marsilius (a layman) spiritual vicar of Rome. Marsilius died in Munich sometime around 1343, abandoned by the emperor, who by then had made peace with the papacy.

The Defender of Peace is a landmark in political thought, both for its argument that all legitimate political power lies originally with the people and for its powerful case against church rule over secular matters. According to Marsilius, Jesus did not claim any political power and did not intend his followers to exercise any. Anticipating arguments that became commonplace in the Reformation, Marsilius argued that Peter was not the first pope and that popes have no special authority in the church. Although *The Defender of Peace* was not widely read prior to the sixteenth century, it was frequently invoked during the Reformation by critics of the papacy. Likely influenced by Marsilius, Richard Hooker (1554–1600) defended a version of original popular sovereignty in his classic *Of the Laws of Ecclesiastical Polity* (1593). Hooker, in turn, was a major influence on John Locke (1632–1704), whose notion of popular sovereignty strongly influenced America's founding fathers.

SEE ALSO The Reformation Begins (1517), Human Rights (1689)

The title page of Marsilius's Defensor Pacis (The Defender of Peace), *from a 1592 edition published in Frankfurt, Germany.*

DEFENSOR PACIS:

SIVE

ADVERSVS

VSVRPATAM ROM.

PONTIFICIS IVRISDICTIO-
nem, MARSILII PATAVINI PRO
inuictiss. & constantiss. Rom. Imperatore LV-
DOVICO IV. BAVARICO, à *tribus*
Rom. *Pontificibus* indigna
perpesso,

APOLOGIA;

Qua politicæ & ecclesiasticæ potestatis limites ·
doctissime explicantur : circa annum
DOMINI M CCC XXIV.
conscripta.

NVNC *vero ad omnium Principum, Magistratuum &*
ecclesiæ Catholicæ, ac nominatim Christianiss.
Galliarum & Nauarræ Regis, &c. HENRICI IV.
(*à* tribus *etiam Rom.* Pontificibus *inique oppu-*
gnati) *eiusque regni & ecclesiarum auctorita-*
tem ac libertatem demonstrandam vtilissima.

FRANCISCVS GOMARVS BRV-
GENSIS recensuit: Capitum argumentis &
NOTIS ad marginem illustrauit.

FRANCOFVRTI
Excudebat IOANNES WECHELVS,
Vænit in officina Vignoniana.

CIƆIƆXCII.

The Renaissance Begins

The Renaissance produced few first-rank philosophers, but it created the conditions for the birth of modern philosophy in the age that followed. Beginning in Italy around the 1350s, the Renaissance marks the rebirth of classical literature and a renewed sense of the value and joys of earthly existence. Whereas the characteristic notes of the Middle Ages were self-abnegation, otherworldliness, preoccupation with sin, and fear of divine punishment, the spirit of the Renaissance was one of discovery, optimism, and belief in the dignity of human nature.

Several things occurred during the Renaissance that set the stage for the genesis of modern philosophy. One was the recovery of the writings of Plato and other Greek and Roman philosophers. This helped to reduce the dominance of Aristotle on the European mind and offered new avenues for philosophical thought. Another important event was the decline of medieval Scholasticism. Thinkers like Petrarch (1304–1374) and Erasmus (1469–1536) attacked what they saw as the arid intellectualism, hair-splitting logic, and excessively theoretical focus of thirteenth-century Scholastics such as Aquinas and Duns Scotus. For Petrarch, the whole point of philosophy was to teach the art of living happily and well, and he condemned Scholasticism for losing sight of this practical purpose. A third significant development was the rise of modern science. Discoveries by such sixteenth-century giants as Nicolaus Copernicus, Johannes Kepler, and Galileo Galilei served to further weaken the authority of Aristotle and provided thinkers like Francis Bacon (1561–1626) and René Descartes (1596–1650) with a new evidence-based paradigm of reliable inquiry.

Finally, the Renaissance—together with the Reformation—opened the door to greater freedom of thought, particularly in Protestant countries. In England, for example, the works of Montaigne (1533–1592) and Machiavelli (1469–1527) were widely read, despite the fact that both writers were on the Catholic Church's "Index of Prohibited Books." The Italian philosopher Giordano Bruno (1548–1600) lived and wrote freely in England for several years, though he was later burned as a heretic by the Inquisition in Rome. Decades later, Descartes and Spinoza (1632–1677) were able to reside and publish largely unmolested in Holland. Such freedoms would have been unthinkable prior to the Renaissance and Reformation.

SEE ALSO The Recovery of Platonism (1468), The Reformation Begins (1517)

Sandro Botticelli's The Birth of Venus, *c. 1482–1485; one of the world's greatest artistic treasures, it was created during the Renaissance.*

The Synthesis of Opposites

Nicholas of Cusa (1401–1464)

Fifteenth-century philosophy and theology was dominated by various forms of Christian Aristotelianism, but there were important thinkers who favored Plato over Aristotle. One of them was Nicholas of Cusa, a brilliant and original thinker who stressed the limits of human understanding and argued for a mystical, Platonic vision of God and the universe.

Nicholas was born in the beautiful German riverfront town of Cusa (present-day Bernkastel-Kues), not far from Trier, where his father was a prosperous merchant. Though trained as a canon lawyer, Nicholas developed a keen interest in Neoplatonic thought, especially that of Pseudo-Dionysius (fl. c. 500), Proclus (d. 485), and John Scotus Eriugena (d. c. 877). Following a visit to Constantinople to promote Christian unity, Cusa wrote a series of books, beginning with *On Learned Ignorance* (1440), which emphasized the transcendence, infinity, and incomprehensibility of God, and the inability of the human mind to attain complete truth about any part of God's creation. Toward the end of his life, Cusa served as both a bishop and a cardinal of the Church.

Cusa's key idea is that of God as a "synthesis of opposites" (*coincidentia oppositorum*). Aristotle had taught that the principle of noncontradiction (the idea that no statement can be both true and false at the same time) is a self-evident principle that lies at the foundation of all thought and reality. Cusa stunned his contemporaries by denying this principle. In God, he argued, one finds a perfect unity of opposites. For example, God is both the greatest being (because he possesses all perfections and is the source of all reality) and also the least of beings (because he has no size and none of the physical qualities we typically associate with greatness). As an infinite being and a synthesis of opposites, God cannot be grasped by the finite human mind. All human learning involves comparing what we know with something we are trying to understand. But there is no comparison between the infinite and the finite. Thus, as Pseudo-Dionysius had argued, the best way to approach God is through "the way of negation." By denying that God is this or that, we recognize the deepest truth: that God infinitely transcends all human attempts to understand him.

SEE ALSO Mystical Theology (c. 1300)

Cardinal Nicholas of Cusa arrives in the Netherlands, *1451, by Dutch engraver Caspar Luyken, c. 1700. Cusa was sent to Germany and the Netherlands in 1450–1452 as a papal legate to preach and reform.*

The Recovery of Platonism

Marsilio Ficino (1433–1499)

Generally speaking, Plato was the most highly regarded Greek philosopher in ancient times, both in pagan and in Christian circles. However, he had little influence in the Christian West during the Middle Ages; after the beginning of the Dark Ages, no one in the West could read Plato because none of his writings, except for part of the *Timaeus*, were available in Latin. It was not until the fifteenth century that Latin translations began to appear. The most important figure in this vital effort was the Italian humanist Marsilio Ficino.

When Ficino was in his twenties, he gained the patronage of Cosimo de' Medici, the de facto ruler of Florence. Byzantine scholars like Manuel Chrysoloras, George Gemistus Plethon, and John Argyropoulos had come to Italy in the early- and mid-1400s and created an intense interest in ancient Greek literature, including the philosophy of Plato. In response, Cosimo founded the Platonic Academy in Florence in 1462 and appointed Ficino as its head. Ficino practically worshipped Plato, believing that he literally had been divinely inspired. By 1468, Ficino had translated (in draft) the complete works of Plato into Latin. He added a series of commentaries to the translations, and the whole work was published in 1484. Now, for the first time in nearly a thousand years, people in the Christian West could read the works of Plato. The effect was profound, not only in philosophy, but in literature, art, and theology as well.

Ficino was a Catholic priest, and his passion for Plato was partly based on his belief in the essential harmony of Platonic and Neoplatonic philosophy with Christianity. He saw Platonism as teaching many of the same basic truths as Christianity and also as providing extra ammunition to bring atheists and skeptics to Christ. For example, in his own major work of original philosophy, the *Platonic Theology* (written 1469–1474), he offers a series of Plato-inspired arguments for the immortality of the soul and the existence of a heavenly afterlife. By such means he hoped to incline those who rejected Christian revelation to give it a fresh look.

SEE ALSO Neoplatonism (c. 250), The Last Great Greek Philosopher (c. 460)

An engraving of Marsilio Ficino by French illustrator Esme de Boulonois, 1682, after Dutch engraver Philip Galle.

Utopia

Sir Thomas More (1478–1535)

Thomas More is among the most dynamic figures of the Renaissance. Humanist, historian, statesman, martyr, and saint, More is best remembered as the author of *Utopia*, a kind of philosophical novel (in Latin) about a fictional island in the South Atlantic. In Greek, the word *utopia* means "nowhere place" while *eutopia* means "happy place." Like Plato's *Republic*, on which it is partly modeled, More's *Utopia* is offered as a blueprint of what a rational and just state would be like. It is also held up a satirical mirror to the follies and vices of the Christian Europe of More's time.

In More's tale, Utopia is a crescent-shaped island 500 miles long by 200 miles wide. On the island are 54 identical-looking cities, each with outlying farms. There is no private property and no money. (There is gold, but it is despised and used only for chamber pots and prisoners' chains.) The people live in large, identical state-owned households and eat their meals in big cafeterias. Clothing is simple and sturdy, and all citizens dress pretty much alike. There are no idlers and everyone who can works, but the workday is only six hours long so there is plenty of time for leisure and cultural activities. Besides working in the fields, every citizen learns a craft, such as shoemaking. These craft-products are stockpiled and offered free to whoever needs them. The government is a form of representative democracy, punishments are mild, and wars are fought only for self-defense or to punish aggressors. Most Utopians worship an ineffable higher power they call "the father of all." Other religions are tolerated, though civil penalties are imposed on those who deny the existence of God or the immortality of the soul. Priests are elected by popular vote, and some priests are women. As for morality, Utopians reject fasting and other forms of self-denial; "No kind of pleasure is forbidden, provided harm does not come of it."

As one would expect, there are many features of More's *Utopia* that strike modern readers as less than ideal. But it cannot be denied that in many ways More was far ahead of his times.

SEE ALSO Plato's *Republic* (c. 380 BCE)

Pages from an original 1516 edition of More's Utopia, *published in Flanders, showing a map of the island of Utopia on the left page and the "Utopian alphabet" on the right.*

3

VTOPIAE INSVLAE FIGVRA

VTOPIENSIVM ALPHABETVM.

a b c d e f g h i k l m n o p q r s t v x y

ⵔⵔ ... (Utopian alphabet glyphs)

Tetrastichon vernacula Vtopiensium lingua.

Vtopos   ha   Boccas   peu   la

chama   polta   chamaan

Bargol   he   maglomi   baccan

soma   gymno   sophaon

Agrama   gymnosophon   labarembacha

bodamilomin

Voluala   barchin   heman   la

lauoluola   dramme   pagloni.

Horum versuum ad verbum hæc est sententia.

Vtopus me dux ex non insula fecit insulam

Vna ego terrarum omnium absq́ philosophia

Ciuitatem philosophicam expressi mortalibus

Libéter impartio mea, nó grauatim accipio meliora,

The Reformation Begins

Martin Luther (1483–1546)

On October 31, 1517, when Martin Luther launched the Protestant Reformation by nailing his ninety-five theses to the door of the Schlosskirche (Castle Church) of Wittenberg, Saxony (in present-day eastern Germany), no one could have predicted the far-reaching intellectual and cultural consequences. Though Luther himself was generally hostile to philosophy, the Reformation turned out to be a tremendous boon to both philosophy and science. Luther, who was born of peasant stock in the Saxon town of Eisleben, revolted against the Aristotelian version of Scholastic philosophy he was taught in college. Aristotle, he said, was a "damned, conceited, rascally heathen" whom God sent as "a plague upon us for our sins." Trained in the Ockhamist tradition of Scholastic philosophy, Luther exalted revelation over reason, even going so far as to call reason "the devil's whore."

For nearly a century after the Reformation began, little first-rate philosophy was produced in either Catholic or Protestant countries. But the Reformation set the stage for the great flowering of philosophy in the seventeenth century, in four major ways: First, there was greater freedom of thought in Protestant countries like England and Holland than in Catholic nations like Italy and Spain. Philosophers such as Hobbes, Spinoza, and Hume, who challenged conventional religious beliefs, wouldn't have been permitted to publish in Catholic countries. Second, Protestant universities broke with the Catholic tradition of Scholastic philosophy and encouraged new ways of thinking. Third, the Protestant doctrine of the right of private judgment encouraged believers in Protestant countries to use reason in forming their religious views. Finally, the endless theological controversies spawned by the Reformation led to a deep examination of the foundations of human knowledge. Both Descartes and Locke, for example, believed that no secure foundation for philosophy or religion could be found until certain basic epistemological questions were answered: What are the sources of human knowledge? What is the human mind capable of knowing? Can anything be known with certainty? This led to a strong, new focus in early modern philosophy on problems of knowledge that philosophers refer to as "the epistemological turn." For all these reasons, the Reformation proved to be a major stimulus to philosophy.

SEE ALSO Ockham's Razor (c. 1320), The Renaissance Begins (c. 1350), The Father of Modern Philosophy (1637)

A stained glass window featuring Martin Luther adorns a thirteenth-century cathedral in Greifswald, Germany.

Hier stehe ich, ich kann nicht anders.
Gott helfe mir. Amen

The Humanist Ideal

Desiderius Erasmus (c. 1466–1536)

Renaissance humanists were not, as a rule, secular humanists. They were Christian humanists who celebrated the educational and formative values of "humane letters" (that is, the Greek and Roman classics) while remaining in the Christian fold. The greatest figure of Renaissance Christian humanism was the Dutch scholar Desiderius Erasmus.

Erasmus was born out of wedlock in Rotterdam, Holland. After receiving an excellent grounding in Latin classics in Deventer, Erasmus was orphaned when the plague killed his parents. He was reluctantly persuaded by his guardians to become an Augustinian monk. After six years he left the monastery, studied at the University of Paris, and became an itinerant scholar. Many of Erasmus's works, including *Adagia* (1500), *Colloquia* (1518), and *Encomium Moriae* (*The Praise of Folly*) (1511), became best sellers.

As a humanist, Erasmus endlessly sang the praises of a classical education and of Ciceronian over medieval Latin. As a Christian, he strongly disliked Scholastic theology and favored a return to a simpler, less dogmatic form of Christian piety. He was such a staunch supporter of church reform that many expected him to join Luther's Protestant revolt when it broke out in 1517. Erasmus's answer came in 1524 when he published *De libero arbitrio . . .* (*On Free Will . . .*), directly challenging Luther's core teachings of divine predestination, total depravity, and God's absolute sovereignty. It is widely considered to be Erasmus's most important philosophical work.

In addition to citing reams of quotations from the Bible and fathers of the Church supporting the idea of free will, Erasmus argues that the denial of human freedom is inconsistent with the idea of a just and loving God. How could a just God punish us for sins we could not help committing? If God completely determines all our thoughts and actions, must he not be the ultimate author of sin? How is being a puppet on God's string consistent with Christian ideals of human dignity? In 1525, Luther responded in *De servo arbitrio* (*On the Bondage of the Will*), an uncompromising denial of free will and a defense of God's absolute sovereignty. Most of Luther's contemporaries thought he won the argument.

SEE ALSO The Renaissance Begins (c. 1350), The Reformation Begins (1517)

A copy of a portrait of Erasmus, after Flemish painter Quinten Massijs, c. 1535.

The Silver Age of Scholasticism

Luis de Molina (1535–1600), **Francisco Suárez** (1548–1617)

During the golden age of Medieval Scholasticism (roughly 1250 to 1350), philosophical giants such as Albertus Magnus, Thomas Aquinas, St. Bonaventure, John Duns Scotus, and William of Ockham struggled to integrate the philosophy of Aristotle with Christian teachings and tried to work out what unaided human reason could know about God, the soul, and a possible afterlife. Two centuries later, a second flowering of Scholastic thought occurred. This was the so-called Silver Age of Scholasticism, when Catholic philosophers based mainly in Spain sought to create a new synthesis of faith and reason from among the discordant schools of medieval and Renaissance philosophy and in response to the new challenge of Protestantism. The greatest philosophers of this age were two Spanish Jesuits, Luis de Molina and Francisco Suárez.

Molina is famous for offering an ingenious solution to the classic theological problem of how to reconcile free will with divine grace, divine foreknowledge, and providence. In his greatest work, *Concordia* (1588), Molina argues that humans can possess free will even though God infallibly foreknows every human choice and actively "concurs" in the causal sequences that result in those choices. Free will is possible because God's foreknowledge and causal concurrence doesn't *force* anyone to make any particular choice. Before God even created the world, he had complete knowledge of every possible choice that every possible person might make in every possible situation. Molina calls this kind of divine foreknowledge "middle knowledge." In virtue of his middle knowledge, God can guarantee that everything that happens in the world fits with his holy master plan. This is consistent with free will, Molina claims, because God does not causally control anyone's thoughts or will. The choices we make remain our own.

Suárez was primarily a theologian, but he was also the author of two great philosophical works, *Metaphysical Disputations* (1597) and *Treatise on Laws and God the Lawgiver* (1612). The two-volume *Disputations* became a standard text at both Catholic and Protestant universities for over two centuries. The voluminous *Treatise on Laws* was a classic work of jurisprudence that strongly influenced Hugo Grotius (1583–1645) and other early modern architects of natural and international law.

SEE ALSO The Birth of Scholasticism (1121), The Great Medieval Synthesis (c. 1265), *On the Law of War and Peace* (1625)

An early-twentieth-century commemorative relief of Francisco Suárez on the facade of the Palacio Arzobispal (Archbishop's Palace) in Granada, where Suárez was born in 1548.

P. FRAN°. SUAREZ S.J.
GRANADINO ILUSTRE
FILOSOFO, TEOLOGO, JURISTA
Y APOLOGISTA INSIGNE
MAS INSIGNE AUN POR SUS VIRTUDES
V ENERO MDXLVIII
† XXV SEPTIEMBRE MDCXVII
EN EL III CENTENARIO DE SU
MUERTE. SUS DISCIPULOS
Y SUS ADMIRADORES
XXV SEPTIEMBRE MCMXVII

The Prince

Niccolò Machiavelli (1469–1527)

Machiavelli's *The Prince* (written in 1513 but not published until 1532) is the bible of power politics. Reviled by many as a godless and amoral cynic, praised by others as a far-seeing prophet who dared to tell the truth about power, Machiavelli remains a towering figure with whom all students of political thought must come to terms.

Machiavelli was born in Florence, the son of a moderately prosperous lawyer. From a young age his great passions were the Latin classics (particularly the Roman historians) and politics. For fourteen years he served as a diplomat and army organizer under the Florentine republic. In 1512, the republic was overthrown by the armies of Pope Julius II; Machiavelli was captured, tortured, and exiled. It was during his years of enforced retirement that he wrote his two great works of political theory, *The Prince* and *Discourses* (written c. 1517, published 1531).

The Prince is a practical manual on how to keep and preserve power in the world of realpolitik. Machiavelli believed that sound political thinking must begin with the recognition that all men are essentially selfish, acquisitive, and vicious. Many previous political thinkers had written utopian fantasies or sermonized about the moral duties of Christian rulers. Machiavelli considered all of that a waste of ink. In the real world of Italian politics that he knew, a sheepish prince would quickly be eaten up by his wolfish neighbors.

Some have suggested that *The Prince* is simply a piece of descriptive, value-free analysis of how to play the game of power politics successfully. In fact, the work reflects an ethic that looks back to the ancient Roman ideal of *virtus*—masculinity, strength of character, courage, boldness—but taken a step further. Effective rulers possess what Machiavelli calls *virtù*—meaning they are prepared to set aside considerations of morality or religion whenever the safety of the state or the imperatives of power demand it. Like Nietzsche (1844–1900), Machiavelli rejected the Christian virtues of gentleness, meekness, humility, and contempt for worldly things. Given the natural wickedness of man, this simply makes the weak the prey of the strong. He much preferred the sterner virtues of courage, energy, strength, boldness, and crafty intelligence.

SEE ALSO The Renaissance Begins (c. 1350), The Revaluation of Values (1887)

An author portrait of Machiavelli from a 1769 edition of The Prince, *published in Italy.*

The Rights of Native Peoples

Francisco de Vitoria (c. 1486–1546)

On a visit to Bolivia in July 2015, Pope Francis apologized to the indigenous people in Latin America, saying that "many grave sins were committed against the native peoples of America in the name of God." The pope's words were a vindication of arguments made in 1539 by the Spanish theologian Francisco de Vitoria.

Vitoria was a Dominican who studied and taught in Paris for over fifteen years. In 1523, he returned to Spain, where he taught theology and Scholastic philosophy until his death in 1546. Though Vitoria published nothing himself, notes of his lectures were published by his students. Among these was a course of lectures Vitoria gave in 1539 titled *De Indis* (*On the American Indians*). There he drew upon just war theory, his own theory of the law of nations, and Aquinas's natural-law ethics to refute common arguments for the conquest, enslavement, and forced conversion of native peoples in the New World.

Vitoria denied that either the pope or the Holy Roman emperor (Charles V at the time) were the rightful rulers of native peoples' lands in the New World. Thus, conquest could not be justified on the ground that indigenous peoples were wrongfully occupying lands that really belonged to the pope or emperor. Could it be argued that the lands are "unoccupied" because only rational beings can own property and the Indians lack reason? No, Vitoria countered, the native peoples have complex social and economic systems, proving that they are rational beings with intrinsic value and dignity. What about the fact that the native peoples are pagans? Might they be enslaved and forcibly converted to Christianity to punish them for the sin of unbelief? No, he argued, unbelief is a sin only if missionaries have presented the native peoples clear proof that Christianity is the one true religion, which he argued hasn't been the case. Might they be enslaved as punishment for their "sins against nature" (fornication, theft, and the like)? By such logic, Vitoria pointed out, native peoples would be justified in conquering and enslaving Europeans for their sins.

Unfortunately, the attempts by Vitoria and later Spanish theologians to stop atrocities in the New World had little impact on the harsh realities of colonization.

SEE ALSO The Birth of Scholasticism (1121), The Silver Age of Scholasticism (c. 1525), *On the Law of War and Peace* (1625)

An illustration depicting atrocities against indigenous peoples by Flemish-German engraver Theodor de Bry from A Short Account of the Destruction of the Indies, 1552, *by Dominican reformer Bartolomé de las Casas (c. 1484–1566), a contemporary of Vitoria*

The Birth of Modern Science

Nothing has had a greater impact on the course of Western philosophy than the rise of modern science, which can be said to have begun with the publication of Nicolaus Copernicus's great work, *On the Revolutions of the Celestial Spheres*, in 1543. The scientific revolution, spanning the fifteenth to seventeenth centuries and brought about by men such as Copernicus, Kepler, Bacon, Galileo, Descartes, and Newton, led to the overthrow of the medieval worldview.

Prior to the scientific revolution, the reigning paradigm of Scholastic Aristotelianism was so hidebound by tradition and respect for authority that it produced little in the way of original thought. The rise of modern science led to a new birth of intellectual freedom. Philosophers such as Descartes and Hobbes threw off the straightjacket of ossified Scholasticism and struck out in bold new directions. Philosophy was no longer seen as simply the handmaid of theology. It had a charter and an agenda of its own.

The scientific revolution also led to a sharper separation of science and philosophy. Increasingly, philosophers left scientific problems to the scientists and focused on what Bertrand Russell (d. 1970) called the "No Man's Land" of speculative thought on which definite knowledge is difficult or impossible to attain. Philosophy came to be regarded as what John Locke called an "under-laborer" for science, charged with clearing obstacles and "rubbish" that impeded its growth. The remarkable success science had achieved through observation and experimentation inspired the growth of British empiricism. On the continent, the mathematical and deductive aspects of modern science fueled the rise of rationalism in mathematically oriented thinkers like Descartes and Spinoza. The mechanical explanations of natural phenomena favored by scientists such as Galileo, Robert Boyle, and Isaac Newton led to atomistic philosophies of nature in thinkers like Hobbes and Descartes. The heady triumphs of natural science inspired philosophers such as Hume to apply "the experimental method of reasoning" to "moral subjects" such as psychology and sociology. Finally, science has contributed to a steady growth of secularism among philosophers in the modern era. Whereas prior to the scientific revolution, nearly all Western philosophers were theists, today a clear majority of them are naturalists. The growth of science, no doubt, is a major reason for the shift.

SEE ALSO The Renaissance Begins (c. 1350), The Enlightenment Begins (1620), The Father of Modern Philosophy (1637)

"Scenography of the Copernican World System," a plate from Harmonia Macrocosmica . . . , *a major astronomical atlas published by Dutch-German cartographer Andreas Cellarius in 1660.*

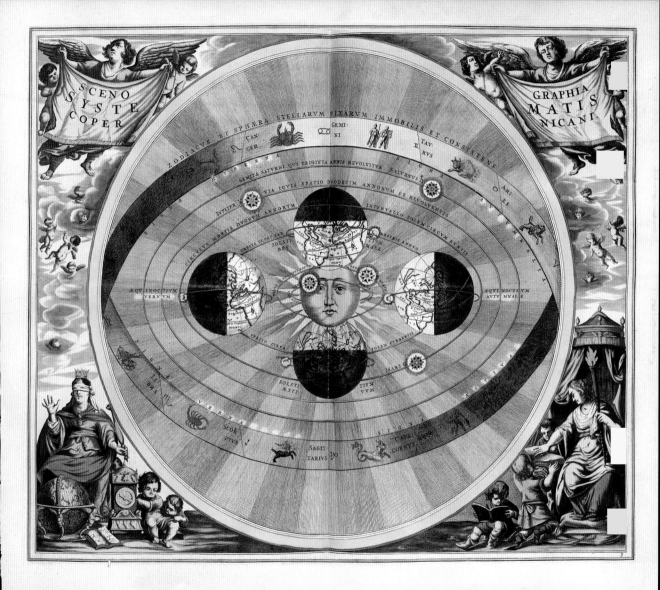

Revival of Classical Skepticism

Michel de Montaigne (1533–1592)

There were two schools of skepticism in ancient Greece and Rome: Academic Skepticism and Pyrrhonian Skepticism. Very little was known about these forms of skepticism during the Middle Ages. Sometime around 1432, *Lives of the Eminent Philosophers*, by third-century biographer Diogenes Laërtius, was translated into Latin, providing some insights into the thought of prominent Greek skeptics such as Pyrrho, Arcesilaus, and Carneades. In the 1560s, the writings of the Pyrrhonian Skeptic Sextus Empiricus were translated into Latin. One person who read Sextus's works was the acclaimed French essayist Michel de Montaigne. Montaigne, a Catholic, was shaken by this encounter, and in response he wrote his longest and perhaps greatest essay, the "Apology for Raymond Sebond."

Montaigne was born on his family château near Bordeaux. After a successful career as a lawyer, he retired on his thirty-eighth birthday into "the bosom of the learned Virgins," meaning the Muses that inspired the great Greek and Roman writers. He spent the rest of his life (except for two stints as mayor of Bordeaux) happily ensconced in the round tower on his château, surrounded by his 1,000-book library. Montaigne invented a new literary form, the essay, to write charming conversational reflections on his favorite subject: himself. His major impact on philosophy was to revive interest in ancient Greek skepticism by means of his vigorous (if qualified) defense of Pyrrhonian Skepticism.

What Montaigne tries to do in the "Apology" is use skeptical arguments borrowed from Sextus to show the frailty of human reason. Montaigne offers a barrage of arguments to demonstrate that we cannot have any confident knowledge of reality unless God deigns to reveal the truth to us. He concludes with a pious and possibly ironical reaffirmation of his Christian faith.

It wasn't lost on Montaigne's readers that his skeptical arguments undermined faith in Christianity just as it did every other big-picture theory of reality. The result was a "Pyrrhonian crisis" that swept Europe around the beginning of the seventeenth century. Major thinkers like Descartes and Locke sought to show that Montaigne's skeptical doubts were excessive. Scholars still debate whether they were successful.

SEE ALSO Carneades on Justice (155 BCE), *Outlines of Pyrrhonism* (c. 200)

This striking engraving of Michel de Montaigne by C. E. Wagstaff appeared in a reference book published in London in 1833, titled The Gallery of Portraits: With Memoirs.

The Advancement of Learning

Francis Bacon (1561–1626)

Francis Bacon was the most important English thinker of the Renaissance. A leading critic of Aristotelian science and medieval Scholasticism, he contributed mightily to the growth of modern science and to a fresh, more empirical approach to philosophy. Like his contemporary Descartes, Bacon believed that a total reconstruction of knowledge was necessary to provide a firm foundation for science, philosophy, and human progress. He first pointed the way to such a reconstruction in *The Advancement of Learning* (1605).

Bacon was born in London, the son of Queen Elizabeth's keeper of the great seal. Educated at Cambridge and trained as a lawyer, Bacon held a series of prominent public offices under King James I, eventually serving as lord chancellor. After pleading guilty to bribery in 1621, Bacon retired to his luxurious country home and devoted the rest of his days to writing. Among his important works are the *Essays* (1597), the *Novum Organum* (1620), and the posthumous *New Atlantis* (1627).

In *The Advancement of Learning*, Bacon speaks eloquently of the dignity of learning, offers a diagnosis of why European science and philosophy have remained stagnant, proposes a new classification of the fields of knowledge, and pleads for major investments in education and research. For too long, he argues, have scholars engaged in idle speculation, groundless pseudoscience, and vain disputation. The main purpose of knowledge is practical: to improve the human condition. To attain this, we must achieve mastery over nature. Only by conquering nature and harnessing its powers through novel technologies and inventions can real progress be made toward a bright new future. In these pages we hear many of the characteristic notes of the "Age of Reason": a sharp break with the superstitious and unproductive past, giving way to empirical science, organized research, practical inquiry, technological advancement, and mastery over nature. Mathematician and philosopher Alfred North Whitehead (1861–1947) rightly called Bacon "one of the great builders who constructed the mind of the modern world." Bacon was (in his own words) the great "bell-ringer" who called mankind to embrace a radically new vision of the human condition. It took many years for people to see that there are major downsides to efforts to "conquer nature."

SEE ALSO The Birth of Modern Science (1543), The Enlightenment Begins (1620), The Father of Modern Philosophy (1637)

A portrait of Francis Bacon, c. 1647, by Dutch engraver Simon van de Passe.

MEDIO FIRMA
CRIA

The Enlightenment Begins

Francis Bacon (1561–1626)

Immanuel Kant (1724–1804) famously defined the Enlightenment as "man's release from his self-incurred tutelage" and declared its motto to be "*Sapere aude!* [Dare to know!] Have courage to use your own understanding."

The Enlightenment of the seventeenth and eighteenth centuries was a complex intellectual and cultural movement, but several salient themes stand out. These include a rejection of authoritarianism and gloomy superstition in matters of belief; faith in the power of reason and science to discover truth and to improve the human condition; a commitment to toleration, political freedom, and human rights; and a belief in progress through reason, science, and education. Leading Enlightenment figures include Francis Bacon, René Descartes, Baruch Spinoza, John Locke, Isaac Newton, Voltaire, Denis Diderot, David Hume, Benjamin Franklin, and Thomas Jefferson.

Scholars debate when the Enlightenment began, but a good case can be made that it started with the publication of Francis Bacon's *Novum organum* in 1620. There, Bacon attacks medieval science, logic, and philosophy, arguing that the only reliable way of forming beliefs about the natural world is through patient scientific induction. Doing such rigorous empirical science is difficult, in part because of certain biases and preconceptions that affect our observations and distort our inferences. Bacon calls these distorting factors "idols," and he identifies four main varieties: idols of the tribe (errors that flow from inherent tendencies in the human mind, such as wishful thinking), idols of the cave (errors that derive from one's own personal biases, temperament, and predispositions), idols of the marketplace (errors that stem from confusions of language), and idols of the theater (errors due to uncritical acceptance of false philosophies of the past).

The heyday of the Enlightenment lasted until the emergence of Romanticism in the late eighteenth century, but in many ways we continue to be children of the Enlightenment. Though faith in progress, science, and reason may have waned somewhat since the heady days of Locke and Jefferson, belief in toleration, political freedom, and human rights has grown, and few today would question the value of independent judgment and "critical thinking" in forming one's beliefs.

SEE ALSO The Birth of Modern Science (1543), *The Advancement of Learning* (1605)

Title page for a 1645 edition of Bacon's Novum organum scientiarum (New Instrument of Science), *published in Leiden, Holland. The Latin phrase under the ship,* Multi pertransibunt & augebitur scientia, *translates as "Many will travel and knowledge will be increased."*

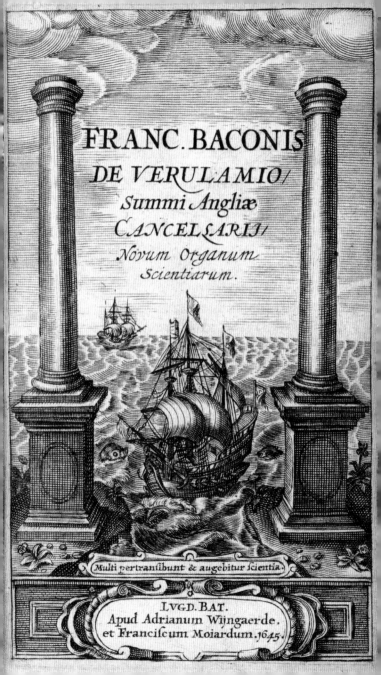

FRANC. BACONIS

DE VERULAMIO,

Summi Angliæ

CANCELLARIJ,

Novum Organum

Scientiarum.

Multi pertransibunt & augebitur scientia.

LVGD. BAT.
Apud Adrianum Wijngaerde,
et Franciscum Moiardum. 1645.

On the Law of War and Peace

Hugo Grotius (1583–1645)

In the early seventeenth century, Europe was plagued by incessant and increasingly destructive wars. In 1618, the Thirty Years' War broke out, causing unprecedented devastation and loss of life across Germany and parts of northern Europe. In response, the brilliant Dutch scholar Hugo Grotius published *On the Law of War and Peace* (1625), the first systematic attempt to lay the foundations of international law and to spell out the conditions for the just and humane conduct of war. It remains a foundational text of modern international politics and the law of war.

Grotius was born in Delft, Holland, the son of a well-educated man. A child prodigy, Grotius was hailed at age fifteen by the king of France as "the miracle of Holland" for his astounding erudition. After serving in a variety of important political posts in Holland, Grotius was imprisoned for three years because of his involvement in a Protestant religious dispute. Aided by his wife, he escaped from prison in a wooden chest and spent most of the rest of his life living in exile in various European countries.

Drawing upon both classical and Scholastic writers, Grotius sought to construct a framework of international law composed of two elements: natural law (*ius naturale*) and the law of nations (*ius gentium*). Grotius followed Aquinas (d. 1274) in thinking of natural law as basic moral principles, rooted in reason and human nature, which have God as their author and enforcer. Among the binding principles of natural law in international relations are that promises should be kept and treaties should not be violated. The law of nations is a loose collection of customs and traditions that most developed nations have observed in their relations with one another (e.g., the treatment of ambassadors). Unlike principles of natural law, the law of nations can be modified by international agreement.

Probably the most influential part of Grotius's text is his extensive discussion of the ethics and lawfulness of war. Grotius laid down stringent conditions for when war may be legally and ethically waged and how it should be conducted. Though frequently ignored, many of those principles are now well-established rules of the law of war.

SEE ALSO Natural Law (c. 1270), The Silver Age of Scholasticism (c. 1525), The Rights of Native Peoples (1539)

The Victory of Fleurus, 1634, by Italian painter Vincenzo Carducci, depicts the Battle of Fleurus (in present-day Belgium), fought on August 29, 1622, during the Thirty Years' War (1618–1648).

The Father of Modern Philosophy

René Descartes (1596–1650)

The seventeenth century marks the birth of modern philosophy. The most important figure in the transition from medieval to modern philosophy was the French philosopher, scientist, and mathematician René Descartes. With him, philosophy made a fresh start.

Descartes was born in La Haye en Touraine (now called Descartes) in central France. After receiving a fine liberal arts education at the Jesuit college of La Flèche, he traveled widely and briefly served as a soldier, desiring to learn from "the great book of the world," as he later said. As a young man, Descartes dedicated himself to the monumental task of constructing a universal science, built on the model of mathematics. Coming from a well-to-do family, he was able to pursue this goal single-mindedly, without the distraction of needing to earn a living. He lived a quiet, scholarly life, in accordance with his personal motto: "He has lived well who has hidden well."

Descartes believed that philosophy was stuck in a rut and could never achieve solid results until it became as rigorous as mathematics. In his classic *Discourse on Method* (1637), he laid down four rules for conducting careful intellectual inquiry. The first of these was to accept nothing as true that one does not clearly and distinctly perceive to be true.

Descartes is rightly called "the father of modern philosophy" for several reasons. First, he broke sharply from medieval philosophy and proposed a new model for doing philosophy, one founded on clear definitions and rigorous reasoning from indisputable starting points. Second, he shifted the main focus of philosophy from questions of being or existence to questions of knowledge, thus initiating what is known as the "epistemological turn" in early modern philosophy. Third, Descartes exalted the power of human reason, claiming that all sorts of fundamental truths about reality could be discovered just by thinking, without the aid of the senses. In so doing, he launched a powerful movement in philosophy known as "rationalism." Finally, he rejected the dense, jargon-ridden writing style of the medieval Scholastics. Descartes wrote elegantly and clearly, setting an admirable pattern that most European philosophers followed until the close of the eighteenth century.

SEE ALSO *Meditations on First Philosophy* (1641), *Ethics* (1677)

René Descartes in his study, a portrait created in 1687–1691, by Dutch engraver Cornelis A. Hellemans.

Meditations on First Philosophy

René Descartes (1596–1650)

Descartes's *Meditations on First Philosophy* (1641) is one of the undisputed classics of philosophy. More than 375 years after it was first published, it remains one of the most widely read texts in introductory philosophy courses.

Part of the charm of the *Meditations* is its personal touch. It is an existential quest rather than a dry treatise. Its basic narrative arc is that of a man who thinks his way from a state of doubt and confusion to one of triumphant and secure self-understanding.

The goals of the *Meditations* are incredibly ambitious: to determine if anything can be known with complete certainty; to refute skepticism and materialism; to provide new and secure foundations for science, philosophy, and theology; to replace Aristotle's philosophy of nature; and to prove the existence of God and the immortality of the soul.

The book begins with Descartes's famous "method of doubt": to doubt everything except what is absolutely certain and indubitable. Over the course of the six meditations, readers encounter some of the most iconic memes in all of philosophy. Could our senses systematically deceive us? Might life be simply a dream? Could what we call reality actually be a cruel hoax perpetrated by an "evil genius"? Could even reason and logic be deceptive? Is my own existence the one rock-solid certainty ("I think therefore I am")? Can God's existence be proved simply by reflecting on the idea of God? Would a good and truthful God allow human beings to be systematically deceived about the nature of reality? Are human beings simply material creatures, or do we have a nonphysical soul that is distinct from the body and capable of surviving after the body dies?

Few philosophers today believe that Descartes was successful in proving his desired conclusions. Most are unconvinced, in particular, by his arguments for the existence of God and an immaterial soul. Nonetheless, the *Meditations* remains one of the enduring classics of philosophy because of the fascinating questions it poses, its readability, and its engaging first-person narrative structure.

SEE ALSO Carneades on Justice (155 BCE), *Outlines of Pyrrhonism* (c. 200), The Father of Modern Philosophy (1637)

The title page of a 1670 edition of Descartes's Meditationes de prima philosophia *(Meditations on First Philosophy), published in Amsterdam.*

RENATI DES CARTES
MEDITATIONES
De Prima
PHILOSOPHIA,

In quibus Dei existentia, & animæ humanæ à
corpore distinctio, demonstrantur.

*His adjunctæ sunt variæ objectiones doctorum virorum in istas
de Deo & anima demonstrationes ;*

CUM RESPONSIONIBUS AUCTORIS.

Editio ultima prioribus auctior & emendatior.

AMSTELODAMI,
Apud DANIELEM ELZEVIRIUM.
cIↃ IↃC LXX.

Leviathan

Thomas Hobbes (1588–1679)

Thomas Hobbes's *Leviathan* is a bold and original work. In his day, Hobbes was widely seen as a dangerous thinker because of his support for materialism, determinism, egoistic psychology, government control of religion, and an all-powerful state. *Leviathan* was a major influence on later English moral and political theory. Among its most influential ideas is that of the social contract as the basis of government.

Hobbes was born in Westport, England, a former village near Malmesbury. After graduating from Oxford, Hobbes became a private tutor in the household of the Earl of Devonshire. In 1640, when his views on absolute royal power became known, Hobbes fled to France for eleven years to avoid possible persecution. There he tutored the future Charles II and wrote a reply to Descartes's *Meditations*. Hobbes returned to England shortly after *Leviathan* was published in 1651. He lived to the ripe age of ninety-one, a fact that he attributed to his nightly habit of singing lustily in bed.

Leviathan is a wide-ranging, lucidly written book that tackles a broad range of philosophical issues. What it is best remembered for today is its account of how society and government are formed. Long ago, Hobbes says, humans lived in small bands without any sort of social organization or government. Hobbes calls this aboriginal condition "the state of nature." Because humans are naturally selfish, violent, and power hungry, this state of nature was a state of perpetual violence in which most people lived lives that were "solitary, poor, nasty, brutish, and short." To escape this dire condition, people decided to create an organized society with government and laws. They agreed on a "social contract" that vested virtually total power in a king or a small group of rulers. Only if the sovereign possesses near-absolute power, Hobbes argued, can it guarantee peace and security.

Hobbes's notions of the state of nature and the social contract were powerful ideas that sparked a great deal of discussion. Later thinkers, like John Locke (1632–1704) and Jean-Jacques Rousseau (1712–1778), offered their own versions of social-contract theory, and today it is widely accepted that just governments rest "on the consent of the governed."

SEE ALSO Human Rights (1689), *The Social Contract* (1762), *A Theory of Justice* (1971), Political Libertarianism (1974)

The original edition of Hobbes's Leviathan, *published in London in 1651, featured this elaborate illustration by French engraver Abraham Bosse.*

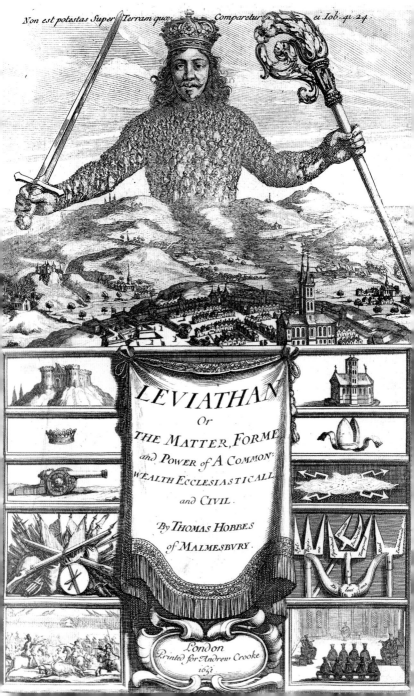

Non est potestas Super Terram quæ Comparetur ei Iob. 41. 24.

LEVIATHAN
Or
THE MATTER, FORME
and POWER of A COMMON-
WEALTH ECCLESIASTICALL
and CIVIL.

By THOMAS HOBBES
of MALMESBVRY.

London
Printed for Andrew Crooke
1651

Free Will and Determinism Are Compatible

Thomas Hobbes (1588–1679)

Many thinkers impressed by the march of modern science have claimed that every event in the universe is an inevitable consequence of prior causes. This is a view called "determinism." On the face of it, determinism seems to rule out any idea of free will. After all, if determinism is true, then all of our acts and choices are the inevitable outcome of antecedent causes, some stretching back to before we were born. But if all our acts and choices are necessitated by prior causes, it seems that those acts and choices are not up to us. And if they are not up to us, how can they be free?

Hobbes was one of the first in a long line of modern thinkers who deny that free will is incompatible with determinism. Hobbes argues for "compatibilism," the view that determinism is not inconsistent with free will. Hobbes accepted determinism. He thought that since "every act of man's will, and every desire and inclination, proceed from some cause, and that from another cause, in a continual chain (whose first link is in the hand of God, the first of all causes), they proceed from *necessity*." But just because an act is necessitated does not mean that it is not free. A person acts freely if "he finds no stop in doing what he has the will, desire, or inclination to do." In other words, we are "free" if we are able to do as we wish without constraint or impediment. Many acts are free in this sense even if determinism is true.

Many philosophers have challenged Hobbes's definition of "free will." Suppose I hypnotize you and say, "When I clap my hands three times, quack like a duck." I clap my hands three times and you say, "Quack, quack." You were able to do what you wanted. There was "no stop" in your ability to do what you had "the will, desire, or inclination to do." Yet it seems clear that your act was not free.

Modern compatibilists have come up with a variety of sophisticated responses to criticisms of this sort. Whether any of them succeed is still a matter of lively debate.

SEE ALSO Stoicism (c. 300 BCE)

Thomas Hobbes is depicted in an engraving from 1665 by noted etcher Wenceslaus Hollar of Prague, after J. B. Caspar.

en! quam modicè habitat Philosophia.

Verà & Vivà Effigies THOMÆ HOBBES Malmesburiensis.
Ætati: suæ 92. obiit 4. Dece̅ 1679.

Pascal's Wager

Blaise Pascal (1623–1662)

The American intellectual Allan Bloom (1930–1992) wrote that "there are two writers who between them shape and set the limits to the minds of educated Frenchmen." One is Descartes, who celebrated the power of reason, and the other is Blaise Pascal, who stressed the limitations of reason and the wretchedness of human beings without God.

Pascal was a universal genius who made important contributions to mathematics, probability theory, and science. Today he is best remembered as the author of two masterpieces of classic French prose: *The Provincial Letters* (1656–1657) and the unfinished, posthumously published *Pensées* (*Thoughts*) (1670). Despite its fragmentary condition, the *Pensées* is highly readable and filled with brilliant insights. Its central theme is the paradoxical nature of humanity (at once brutish and angelic) and the weakness of human reason. Left to itself, Pascal argues, reason quickly bogs down in a morass of unintelligibility and doubt. Reason cannot prove God's existence, the soul's immortality, the reality of moral truth, the meaningfulness of existence, or the reliability of the Scriptures. Ultimately, we must trust "the reasons of the heart" rather than reason alone. Only in faith and in divine revelation can we find the answers and the healing we seek.

In the *Pensées*, Pascal offers his famous "wager argument" for belief in God: No one can truly know, through reason alone, whether God exists or not. Still, it makes sense to "bet" that God exists because we have everything to gain if He does and little or nothing to lose if He doesn't. If we believe in God, and He exists, we gain eternal happiness and bliss. If we don't believe in God, and He does exist, we risk eternal loss and damnation. Finally, if God doesn't exist, there's no big gain or loss whether we believe that He exists or not. Given these alternatives, the smart thing to do is bet on God, live a religious life, and hope for the best.

Is Pascal's Wager sound? Many philosophers have rejected it with scorn and indignation. Certainly some of his assumptions about the relevant options can be questioned. But if you begin from Pascal's starting points, the argument may be compelling.

SEE ALSO "The Will to Believe" (1897)

A marble statue from 1785 by French sculptor Augustin Pajou shows Blaise Pascal studying a tablet; the stacked papers at his feet are his Pensées (Thoughts), *and the open book is his* Lettres provinciales (Provincial Letters).

Occasionalism

Nicolas Malebranche (1638–1715)

Occasionalism is the view that God is the only genuine cause of events, and that finite creatures like us are merely the "occasion," or nominal trigger, of God's causal activity in the world. This may sound like an implausible view, but a number of leading philosophers have embraced or seriously entertained it, including the Islamic thinker al-Ghazālī (d. 1111) and (in qualified form) George Berkeley (d. 1753). By far the most famous defender of occasionalism is the seventeenth-century French philosopher and theologian Nicolas Malebranche.

Malebranche was a Parisian Oratorian priest and a prolific writer who today is increasingly being recognized as a major early modern philosopher. His most notable work, *The Search after Truth* (1674–1675), is heavily influenced by Descartes. (Reportedly, Malebranche was so excited when he first encountered Descartes's works at a Paris bookstall that he had "such violent palpitations of the heart that he was obliged to leave his book at frequent intervals, and to interrupt his reading of it in order to breathe more easily.") The main focus of *The Search after Truth* is how human errors arise and what we can do to avoid them. Along the way, however, Malebranche defends his bold claim that God is the one and only true cause in the universe.

Malebranche offers a slew of arguments for his occasionalist view. Like several of Descartes's followers, he found it unfathomable that matter could causally interact with mind, and so he threw out the inexplicable middle man, so to speak, by declaring matter to be causally inert. Malebranche also argued that all true causes must necessitate their effects. So-called finite (natural, nondivine) causes cannot do this, he maintained, because God can always perform a miracle that will disrupt the normal connection between cause and effect. Only God, he claimed, can truly necessitate a given effect.

Malebranche made few converts with his occasionalism, but he did have some attentive readers. One was David Hume (d. 1776), who in his *A Treatise of Human Nature* (1739–1740) appropriated Malebranche's doubts about necessary causal connections and wove them into his powerful critique of traditional accounts of causation.

SEE ALSO *The Incoherence of the Philosophers* (c. 1093), *A Treatise of Human Nature* (1739)

A detail of the fresco God the Father in Glory, *painted in 1716 on the chapel ceiling at Versailles, by French painter Antoine Coypel. According to Malebranche, God can always perform a miracle that will disrupt the normal connection between cause and effect.*

Ethics

Baruch Spinoza (1632–1677)

Bertrand Russell (d. 1970) described the Dutch philosopher Baruch Spinoza as "the noblest and most lovable of the great philosophers." Characteristically, Russell adds: "As a natural consequence, he was considered, during his lifetime and for a century after his death, a man of appalling wickedness." Like many profoundly original thinkers, Spinoza has always attracted fervent critics and admirers.

Spinoza was born in Amsterdam into a well-to-do family of Portuguese Jewish merchants. At an early age he became interested in philosophy and began to have doubts about the religion he'd been taught. When he refused to conform, he was cursed and solemnly excommunicated from the Jewish community and disowned by his family. Thereafter he lived quietly and simply in rented rooms, making ends meet by grinding lenses for glasses and optical instruments. In 1670, he published (anonymously) the *Tractatus Theologico-Politicus*, a critique of conventional religion and a landmark in modern biblical criticism. His major work, *Ethics*, was published in 1677, following his early death from tuberculosis.

The *Ethics* is a remarkable book in both style and substance. Its central idea is that only one reality ("substance") exists, which Spinoza calls "God or Nature." This reality is infinite, eternal, and perfect, but is not a personal god in the sense of traditional theism. God has an infinite number of attributes, including thought and extension. The universe is God's body, and what we ordinarily think of as separate "things," like stars, cabbages, and human beings, are simply "modes" of God. The supreme good of human existence is to free ourselves from the bondage of worldly lusts and constraining emotions and achieve wisdom and blessedness by identifying ourselves with the infinite, accepting the necessitated course of things, and devoting ourselves to the "intellectual love" of God.

All of this Spinoza claimed to prove with rigorous, airtight reasoning. The *Ethics* is written like a geometry text. It begins with definitions and axioms, and proceeds to prove its numbered conclusions with mathematical exactitude. This makes the *Ethics* a difficult but absorbing book to read. As Spinoza himself said, "all excellent things are as difficult as they are rare."

SEE ALSO The Vedas (c. 1500 BCE), Monism (c. 810)

A 1784 engraving by Dutch engraver Noach van der Meer showing Spinoza being forced out of Amsterdam in 1667.

Human Rights

John Locke (1632–1704)

As historian Frederick Copleston (d. 1994) noted, the political writings of John Locke are "a standing disproof of the notion that philosophers are ineffectual." Though considered radical in their day, Locke's core political ideas are now widely accepted. Among these is the idea of human rights.

Locke was born near Bristol, England, and educated at Westminster School and Christ Church, Oxford. For several years he taught at Christ Church, but most of his life was spent in government service, practicing medicine, and in other nonacademic pursuits. For reasons of health and safety, Locke spent most of the period between 1675–1688 in France and Holland. This gave him time to write. His major works include *Two Treatises of Government* (1689), *An Essay Concerning Human Understanding* (1689), *A Letter Concerning Toleration* (1689), and *The Reasonableness of Christianity* (1695).

In the *Two Treatises*, Locke critiques the philosophy of political theorist Robert Filmer (c. 1588–1653), who posited that kings possess a God-given right to rule ("the divine right of kings"). Locke argues that government rests on the consent of the governed. Originally, as Hobbes held, humans lived in a "state of nature" without governments or laws. But Locke's picture of the state of nature is very different from Hobbes's—it isn't a *Hunger Games*–like war of all against all; humans are naturally sociable and rational, and they recognize a binding natural moral law, "the law of nature." This law teaches that all humans are naturally free and equal, and that they possess basic rights to life, freedom, and property that may not be rightfully infringed. These basic, universal, pre-political rights are what the American Declaration of Independence calls "inalienable rights." Today we call them human rights.

Locke famously argues that governments were created when people decided to try to better their lives by leaving the state of nature and forming governments by means of a "social contract." Since the very purpose of governments is to protect basic rights and freedoms, they may be forcibly overthrown (if necessary) whenever there is a flagrant failure to do so. This became a rallying cry in the American Revolution and in many later political movements.

SEE ALSO Natural Law (c. 1270), *Leviathan* (1651), *The Social Contract* (1762), Political Libertarianism (1974)

A mezzotint of John Locke, 1721, by John Smith, after Dutch-English portrait painter Sir Godfrey Kneller.

Religious Liberty

John Locke (1632–1704)

Despite centuries of attacks on "the civil rights and worldly goods of each other upon pretence of religion" that inevitably resulted in what Locke termed "endless hatreds, rapines, and slaughters," few Europeans in his day believed in any kind of robust religious freedom. Locke's was one of the earliest and most influential voices for allowing people to believe and worship as they choose.

In late 1685, while Locke was living in political exile in Amsterdam, he wrote a long Latin letter to his Dutch friend Philip von Limborch, which was later published anonymously in May 1689 under the title *Epistola de Tolerantia* (*A Letter Concerning Toleration*). Locke was moved by the plight of French Huguenots fleeing persecution in France following the revocation of the Edict of Nantes in October 1685. He was also worried that the new Catholic king of England, James II, might prove intolerant to non-Catholics in England. Locke had seen firsthand how successfully religious toleration worked in Holland; his hope was that England would follow the Dutch example.

In *Epistola* he argues that the "care of souls" is simply not the state's business. The purpose of government is to protect basic rights and freedoms, not to impose religious beliefs. To insist that force may be used to coerce religious conformity is to sow a pernicious "seed of discord and war." Moreover, "only light and evidence . . . can work a change in men's opinions"; coercion produces hypocrites and martyrs, not sincere believers. Finally, the Gospels and apostles teach that "no man can be a Christian without charity, and without that faith which works, not by force, but by love."

Locke was not an advocate of complete religious freedom. He argued that governments should not tolerate religions that cause concrete harms or seek to undermine the foundations of society. Nor should they tolerate atheists (who lack the moral backbone to be reliable citizens) or Roman Catholics (who profess allegiance to a foreign power, the pope). Here Locke was a step behind the farsighted American Puritan Roger Williams (c. 1603–1683), who argued for complete religious liberty, even for "paganish, Jewish, Turkish or anti-Christian consciences and worships," in his remarkable *Bloudy Tenent of Persecution* (1644).

SEE ALSO Human Rights (1689)

The title page of the first edition John Locke's A Letter Concerning Toleration, *published in London in 1689.*

A

LETTER

CONCERNING

Toleration:

Humbly Submitted, &c.

LICENSED, *Octob.* 3. 1689.

LONDON,

Printed for *Awnsham Churchill,* at the *Black Swan* at *Amen-Corner.* 1689.

Empiricism

John Locke (1632–1704)

In Locke's day, most philosophers believed that some ideas are innate—that is, present in the mind (at least implicitly or inchoately) from birth. Popular candidates for inborn ideas included the idea of God, basic moral concepts, and fundamental logical principles like "no proposition can be both true and false." Locke argued that there are no innate ideas or principles. All ideas come from experience—chiefly sense experience. Locke's forceful and influential arguments for this view made him "the father of modern empiricism."

In *An Essay Concerning Human Understanding* (1689), Locke argued that if innate ideas exist, then literally everybody would have them. But there is no reason to think that infants, for example, have an idea of God or a knowledge of right and wrong. If it is retorted that such ideas are "virtually" or "seminally" innate in babies' minds, this is either trivially true or nonsensical. It is trivially true if what is meant is that babies are capable of forming such ideas when they get older. No one denies that. And it is nonsensical if what it meant is that babies have such ideas but are not yet able to consciously access them. It makes no sense, Locke argues, to say you "have" an idea that is totally unconscious and unavailable.

As an empiricist, Locke believed that all ideas come either from the senses or through introspection on our own thoughts and feelings—what he calls "ideas of reflection." Locke also argues that we have no direct knowledge of the world as it exists outside our heads; all we ever know directly are our own ideas and sensations. In other words, all awareness of the world is mediated awareness; all we know directly is how the world *appears* to us. This raises an obvious opening for skepticism. How do we know that we are not dreaming or that which we call "life" is not some huge hoax perpetrated by a mind-controlling demon or evil extraterrestrial scientists? Locke dismisses such doubts as mere academic pettifogging. But other empiricists, like Berkeley and Hume in the eighteenth century, would take them much more seriously.

SEE ALSO To Be Is to Be Perceived (1713), *A Treatise of Human Nature* (1739), *Pragmatism* (1907)

An engraving of the personification of Idea, with a baby at her breast symbolizing nature, from Iconologia: or, Moral Emblems, 1709, by Italian writer Cesare Ripa.

192. Idea.

Preestablished Harmony

Gottfried Wilhelm Leibniz (1646–1716)

As the father of modern philosophy, Descartes launched a good many newly built ships onto the philosophical waters. One of these was the tradition of continental rationalism. Rationalists claim that we can discover many important truths about reality by reason alone, without the aid of the senses. There were three great rationalists in early modern philosophy: Descartes, Spinoza, and Leibniz. Of these, Leibniz had the least influence. For sheer brainpower, though, he may have been the most brilliant.

Leibniz was born in Leipzig, Germany, where his father was an ethics professor. A studious boy, Leibniz had the run of his father's extensive library and became something of a boy genius. At the young age of twenty-one, Leibniz was awarded a doctorate in law and was offered a university post. He chose instead to pursue a nonacademic career as a diplomat, councilor, librarian, and all-purpose savant, mostly at the court of Hanover. During his lifetime, Leibniz was best known as a mathematician, sharing with Newton the honor of discovering differential calculus. Today he is mostly remembered as a philosopher and logician. Much of his important work in philosophy was published only after his death.

Leibniz developed an impressive metaphysical system in which the basic constituents of reality are soul-like immaterial entities that he called "monads." Reality consists of an infinite number of unique monads, ranged in a hierarchy depending on the clarity with which they "mirror" the rest of reality. Monads are "windowless" in the sense that they do not causally interact with one another; each contains its own pre-programmed source of activity within itself. The world appears to involve cause-and-effect relationships because God has created a preestablished harmony between monads, like a collection of alarm clocks set to go off at predetermined times. The physical universe is an appearance, rather than real. Though the universe contains much suffering and evil, Leibniz famously argues that it must nevertheless be "the best of all possible worlds." An infinitely perfect God, surveying all the possible worlds He could create, would necessarily pick the one that has the greatest possible balance of good over evil. This view was mercilessly lampooned by Voltaire in his classic novella *Candide* (1759).

SEE ALSO The Father of Modern Philosophy (1637), *Candide* (1759)

A nineteenth-century engraving of Gottfried Wilhelm Leibniz.

To Be Is to Be Perceived

George Berkeley (1685–1753)

There were three great British empiricists in early modern philosophy: John Locke, who was English; George Berkeley, who was Irish (of English descent); and David Hume, who was Scottish. Locke and Hume are mostly on the same page, though Hume takes empiricism in a much more skeptical direction than Locke does. Berkeley is in many ways the odd man out. He was an Anglican bishop and a staunch defender of Christian orthodoxy against atheists, skeptics, and freethinkers. Yet he argued for the seemingly irrational view that matter does not exist. All that exists, Berkeley contends, are spirits (God, human souls, and angels) and their ideas. For so-called physical objects, such as rocks and stars and trees, his theory was *esse is percipi* (to be is to be perceived). This is a view called "Idealism" or "Immaterialism." Berkeley's greatness as a philosopher lies in how ingeniously he argues for this seemingly paradoxical view. It helped that he was also perhaps the greatest writer of English philosophical prose who ever lived.

Berkeley was born near Kilkenny, Ireland. After graduating from Trinity College, Dublin, he became a fellow there in 1707. All of his most important philosophical work was written before he was thirty years old. His greatest work, *A Treatise Concerning the Principles of Human Knowledge*, was published in 1710. Disappointed by its reception, Berkeley published a more popular version of his idealist theory in *Three Dialogues between Hylas and Philonous* in 1713. From 1728 to 1732, Berkeley waited in vain in Newport, Rhode Island, for funds from the British government to found a college in Bermuda. In 1734, he was appointed bishop of Cloyne, in southern Ireland, where he served until he retired to Oxford in 1752.

Berkeley offered a battery of arguments to try to show that the concept of matter was unintelligible, unneeded, and dangerous to religion. Some of the arguments he advanced against the idea of material substance applied just as well to the notion of spiritual substance. It was left to the next great empiricist, David Hume, to throw out the concept of substance altogether.

SEE ALSO Empiricism (1689), *A Treatise of Human Nature* (1739), *An Idealist View of Life* (1929)

All that exists, according to George Berkeley, are spirits (God, human souls, and angels) and their ideas. Here, God the Father holds court among a choir of angels; below, biblical scenes include Adam and Eve being driven out of Paradise (center), and the Annunciation (right). This engraving is by Flemish artists Maerten de Vos and Jan Collaert II, c. 1590.

Gloria in altißimis Deo.

Ter Sanctus vnus Deus.

LEX

The Moral Sense

**Anthony Ashley-Cooper, 3rd Earl of Shaftesbury (Lord Shaftesbury)
(1671–1713), Francis Hutcheson (1694–1746)**

Most people would say they *know* certain moral truths, such as that cruelty to animals is wrong. But *how* do we know such things? What "faculty" or mental processes do we use in making such judgments? Prior to about 1700, the conventional answer among Western philosophers was that we use *reason*. We obtain moral knowledge by using the same methods of reasoning and intuition that we use in math or science, a view known as "moral rationalism." In the eighteenth century, moral rationalism came under attack from a group of British thinkers known today as "moral-sense theorists" or "moral sentimentalists." The four most important moral-sense theorists were Lord Shaftesbury, Francis Hutcheson, David Hume (d. 1776), and Adam Smith (1723–1790). Shaftesbury sketched a version of moral-sense theory in *Characteristics of Men, Manners, Opinions, Times* (1711), but the first systematic presentation of the theory was offered by Hutcheson in *An Inquiry into the Original of Our Ideas of Beauty and Virtue* (1725).

Shaftesbury and Hutcheson were struck by the fact that often our moral reactions are immediate and involuntary. For example, if we see someone mistreating a child, we instantly get upset and have strong feelings of moral disapproval. Yet reason operates too slowly to explain these reactions. Moreover, if all our ideas come from experience, as Locke was thought to have shown, where do we get our ideas of moral goodness and badness? Presumably from the senses. But not from our five ordinary senses, which only reveal physical properties of things. So our ideas of moral goodness and badness must come from a special faculty of sensation, the moral sense. God, they believed, has endowed us with a conscience, or moral sense, that perceives moral beauty and ugliness, much as our aesthetic sense perceives artistic beauty or ugliness. Reason may come into play later to verify or to systematize the intimations of moral sense, but moral sense is primary.

Shaftesbury and Hutcheson's moral-sense theory provoked a huge century-long debate in British philosophy between defenders of moral rationalism, such as Joseph Butler (d. 1752), John Balguy (1686–1748), and Richard Price (1723–1791), and the new upstart moral sentimentalists. In some ways, the debate continues today.

SEE ALSO Natural Law (c. 1270), Morality Is Rooted in Feeling (1751), Ethical Intuitionism (1903)

Anthony Ashley-Cooper, 3rd Earl of Shaftesbury, by French engraver Simon Gribelin, after German painter John Closterman, 1702.

The Right Honorable Anthony Ashley Cooper Earl of Shaftesbury, Baron Ashley of Winbourn St. Giles, & Lord Cooper of Pawlett.

J. Closterman Pinx.   Sim: Gribelin Sculp.

Deism

Matthew Tindal (1657–1733)

There are two views that commonly go by the name of "deism." One is the idea of an absentee or clockmaker God who made the world, gave it its laws, and then left it to run on its own. The other is the view that true religion is "natural religion," that is, truths about God can be learned solely by means of reason and the observation of nature, without resort to any alleged divine revelation. This latter form of deism was defended by a number of important seventeenth- and eighteenth-century thinkers, including John Toland (1670–1722), Anthony Collins (1676–1729), Voltaire (d. 1778), and Thomas Paine (1737–1809). Philosophically, the most important defense of deism was Matthew Tindal's 1730 book, *Christianity as Old as the Creation*.

An Oxford don and lawyer, Tindal argued that an all-wise and all-good God would not have revealed his will and essential truths of religion to only a small percentage of mankind. The Bible, therefore, is not the word of God. The core truths of religion can be discerned by the pure light of reason alone. Those core truths are simply that an infinitely perfect Creator exists, that God wishes us to be happy, and that we serve God best by trying to do as much good as we can. This simple creed is what true Christianity is all about. Such a creed has been evident throughout human history. Accordingly, Christianity is "as old as the creation."

Tindal's book created a firestorm. Within a few years, over 150 replies were published, including William Law's *The Case of Reason* (1731), George Berkeley's *Alciphron* (1732), and Joseph Butler's *The Analogy of Religion* (1736).

A number of America's founding fathers were deists, including Benjamin Franklin and Thomas Jefferson. Franklin stated that he believed in "one Supreme most perfect being," but doubted that such a being "does in the least regard such an inconsiderable nothing as man." Jefferson advised his nephew to "fix reason firmly in her seat, and call to her tribunal every fact, every opinion. Question with boldness even the existence of a God; because, if there be one, he must more approve the homage of reason than of blindfolded fear."

SEE ALSO *The Analogy of Religion* (1736), Hume's *Dialogues* (1779)

The title page of a 1732 edition of Tindal's Christianity as Old as the Creation, *published in London.*

Chriſtianity as Old as the Creation:

OR, THE

GOSPEL,

A

REPUBLICATION

OF THE

Religion of NATURE.

The SECOND EDITION *in Octavo.*

Eſt autem Jus naturale adeo immutabile, ut ne quidem à Deo mutari poteſt.
Grot. de Jure Belli & Pacis. l. 1. *c.* 1. §. 10. *n.* 5.

The Gentiles, which have not the Law, do by Nature the Things contained in the Law. Rom. ii. 14.

———— *God is no Reſpecter of Perſons; but in every Nation, he that feareth him, and worketh Righteouſneſs is accepted with him.* Acts x. 34, 35.

Proinde perfectam illam Religionem, quæ Chriſti prædicatione nobis tradita eſt, non Novam aut Peregrinam, ſed ſi verum dicere oportet, primam, ſolam, veramque eſſe liquido apparet.
Euſeb. Eccl. Hiſt. l. 1. c. 4. *Valeſius's* Tranſl.

Res ipſa, quæ nunc Chriſtiana Religio nuncupatur, erat & apud Antiquos, nec defuit ab Initio generis humani, quouſque ipſe Chriſtus veniret in carne; unde vera Religio quæ jam erat, cœpit appellari Chriſtiana.
Aug. Oper. Tom. 1. p. 17. c. --*Retract.* l. 1. c. 13.

The Religion of the Goſpel, is the true original Religion of Reaſon and Nature ——And its Precepts declarative of that original Religion, which was as old as the Creation.
Serm. for prop. the Goſp. in for. Parts, by Dr. Sherlock, now Bp. of *Bangor.* p. 10, and 13.

God does nothing in the Government of the World by mere Will and Arbitrarineſs.——The Will of God always determines itſelf to act according to the eternal Reaſon of Things.—— All rational Creatures are oblig'd to govern themſelves in ALL their Actions by the ſame eternal Rule of Reaſon.
Dr. *S. Clarke's* Unchang. Oblig. of Nat. Relig. Edit. 4. p. 47, 48, 49.

LONDON:

Printed in the Year M. DCC. XXXII.

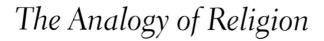

The Analogy of Religion

Joseph Butler (1692–1752)

The English deists' attack on organized religion provoked a flurry of able responses. One of the best was Joseph Butler's *The Analogy of Religion* (1736).

Butler was born in Berkshire, the son of a Presbyterian linendraper. After converting to Anglicanism in his teens, he attended Oxford and was ordained an Anglican priest. Though introverted and cerebral by nature, Butler served in a series of important church posts, including clerk of the closet to Queen Caroline, dean of St. Paul's, and bishop of Durham. His two most important works are *Fifteen Sermons Preached at the Rolls Chapel* (1726) and *The Analogy of Religion*. Today Butler is best known for his ethics, his critique of psychological egoism (the claim that all human actions are ultimately motivated by self-interest), and his criticism of Locke's theory of personal identity. But in the eighteenth century, Butler's *Analogy* was regarded as his masterpiece. Deists commonly argued that Scripture was obscure and full of perplexities and barbarities, but that nature revealed clearly the existence of a benevolent intelligent designer. In *The Analogy of Religion*, Butler tried to turn the tables on the deists in an interesting way. Conceding that revealed religion (based on revelation) is replete with problems and mysteries, Butler argued that natural religion fares little better. Nature, with its waste and cruelty, does not appear on its face to be the product of an infinitely wise and good Creator. Yet Butler and his deist opponents agreed that it is reasonable to infer the existence of an infinitely perfect God from the order, complexity, and beauty of nature, despite apparent evidence to the contrary. Thus, there is an analogy, or similarity, between natural and revealed religion. Both present significant mysteries and perplexities but are otherwise reasonable and credible. Therefore, it is inconsistent to favor natural religion over revealed religion. Both are in the same boat and must sink or swim together.

Contemporary critics of Butler quickly noted how risky his argumentative strategy was. If nature and Scripture are both full of insoluble mysteries, why not reject both and embrace atheism? Indeed, this was precisely the approach taken by David Hume and other eighteenth-century religious skeptics.

SEE ALSO Deism (1730), Hume's *Dialogues* (1779)

A c. 1900 photochrom of the Thames River winding through the rolling hills of Oxfordshire, England; "the beauty of nature" likely little changed from Joseph Butler's day.

A Treatise of Human Nature

David Hume (1711–1776)

David Hume is widely considered to be the greatest of all British philosophers. He was born in Edinburgh, Scotland, and educated at the University of Edinburgh. His first book, *A Treatise of Human Nature*, made little splash when it was first published, though it is now generally considered to be his masterwork. Other than the *Treatise*, Hume's three most important philosophical works are *An Enquiry Concerning Human Understanding* (1748), *An Enquiry Concerning the Principles of Morals* (1751), and the *Dialogues Concerning Natural Religion* (1779).

In his momentous early work *A Treatise of Human Nature* (1739–1740), Hume sought to apply the "experimental method" of investigation that had proved so successful in the natural sciences to the study of human subjects. In the process, Hume showed how empiricism leads ineluctably to various forms of skepticism. If all human ideas derive from experience, then any apparent idea that cannot be traced back to experience must be a pseudo-idea. This is a notion that later philosophers have dubbed "the empirical criterion of meaning." According to this test, all genuine or meaningful ideas can in principle be traced to some original sensory or introspective impression. Hume wields this empirical criterion of meaning like a sword to cut through huge swaths of traditional philosophy, including ideas of causation, the self, objective morality, and an independently existing external world.

Consider causation. The ordinary notion of causation supposes that some events cause other events by means of some kind of causal "power" or "necessary connection." But do we ever actually experience causal power or necessity? No, Hume argues; all we ever perceive are regular sequences of events: A is always followed by B. For all we know, A and B might be totally unrelated events that are part of a story that some mind controller has planted in our heads. Thus, Hume argued, the traditional idea of causation is empirically unwarranted. The only meaningful idea of causation we have is that of "constant conjunction": A, in our experience, has always been followed by B, and we have a strong psychological propensity to believe that this pattern will continue in the future.

SEE ALSO The Problem of Induction (1739), Morality Is Rooted in Feeling (1751), Logical Positivism (1936)

The title page from Of the Understanding, *volume I of Hume's* A Treatise of Human Nature, *1739, published in London.*

A

TREATISE

OF

Human Nature:

BEING

An ATTEMPT to introduce the experimental Method of Reasoning

INTO

MORAL SUBJECTS.

Rara temporum felicitas, ubi sentire, quæ velis; & quæ sentias, dicere licet. TACIT.

VOL. I.

OF THE

UNDERSTANDING.

LONDON:

Printed for JOHN NOON, at the *White-Hart,* near *Mercer's-Chapel,* in *Cheapside.*

MDCCXXXIX.

The Problem of Induction

David Hume (1711–1776)

One of the many powerful skeptical challenges offered in Hume's *Treatise of Human Nature* (1739–1740) is what is now called the "problem of induction." The problem centrally involves reasoning that tries to predict the future based on things we have observed in the past. Hume's stunning conclusion is that no such predictions can be rationally justified.

Hume's account of the problem of induction is a bit complex, so let me briefly sketch the problem in more contemporary terms. Consider our belief that the law of gravity will continue to operate tomorrow. What evidence do we have for this? Well, in the past the law of gravity has always held true, so is it not reasonable to suppose it will continue to operate tomorrow? But here Hume noticed something very interesting. Why is the past any guide to the future at all? If nature were totally anarchic and the laws of nature changed every half-second, the past would not be a reliable guide to the future. So whenever we make predictions we are assuming that nature is substantially uniform, that the future will (substantially) resemble the past. Call this assumption "the principle of uniformity." Now Hume asks, what evidence do we have that the principle of uniformity is true? Because it has held true in the past? But then we are assuming that the past is a reliable guide to the future, which means we are using the principle of uniformity to try to prove the principle of uniformity, which is reasoning in a circle. It seems, in fact, that there is no noncircular way of arguing for the principle of uniformity at all. Not a single bit of real evidence can be produced that it is true. Yet the principle of uniformity is not self-evident; we can easily imagine it turning out to be false. Hume's conclusion is that all inductive (that is, probabilistic) inferences that try to predict the future are based on what he calls "instinct" or "custom," not reason. Nature has just hardwired us, as it has many animals, to expect the future to go on much like the past. As Hume sees it, reason plays a much less significant role in human existence than most philosophers have thought.

SEE ALSO *A Treatise of Human Nature* (1739), The New Riddle of Induction (1954)

David Hume, in an 1837 engraving.

An Attack on Miracles

David Hume (1711–1776)

In Section X of *An Enquiry Concerning Human Understanding* (1748), Hume offers a famous argument against miracles. He does not argue that miracles are impossible, a claim that would be at odds with his empiricist starting points. His contention, rather, is that it is never reasonable to believe that a miracle has occurred, no matter how strongly it may appear to be supported by human testimony. His argument has two parts: First he gives a general argument why the burden of proof is extremely high in cases of alleged miracles. Then he offers some specific reasons for thinking that this burden of proof has never, in fact, come close to having been met.

The specific reasons Hume mentions are mostly conventional worries about the credibility of miracle stories (for example, the fact that they "are observed chiefly to abound among ignorant and barbarous nations"). Of greater interest and originality is the preliminary argument Hume gives for why we should be highly suspicious of miracle stories in general. A miracle, Hume says, is a violation of a law of nature. Nothing is called a law of nature unless it is supported by abundant and absolutely uniform evidence. Such evidence, Hume argues, amounts to a certainty, or what he calls a "proof," that such laws will continue to operate without exceptions. Whenever we hear or read about an alleged miracle, we must balance this proof against the likelihood that the witness is either lying or mistaken. At best, Hume argues, any human testimony for a miracle can amount only to a "probability," not to a proof. A wise man proportions his belief to the evidence. Proofs provide stronger evidence than do probabilities. So a wise man will always disbelieve testimony for a miracle unless the falsehood of the report would be even more miraculous than the alleged miracle itself. Such a high burden of proof, Hume argues, has never remotely been met. With every actual miracle report, it is always much more likely that the testifier is lying or mistaken than that a law of nature has been broken.

SEE ALSO *A Treatise of Human Nature* (1739), The Problem of Induction (1739)

An eighteenth-century engraving depicting crowds of sick pilgrims gathering in the cemetery of St. Médard, Paris, at the tomb of François de Pâris (1690–1727), an ascetic French Catholic deacon. A fervor erupted when hundreds were supposedly miraculously cured at his gravesite in 1731.

1748

The Spirit of the Laws

Charles Louis de Secondat, Baron de la Brède et de Montesquieu (1689–1755)

Like a modern rock star, Charles Louis de Secondat, Baron de la Brède et de Montesquieu, is generally known by a single moniker: Montesquieu. Born in southwestern France to noble parents, Montesquieu became a lawyer and a distinguished public servant before retiring to his moated château in his early forties to devote himself to writing. His first book, *The Persian Letters* (1721), was a tremendous success, bringing him honors and fame. In 1748, after twenty years of labor, Montesquieu published his masterwork, *The Spirit of the Laws*. It was instantly recognized as a classic of political and legal theory.

Montesquieu's basic aim was to construct a kind of science of legal theory and social institutions. He believed there are regularities in human affairs that can be studied in a scientific spirit. His book argues, for instance, that climate influences human character and social structures in ways that history and experience confirm. He also believed that it can be shown that some sorts of government are suitable for some societies but not for others. There are, he claimed, three basic forms of government: monarchy, despotism, and republican (which can be either democratic or aristocratic). Republican governments tend to work only in small states where the citizens are animated by a strong sense of patriotism and civic virtue. Despotisms, on the other hand, are practically inevitable in areas where climate, geography, or cultural mores make it difficult to impose effective checks on tyrannical rulers.

Montesquieu was an important influence on America's founding fathers. The authors of *The Federalist* (1787–1788) quote him more often than any other writer. They frequently invoke him in support of the claim that only a republican form of government comports with what James Madison calls "the genius of the people of America." However, the most important idea the founders got from Montesquieu is that of the separation of political powers. He argued that the powers given to the legislative, executive, and judicial branches of government must be separated, so that power grabs by one branch can be effectively checked by another. History has borne out the wisdom of Montesquieu's idea, and it has been widely adopted by constitution-makers around the world.

SEE ALSO *The Federalist* (1787)

A statue of Montesquieu in Bordeaux, France, created in 1858 by Italian sculptor Dominique Fortuné Maggesi.

Morality Is Rooted in Feeling

David Hume (1711–1776)

As we have seen, there was a long-running debate in eighteenth-century Britain between moral rationalists, who believed that ethics is based in reason, and moral sentimentalists, who believed that ethics is rooted in feeling. In 1751, David Hume published *An Enquiry Concerning the Principles of Morals*. There, Hume offered powerful support for the sentimentalist view.

Like Francis Hutcheson (d. 1746), to whom Hume was heavily indebted in ethics, Hume was struck by the similarity between judgments of beauty and judgments of morality. Hume believed that Hutcheson had convincingly demonstrated that aesthetic and moral qualities are subjective, or perceiver dependent, in the same way that sounds, tastes, and colors are. As a strict empiricist, Hume held that there was no viable basis for belief in objective moral properties. Our senses cannot perceive objective moral properties, nor can our reason, which Hume claimed deals only with "relations of ideas" (like math and logic) and "matters of fact" (that is, factual beliefs that are based on sense impressions). As Hutcheson claimed, morality is rooted in human nature—specifically in feeling or sentiment. Hume identifies two natural human feelings that he believed lay at the root of ethics: benevolence and sympathy. Humans naturally approve of acts of kindness and beneficence, and feel distress when observing others in pain. What we call "virtues" are qualities like justice, honesty, and cheerfulness that are "either useful or agreeable to the person himself or to others." This makes morality subjective in the sense that moral judgments depend on feeling rather than on rational insight or perception of mind-independent moral qualities. But morality is also objective inasmuch as it is rooted in more or less universal human feelings and instincts.

One striking conclusion that follows from Hume's view is a complete reversal of the traditional conception of the relationship between reason and emotion. Since Plato, Western philosophers had generally agreed that emotion must be subordinate to reason. Hume inverted this, claiming that "reason is, and ought only to be, the slave of the passions." And this is true not only in ethics. As Hume saw it, pretty much the entire structure of human belief is rooted in feeling and instinct.

SEE ALSO The Moral Sense (1725), *A Treatise of Human Nature* (1739)

A tranquil scene of famed philosophers and authors conversing in Elysium, by French engraver Bernard Picart, 1727. In An Enquiry, *Hume writes: "When poets form descriptions of Elysian fields, where the blessed inhabitants stand in no need of each other's assistance, they yet represent them as maintaining a constant intercourse of love and friendship."*

America's First Major Philosopher

Jonathan Edwards (1703–1758)

America has produced many first-rate philosophers, but it took a while for this process to get rolling. Jonathan Edwards, a Puritan minister, is generally regarded as America's first philosopher of distinction.

Edwards was born in East Windsor, Connecticut, the son of a pastor. A precocious boy, Edwards enrolled at Yale University at the age of thirteen. There he thoroughly absorbed the "new philosophy" of Newton and Locke. Incredibly, Edwards reported that when he read Locke's *Essay Concerning Human Understanding* (1689) at age fourteen he experienced more enjoyment "than the most greedy miser finds, when gathering up handfuls of silver and gold." In 1727, Edwards became pastor of a Puritan church in Northampton, Massachusetts. There he played a major role in the Great Awakening, the revivalist movement that swept America in the 1740s. His first major work, *A Treatise Concerning Religious Affections* (1746), was written as a defense of the kind of "heart religion" typified by the emotionalism of this period. In 1750, Edwards's stern religious convictions caused him to be dismissed by his congregation. This gave Edwards time to write, and the books he wrote over the next several years, most notably *Freedom of Will* (1754), made him the preeminent American thinker of his day. He died in 1758, shortly after being appointed president of what later became Princeton University.

Edwards recognized that Locke and Newton had undermined the old Scholastic foundation of Puritan theology. His goal was to provide a new foundation that drew not only on Lockean empiricism and Newtonian mechanics but also on the Puritan Platonism that flowed from such thinkers as Peter Ramus (1515–1572). Like George Berkeley (d. 1753), Edwards embraced a form of idealism that held that only minds are real. He vigorously defended the Puritan doctrines of God's absolute sovereignty, universal determinism, and total depravity. His defense of compatibilism—the idea that free will is consistent with causal determinism—was the most detailed and sophisticated defense offered up to that time. His view that religious believers have a special faculty of spiritual perception, a "sense of the heart," influenced a number of twentieth-century religious epistemologists, including Alvin Plantinga and William Alston.

SEE ALSO The Birth of Modern Science (1543), Free Will and Determinism Are Compatible (1651), *The Varieties of Religious Experience* (1902)

The title page of a fourth edition of Edwards's Freedom of Will, *published in Wilmington, Delaware, in 1790.*

A

CAREFUL and *STRICT*

INQUIRY

INTO

The *modern* prevailing Notions

OF THAT

FREEDOM *of* WILL,

Which is supposed to be essential

TO

MORAL AGENCY, VIRTUE and VICE,
REWARD and PUNISHMENT, PRAISE
and BLAME.

By the late Reverend and Learned

JONATHAN EDWARDS, A. M.

President of the College of *New-Jersey.*

Rom. ix. 16. *It is not of him that willeth——*

The FOURTH EDITION.

WILMINGTON, (*Delaware*)
Printed and Sold by JAMES ADAMS, in *High-street,*
M.DCC.XC.

Candide

François-Marie Arouet (Voltaire) (1694–1778)

In trying to make sense of our world from a religious perspective, many philosophers have taught either that there are no genuine evils (because what appears to be evil is actually good) or that there are no "pointless" or "gratuitous" evils, that is, evils that do not result in greater goods. This latter idea was encapsulated in Leibniz's (d. 1716) famous slogan that God has created "the best of all possible worlds." In *Candide, ou l'optimisme* (1759), the French writer and philosopher Voltaire satirizes this kind of baseless optimism in one of the great short stories of all time.

Voltaire (the pen name of François-Marie Arouet) was a controversial figure during his lifetime and remains so today. As a writer, he was loved for his wit, vitality, and sparkling storytelling skills. Yet his unrelenting attacks on organized religion, autocratic government, war, religious intolerance, and an inhumane criminal justice system made him many enemies.

Candide is a madcap tale of the incredible misadventures of a young man named Candide; his eternally optimistic tutor, Professor Pangloss; Candide's love-interest, Cunégonde; and Candide's faithful servant, Cacambo, as they travel the world meeting with one tragic misfortune after another. No matter what calamity strikes them, Professor Pangloss sticks to his Leibnizian optimism, always managing to find some redeeming good in every personal tragedy. By the end of the book, however, Candide's eyes have been opened; his final enigmatic advice in this world of follies and woe is to "cultivate our garden."

Philosophically, the most interesting question *Candide* raises is whether theism implies that this is the best of all possible worlds. Leibniz argues that it does, claiming that an all-powerful, all-wise, and all-good God would survey all the possible universes he could create and actualize that one that has the best overall balance of good over evil. In advancing his argument, Leibniz assumes first that there is some maximally good world, and secondly that a perfectly good God would follow a utilitarian strategy of maximizing net happiness. Both of these assumptions can be questioned. Thus, contrary to Leibniz, there may be ways of reconciling belief in a perfect God with the existence of an obviously imperfect world.

SEE ALSO The Book of Job (c. 500 BCE), Soul-Making Theodicy (1966)

A c. 1800 color aquatint of Voltaire by French engraver Pierre-Michel Alix, after Jean-François Garneray.

F. M. AROUET DE VOLTAIRE.

The Birth of Romanticism

Jean-Jacques Rousseau (1712–1778)

Romanticism was a complex and multifaceted cultural movement in Western history that extended from roughly the 1760s to the late 1850s. Broadly, it was a revolt against Enlightenment rationalism. Romantics exalted feeling over reason, art over science, nature over civilization, solitude over society, mysticism over organized religion, and individual freedom over social order. The Romantic movement had a profound impact on literature, art, architecture, music, education, politics, environmentalism, theology, and philosophy. Though its beginnings were complex, one important early influence was Rousseau, particularly his sentimentalist novel *Julie, or the New Heloise* (1761), his novelistic educational treatise *Emile* (1762), and above all, his shockingly outspoken autobiography, *The Confessions* (1782). Throughout these works, Rousseau pounds home the notion that feelings are a better guide to truth than reason is.

Rousseau's ideas on democracy, popular sovereignty, and equality strongly influenced the politics of the French Revolution. In Germany, Immanuel Kant stressed the limits of human reason and grounded religion in moral feeling, and Arthur Schopenhauer's exaltation of the will and of art breathed the very spirit of Romanticism. In America, the transcendentalist movement of Ralph Waldo Emerson and Henry David Thoreau reflected clearly the individualistic, mystical, and nature-centered themes of the Age of Feeling. The influences of Romanticism are reflected in the Rousseauian educational thought of J. H. Pestalozzi and Friedrich Fröbel, Samuel Taylor Coleridge's distinction between spirit-attuned Reason and spirit-blind Understanding, and the nature-mysticism of John Muir.

The decline of Romanticism can be dated roughly to the publication of Charles Darwin's *Origin of Species* in 1859. Romanticism was at bottom a revolt against the horrors of the Industrial Revolution and the cold, mechanistic world that science seemed to have revealed. As economic conditions improved in the latter half of the nineteenth century and the prestige of science grew, philosophers in both Europe and America increasingly returned to Enlightenment ideals of reason, science, and optimism, though the impact of Romanticism continued to be felt.

SEE ALSO The Enlightenment Begins (1620), *Emile* and Natural Education (1762)

Dawn in the Valleys of Devon, *1832, by major English Romantic painter J. M. W. Turner.*

The Social Contract

Jean-Jacques Rousseau (1712–1778)

Rousseau had a profound impact not only on philosophy, but also on politics, literature, art, education, and manners. His influence on Romanticism and education will be considered in other entries. Here we look at his political thought, particularly as expressed in *The Social Contract*, his most important book.

Rousseau, who led a turbulent and troubled life, was born in Geneva, Switzerland, in 1712, the son of a poor watchmaker. After his father abandoned the family around 1724, Rousseau largely raised and educated himself. His first book, *Discourse on the Arts and Sciences* (1750), shocked French Enlightenment thinkers such as Diderot and Voltaire by attacking civilization, science, and reason. His next major work, *Discourse on the Origins of Inequality* (1755), argued that humans are naturally good; painted an idyllic picture of a primitive, pre-social state of nature; and blamed private property as the origin of oppressive inequalities. In *The Social Contract* (1762), Rousseau made clear that he wasn't attacking government and social order per se. On the contrary, he argued, only through organized communities can humans truly be ethical and free.

The problem Rousseau wrestles with in *The Social Contract* is how to reconcile government and freedom. When humans decide to leave the state of nature by creating governments and laws, they surrender their "natural liberty" to do as they please, unhindered by laws or other people. But in creating governments they acquire a higher type of freedom that Rousseau calls "civil liberty." True liberty, he argues, is living under laws that we ourselves have made. When humans elect to leave the state of nature and form a community they create an artificial person, a sovereign body, with a will of its own—"the general will"—which is basically the collective desire to promote the common good. Fostering the communal good, he says, is also our own "real will," what all of us explicitly or implicitly desire. Therefore there is no real sacrifice of freedom when we obey laws, even those with which we may strongly disagree. In fact, lawbreakers may be "forced to be free" by state coercion, a notion that many contemporary philosophers regard as paradoxical and fraught with peril.

SEE ALSO *Leviathan* (1651), Human Rights (1689), The Birth of Romanticism (c. 1760)

A detail of a statue of Jean-Jacques Rousseau by Swiss-French sculptor James Pradier, created in 1835; it is located on the Île Rousseau, an island named after the philosopher on the Rhône in Geneva.

Emile and Natural Education

Jean-Jacques Rousseau (1712–1778)

Rousseau is the fountainhead of many important developments in the modern world, including what we today call child-centered education. His vision of education is laid out in his charming book, *Emile, or on Education* (1762). Like everything Rousseau wrote, it is full of exaggerations and absurdities, but it remains a seminal work of educational theory.

Emile is the story, written in novelistic form, of a rich young boy (Emile) and his dedicated tutor, who devotes over twenty years to Emile's private education. Rousseau believed that humans are naturally good and that civilization corrupts. As he saw it, the proper task of education is thus to preserve and develop a child's natural goodness to the greatest degree possible. To do this, Emile's tutor raises him in the country, far from the vicious influences of the city. Emile's education is divided into three stages: childhood (ages 0–12), youth (ages 13–20), and young adulthood (21 until roughly 25). The first stage is completely nonintellectual. Its goal is to preserve the heart from vice and the mind from error by keeping the mental faculties inactive until they have matured. The motto at this stage is "Let childhood ripen in children." What learning takes place occurs mostly through outdoor play, active doing, feeling, and firsthand experience, not through books or verbal lessons.

Emile's formal education begins in early adolescence. At this time he is introduced to books, but mostly he learns by doing and experience. He also learns a useful trade so that he can earn a living if necessary. He knows nothing at this stage about history, philosophy, or religion. When Emile is taught religion it is only a simple theistic creed; he is left to choose whether he wishes to follow any particular sect. It is only in the young-adult period of education that Emile studies history and develops his own sense of taste, mingles in society, travels, and actively prepares for married life. The last book of *Emile* is devoted to the largely domestic education of Emile's ideal mate, Sophie. According to Rousseau, a woman's essential role in life is to be a sweet, useful, and agreeable stay-at-home helpmate.

SEE ALSO Progressive Education (1916)

An illustration from an eighteenth-century edition of Rousseau's Emile, or on Education.

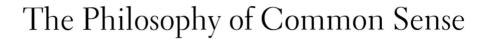

The Philosophy of Common Sense

Thomas Reid (1710–1796)

There were many eighteenth-century philosophers who were deeply troubled by David Hume's corrosive skepticism, but few appreciated the full force of Hume's arguments and made a serious attempt to meet them. One notable exception was the Scottish philosopher Thomas Reid.

Reid was born in Strachan, Scotland, the son of the village's long-serving Presbyterian minister. Like his father, Reid was educated at the University of Aberdeen and entered the ministry. In his early forties, Reid was appointed professor of philosophy at Aberdeen, and in 1764 he succeeded Adam Smith as professor of moral philosophy at the University of Glasgow. Reid published his major work, *An Inquiry into the Human Mind on the Principles of Common Sense*, in 1764. After retiring from teaching, he published two books on human intellectual and active powers.

Reid made significant contributions to debates on free will and personal identity, but what he is best remembered for is his response to Hume. Reid described Hume as the greatest metaphysician of the age, but he thought Hume was dead wrong in his starting points. Like Locke, Hume accepted a "representationalist" view of knowledge, which claims that the only things we directly know are our own ideas. This "theory of ideas," Reid argues, is based on a fiction and leads straight to skepticism. To avoid skepticism we should start from the commonsense assumptions that we do perceive physical objects, that we can trust our senses, our memory, our moral intuitions, and our belief in induction. Hume trusts reason and consciousness, but inconsistently casts doubt on other sources of knowledge that come "out of the same workshop." In contemporary terms, Reid argues that trust in reason, the senses, memory, and induction are "properly basic beliefs" that we are rationally entitled to accept without evidence and to treat as foundational to our beliefs. This commonsense approach to knowledge was highly influential in Scotland and the United States in the eighteenth and nineteenth centuries. After being unfairly neglected for much of the twentieth century, Reid is again widely regarded as a major thinker.

SEE ALSO Empiricism (1689), *A Treatise of Human Nature* (1739), The Problem of Induction (1739)

The table of contents from an 1801 edition of Reid's An Inquiry into the Human Mind on the Principles of Common Sense. *Each of the book's main chapters is devoted to one of the five senses.*

CONTENTS.

CHAPTER I.
INTRODUCTION.

CHAP. II.
OF SMELLING.

A Godless, Mechanistic Universe

Paul-Henri Thiry, Baron d'Holbach (1723–1789)

In the middle of the eighteenth century, a group of like-minded public intellectuals called the "philosophes" popularized Enlightenment ideals in France. Many of these thinkers were associated with the famous *Encyclopédie* (1751–1772) edited by Denis Diderot and Jean d'Alembert. The philosophes were opposed to the established political order and to organized religion, particularly the Catholic Church. Though some of the philosophes were deists, others were agnostics or atheists. The most outspoken atheist was Paul-Henri Thiry, Baron d'Holbach.

Holbach was born in Germany, the son of a vintner, but he was raised in Paris by his uncle, a rich stock speculator and French nobleman. After graduating from the University of Leiden in Holland, Holbach married and began contributing numerous articles to the *Encyclopédie*. In 1753, Holbach inherited his uncle's title and estate, making him wealthy for life. The following year, Holbach's wife died. He later married his wife's younger sister. In 1761, Holbach published *Christianity Unveiled*, an attack on Christianity and its moral influences. Thereafter, Holbach poured out a constant stream of antireligious books, including his most important work, *The System of Nature* (1770), referred to as "the Bible of atheism" by his opponents. All of his books were published anonymously or under false names.

Holbach was a materialist who believed that nothing exists except matter in motion. He was also a strict determinist, claiming everything that occurs in nature is necessitated by prior events and that free will is an illusion. Any fully satisfactory explanation of events, he claimed, must be mechanistic, referring only to matter, motion, and the laws that govern the movement of material particles.

Holbach used his great wealth to host fabulous parties at his townhouse in Paris and his country estate at Grandval in southern France. Many leading philosophes and distinguished guests met at Holbach's salon. Among Holbach's famous guests was David Hume. The first time Hume dined with Holbach he remarked that he had never met a real atheist. Holbach responded that of the eighteen other guests at the table fifteen were avowed atheists and three had not yet made up their minds.

SEE ALSO Atoms and the Void (c. 420 BCE), *On the Nature of Things* (c. 55 BCE), The Enlightenment Begins (1620), The New Atheists (2004)

A page from English biologist John T. Needham's 1750 treatise that included his "spontaneous generation" of life experiment on tainted wheat. Holbach cited Needham's "microscopical observations" in The System of Nature, *noting: "The production of a man . . . would not be more marvelous than that of an insect with flour and water."*

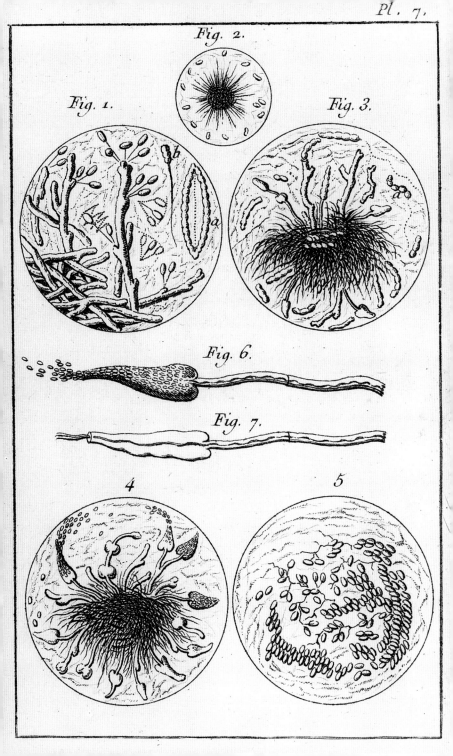

Pl. 7.

Fig. 2.

Fig. 1.

Fig. 3.

Fig. 6.

Fig. 7.

4

5

Hume's *Dialogues*

David Hume (1711–1776)

In the eighteenth century it was widely believed that the wonderful order, complexity, and beauty of the world provides clear evidence of the existence of God. This so-called argument from design was powerfully challenged in David Hume's posthumously published *Dialogues Concerning Natural Religion* (1779).

There are three participants in the *Dialogues*: Demea, an orthodox Christian who tries to prove God's existence as the first cause of the universe; Cleanthes, a deist who defends the argument from design; and Philo, a skeptic, who denies that God's existence can be proved. Most scholars believe that it is Philo who speaks most directly for Hume.

Hume offers a barrage of arguments against the argument from design. How can we reconcile the idea of an all-benevolent God with all the pain and suffering we see in the world? How can we infer the existence of an all-perfect God from a far-from-perfect world? If order and complexity imply intelligent design, what explains the order and complexity of ideas in God's mind? Finally, how strong is the analogy between human-made machines and a God-made world-machine? Machines are usually built by many workers. Why suppose that only a single god made the world? How do we know that the world is not "the production of old age and dotage in some superannuated Deity" who has long since expired or "the first rude essay of some infant deity, who afterwards abandoned it"? Why should not many universes "have been botched and bungled, throughout an eternity, ere this system was struck out"? At best, Hume argues, the argument from design shows that "the cause or causes of order in the universe probably bear some remote analogy to human intelligence." Beyond this vague and tentative supposition, not a single step can be taken.

Despite Hume's powerful attack, the argument from design continued to attract influential defenders. Less than a quarter-century after Hume's *Dialogues* appeared, English cleric and philosopher William Paley (1743–1805) published his famous work, *Natural Theology* (1802), which offered an elaborate defense of the argument. It was Darwin, not Hume, however, who delivered the most serious blow to the argument from design.

SEE ALSO Mind Organizes Nature (c. 460 BCE), The Five Ways (c. 1265), Deism (1730), Darwin's *Origin of Species* (1859)

Hume wondered how strong the analogy is between human-made machines, such as this steam engine invented by British engineer Thomas Newcomen in 1712, and a God-made world-machine.

Critique of Pure Reason

Immanuel Kant (1724–1804)

Immanuel Kant's *Critique of Pure Reason* was a huge watershed in philosophy. The book's central idea—that the world as we experience it is mostly a construct of the human mind—dominated nineteenth-century thought and is still accepted by many philosophers today.

Kant's life will never be made into a movie; it was rich in ideas but not in adventures. He was born in Königsberg (then part of East Prussia but now Kaliningrad, in a noncontiguous part of Russia). Aside from a few short trips, Kant lived his entire life in his native city, where he taught at the University of Königsberg for many decades. A late bloomer, Kant published all of his major philosophical works after the age of fifty-six. His most important books are the *Critique of Pure Reason* (1781), *Groundwork of the Metaphysics of Morals* (1785), *Critique of Practical Reason* (1788), and *Critique of Judgment* (1790). Like many great philosophers, he never married.

Kant was troubled by both Hume's corrosive skepticism and the failure of traditional metaphysics to provide a secure foundation for belief in God, objective morality, free will, and life after death. Unlike Hume, Kant believed that we know necessary truths about empirical and moral reality (for example, we know that every event *must* have a cause). As Hume had argued, it is impossible for us to acquire such knowledge through experience. Kant's solution was to say that the human mind has certain innate, built-in structures that automatically process all possible experiences into certain predetermined forms. The mind, as it were, has certain hardwired cookie-cutter patterns that it imposes on all possible experiences. The upshot is that we can never know reality as it is itself (what Kant calls "noumenal reality"); we can only know "phenomenal reality," reality as it appears to us. Ultimately, Kant argues, reason cannot prove that God exists or that we have free will or that there will be an afterlife. However, our moral experience makes no sense without these underpinning beliefs, so they can be supported by a kind of rational faith.

SEE ALSO *A Treatise of Human Nature* (1739), The Problem of Induction (1739), The Beginnings of German Idealism (c. 1795)

This statue of Kant stands in front of the Immanuel Kant Baltic Federal University, in Kaliningrad, Russia. The original sculpture, by nineteenth-century German sculptor Christian Daniel Rauch, was destroyed in 1945; the replica shown here was made by Harald Haacke.

The Categorical Imperative

Immanuel Kant (1724–1804)

Kant is an important ethicist for a number of reasons. First, he is the founding father of deontological, or duty-centered, ethics, which has been a leading moral theory for over two centuries. Second, he is a major influence on modern ethical theories that emphasize the inherent dignity or worth of all human beings. Finally, he formulated a basic moral principle, the so-called categorical imperative, which has generated a great deal of interest and discussion.

Kant was raised in a pious Protestant family, and he believed that the Golden Rule of Jesus—do unto others as you would have others do unto you—captured something at the heart of morality. But Kant noted that the Golden Rule has certain limitations. For instance, it says nothing about duties to self, such as the obligations not to waste one's talents and not to commit suicide. So Kant reformulated the Golden Rule in a way that made it more general and (he believed) more precise. He called this reformulation the categorical imperative to emphasize both that it is a *law* ("imperative" is another word for "command") and that it *binds unconditionally*. Confusingly, Kant offers four different formulations of the categorical imperative. The first and most famous version is this: "I should never act in such a way that I could not also will that my maxim should be a universal law."

It is uncertain how exactly this should be interpreted. Kant is not very clear what he means by a "maxim" or how we should go about formulating the maxims that implicitly underlie our contemplated actions. But Kant's general drift is clear enough: It is wrong to do something that you would not want others to do in your exact situation. Put otherwise, it is unethical to treat yourself as a "special case," exempt from moral rules that you yourself admit are reasonable and just. There are difficulties when you apply Kant's categorical imperative to certain cases. In particular, it is not clear that Kant's principle will rule out all immoral acts or produce the kinds of universally applicable moral standards Kant seeks. But the core insight expressed by the categorical imperative has great intuitive appeal.

SEE ALSO Reciprocity (c. 500 BCE), Deontological Intuitionism (1930)

La Justice, c. 1800, by French painter Bernard d'Agesci. The allegorical figure holds the scales of justice in one hand and, in the other, a book with the Golden Rule written on the right page.

The Federalist

Alexander Hamilton (1755/57–1804), **James Madison** (1751–1836), **John Jay** (1745–1829)

Thomas Jefferson—no slouch as a political thinker—described *The Federalist* in 1787 as "the best commentary on the principles of government which ever was written." Together with the Declaration of Independence, the U.S. Constitution, the Bill of Rights, and the Gettysburg Address, it remains one of the foundational documents of American government. *The Federalist* (or *Federalist Papers*) consists of eighty-five essays, most of which were published in New York City newspapers between October 1787 and April 1788. The purpose was to build support for the ratification of the new Constitution that had been proposed by the Philadelphia Convention in September 1787. New York County assemblyman Alexander Hamilton—soon to be the first secretary of the treasury—proposed the project and wrote the lion's share of the articles. Virginia delegate and future U.S. president James Madison contributed about thirty essays, including some of the most brilliant. New York lawyer John Jay, who later became the nation's first chief justice, wrote five.

The Federalist is a masterpiece of political debate. Its combination of learning, eloquence, and powerful compact reasoning overwhelmed the Constitution's numerous opponents and helped secure ratification in closely fought states like New York and Virginia. As a contribution to political philosophy, *The Federalist* is most important for its sustained case for a new vision of republican government. At the time, it was widely believed that any large state would inevitably become unjust and undemocratic. *The Federalist* authors successfully rebutted this assumption by arguing that the proposed Constitution's elaborate safeguards—including checks and balances, separation of powers, and staggered and indirect elections—allowed for an energetic national government that wouldn't trample on people's rights. Moreover, as Madison famously argued in Federalist No. 10, the great diversity of American life would make it difficult for oppressive "factions" to unite to cause mischief at the federal level. Today, we recognize that some of *The Federalist*'s predictions were overly rosy, and that original Constitution was not perfect. But Americans continue to feel great pride in what is the oldest written charter of government in the world. A good deal of credit for that is due to *The Federalist*.

SEE ALSO Human Rights (1689), *The Spirit of the Laws* (1748)

Two pages from The Federalist, *showing part of article numbers I (Introduction) and XXI (Further Defects of the Present Constitution).*

THE

FEDERALIST:

ADDRESSED TO THE

PEOPLE OF THE STATE OF NEW-YORK.

NUMBER I.

Introduction.

AFTER an unequivocal experience of the inefficacy of the subsisting federal government, you are called upon to deliberate on a new constitution for the United States of America. The subject speaks its own importance; comprehending in its consequences, nothing less than the existence of the UNION, the safety and welfare of the parts of which it is composed, the fate of an empire, in many respects, the most interesting in the world. It has been frequently remarked, that it seems to have been reserved to the people of this country, by their conduct and example, to decide the important question, whether societies of men are really capable or not, of establishing good government from reflection and choice, or whether they are forever destined to depend, for their political constitutions, on accident and force. If there be any truth in the remark, the crisis, at which we are arrived, may with propriety be regarded as the æra in which

A   that

nounces in the present case, is, that a sovereignty over sovereigns, a government over governments, a legislation for communities, as contradistinguished from individuals; as it is a solecism in theory; so in practice, it is subversive of the order and ends of civil polity, by substituting *violence* in place of *law*, or the destructive *coertion* of the *sword*, in place of the mild and salutary *coertion* of the *magistracy*.

PUBLIUS.

NUMBER XXI.

Further Defects of the present Constitution.

HAVING in the three last numbers taken a summary review of the principal circumstances and events which depict the genius and fate of other confederate governments; I shall now proceed in the enumeration of the most important of those defects, which have hitherto disappointed our hopes from the system established among ourselves. To form a safe and satisfactory judgment of the proper remedy, it is absolutely necessary that we should be well acquainted with the extent and malignity of the disease.

The next most palpable defect of the existing confederation is the total want of a SANCTION to its laws. The United States as now composed, have no power to exact obedience, or punish disobedience to their resolutions, either by pecuniary mulcts, by a suspension or divestiture of privileges, or by any other constitutional means. There is no express delegation of authority to them to use force against delinquent members; and if such a right should be ascribed to the federal head, as resulting from the nature of the social compact between the states, it must be by inference and construction, in the face of that part of the second article, by which it is declared, "that

" each

Utilitarianism

Jeremy Bentham (1748–1832)

Several eighteenth-century thinkers, including David Hartley (1705–1757) and Francis Hutcheson (d. 1746), defended versions of the principle of utility, also called the greatest happiness principle. According to this principle, an act is morally right if and only if it produces "the greatest happiness of the greatest number," or, more precisely, brings about more net happiness than any alternative action could have produced. The thinker who first popularized the principle of utility was the English philosopher and political reformer Jeremy Bentham.

Bentham was a brilliant but odd man. Born in London, he was a precocious child, graduating from the University of Oxford at the age of fifteen. After obtaining a law degree, Bentham was appalled by the inhumane and incoherent condition of English law and decided to devote his life to legal and political reform. He became the leader of a group of reformers known as the Philosophical Radicals, or Benthamites, cofounded a journal (the *Westminster Review*), and wrote tirelessly. For some strange reason, he left many of his works unfinished and only published a tiny proportion of what he wrote. Probably the most important work he did publish is *An Introduction to the Principles of Morals and Legislation* (1789). There he explains and defends the principle of utility and works out a system of ethics and law based on that principle.

Bentham was a systematizer. He loved to work out elaborate classifications in which everything was fleshed out properly and had its logical cubbyhole. One example of this is his so-called hedonic, or felicific, calculus. This is a method for figuring out which act, of all those one could perform, is likely to produce the greatest amount of pleasure. There are seven factors that must be considered: the intensity of the pleasure, its duration, its certainty, its propinquity (how soon the pleasure will occur), its fecundity (how likely it is to produce other pleasures), its purity (whether it is entirely pleasurable or mixed with some pain), and its extent (how many people are affected by it). By means of this calculus, Bentham hoped to make a kind of science of pleasure. And certainly if pleasure is your goal, these are the sorts of factors you should consider.

SEE ALSO Cyrenaic Hedonism (c. 400 BCE), Epicureanism (c. 300 BCE), Refined Utilitarianism (1863)

Jeremy Bentham codified his science of pleasure onto a large folding diagram, published in 1817, a detail of which is shown here. He described it as follows: "Table of the Springs of Action: shewing the several species of Pleasures and Pains, of which Man's Nature is susceptible: together with the several Species of Interests, Desires, and Motives, respectively corresponding to them."

and *Dyslogistic*, by which each Species of *MOTIVE* is wont to be designated: to which are added EXPLANATORY
Basis or *Foundation*, of and for the Art and Science of MORALS, otherwise termed ETHICS,—whether *PRIVATE*, or *PUBLIC alias* POLITICS—(inclu
(which coincides mostly with *THEORETICAL*), or *CENSORIAL*, which coincides mostly with DEONTOLOGY: also of and for PSYCHOLOGY, in so far as co
View.

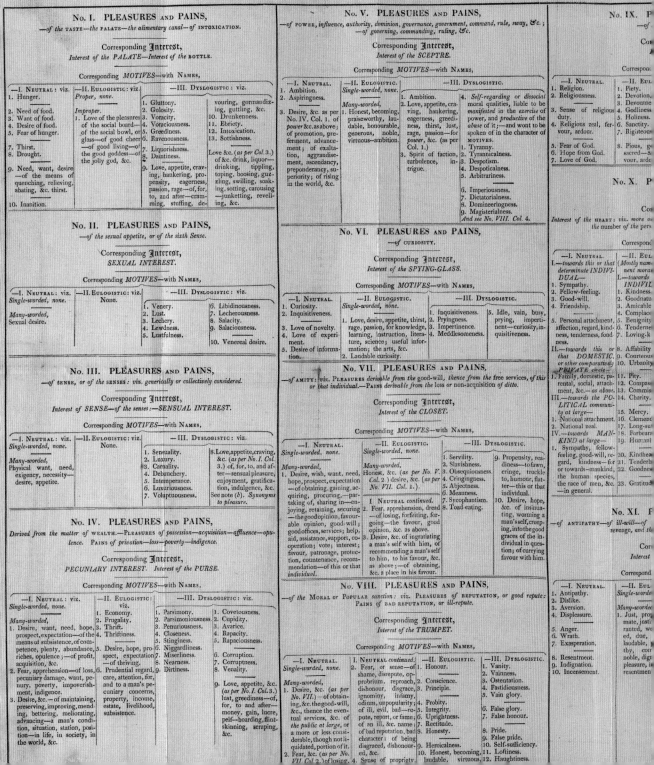

No. I. PLEASURES AND PAINS,

—of the TASTE*—the palate—the alimentary canal—of* INTOXICATION.

Corresponding **Interest**,

Interest of the PALATE—Interest of the BOTTLE.

Corresponding *MOTIVES*—with NAMES,

—I. NEUTRAL: viz.
1. Hunger.

2. Need of food.
3. Want of food.
4. Desire of food.
5. Fear of hunger.

7. Thirst.
8. Drought.

9. Need, want, desire—of the means of quenching, relieving, abating, &c. thirst.

10. Inanition.

—II. EULOGISTIC: viz.
Proper, none.

Improper.
1. Love of the pleasures of the social board—of the social bowl, or glass—of good cheer—of good living—of the good goddess—of the jolly god, &c.

—III. DYSLOGISTIC: viz.
1. Gluttony.
2. Gulosity.
3. Voracity.
4. Voraciousness.
5. Greediness.
6. Ravenousness.

7. Liquorishness.
8. Daintiness.

9. Love, appetite, craving, hankering, propensity, eagerness, passion, rage—of, for, to, and after—cramming, stuffing, devouring, gormandizing, guttling, &c.
10. Drunkenness.
11. Ebriety.
12. Intoxication.
13. Sottishness.

Love &c. (*as per Col.* 3.) of &c. drink, liquor—drinking, tippling, toping, boosing, guzzling, swilling, soaking, sotting, carousing—junketting, revelling, &c.

No. II. PLEASURES AND PAINS,

—of the sexual appetite, or of the sixth Sense.

Corresponding **Interest**,

SEXUAL INTEREST.

Corresponding *MOTIVES*—with NAMES,

—I. NEUTRAL: viz.
Single-worded, none.

Many-worded,
Sexual desire.

—II. EULOGISTIC: viz.
None.

—III. DYSLOGISTIC: viz.
1. Venery.
2. Lust.
3. Lechery.
4. Lewdness.
5. Lustfulness.
6. Libidinousness.
7. Lecherousness.
8. Salacity.
9. Salaciousness.

10. Venereal desire.

No. III. PLEASURES AND PAINS,

—of SENSE, *or of the* SENSES: *viz. generically or collectively considered.*

Corresponding **Interest**,

Interest of SENSE—of the senses:—SENSUAL INTEREST.

Corresponding *MOTIVES*—with NAMES,

—I. NEUTRAL: viz.
Single-worded, none.

Many-worded,
Physical want, need, exigency, necessity—desire, appetite.

—II. EULOGISTIC: viz.
None.

—III. DYSLOGISTIC: viz.
1. Sensuality.
2. Luxury.
3. Carnality.
4. Debauchery.
5. Intemperance.
6. Luxuriousness.
7. Voluptuousness.
8. Love, appetite, craving, &c. (*as per No. I. Col.* 3.) of, for, to, and after—sensual pleasure, enjoyment, gratification, indulgence, &c.

See note (*b*). *Synonyms to pleasure.*

No. IV. PLEASURES AND PAINS,

Derived from the matter of WEALTH.—PLEASURES *of possession—acquisition—affluence—opulence.* PAINS *of privation—loss—poverty—indigence.*

Corresponding **Interest**,

PECUNIARY INTEREST. Interest of the PURSE.

Corresponding *MOTIVES*—with NAMES,

—I. NEUTRAL: viz.
Single-worded, none.

Many-worded,
1. Desire, want, need, hope, prospect, expectation—of the means of subsistence, of competence, plenty, abundance, riches, opulence;—of profit, acquisition, &c.
2. Fear, apprehension—of loss, pecuniary damage, want, penury, poverty, impoverishment, indigence.
3. Desire, &c.—of maintaining, preserving, improving, mending, bettering, meliorating, advancing—a man's condition, situation, station, position—in life, in society, in the world, &c.

—II. EULOGISTIC: viz.
1. Economy.
2. Frugality.
3. Thrift.
4. Thriftiness.

5. Desire, hope, prospect, expectation—of thriving.
6. Prudential regard, care, attention, for, and to a man's pecuniary concerns, property, income, estate, livelihood, subsistence.

—III. DYSLOGISTIC: viz.
1. Parsimony.
2. Parsimoniousness.
3. Penuriousness.
4. Closeness.
5. Stinginess.
6. Niggardliness.
7. Miserliness.
8. Nearness.
9. Dirtiness.

1. Covetousness.
2. Cupidity.
3. Avarice.
4. Rapacity.
5. Rapaciousness.

6. Corruption.
7. Corruptness.
8. Venality.

9. Love, appetite, &c. (*as per No. I. Col.* 3.) lust, greediness—of, for, to and after—money, gain, lucre, pelf—hoarding, flint-skinning, scraping, &c.

No. V. PLEASURES AND PAINS,

—of POWER, *influence, authority, dominion, governance, government, command, rule, sway, &c.; —of governing, commanding, ruling, &c.*

Corresponding **Interest**,

Interest of the SCEPTRE.

Corresponding *MOTIVES*—with NAMES,

—I. NEUTRAL.
1. Ambition.
2. Aspiringness.

3. Desire, &c. as per No. IV. Col. 1. of *power* &c. as above; of promotion, preferment, advancement; of exaltation, aggrandisement, ascendancy, preponderancy, superiority; of rising in the world, &c.

—II. EULOGISTIC.
Single-worded, none.

Many-worded,
1. Honest, becoming, praiseworthy, laudable, honourable, generous, noble, virtuous—ambition.

—III. DYSLOGISTIC.
1. Ambition.
2. Love, appetite, craving, hankering, eagerness, greediness, thirst, lust, rage, passion—for *power*, &c. (as per Col. 1.)
3. Spirit of faction, turbulence, intrigue.

4. *Self-regarding* or *dissocial* moral qualities, liable to be *manifested* in the *exercise* of power, and *productive* of the *abuse* of it;—and wont to be spoken of in the character of MOTIVES.
1. Tyranny.
2. Tyrannicalness.
3. Despotism.
4. Despoticalness.
5. Arbitrariness.

6. Imperiousness.
7. Dictatorialness.
8. Domineeringness.
9. Magisterialness.

And see No. VIII. Col. 4.

No. VI. PLEASURES AND PAINS,

—of CURIOSITY.

Corresponding **Interest**,

Interest of the SPYING-GLASS.

Corresponding *MOTIVES*—with NAMES,

—I. NEUTRAL.
1. Curiosity.
2. Inquisitiveness.

3. Love of novelty.
4. Love of experiment.
5. Desire of information.

—II. EULOGISTIC.
Single-worded, none.

1. Love, desire, appetite, thirst, rage, passion, for knowledge, learning, instruction, literature, science; useful information; the arts, &c.
2. Laudable curiosity.

—III. DYSLOGISTIC.
1. Inquisitiveness.
2. Pryingness.
3. Impertinence.
4. Meddlesomeness.
5. Idle, vain, busy, prying, impertinent—curiosity, inquisitiveness.

No. VII. PLEASURES AND PAINS,

—of AMITY: *viz.* PLEASURES *derivable from the* good-will, *thence from the* free services, *of this or that individual.*—PAINS *derivable from the* loss *or* non-acquisition *of ditto.*

Corresponding **Interest**,

Interest of the CLOSET.

Corresponding *MOTIVES*—with NAMES,

—I. NEUTRAL.
Single-worded, none.

Many-worded,
1. Desire, wish, want, need, hope, prospect, expectation—of obtaining, gaining, acquiring, procuring,—partaking of, sharing in—enjoying, retaining, securing—the good opinion, favourable opinion, good-will; good offices, services; help, aid, assistance, support, cooperation; vote; interest; favour, patronage, protection, countenance, recommendation—of this or that *individual*.

—II. EULOGISTIC.
Single-worded, none.

Many-worded,
Honest, &c. (*as per No. V. Col.* 2.) desire, &c. (*as per No. VII. Col.* 1.).

I. NEUTRAL *continued*.
2. Fear, apprehension, dread—of losing, forfeiting, forgoing—the favour, good opinion, &c. as above.
3. Desire, &c. of ingratiating a man's self with him, of recommending a man's self to him, to his favour, &c. as above;—of obtaining, &c. a place in his favour.

—III. DYSLOGISTIC.
1. Servility.
2. Slavishness.
3. Obsequiousness.
4. Cringingness.
5. Abjectness.
6. Meanness.
7. Sycophantism.
8. Toad-eating.
9. Propensity, readiness—to fawn, cringe, truckle to, humour, flatter—this or that individual.
10. Desire, hope, &c. of insinuating, worming a man's self, creeping, into the good graces of the individual in question; of currying favour with him.

No. VIII. PLEASURES AND PAINS,

—of the MORAL *or* POPULAR *sanction: viz.* PLEASURES *of* REPUTATION, *or good repute:* PAINS *of* BAD REPUTATION, *or ill-repute.*

Corresponding **Interest**,

Interest of the TRUMPET.

Corresponding *MOTIVES*—with NAMES,

—I. NEUTRAL.
Single-worded, none.

Many-worded,
1. Desire, &c. (*as per No. VII.*)—of obtaining, &c. the good-will, &c., thence the eventual services, &c. of *the public at large*, or a more or less considerable, though not liquidated, portion of it.
2. Fear, &c. (*as per No. VII. Col.* 2.) of losing,

I. NEUTRAL *continued*.
2. Fear, or sense—of shame, disrepute, opprobrium, reproach, dishonour, disgrace, ignominy, infamy, odium, unpopularity; of ill, evil, bad—repute, report, or fame; of an ill, &c. name; of bad reputation, bad character: of being disgraced, dishonoured, &c.
4. Sense of propriety,

—II. EULOGISTIC.
1. Honour.

2. Conscience.
3. Principle.

4. Probity.
5. Integrity.
6. Uprightness.
7. Rectitude.
8. Honesty.

9. Heroicalness.
10. Honest, becoming, laudable, virtuous,

—III. DYSLOGISTIC.
1. Vanity.
2. Vainness.
3. Ostentation.
4. Fastidiousness.
5. Vain glory.

6. False glory.
7. False honour.

8. Pride.
9. False pride.
10. Self-sufficiency.
11. Loftiness.
12. Haughtiness.

No. IX. P

—of

Co

Correspon

—I. NEUTRAL.
1. Religion.
2. Religiousness.

3. Sense of religious duty.
4. Religious zeal, fervour, ardour.

5. Fear of God.
6. Hope from God.
7. Love of God.

—II. EUL
1. Piety.
2. Devotion.
3. Devoutne
4. Godliness
5. Holiness.
6. Sanctity.
7. Righteous

8. Pious, g sacred—& vour, ardo

No. X. P

Co

Interest of the HEART: *viz. more o the number of the pers*

Correspon

—I. NEUTRAL.
I.—*towards this or that determinate INDIVIDUAL—*
1. Sympathy.
2. Fellow-feeling.
3. Good-will.
4. Friendship.

5. Personal attachment, affection, regard, kindness, tenderness, fondness.

II.—*towards this or that DOMESTIC, or other comparatively PRIVATE circle—*
1. Family, domestic, parental, social, attachment, &c.—*as above.*

III.—*towards the POLITICAL community at large—*
1. National attachment.
2. National zeal.

IV.—*towards MANKIND at large—*
1. Sympathy, fellow-feeling, good-will, regard, kindness—for or towards—mankind, the human species, the race of men, &c.—in general.

—II. EUL
(*Mostly nam nent mora*
I.—*towards INDIVIL*
1. Kindness.
2. Goodnatu
3. Amicable
4. Complace
5. Benignity
6. Tenderne
7. Loving-k
8. Affability
9. Courteous
10. Urbanity
11. Pity.
12. Compass
13. Commis
14. Charity.
15. Mercy.
16. Clemenc
17. Long-su
18. Forbeara
19. Humani
20. Kindhea
21. Tenderh
22. Goodnes
23. Gratitud

No. XI. F

—of ANTIPATHY*—of ill-will—of revenge, and th*

Cor

Interest

Correspond

—I. NEUTRAL.
1. Antipathy.
2. Dislike.
3. Aversion.
4. Displeasure.

5. Anger.
6. Wrath.
7. Exasperation.

8. Resentment.
9. Indignation.
10. Incensement.

—II. EUL
Single-worde

Many-worde
1. Just, prop mate, justi ranted, we ed, due, laudable, thy, com noble, dig pleasure, i resentmen

Critique of Judgment

Immanuel Kant (1724–1804)

Aesthetics is the branch of philosophy that studies art and beauty. One of the key questions in aesthetics is whether beauty is simply "in the eye of the beholder," that is, purely subjective. Here we seem to be pulled in different directions. On the one hand, we recognize that judgments of beauty and artistic merit cannot be "proved" to be correct. As the Romans used to say, *de gustibus non est disputandum* (there is no disputing about tastes). On the other hand, we do argue about matters of beauty and art, and it is generally admitted that some people are better and more discriminating judges of art and literature than others. How can we make sense of these conflicting intuitions? One classic solution is offered in Immanuel Kant's great contribution to aesthetics in his *Critique of Judgment* (1790).

Kant argues that aesthetic judgments are partly subjective and partly objective. They are subjective because they are rooted in feeling rather than in the intellect. Aesthetic qualities like beauty, Kant believes, are not inherent properties of things; rather, they are emotionally charged ways that we respond to things. We call things "beautiful" that awaken in us a certain kind of "disinterested" pleasure. In aesthetic experience we contemplate or enjoy beauty for its own sake, without distracting desires or thoughts about how we might use or possess the object. This disinterested response is subjective because it is based in feeling and cannot be brought under any rule or concept provided by the intellect. In fact, Kant says that aesthetic judgments are not cognitive judgments at all. Nevertheless, he argues, there is a certain objectivity to judgments of beauty and artistic merit. Because pure aesthetic judgments are disinterested, there is nothing personal or idiosyncratic about them. Consequently, when we say, for example, that a particular statue is beautiful, we are tacitly saying that *anyone* who views it disinterestedly should also find it beautiful. This implicit "go and do likewise" component of aesthetic judgment confers a kind of objectivity on such judgments, and it explains why we can intelligibly communicate and reason and argue about standards of taste and beauty.

SEE ALSO *Critique of Pure Reason* (1781)

A replica statue of Mars at Hadrian's Villa, second century CE, in Tivoli, Italy. In Critique of Judgment, *Kant states: "The art of sculpture . . . has excluded from its creations the direct representation of ugly objects, and, instead, only sanctions, for example, the representation of death (in a beautiful genius), or of the warlike spirit (in Mars), by means of an allegory, or attributes which wear a pleasant guise."*

Forefather of Conservatism

Edmund Burke (1729–1797)

Edmund Burke, the great Anglo-Irish orator and statesman, is remembered for many things, including his support for the American Revolution and the rights of Catholics. But his most enduring legacy is as the philosophical forefather of conservatism.

Burke was born in Dublin, the son of a successful Protestant lawyer and a Catholic mother. After graduating from Trinity College in Dublin, Burke moved to England, where he briefly practiced law before turning to writing and politics. In 1757, he published *A Philosophical Inquiry into the Origin of Our Ideas of the Sublime and Beautiful*, a major contribution to aesthetics that was highly regarded by Kant. In 1765, Burke entered Parliament, where he served with distinction for over thirty years. A gifted orator with an encyclopedic mind, Burke became an eloquent defender of aristocracy, monarchy, property, and the established Anglican Church, despite always being seen as something of an outsider due to his Irish birth, middle-class origins, and suspected Catholic sympathies.

Though Burke wrote no systematic political treatise, the core elements of his conservative thought are on display in his major work, *Reflections on the Revolution in France* (1790). Burke condemned the French Revolution as a triumph of theory-mad fanatics, blind to the accumulated wisdom of tradition. Complex social orders are not the product of abstract speculation; they grow slowly over time and are built on practical experience rather than on any doctrinaire logic or preordained template. Though jerry-built and held together by expedience, custom, and "prejudice," established social orders embody an implicit wisdom that is easily overlooked by would-be revolutionaries. The cardinal virtue in politics is prudence, and this requires a go-slow approach to reform and a healthy distrust of theory and individual judgment. "The individual is foolish. The multitude, for the moment, is foolish, when they act without deliberation; but the species is wise, and when time is given to it, as a species it almost always acts right." Though most would agree that Burke was on the wrong side of history in his total condemnation of the French Revolution, he made a lasting contribution to political thought by deepening the debate over that watershed event in modern history to the level of first principles.

SEE ALSO *The Federalist* (1787)

A British political cartoon from 1790, captioned "Frontispiece to Reflections on the French Revolution," depicts Edmund Burke on bended knee before a vision of Marie Antoinette. A cherub taps him with a firebrand, setting off sparks of romance.

London Pub.d Novem.r the 3, 1796 by Will.m F.Holland N.º 50, Oxford S.t in. whose rooms may be seen the largest Collection in Europe of Caricatures. Admit. 1.S.

FRONTISPIECE to REFLECTIONS on the FRENCH REVOLUTION.

It is now sixteen or seventeen years since I saw the Queen of France, then the Dauphiness, at Versailles:
and surely never lighted on this orb, which she hardly seemed to touch, a more delightful vision. I saw her just above the horizon
decorating and cheering the elevated sphere she just began to move in, — glittering like the morning star, full of life and
splendor, and joy. Oh! what a revolution! and what an heart must I have, to contemplate without emotion that elevation
and that fall! Little did I dream that, when she added titles of veneration to those of enthusiastic, distant, respectful love, that she should
ever be obliged to carry the sharp antidote against disgrace concealed in that bosom; little did I dream that I should have lived to see
such disasters fallen upon her in a nation of gallant men, in a nation of men of honour: and of cavaliers. I thought ten
thousand swords must have leaped from their scabbards to avenge even a look that threatened her with insult. — But the age of
chivalry is gone.
Burke on the Revolution on France Page 112.

A Vindication of the Rights of Woman

Mary Wollstonecraft (1759–1797)

Mary Wollstonecraft's reputation long suffered from the shocking memoir her husband, William Godwin, published a year after her death. Godwin's indiscreet tales of her illicit affairs, a child born out of wedlock, and two suicide attempts made her a scandalous figure whom few were willing to take seriously. Today, however, she is regarded as an important political thinker and a pioneering advocate of women's rights.

Wollstonecraft led a tumultuous and often unhappy life. Born in London to an abusive and irresponsible father, Wollstonecraft left home early to support herself as a lady's companion, governess, and schoolteacher. Entirely self-educated, Wollstonecraft taught herself French and German and was determined to make a living as a writer. In 1790, she published *A Vindication of the Rights of Men*, a reply to Edmund Burke's *Reflections on the Revolution in France* that brought her considerable notice. Two years later she published her most influential work, *A Vindication of the Rights of Woman*. After two unhappy affairs and a multitude of what John Stuart Mill (1806–1873) famously called unconventional "experiments in living," Wollstonecraft married William Godwin (1756–1836), the well-known anarchist and author of *Political Justice* (1793). She died shortly after giving birth to a daughter, Mary, Shelley's future wife and the author of *Frankenstein*.

Wollstonecraft's radical conclusions in *A Vindication of the Rights of Woman* are grounded in conventional views of God and human nature. Human dignity, which ultimately flows from God, is rooted in our capacities for reason, virtue, and knowledge. These noble capacities are not unique to men; they are *human* potentialities that should be cultivated by all. Yet men have used their power over women to stunt women's capacities for reason and knowledge and to enfeeble their characters by substituting pseudovirtues (such as complaisance, timidity, and womanly "sensibility") over genuine ones. Liberating women from such false ideals and educating them as equals would improve their usefulness to society, strengthen marriages, enable them to be better parents and educators of their children, and allow them to achieve their God-given potential as rational and moral agents.

SEE ALSO *The Subjection of Women* (1869), Emergence of Feminist Philosophy (c. 1976)

Mary Wollstonecraft (Mrs. William Godwin), *c. 1790–1791, by Cornish painter John Opie.*

The Beginnings of German Idealism

Johann Gottlieb Fichte (1762–1814), **Friedrich Wilhelm Joseph von Schelling** (1775–1854)

By the mid-1790s, Kant's philosophy had taken the German intellectual world by storm. Yet some thinkers saw problems with Kant's system and sought to develop it in a different direction. One issue was how the noumenal world (the world of mysterious and utterly unknowable "things in themselves") was related to the phenomenal world of appearance. Kant said that things in themselves provide the raw materials that the human mind uses to construct the phenomenal world. In other words, things in themselves *cause* us to perceive objects in space and time. Yet Kant claims that causation is one of the built-in categories that the human mind uses to organize all possible experiences of the world. The categories apply only to phenomena, not to things in themselves. How, then, can Kant say that things in themselves cause events in the phenomenal world? To solve this apparent contradiction, German thinkers like J. G. Fichte and F. W. J. von Schelling threw out the idea of things in themselves and embraced forms of idealism that claim that ultimately only mind or spirit is real.

Fichte and Schelling came from very different backgrounds. Fichte was born poor, the son of a Saxon ribbon weaver. Through the generosity of a wealthy baron, Fichte was able to get an education. After his appointment to a philosophy post at the University of Jena in 1794, Fichte published a series of major works that made him the most important philosopher in Germany and the father of German idealism.

Schelling was born near Stuttgart, the son of a learned and well-to-do Lutheran pastor. His thought passed through several phases, with most of his important work being completed before he was thirty-five. Schelling worked out a dense and complex version of idealism that views mind and matter as two attributes of a single reality. In one stream of his thought, he theorized that the physical world originated in a free, timeless "leap" of divine ideas into the world of finite nature; history and nature are an attempt to reunite these ideas with God. Schelling's thought was always evolving and never took the form of a finished system, yet it greatly inspired English poet-philosopher Samuel Taylor Coleridge (1772–1834), thereby influencing English and American Romanticism.

SEE ALSO *Critique of Pure Reason* (1781), *The Phenomenology of Spirit* (1807), American Transcendentalism (1836), The Rise of British Idealism (c. 1865)

Woman before the Rising Sun (Woman before the Setting Sun), 1818–1820, by German Romantic painter Caspar David Friedrich. Friedrich was a friend of Schelling's and inspired by his work.

The Phenomenology of Spirit

Georg Wilhelm Friedrich Hegel (1770–1831)

The nineteenth century saw a growing awareness of the historically conditioned character of human thought and an increased interest in the philosophy of history. Many thinkers asked whether there was any meaning or pattern to human history. The most ambitious attempt to lay bare the inner meaning of history is found in the thought of the German philosopher Georg Wilhelm Friedrich Hegel.

Hegel was born in Stuttgart, the oldest child of a middle-class family. After studying theology at Tübingen, Hegel worked as a family tutor for several years before obtaining a teaching post at the University of Jena. There he published his greatest work, *The Phenomenology of Spirit*, in 1807. Later he taught at the universities of Heidelberg and Berlin, where he came to dominate German intellectual life. In works such as *The Science of Logic* (1812–1816) and the *Encyclopedia of the Philosophical Sciences* (1817), Hegel presented a complex and grandiose picture of history as a process by which God (or what Hegel called the Absolute or Spirit) achieves self-consciousness and self-actualization. A difficult thinker, Hegel's most readable works were compiled from his lectures and published after his death.

Hegel's *Phenomenology of Spirit* is an absorbing drama of the human spirit. For Hegel, history is not a meaningless jumble of events, but a rational process with an inner logic that can be grasped by the human mind. All the great nation-states of history and all the great philosophies and religions of the world are stages in the "struggles of Spirit to know itself and to find itself." What drives this process is a continual interplay of conflicting opposites that Hegel calls "dialectic." Every idea, Hegel claims, is partial, is limited, and contains hidden contradictions. The history of human thought has been a repeated process in which ideas arise, pass over into their opposites, and are eventually transcended and unified in some higher idea. This triadic process of what Hegel calls thesis, antithesis, and synthesis results in ever-greater levels of self-consciousness and a growing awareness of freedom. The end result will be a kind of complete truth, an absolute knowledge, in which the Spirit will achieve infinite self-consciousness and know itself in the form of Spirit.

SEE ALSO The Beginnings of German Idealism (c. 1795), The Real Is the Rational (1821), The Rise of British Idealism (c. 1865)

This nineteenth-century bust of Georg Wilhelm Friedrich Hegel, by German sculptor Gustav Bläser, is displayed in a plaza named after the philosopher in Berlin.

G.W.F.HEGEL.

The Philosophy of Pessimism

Arthur Schopenhauer (1788–1860)

The nineteenth century was generally a period of optimism and belief in progress. But one great philosopher, the German thinker Arthur Schopenhauer, bucked this trend and defended an uncompromising pessimism. Like Buddha, Schopenhauer believed that life is essentially suffering. But Schopenhauer was much more pessimistic than Buddha about a panacea.

Schopenhauer was born in Danzig (now Gdańsk, Poland). His family was wealthy, which allowed him to spend his life as he wished: as an independent scholar and writer. After obtaining a PhD in philosophy from the University of Jena, Schopenhauer moved to Dresden, where he wrote his masterwork, *The World as Will and Representation* (1819). Like all of his early writings, it was largely ignored. A brilliant writer, he finally achieved literary success as an essayist. Vain, egotistic, and quarrelsome, Schopenhauer never married and lived alone with a succession of poodles.

Schopenhauer was a great admirer of Kant. Like Kant, he believed that what we call "the world" is mostly a construct of the human mind. Kant held that true reality (what he called the noumenal world) is forever unknowable by the human mind. Schopenhauer disagreed. We ourselves have a true or noumenal self, so we can know true reality through introspection of our own inner experiences. True reality is a timeless and spaceless "force" that Schopenhauer calls Will. In the world as we experience it, Will manifests itself as a blind, restless striving and instinct for survival. When we look at the universe honestly, we see that life is full of violence, conflict, and unsatisfied wants. As Buddha noted, the root cause of suffering is desire. Art can provide a temporary respite from suffering. Longer-lasting relief can be obtained by a Hindu-like resignation in which we accept the inevitability of suffering and curb our desires. But Schopenhauer, unlike the Eastern thinkers he admired, did not believe in any kind of permanent liberation or nirvana. As he saw it, Macbeth got it right: "Life's but a walking shadow, a poor player / That struts and frets his hour upon the stage / And then is heard no more: it is a tale / Told by an idiot, full of sound and fury, / Signifying nothing."

SEE ALSO The Four Noble Truths (c. 525 BCE), *Critique of Pure Reason* (1781)

A photograph of Arthur Schopenhauer from 1859, at age seventy-one.

The Real Is the Rational

Georg Wilhelm Friedrich Hegel (1770–1831)

Hegel worked out a complex, systematic picture of reality called absolute idealism. His core idea was that reality is ultimately mental; what we call the physical world is an expression of a divine reality, which Hegel called the Absolute or Spirit. How does Hegel support such a view?

Kant said that knowledge of super-sensible realities such as God and the soul is impossible because the human mind is not equipped to know such realities. Our minds are limited by certain hardwired "categories" that apply only to the phenomenal world of space and time, not to things in themselves. Like his fellow idealists Fichte and Schelling, Hegel scrapped the idea of things in themselves and said that all reality is mental. Because we are Spirits ourselves, we can know Spirit. Thus, Kant was wrong in claiming that metaphysics is impossible.

Hegel sees Kant's categories not as structures of the human mind but as structures of reality itself. The elaborate metaphysics he worked out—his so-called Logic—is an attempt to deduce the categories that characterize Absolute Mind and its self-development through nature and history. The technique Hegel uses for deducing the categories is the "dialectical" method of thesis, antithesis, and synthesis discussed in the previous Hegel entry. To give one quick example of Hegel's method: The most general concept of reality that we have is that of pure being. But the bare idea of being without any qualities is practically indistinguishable from the empty idea of nothing. From this collision of thesis ("reality is being") and antithesis ("reality is unbeing") arises a higher and truer synthesis ("reality is becoming"). By endlessly repeated applications of this triadic formula, Hegel deduces what he sees as the logically necessary structure of reality.

One striking consequence of Hegel's idealism is a kind of optimism that Hegel expresses in his famous dictum in *The Philosophy of Right* (1821) that "what is actual is rational" (frequently paraphrased as "the real is the rational"). If ultimate reality, as Hegel claims, is the totality of rational concepts, a structure that reveals itself in the world and in human experience, then all reality is knowable and everything that occurs in the world is rational and ultimately for the greater good.

SEE ALSO The Beginnings of German Idealism (c. 1795), *The Phenomenology of Spirit* (1807), The Rise of British Idealism (c. 1865)

Hegel is pictured here in one of a set of German stamps that was created in 1970 to mark the two-hundredth anniversary of the philosopher's birth.

Positivism

1830

Auguste Comte (1798–1857)

Auguste Comte was half genius, half crackpot. Today he is mostly remembered as one of the founders of sociology, an important forerunner of logical positivism and scientific antirealism, and a tireless advocate of harnessing science to improve the human condition. His nutty ideas about a "religion of humanity," with himself as the self-appointed high priest, are remembered as a cautionary tale of the silly things smart, theory-besotted philosophers can say.

Comte was born in Montpellier and attended the great French military academy, the École polytechnique. Expelled for his antiroyalist leanings in 1816, Comte lived as a tutor and private scholar most of his life. Plagued by poverty, mental illness, and a bad marriage, Comte published a steady stream of books promoting his vision of a new "positivistic" conception of science and a total reorganization of society based on that new learning. He died poor, wretched, and largely forgotten in 1857.

Comte was an agnostic and a huge admirer of science. He believed that the human mind had progressed through three stages: a theological stage, when events were explained by supernatural forces; a metaphysical stage, when fanciful abstractions like "the force of gravity" or "the social contract" were used to explain things; and an age of positivistic science, which Comte believed that he himself was inaugurating. True science, Comte argued, was positivistic science, meaning it was concerned only with prediction and control based on observable facts. True science makes no attempt to explain "the real nature" or "true causes" of things; it deals only with hard empirical facts and observed regularities in nature. Comte's ambition was to apply positivist science to human behavior and human social relations, and thus provide the know-how to create a new and better society that would be run much along the lines of Plato's *Republic*, by unelected and unaccountable scientific experts. To provide the religious "glue" needed for the cohesiveness of such a society, Comte proposed an elaborate new religion, the religion of humanity, modeled on Catholicism and dedicated to the worship of the "Supreme Being" (i.e., man himself). Chapels were built by Comte's devoted followers, and in various guises the cult persists to this day.

SEE ALSO Logical Positivism (1936)

A calendar listing Auguste Comte's "religion of humanity" positivism festivals, from The Positivist Calendar: or, Transitional System of Public Commemoration, *published in New York in 1856 by Comte disciple Henry Edger.*

LOVE for Principle ;
ORDER for Basis, and
PROGRESS for End.
} SOCIOLATRICAL TABLEAU, {
Live for others.
[Family, Country,
Humanity.]

SUMMING UP IN 81 ANNUAL FESTIVALS

THE UNIVERSAL ADORATION OF HUMANITY.

FUNDAMENTAL BONDS.

1st Month. HUMANITY...
- 1st day of the year · · { Synthetic Festival of the Great Being.
- Hebdomadal Festivals of Social Union,
  - religious.
  - historical.
  - national.
  - communal.

2d Month. MARRIAGE...
- complete.
- chaste.
- unequal.
- subjective.

3d Month. PATERNITY..
- complete........... { natural. / artificial.
- incomplete. .... { spiritual. / temporal.

4th Month. FILIATION.... *Same subdivisions.*

**5th Month. FRATERNITY.. ** *Idem.*

6th Month. DOMESTICITY
- permanent. .... { complete. / incomplete.
- transient........... *same subdivision*

PREPARATORY STATES.

7th Month. FETICHISM.
- spontaneous { nomadic... *Festival of the Animals* / sedentary... *Festival of Fire.*
- systematic... { sacerdotal. *Festival of the Sun.* / military... *Festival of Iron.*

8th Month. POLYTHEISM.
- conservative...........*Festival of the Castes.*
- intellectual. (*Salamis*) { esthetic. *Homer, Æschylus, Phidias.* / theoretical { *Thales, Pythagoras, Aristotle, Hippocrates, Archimedes, Apollonius, Hipparchus.*
- social.............*Scipio, Cæsar, Trajan.*

9th Month. MONOTHEISM.
- theocratic.........*Abraham, Moses, Solomon.*
- catholic........... { *Saint Paul. / Charlemagne. / Alfred. / Hildebrand. / Godfrey. / Saint Bernard.*
- islamite... (*Lepanto*) *Mahomet.*
- metaphysical........ { *Dante, / Descartes, / Frederick.*

NORMAL FUNCTIONS.

10th Month. WOMAN. ....
Moral Providence.
- mother.
- wife.
- daughter.
- sister.

11th Month. THE PRIESTHOOD.
Intellectual Providence.
- incomplete.........*Festival of Art.*
- preparatory... .....*Festival of Science.*
- definitive. { secondary. / principal. *Festival of the Elders.*

12th Month. THE PATRICIATE.
Material Providence
- banking.............*Festival of the Chevaliers*
- commerce.
- fabrication.
- agriculture.

13th Month. THE PROLETARIATE
General Providence.
- active... *Festival of Inventors: Guttenberg, Columbus, Vaucanson, Watt, Montgolfier.*
- affective.
- contemplative.
- passive.....*Saint Francis of Assisi*

**Complementary Day ..... ** Universal Festival of THE DEAD.

Bissextile Day......... General Festival of HOLY WOMEN.

Paris, Saturday, 7 Archimedes, 66. (1st April, 1854.)

AUGUSTE COMTE.

(10, Rue Monsieur-le-Prince.)

Law and Morality Are Separate

John Austin (1790–1859)

Prior to the nineteenth century, the dominant theory of law for over a millennium was natural law theory. In this view, law and morality are necessarily connected; law is rooted in a natural and divine moral order and is inherently normative and binding. Any human "law" that seriously conflicts with natural or divine law is not morally obligatory and is not fully or truly law.

Natural law theory was challenged by Thomas Hobbes (d. 1679) and Jeremy Bentham (d. 1832), but the first person to offer a full-scale alternative was the English legal theorist John Austin. Austin defended a theory of law that is now known as "legal positivism." According to Austin, laws are essentially just orders backed by threats, and may or may not be morally good or just.

Austin was an odd but gifted man. Born the son of a prosperous miller, Austin served for several years in the British army before deciding to study law. Impressed with the writings of Bentham, Austin became a committed utilitarian and was appointed to the newly founded chair of jurisprudence at the University of London in 1827. His lectures, which were dense and almost painfully meticulous, were not a success, and Austin resigned from his university post in 1835. Thereafter, he published virtually nothing, being plagued by what British legal philosopher H. L. A. Hart (1907–1992) termed "recurrent bouts of nervous illness, depression and self-distrust." Following his death, Austin's positivist theory of law was widely embraced in English and American jurisprudence.

Austin believed that it was crucial not to confuse "what the law is" with "what the law ought to be." What the law is, he argued, is a system of commands issued by someone with de facto authority ("the sovereign") who has the power to punish those who fail to comply. Whether a law exists or not is therefore entirely a factual question. The fact that a law may be immoral or unjust does not mean that it is not, in fact, a valid law. In Austin's view, it invites confusion and debate to call something "law" only if it comports with the divine will or meets a certain standard of moral correctness.

SEE ALSO Universal Moral Law (51 BCE), Natural Law (c. 1270), Legal Positivism (1961), *Taking Rights Seriously* (1977)

This gold statue of Lady Justice, 1902, by British sculptor F. W. Pomeroy, sits on top of the Old Bailey, the Central Criminal Court of England and Wales in London.

American Transcendentalism

Ralph Waldo Emerson (1803–1882)

Transcendentalism was the most significant American intellectual movement of the second third of the nineteenth century. At its core, transcendentalism was a Romantic revolt against Puritanism and Enlightenment rationalism and a fervent affirmation of individualism, the divinity of man and nature, and direct spiritual communion with God. Prominent transcendentalists of that time included Henry David Thoreau, Bronson Alcott, Theodore Parker, Margaret Fuller, George Ripley, and Orestes Brownson. But the unofficial leader and prophet of the movement was "the sage of Concord," Ralph Waldo Emerson.

Emerson was born in Boston, the son of a leading Unitarian minister. After graduating from Harvard Divinity School, Emerson served as pastor of a Unitarian church, before resigning in 1832 due to his doubts about Christianity and organized religion. For the rest of his life, Emerson supported himself by lecturing and writing, becoming one of America's best-known authors. His 1836 long essay, *Nature*, became something of a credo for the transcendentalist movement.

Strongly influenced by English Romantics such as William Wordsworth (1770–1850) and Samuel Taylor Coleridge (d. 1834), Emerson embraced a form of idealism that views nature as a symbol of spirit, recognizes an element of divinity in the human soul, and sees everything as being (in some mysterious way) "part or parcel of God," or what he sometimes calls the One or the Over-soul. Like many Romantics in that period, Emerson was troubled by the skeptical implications of John Locke's (d. 1704) empiricist approach to knowledge. If all our ideas about external reality come from the senses, how is religious experience or moral knowledge possible? To provide a basis for faith and spiritual cognition, Emerson relied on Coleridge's distinction between Reason and Understanding. Reason is the eye of the spirit, the faculty by which super-sensuous truths are perceived. Understanding is the faculty that measures, classifies, and arranges information provided by the senses. Emerson essentially identifies Reason with God, thereby divinizing man and making direct spiritual communion possible for everyone. This was a heady doctrine, which caught the spirit of the age and resonated well with American ideals of individualism, democracy, self-reliance, and optimism.

SEE ALSO The Birth of Romanticism (c. 1760), *Walden* (1854)

A nineteenth-century engraving of Ralph Waldo Emerson by American artist John Angel James Wilcox.

Idealism Is Turned Upside Down

Ludwig Feuerbach (1804–1872)

Hegel's soaring cathedral of idealist philosophy did not impress everybody. Søren Kierkegaard (1813–1855) attacked it for burying the individual under a mass of abstractions. Schopenhauer blasted it as "the most barefaced general mystification that has ever taken place, with a result which will appear fabulous to posterity, and will remain as a monument to German stupidity." And even former allies, such as the left-leaning and anti-religious Young Hegelians, rejected key aspects of Hegel's thought. Karl Marx (1818–1883) was destined to become the most famous Young Hegelian, but Ludwig Feuerbach was another hugely important figure in the movement.

Feuerbach was born in southeastern Germany, the son of a prominent lawyer. As a college student, Feuerbach was first interested in theology but switched to philosophy after he heard Hegel lecture at the University of Berlin. After obtaining a doctorate in philosophy, Feuerbach taught briefly at the University of Erlangen but sabotaged his own career with his outspokenness against the brand of Lutheranism that was dominant there. Thereafter he lived as a private scholar, making his living writing books. His most famous book was *The Essence of Christianity* (1841), which electrified Marx and his fellow Young Hegelians.

Like Marx, Feuerbach was an atheist and a materialist who completely rejected Hegel's spiritual Absolute. But Feuerbach believed that Hegel was a deep and profound thinker nonetheless. Hegel thought he was revealing the nature of a spiritual entity, the Absolute, but what he was really doing, Feuerbach claimed, was laying bare the nature of humanity. This is because religion is an unconscious projection of man's idealized self onto a fictitious being, God. As Xenophanes argued, humans make God in their own image, taking their desire for ultimate power, ultimate knowledge, immortality, and so forth and hypostasizing them into the idea of a perfect, holy being. In so doing, humans engage in a process of self-alienation, making God the epitome of perfection and themselves miserable worms. The solution lies in realizing our true condition and adopting a humanistic spirituality based on love for our fellow man. Only in this way can we overcome our self-alienation and achieve true fulfillment.

SEE ALSO Anthropomorphization (c. 530 BCE), The Real Is the Rational (1821), *The Communist Manifesto* (1848)

This engraved portrait of Ludwig Feuerbach appeared in the nineteenth-century German magazine Die Gartenlaube *(The Garden Arbor).*

Ludwig Feuerbach.

Existentialism

Søren Kierkegaard (1813–1855)

One of the most intriguing philosophies of the twentieth century was existentialism, which reached its heyday in the 1940s and 1950s, particularly in Europe. Existentialism is not a single, unified philosophy but a cluster of related themes and concerns. It arose as a response both to the challenges of being an authentic individual in an increasingly cookie-cutter world and to the aridity and abstractness of much nineteenth- and twentieth-century philosophy. A major forerunner of existentialism was the nineteenth-century Danish philosopher Søren Kierkegaard.

Kierkegaard epitomized the existentially anguished philosopher. His wealthy father, Michael, was a melancholic and guilt-ridden man, and Søren struggled all his life with similar feelings. In his college days, Kierkegaard was a dandified socialite, and it took him ten years to finally graduate with a theology degree. Shortly before he graduated, Kierkegaard fell in love with fourteen-year-old Regina Olsen. Three years later they became engaged, but Kierkegaard broke off the engagement in the belief that God had called him to take a different, more arduous path. He spent most of the next ten years pouring out a steady stream of books exploring various dimensions of what it means to be an authentic person and a true Christian. He died young, totally spent by his efforts.

In Kierkegaard's philosophy most of the key existentialist themes are sounded, including freedom, individuality, authenticity, choice, commitment, dread, and despair. His central theme is that human existence is plagued by a pervasive sense of anxiety, sin, and despair, and that the only cure for this is a leap of faith and an absolute, all-in commitment to God. Making such a leap is frightening and it is not "rational," Kierkegaard believes. It requires us to stake everything on something that looks quite improbable from the standpoint of logic and common sense. This is why, in Kierkegaard's famous phrase, the life of faith is like floating on the deep over "seventy thousand fathoms" of water. For Kierkegaard, faith is not a stasis, a calm oasis in the desert. It is a constantly renewed recommitment, a leap into the dark that seems crazy by the world's standards. Thus, only in the transcendent is there true respite from anxiety and dread.

SEE ALSO Truth Is Subjectivity (1846), Existential Defiance (1942), Atheistic Existentialism (1946)

A sculpture of Søren Kierkegaard created in 1879 by Danish sculptor Louis Hasselriis, at the Royal Library Garden in Copenhagen..

A System of Logic

John Stuart Mill (1806–1873)

John Stuart Mill is the most influential British philosopher of the nineteenth century. His most widely read works today are *On Liberty* (1859) and *Utilitarianism* (1863). But Mill himself believed that his best book, and the one for which he would be longest remembered, was *A System of Logic: Ratiocinative and Inductive* (1843).

Mill was born in London and had an unusual childhood. His Scottish father, James Mill (1773–1836), was a follower of Jeremy Bentham (d. 1832) and a well-known British intellectual. John was educated at home by his father, who put him through an extraordinarily rigorous and fast-paced education focused mainly on the Greek and Roman classics, history, math, and economics. By age seven he was reading Plato's dialogues in the original Greek and talking learnedly with his father about Gibbon's insights into the rise and fall of the Roman Empire. The normal joys of childhood—games, toys, friends—were denied him. Not surprisingly, this hyper-intellectualized upbringing turned out badly. At age twenty he fell into a profound depression that lasted for several years. Only when Mill fell in love and began reading poetry did he recover the emotional balance he had been missing. He went on to serve in Parliament and became one of the best-known British writers of his day.

Mill's *System of Logic* is a highly original work that had a significant impact on subsequent science, logic, and the philosophy of language. Since Aristotle, logicians had focused mainly on deductive logic, especially syllogistic reasoning. Mill gave pride of place to inductive logic, going so far as to say that all true inference is inductive. The most influential part of the book dealt with scientific and causal reasoning. Mill formulated five techniques of inductive inference, which he called the method of agreement, the method of difference, the joint method of agreement and difference, the method of residues, and the method of concomitant variation. Though critics have pointed out various drawbacks with these methods, they still have considerable value in circumstances when they can be effectively employed. Many current logic textbooks include a section on Mill's methods.

SEE ALSO The Invention of Logic (c. 330 BCE), The New Logic (1879)

A photograph of John Stuart Mill from 1870, at age sixty-four.

Truth Is Subjectivity

Søren Kierkegaard (1813–1855)

One of Kierkegaard's most famous sayings is that "truth is subjectivity." He did not mean that truth is just a matter of opinion or that it is OK to believe whatever you want. He meant something much deeper.

Kierkegaard's idea of truth as subjectivity is connected with his view of faith. For Kierkegaard, faith is not a matter of accepting revealed truths on the authority of the Church or the Bible. Faith is a leap, a passionate commitment of one's whole self, to something that appears absurd from the standpoint of objective reason. Jesus said, "I am the truth." Thus, for a Christian existentialist like Kierkegaard, faith and truth are ultimately the same thing: "An objective uncertainty, held fast in an appropriation-process of the most passionate inwardness, is the truth, the highest truth attainable for an existing individual."

In his greatest book, *Concluding Unscientific Postscript* (1846), Kierkegaard made an important distinction between "having the truth" and "being in the truth." Someone who knows all the important truths about religion but makes no effort to live up to them "has" the truth in the sense that he can reel off correct answers on a theology test. But what is far more important is to be "in" the truth by making those religious beliefs operational in one's life. According to Kierkegaard, attempts to reach God by objective reasoning are bound to fail. And even if we could make God an object of objective knowledge, what good would it do us without the reality of a living faith? As Kierkegaard saw it, the really important thing in religion is the quality of the *relationship* one has with God. When we focus on objective knowledge, we concentrate on the object, on whether the searchlight of our minds, so to speak, has hit upon the right thing. But when it comes to God, what matters most is whether we have related ourselves to Him in the right way. Have I taken up the reality of the saving God into my life with the "passionate inwardness" true faith demands? This is the central question Kierkegaard poses for his religious readers.

SEE ALSO Existentialism (1843), *I and Thou* (1923)

The Sun, 1910–1911, *a spiritual mural at Oslo University by Edvard Munch; the Norwegian painter was a great admirer of Kierkegaard.*

1848

The Communist Manifesto

Karl Marx (1818–1883), Friedrich Engels (1820–1895)

Marx and Engels's *The Communist Manifesto* is undoubtedly the most widely read political pamphlet of all time. More than a century and a half after its publication, its sledgehammer rhetoric and burning zeal for the downtrodden still have the power to challenge and inspire.

Marx and Engels were both born in Germany, though each lived for much of their lives in England. Both became radicalized at an early age. In 1848, while living in Brussels, they collaborated on writing *The Communist Manifesto*, though Marx did the majority of the work. Later, when Marx and his family lived in poverty in London, Engels provided critical financial support. They wrote a number of works together, and Engels edited the second and third volumes of *Capital* (1885, 1894) after Marx's death.

The Communist Manifesto begins with a clear statement of Marx and Engels's materialist conception of history: "The history of all hitherto existing society is the history of class struggles." The fundamental clash in modern society is between the bourgeoisie, who own the means of production, and the proletariat, the exploited working class. Marx and Engels argue that the evils of industrial exploitation have now become so dire that the violent overthrow of the bourgeoisie by the proletariat is both inevitable and imminent. Capitalism has produced "its own grave-diggers." After a transitional socialist period in which the means of production will gradually be centralized in the state and many forms of private property will be abolished, a fully classless and stateless communist society will emerge.

Marx and Engels go on to address a number of common objections to communism. They deny that workers would be lazy if private property was abolished and they could not better their condition in life by hard work. If this were true, they argue, then capitalism would long ago have collapsed, because "those who work therein gain nothing, and those who gain do not work." They also deny that communism would lead to the "community [sharing] of women," remarking that the bourgeoisie already have established a de facto system of sexual freebooting by "having the wives and daughters of the proletarians at their disposal" and "seducing each other's wives"!

SEE ALSO *Capital* (1867)

A Soviet stamp depicting Karl Marx and Friedrich Engels, issued in 1948 on the one-hundredth anniversary of The Communist Manifesto.

Walden

Henry David Thoreau (1817–1862)

Was Thoreau a philosopher? Certainly he was a lover of wisdom, which is what the term originally meant to the ancient Greeks. Thoreau himself stated: "To be a philosopher is not merely to have subtle thoughts, nor even to found a school, but so to love wisdom as to live according to its dictates, a life of simplicity, independence, magnanimity and trust." By this definition, Thoreau was a philosopher of the first rank.

Born in Concord, Massachusetts, Thoreau spent nearly his whole life there, making ends meet by surveying, making pencils, and occasionally lecturing. His true life was lived in the fields and woods as a "self-appointed inspector of snow-storms and rain-storms." In his late twenties, he spent twenty-six months in a small cabin he built on the shore of Walden Pond. Out of that experience, he distilled one of the enduring masterpieces of American literature, *Walden* (1854). Like Emerson (d. 1882), Thoreau was a transcendentalist who believed that there was a divine element in every human being, that through this element we can intuit moral and spiritual truths, and that nature was a mirror and symbol of the divine. As a Romantic, Thoreau believed in people's innate goodness and agreed with Wordsworth (d. 1850) about the beneficent moral "impulses" emanating from smiling meadows and sun-dappled woods. As he saw it, "all good things are wild, and free."

Thoreau's essay "Civil Disobedience" (1849) was a major influence on Mahatma Gandhi's anticolonial liberation movement in India and on Martin Luther King Jr.'s campaign of nonviolent protest during the American civil-rights era. Thoreau was among the first to suggest the creation of a national park system, and his writings strongly impacted John Muir (1838–1914) and other key figures in the American environmental movement. Today he acts as an inspiration to the contemporary voluntary simplicity movement, which is sure to grow as we confront the challenges of climate change. Though he died young, he led a life "rich in sunny hours and summer days." He will always speak to those who need "the tonic of wildness" and believe that the true cost of anything is the amount of "life which is required to be exchanged for it."

SEE ALSO Cynicism (c. 400 BCE), The Birth of Romanticism (c. 1760), American Transcendentalism (1836), Environmental Preservationism (1901)

A replica of Henry David Thoreau's cabin at Walden Pond, in Concord, Massachusetts.

On Liberty

John Stuart Mill (1806–1873)

Over the course of human history, threats to individual liberty have come mainly from tyrants, conquerors, and oppressive elites. In *On Liberty* (1859), John Stuart Mill focuses on a relatively new threat to freedom: the "tyranny of the majority." Though widely denounced in Mill's own day, *On Liberty* is now generally recognized as one of the great classics of political philosophy.

The central thesis of *On Liberty* is that society can legitimately restrict individual liberty only in order to prevent one person from harming another. This proposed standard, now called the harm principle, has far-reaching implications. Historically, nearly all societies have had laws that banned conduct simply because it was considered to be offensive, immoral, irreligious, or harmful to oneself. The harm principle excludes all such laws. Only behavior that harms, or threatens harm to, other people can be outlawed or otherwise restricted.

Mill argues for the harm principle not by appealing to individual rights or human dignity, but on utilitarian grounds. Specifically, Mill argues that respect for individual liberty is vital to social progress and the full development of one's individuality and higher capacities.

On Liberty also contains a powerful defense of freedom of thought and expression. A censored opinion, Mill notes, can be either entirely true, partly true, or completely false. By censoring an opinion that is wholly or partly true, we lose the chance to replace error with truth. Even completely false opinions should not be censored, Mill argues, because truths that are protected from all critical scrutiny often fossilize into mere dogmas or meaningless formulae. Mill was a bold thinker, far ahead of his time on issues such as women's rights and participatory democracy. When *On Liberty* was first published, it was widely considered a tissue of radical nonsense that threatened the very foundations of social order. Today we live in an increasingly Millian world. Many nations have liberalized their laws on same-sex marriage, physician-assisted suicide, adultery, recreational drug use, pornography, gambling, prostitution, and other so-called "morals offenses." Mill's *On Liberty* has been a seminal text in this process.

SEE ALSO Political Libertarianism (1974), *The Moral Limits of Criminal Law* (1984)

"The Doom of the Editor—A Legal Barbarity," a political cartoon by Tom Merry, published in the British conservative journal St. Stephen's Review *in 1884. It shows a priest visiting a journalist in prison; the latter waves away a paper labeled "TRUTH." Freedom of the press, which Mill championed in* On Liberty, *remained a controversial issue a decade after his death and is still an issue in many countries today.*

THE DOOM OF THE EDITOR.
A LEGAL BARBARITY.
(SEE LIBRETTO.)

JUDD & Cᵒ LITH. LONDON

Darwin's *Origin of Species*

Charles Darwin (1809–1882)

The publication of *On the Origin of Species* in 1859 by English naturalist Charles Darwin was a huge milestone in philosophy as well as in science. As American philosopher Daniel Dennett (b. 1942) has remarked, Darwin's theory of evolution was a kind of "universal acid" that forced a reappraisal of long-accepted ideas in all areas of intellectual life, including philosophy. In some ways that process of reassessment is ongoing, and its ultimate outcome is uncertain. Looking back, however, we can note several major influences that Darwin had on philosophy. One immediate impact was the emergence of social Darwinism, which sought to apply Darwin's ideas of natural selection and survival of the fittest to business and society. Leading social Darwinists such as Herbert Spencer (1820–1903) and John Fiske (1842–1901) convinced millions that the true lessons of Darwinism were the inevitability of progress and the wisdom of a laissez-faire approach to business regulation—although this movement faded rather quickly (see page 318). More lasting impacts can be seen in areas like ethics and philosophy of knowledge. When Nietzsche sought to justify a rather ruthless-sounding "master morality" by citing the fact that "life itself is *essentially* appropriation, injury, conquest of the strange and weak," the influence of Darwin was obvious. More generally, Darwinism made it difficult to see how an evolved human brain could get in sync with nonnatural, objective moral values. This led to a variety of attempts to "naturalize" ethics, such as emotivism, relativism, ethical naturalism, moral antirealism, and evolutionary ethics.

The impact of Darwinism on epistemology was equally profound. Evolutionary theory sent the traditional "ghost in the machine" Cartesian dualism into a tailspin from which it never recovered. Debates in contemporary epistemology over artificial intelligence, reductionism, foundationalism, conceptual relativism, pragmatism, evolutionary psychology, "emergent" properties, and so forth are all rooted in post-Darwinian efforts to understand the mind as a natural, evolved phenomenon.

These examples barely scratch the surface of Darwin's influence on philosophy. Evolutionary theory was a huge paradigm-shift that led to the wholesale abandonment of many traditional philosophical ideas and debates.

SEE ALSO Social Darwinism (1862), The Revaluation of Values (1887), The Ghost in the Machine (1949)

A photograph of Charles Robert Darwin, 1868, by well-known British portrait photographer Julia Margaret Cameron.

Social Darwinism

Herbert Spencer (1820–1903)

When Charles Darwin's *Origin of Species* was published in 1859, it sent shock waves through almost every field of human thought. In the natural sciences, theology, philosophy, history, and many other disciplines, there were intense efforts to explore the implications of evolution. One effort along these lines was what later came to be called social Darwinism: basically the attempt to apply the lessons of biological evolution to human societies. In nature, it was claimed, progress occurs through a ruthless process of competitive struggle and "survival of the fittest." In a similar way, human progress will occur only if government allows unrestricted business competition and makes no effort to protect the "weak" and "unfit" by means of social welfare laws.

The most influential defender of social Darwinism was the British philosopher and social scientist Herbert Spencer. In 1862, Spencer published *First Principles*, the first volume of his massive ten-volume *System of Synthetic Philosophy*. In this series of books, he argued that there is a general law of evolutionary progress that applies not only to nature, but to human individuals and societies as well.

Though largely forgotten today, Spencer was hugely influential in the late nineteenth century, especially in the United States. Spencer's gospel of progress through struggle and competition struck a nerve in the heady "Gilded Age" of postbellum America.

By the 1890s, social Darwinism was in rapid decline. Critics pointed out that there is no scientific basis for any general law of "evolutionary progress" that reigns at every level of nature and human affairs. They also noted that moral lessons—such as how societies should treat the old or mentally handicapped—cannot be drawn by looking to nature, which is indifferent to moral values. Finally, many people began to see firsthand the toll that unrestricted competition in the industrial age took on ordinary people's lives and the environment. As the Progressive Era dawned, increasing numbers of Americans came to believe that government has a legitimate role to play in addressing social problems such as child labor, safe working conditions, old-age insurance, maximum working hours, monopolistic pricing, and environmental destruction.

SEE ALSO Darwin's *Origin of Species* (1859)

A cartoon from the magazine Puck, *1883, titled "An Appalling Attempt to Muzzle the Watch-Dog of Science," by Friedrich Graetz, imagines Herbert Spencer as an enormous dog guarding the entrance to a public building that emits rays of light labeled "Science"; numerous little men race about trying to silence him, while a flag atop the pole reads "Freedom of Thought."*

VOL. XIII.-No. 314.

MARCH 14, 1883.

Price, 10 Cents.

"What fools these Mortals be!"
MIDSUMMER-NIGHTS DREAM.

Puck

PUBLISHED BY
KEPPLER & SCHWARZMANN.

NEW YORK
TRADE MARK REGISTERED 1878

OFFICE No. 21 - 23 WARREN ST

"ENTERED AT THE POST OFFICE AT NEW YORK, AND ADMITTED FOR TRANSMISSION THROUGH THE MAILS AT SECOND CLASS RATES."

AN APPALLING ATTEMPT TO MUZZLE THE WATCH-DOG OF SCIENCE.

"The Society for the Suppression of Blasphemous Literature proposes to get up cases against Professors Huxley and Tyndall, Herbert Spencer, and others who, by their writings, have sown widespread unbelief, and in some cases rank atheism."—*Tel. London, March 5, 1883.*

1863

Refined Utilitarianism

John Stuart Mill (1806–1873)

Mill's *Utilitarianism*, first published in *Fraser's Magazine* in London in 1861 and then as a book in 1863, is a landmark in ethics. Although there had been defenders of utilitarianism since at least the end of the eighteenth century, it was Mill's book that made it arguably the leading ethical theory in English-speaking countries. Mill was able to accomplish this by refining utilitarianism in ways that made it less at odds with popular morality.

In his youth, Mill had been an ardent disciple of Jeremy Bentham (d. 1832), the most important early defender of utilitarianism. Bentham argued that pleasure is the only thing people ever desire for its own sake and that there are no higher or lower pleasures. Mill rejects both of these claims.

Like Bentham, Mill equates pleasure with happiness and claims that happiness is the only thing people ever desire as an end. But he softens what many saw as Bentham's crude psychology by maintaining that other sorts of goods, such as friendship, knowledge, and virtue, can be desired as *parts* of happiness, or as constitutive of a person's conception of happiness. He also claims that pleasures differ in quality as well as quantity. Like most Victorians, Mill believed that mental pleasures have higher value than pleasures of the body, and that anyone who had experienced both sorts of pleasures would prefer those of the mind.

Mill modifies Bentham's utilitarianism in other ways as well. One was to give a greater place to conventional moral rules. Bentham seemed to hold that rules like "don't lie" and "keep your promises" should play little or no role in moral decision making. Mill disagrees. While he concurs with Bentham that the principle of utility is the ultimate test of moral rightness, he also believes that following moral rules is usually the best strategy for maximizing long-term happiness. Only when moral rules conflict is it necessary to appeal to the principle of utility directly.

Mill succeeded in getting his contemporaries to give utilitarianism a serious hearing. After 150 years, *Utilitarianism* remains as one of the most influential and widely read books on ethics.

SEE ALSO Utilitarianism (1789), *A Theory of Justice* (1971)

The title page from a 1910 omnibus of three of Mill's major works: Utilitarianism *(1863),* On Liberty *(1859),* and Considerations on Representative Government *(1861).*

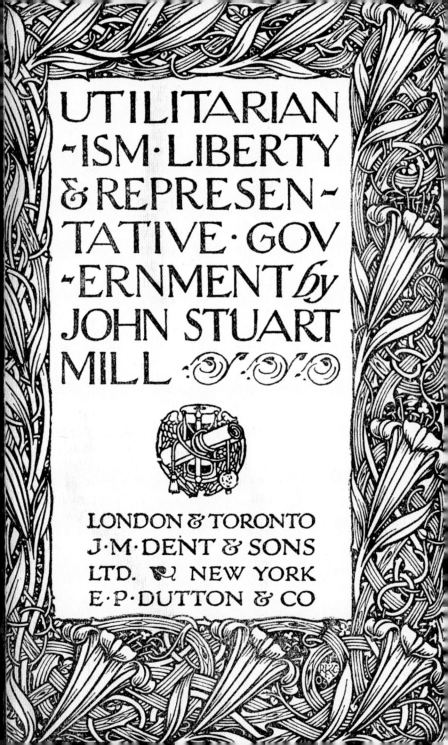

UTILITARIAN
-ISM·LIBERTY
&REPRESEN-
TATIVE·GOV
-ERNMENT by
JOHN STUART
MILL

LONDON & TORONTO
J·M·DENT & SONS
LTD. ✤ NEW YORK
E·P·DUTTON & CO

The Rise of British Idealism

Francis Herbert Bradley (1846–1924)

The second half of the nineteenth century was an age when many people felt troubled by what contemporary poet Matthew Arnold famously termed the "melancholy, long, withdrawing roar" of traditional religious faith. One response was the growth of absolute idealism, a broadly Hegelian philosophy that held that Spirit is the only reality. Beginning in the mid-1860s, many philosophers in both Great Britain and the United States turned to idealism as a spiritual substitute for orthodox Christianity and as a bulwark against the perceived evils of empiricism and materialism. Major figures in the idealist movement included Thomas Hill Green (1836–1882), Bernard Bosanquet (1848–1923), Josiah Royce (1855–1916), and J. M. E. McTaggart (1866–1925). Probably the most brilliant idealist philosopher was the odd British recluse F. H. Bradley.

Bradley was born in London, the son of an evangelical preacher, and educated at University College, Oxford. In 1870, he was elected to a nonteaching fellowship at Merton College, Oxford. In chronic poor health, Bradley lived for fifty-four years at Merton, seldom venturing outside his rooms except for regular trips to seaside resorts. He considered himself a marksman and disliked cats, and is said to have sometimes shot at them from his window. Among his major works are *Ethical Studies* (1876), *The Principles of Logic* (1883), and *Appearance and Reality* (1893).

Like Hegel, Bradley believed that all that exists is a single all-embracing, self-differentiating spiritual reality that Bradley called the "Absolute." Yet unlike Hegel, Bradley denied that the human mind can achieve an adequate grasp of the Absolute. As he saw it, our minds are finite and tie themselves up into knots whenever they carve up reality into discrete objects or try to comprehend the all-inclusive Absolute. When pressed to clarify the rational basis of his idealist philosophy, Bradley candidly admitted that his entire system rested on the assumption that "the object of metaphysics is to find a general view which will satisfy the intellect, and . . . that whatever succeeds in doing this is real and true." To critics like Bertrand Russell (d. 1970) and G. E. Moore (1873–1958) this sounded too much like wishful thinking, and idealism rapidly lost favor after their hard-hitting attacks in the first decade of the twentieth century.

SEE ALSO The Beginnings of German Idealism (c. 1795), The Real Is the Rational (1821), The Analytic-Continental Split (1903)

An eighteenth-century aquatint of the church of Merton College at Oxford; idealist philosopher F. H. Bradley lived at Merton for most of his adult life.

Capital

Karl Marx (1818–1883)

Scholars often distinguish between the "early Marx" and the "mature Marx." The early Marx is reflected in *The Economic and Philosophic Manuscripts* (1844). There, Marx offers a passionate philosophical indictment of capitalism and how it alienates workers from their products, their work, their fellow workers, and their own essential selves. In *Capital (Das Kapital)*, the first volume of which was published in 1867, Marx offers a purportedly scientific analysis of capital, the division of labor, class conflict, modes and relations of production, the inevitability of a violent overthrow of the ruling class, and so forth. Yet Marx in *Capital* does not take back what he said about the alienating effects of capitalism in his youth; the humanistic and scientific analyses are not mutually exclusive.

What is largely new in the mature Marx is a complex economic and historical account of how capitalism works, how it has developed, and how and why it will soon meet its violent end. In *Capital* Marx puts forth his famous "materialist conception of history." In this view, it is ultimately economic factors that drive history and determine what Marx calls the cultural "superstructure" of prevailing ideas of religion, art, law, philosophy, ethics, and politics in a given society. Marx also lays out other important elements of his "scientific" analysis of capitalism, including his labor theory of value (the claim that the economic value of a commodity is determined by the amount of labor that was needed to produce it); his theory of dialectical materialism (the Hegelian-inspired idea that history advances by means of conflicting economic forces, which lead to a higher resolution of those processes); and the theory of surplus value (the view that capitalists make money by paying workers less than they deserve, then skim off the extra value in the form of business profits). Most Western economists now dismiss Marx's supposedly scientific analysis of capitalism as theory-driven utopian pseudoscience. However, one aspect of Marx's account has powerfully influenced left-leaning social thought: his notion of "ideology." Marx believed that dominant ideas of law, politics, philosophy, and so forth, are falsifications because they reflect the economic interests and biases of the ruling class. This has contributed to widespread scholarly distrust of claims to "objectivity," "neutrality," "universality," and the like.

SEE ALSO *The Communist Manifesto* (1848), Power/Knowledge (1975)

The enormous Karl Marx Monument, in Moscow, Russia, by Soviet sculptor Lev Kerbel, was unveiled in 1961 at Theatre Square.

The Subjection of Women

John Stuart Mill (1806–1873)

British philosopher John Stuart Mill was a pioneering thinker who advocated a number of ideas that were widely ridiculed in his lifetime but are commonly accepted today. One is that women should enjoy a "perfect equality" with men.

Mill makes his case for women's rights in his short book, *The Subjection of Women*, written in 1861 but published in 1869. As a utilitarian, Mill grounds his argument on appeals to the general happiness rather than on abstract considerations of justice or fairness. His central argument is that both women *and men* would be happier if they were treated as equals.

In Mill's day, women in Great Britain could not vote, serve in public office or work in most careers outside the home, and in the 1860s there were still many countries that forbade the matriculation of women. Moreover, under British marriage laws wives were almost totally subject to their husbands. Any property or income a wife had belonged by law to her husband. Only husbands had legal rights over a married couple's children. Even if a husband died, the wife had no legal guardianship over her children unless the husband had so provided in his will. If a wife left her husband, even for reasons of physical abuse, she could take nothing with her, and the husband could compel her to return, even by physical force. Mill frankly likened women's marital status to slavery, suggesting that in some ways it was even worse. Slaves, for example, had a right to refuse the unwelcome sexual advances of their masters, but wives did not have a similar right with their husbands.

Mill argued that women would enjoy an "unspeakable gain" in personal happiness if they were treated as equals in marriage and were free to work in whatever profession they wished, to go to college, and so forth. But men would also gain. All of society would benefit if the intelligence and talents of half the population were unleashed. Men would also gain by having wives of equal education and culture. Marriage would then no longer be the "school of despotism" that it was in Mill's day. Instead, it would be a "school of moral cultivation" in which a climate of command and obedience was replaced with equality and mutual respect.

SEE ALSO *A Vindication of the Rights of Woman* (1792), Emergence of Feminist Philosophy (c. 1976)

In The Subjection of Women, *John Stuart Mill espoused the rights of women, including the right to vote. This 1867 political cartoon from the British magazine* Punch *shows Mill clearing the path for a group of suffragettes.*

MILL'S LOGIC; OR, FRANCHISE FOR FEMALES.

"PRAY CLEAR THE WAY, THERE, FOR THESE—A—PERSONS."

The Methods of Ethics

Henry Sidgwick (1838–1900)

Henry Sidgwick's *The Methods of Ethics* (1874) is widely considered one of the greatest works of ethics ever written. It set new standards for clarity and thoroughness, solidified the place of utilitarianism as a leading moral theory, and largely set the agenda for philosophical ethics for the next several decades.

Sidgwick was born in Yorkshire, attended Rugby, and had a brilliant undergraduate career at Trinity College, Cambridge, where he excelled at both mathematics and classics. He remained at Cambridge for the rest of his life, becoming Knightsbridge professor of moral philosophy in 1883. A man of wide-ranging interests, he was an active supporter of women's education and psychical research.

Sidgwick's chief aim in *The Methods of Ethics* is to explore the contents of "commonsense" morality and determine if the various decision-procedures it employs are mutually consistent. He concludes that there are three basic methods used in ordinary morality: utilitarianism (maximize general happiness); egoistic hedonism (maximize personal happiness); and intuitionism (follow self-evident moral principles that prescribe acts—such as truth telling—that are morally obligatory, largely irrespective of consequences). Sidgwick argues that among the few ethical principles that are truly self-evident are (a) that the good of any one individual is no more important than the good of any other individual, and (b) that a rational being ought to "aim at" the general good. It follows that intuitionism, properly construed, can be completely synthesized with utilitarianism. It is more difficult, Sidgwick admits, to harmonize egoism and utilitarianism. Egoists claim that each person ought to seek his or her own greatest good. Given the distinctness of persons, Sidgwick believed that it was reasonable to accept such a principle of prudence. The obvious difficulty is that it seems to conflict with the equally self-evident principle that a rational being should always aim at the general good. Sidgwick suggests that if God exists, he might bring about a perfect harmony of self-interest and service to others. But Sidgwick saw no convincing evidence of God's existence. He thus concluded that it is impossible to make our commonsense moral intuitions fully consistent. We are stuck with what he called a "dualism of the practical reason."

SEE ALSO Utilitarianism (1789), Refined Utilitarianism (1863), Ethical Intuitionism (1903)

A reproduction of a photograph of Henry Sidgwick, c. 1890.

Intentionality

Franz Brentano (1838–1917)

Is there anything that all mental states have in common? Is there something that clearly distinguishes mental things from nonmental things? One influential answer to both questions was offered by the so-called grandfather of phenomenology, the important nineteenth-century German philosopher Franz Brentano. According to Brentano, what is common and peculiar to mental phenomena is that they are "about" objects other than themselves. This claim about the "intentionality" (i.e., object-directedness) of thought has been highly influential in both the analytic and continental traditions (see page 354) of contemporary philosophy.

Brentano was born in Western Germany, near Cologne, and taught for most of his career at the Universities of Würzburg and Vienna. In 1864, he was ordained a Roman Catholic priest, but left the Church in the 1870s. A dynamic teacher, Brentano influenced a number of students who went on to become distinguished philosophers, most notably Edmund Husserl (1859–1938) and Alexius Meinong (1853–1920). In 1874, Brentano published his most influential book, *Psychology from an Empirical Standpoint*, which sets forth his theory of intentionality. He also did important work in ethics, metaphysics, and logic.

Brentano claimed that all mental phenomena—thought, sensation, emotion, judgment, desire, etc.—are focused on some object. When we think, we think about something; when we desire, there is something that we want. Brentano suggests, in fact, that all mental states have both a primary and a secondary intentional object. The primary object is the thing, or set of things, toward which the thought is directed (e.g., the Eiffel Tower). The secondary object is our act of consciousness itself. Consciousness is "reflexive," or turned back on itself. In listening to music, for example, I am aware of my own conscious act of hearing. This claim about the inherent reflexivity of thought would be denied by a number of later phenomenologists. Brentano's claim that only mental states can include things like intentional objects is a common objection to certain physicalistic theories of the mind. Can a configuration of atoms in the brain be "about" anything at all, or is intentionality an inherently nonphysical property of the mind?

SEE ALSO Phenomenology (1900), The Analytic-Continental Split (1903), Mind-Brain Identity Theory (1968)

Brentano claimed that all mental states have both a primary and a secondary intentional object. The primary object is the specific thing, such as the Eiffel Tower (shown here in a c. 1890 photochrom), toward which the thought is directed.

Origins of Pragmatism

Charles Sanders Peirce (1839–1914)

C. S. Peirce was a neglected genius during his lifetime but is now widely regarded as one of America's greatest philosophers. He made important contributions to logic, science, and the philosophy of language, but he is best known as the inventor of pragmatism. He first introduced the idea of pragmatism in an 1878 paper titled "How to Make Our Ideas Clear."

Peirce believed there is a close connection between thought and action. The whole function of thought, he said, is to produce habits of actions. We find ourselves irritated by doubts, uncertain what to believe or do. The goal of thought is to remove these annoyances, to achieve rest through settled belief. Because of the close connection between thought and action, we can achieve maximum clarity in our ideas by unpacking what we take to be the practical consequences of those ideas. In fact, Peirce goes so far as to say our "idea of anything *is* our idea of its sensible effects." This provides the basis for Peirce's pragmatic theory of meaning, which holds that the meaning of an idea is the sum total of its conceived practical consequences.

Peirce's pragmatic theory of meaning has two important implications for the practice of philosophy. First, if two allegedly different ideas have exactly the same practical consequences, they are really the same idea. As an example, Peirce cites the alleged difference between Catholic and Protestant views of the Eucharist. Catholics say that the consecrated bread and wine are no longer bread and wine but have been miraculously transformed into the body and blood of Christ. Protestants reject this doctrine of literal transubstantiation. But do Catholics and Protestants disagree about any of the practical effects of their respective views of the Eucharist? If not, then their disagreement is merely verbal, not real.

The second important implication of Peirce's pragmatic theory of meaning is that ideas and theories that have *no* conceivable practical implications are meaningless. As a hardheaded working scientist, Peirce was not impressed by airy theorizing. In proposing a pragmatic theory of meaning, Peirce hoped to make philosophy more practical and more like science.

SEE ALSO *Pragmatism* (1907), Instrumentalism (1925), The New Pragmatism (1979)

The Institution of the Eucharist, c. 1850, by German engraver Joseph von Keller after J. F. Overbeck. Peirce examines the alleged difference between Catholic and Protestant views of the Eucharist as an example of the pragmatic idea that if two allegedly different ideas have exactly the same practical consequences, they are really the same idea.

The New Logic

Gottlob Frege (1848–1925)

Logic was founded by Aristotle more than 2,300 years ago. So thorough and impressive was Aristotle's achievement that there was relatively little progress in logic until the nineteenth century. Then, in *A System of Logic* (1843), John Stuart Mill significantly advanced our understanding of inductive and scientific reasoning. An even more important contribution was made by the German mathematician and logician Gottlob Frege in his 1879 book *Begriffsschrift* (*Concept-Notation*). Many consider Frege to be the second founder of logic.

Frege was born in Wismar, on the Baltic Sea coast of northern Germany. His father was the headmaster of a local girls' school. At an early age, Frege became interested in mathematics and science. After studying mathematics at the University of Jena, he received his doctorate in math from the University of Göttingen. He spent the rest of his career as a relatively obscure mathematics professor at the University of Jena. According to Bertrand Russell, Frege "remained wholly without recognition" until Russell drew attention to his groundbreaking discoveries in 1903.

Frege is a towering figure in modern philosophy for his contributions to both modern logic and analytic philosophy. In logic, he revolutionized the subject by creating a new system of logical notation that laid the foundation for predicate logic (the form of symbolic logic that involves variables and quantifiers) and provided a better way of expressing the logical form of sentences. Frege is also considered one of the founders of twentieth-century analytic philosophy. In his classic 1892 paper "On Sense and Reference," Frege distinguished two aspects of linguistic signification, *Sinn* (sense) and *Bedeutung* (reference or meaning). Consider these two superficially similar sentences: "The morning star is the morning star," and "The morning star is the evening star." As Frege pointed out, the first sentence is a trivial logical truth, whereas the second is an important astronomical discovery (the planet Venus is the morning star and the evening star). The essential difference, he argued, is this: even though the expressions "the morning star" and the "evening star" have the same reference (they both denote the planet Venus), they have different senses, that is, different ways of referring to the object they denote. Philosophers continue to debate Frege's sense-reference distinction today.

SEE ALSO The Invention of Logic (c. 330 BCE), *A System of Logic* (1843)

A contemporary photograph of a seascape with the moon and Venus—the morning star and the evening star.

"God Is Dead"

Friedrich Nietzsche (1844–1900)

In two of his books, *The Gay Science* (or *Joyful Wisdom*) (1882) and *Thus Spake Zarathustra* (1883–1885), the important nineteenth-century German philosopher Friedrich Nietzsche dramatically declares that "God is dead." This is one of the most famous sayings in philosophy, but what does it mean?

Nietzsche does not, of course, mean that God has literally died—that once God existed, but he has since expired. Nor does he mean, as some have suggested, that authentic belief in God is no longer possible. As he explains in *The Gay Science*, what he means is that God is now "unworthy of belief" in the sense that belief in God has been discredited. There are no longer any rational grounds for affirming that God exists. How did this occur? "We have killed him," Nietzsche says. In his view, all the traditional arguments for God's existence have been thoroughly undermined by science, philosophy, modern biblical criticism, and other corrosive developments in the modern world. Yet Nietzsche notes that "this tremendous event . . . has not yet reached the ears of man." It has not yet truly sunk in, either to the masses or even to most intellectuals. When it does, Nietzsche predicts, the effects will be both calamitous and (for "free spirits") a cause for joy.

Nietzsche does not believe we can give up belief in God and just continue on our merry way; we must also give up all belief in objective moral values, objective meanings, and even objective truth. When the full ramifications of God's death sink in, all traditional moorings will be lost. It will be as though a sponge has "wipe[d] away the entire horizon," the earth has been "unchained" from the sun, and there is no longer "any up or down." Unprecedented wars and violence will break out, and the whole structure of Christian civilization will be destroyed.

Despite this sense of apocalyptic foreboding, Nietzsche saw a bright side to the death of God. With no "anti-life," sin-obsessed God to impose values and meanings, strong, clear-eyed "free spirits" will at last be free to create their life-affirming values and meanings, and an exciting new world will open up.

SEE ALSO Perspectivism (1882), The Revaluation of Values (1887), Atheistic Existentialism (1946)

A c. 1910 drawing created from an iconic photograph of Friedrich Nietzsche.

Perspectivism

Friedrich Nietzsche (1844–1900)

Nietzsche uses the term *perspectivism* to describe his general view of truth and knowledge. Exactly what Nietzsche's perspectivism amounts to is one of the most vexing questions in Nietzsche scholarship, but certain features of his view are clear.

First, Nietzsche views reality as a chaotic flux of "becoming" that we turn into something intelligible by imposing categories such as thing, substance, permanence, object, cause, and attribute. The world, he tells us, "is a mere fiction, constructed of fictitious entities." It follows that there is no perspective-independent "real world" and that there cannot be any objective or absolute truths in the sense of beliefs or statements that correspond to "the way things really are," independent of human perceptions and categorizations. "There are no facts," as he famously puts it, "only interpretations."

Second, Nietzsche supports his perspectivist view by connecting it to his idea of "the will to power." Nietzsche believed that human beings, and indeed all forms of life, are driven by a restless desire to survive, to grow, to enlarge and discharge their powers, and to dominate others. Inevitably, Nietzsche argues, the will to power shapes the way we perceive reality. As a species, we have adopted a commonsense worldview as divided into more or less enduring "things" because we have found this useful in the struggle for survival. As individuals, we adopt various interpretations of reality as "a means of becoming master over something." All seeing and knowing is thus seeing and knowing from a certain vantage point that is significantly shaped by the will to power. Therefore, even if there was a "real world," there could be no objective or perspective-free knowledge of it, because all human attempts to make sense of the world must operate through "lenses" that are fashioned by our will-to-power-driven interests, needs, values, and so forth. These, of course, vary from person to person and culture to culture.

Nietzsche never worked out his perspectivism into a clear and systematic theory. What he does say raises lots of fascinating questions. Many twentieth-century postmodernists, pragmatists, and feminists were influenced by Nietzsche's perspectivism and developed his ideas in various directions.

SEE ALSO "God Is Dead" (1882), Power/Knowledge (1975), Postmodernism (1979)

Napoleon with his Staff, *by Dutch painter Charles Rochussen, c. 1840–1850. Nietzsche considered Napoleon to be one of the "highest human beings," an exemplar of self-mastering the "will to power."*

The Revaluation of Values

Friedrich Nietzsche (1844–1900)

Nietzsche was an iconoclast about ethics. He denied that there are any moral facts, rejected the idea of any objective or universal moral standards, and argued for a "revaluation of all values" in light of the "death of God." He often described himself as an "immoralist" for his radically unconventional views. Just what did Nietzsche's immoralism amount to?

In his sketchy but fascinating 1887 "history" of morals, *On the Genealogy of Morality*, Nietzsche identifies two types of morality: master morality and slave morality. In ancient times, particularly in Homeric Greece and during periods of Roman history, the dominant morality was master morality. This was a noble, aristocratic ethical code that prized virtues like courage, strength, cunning, pride, self-confidence, love of life, love of beauty, self-overcoming, and contempt for the inferior herd. As Nietzsche tells it, this master morality was attacked and largely replaced by a greatly inferior approach to ethics that he calls slave morality or herd morality. Examples of slave morality include Judeo-Christian ethics and utilitarianism. Slave morality is designed to protect "the herd," that is, the weak and powerless, from exploitation by the strong. For this reason, it prizes virtues that smooth social life and promote collective happiness like kindness, humility, pity, benevolence, meekness, hard work, law-abidingness, justice, and equality. Because of the long dominance of Christianity, slave morality in the West has also long-valued religious virtues such as chastity, self-denial, anxious concern for the purity of one's thoughts, contrition, hostility to pleasure and to the senses, and generally a preoccupation with the next life and a contempt for this one.

When Nietzsche says that we should "revaluate all values," what he mainly means is that we should thoroughly reexamine prevailing slave-morality ethical standards. Many of those standards, he believed, make no sense once we recognize that there is no God and no afterlife. For the strong, what Nietzsche calls "us free spirits," maybe some of the old master morality values would be more life affirming and lead to greater forms of excellence. With God out of the picture, he says in *The Gay Science*, the horizon at long last "appears free to us again." "The sea, our sea, lies open again; perhaps there has never been such an 'open sea.'"

SEE ALSO "God Is Dead" (1882), Perspectivism (1882)

"Master morality" and "slave morality" in ancient Rome as exemplified in a relief showing warrior nobles and slave workers, from Trajan's Column, erected in Rome by Emperor Trajan in 113 CE.

The Principles of Psychology

William James (1842–1910)

Though William James is best remembered today as a philosopher, his two-volume work, *The Principles of Psychology* (1890), is widely considered to be his masterpiece. Into it James poured all his polyglot scientific learning, his artistic sensibility, and his immense vitality. Never before had science read so much like literature. For decades it was the most influential text in American psychology and can still be read with interest and profit.

James was born in New York, the oldest child of a wealthy and eccentric father, Henry James Sr. After receiving an MD from Harvard Medical School, James taught anatomy and physiology at Harvard before switching to psychology. Toward the end of his career, James worked mainly in philosophy, publishing such classic works as *The Will to Believe, and Other Essays in Popular Philosophy* (1897), *Pragmatism: A New Name for Some Old Ways of Thinking* (1907), and *The Meaning of Truth* (1909). After more than a century, his *Varieties of Religious Experience* (1902) is still one of the best introductions to the psychology of religion.

According to the historian of psychology Gardner Murphy (1895–1979), James's *Principles* "burst upon the world like a volcanic eruption." Among the things that excited the most interest were its metaphor of consciousness as a "stream," kaleidoscopic and ever changing, an activity rather than a thing or substance; its theory of emotions, the so-called James-Lange theory, which views emotions as aftereffects of physiological reactions; and its eloquent discussion of habit as "the fly-wheel of society," the foundation of social stability and personal success. "Sow an action," he later wrote, "and you reap a habit; sow a habit and you reap a character; sow a character and reap a destiny."

Always a student of human potential and an advocate of what he called "the strenuous life," James peppered the *Principles* with wholesome exhortations aimed at younger, impressionable readers. For example, he urged such readers to "keep the faculty of effort alive in you by a little gratuitous exercise every day. That is, be systematically ascetic or heroic in little unnecessary points . . . so that when the hour of dire need draws nigh, it may find you not unnerved and untrained to stand the test."

SEE ALSO "The Will to Believe" (1897), *The Varieties of Religious Experience* (1902), *Pragmatism* (1907)

A c. 1890 photograph of William James.

"The Will to Believe"

William James (1842–1910)

William James's "The Will to Believe" is probably the most widely read essay on the ethics of belief ever written. It has been both widely praised and widely criticized, and it has been interpreted in sharply conflicting ways.

In some ways, James's argument can be seen as a new and improved version of Pascal's famous wager argument for belief in God. Pascal argued that we should "bet" that God exists, even if it seems highly unlikely that he does, because we have everything to gain if we bet right and little or nothing to lose if we bet wrong. James rejects Pascal's argument, mainly because it licenses a kind of wishful thinking that James believes is both morally and intellectually indefensible. According to James, however, something close to Pascal's Wager, suitably modified, can be defended.

James's basic strategy is to drastically limit the kinds of cases in which Pascal-like appeals to self-interest are legitimate. James imposes two kinds of restrictions: First, the choice between the relevant betting options must be intellectually undecidable. That is, there cannot be compelling evidence in favor of either option. Second, the choice must be what James calls a "genuine option." A genuine option, as James defines it, is one that is "momentous" (has great personal significance), "living" (you could sincerely believe or disbelieve it), and "forced" (you have to "bet" whether you wish to or not). James argues that, for many people, belief in God (or what he somewhat nebulously calls "the religious hypothesis") meets all these conditions. Such people, James argues, have an intellectual and moral right to believe in God even though they have no compelling evidence that he exists.

James's argument was directed in part against certain militant agnostics of his day, including the English mathematician William Kingdon Clifford, who boldly pronounced that "it is wrong always, everywhere, and for anyone to believe anything on insufficient evidence." Whether James succeeds or not in showing that there is a right to believe in God in the face of inconclusive evidence, his essay raises fascinating questions about intellectual standards and the role that evidence should play in forming our beliefs and our ultimate commitments.

SEE ALSO Pascal's Wager (1670)

Mount Ararat, a sacred site in eastern Turkey to many faiths, is said to be the place where Noah—an archetypal model of faith—brought his ark to rest, as written in Genesis.

Phenomenology

Edmund Husserl (1859–1938)

Probably the two most important developments in twentieth-century philosophy were the emergence of analytic philosophy and phenomenology. Edmund Husserl was the father of phenomenology, and for this reason he is one of the most important philosophers of the last century.

Husserl was born in Prossnitz (Prostějeov), in what is now the Czech Republic; his family was Jewish, though Husserl later became a Protestant. Trained as a mathematician, Husserl switched to philosophy after studying with Franz Brentano (d. 1917) in the mid-1880s at the University of Vienna. Husserl went on to teach philosophy at various German universities, including Göttingen and Freiburg. His most important work, *Logical Investigations*, was published in two volumes in 1900–1901. Later books, such as *Ideas* (1913), *Formal and Transcendental Logic* (1929), and *The Crisis of European Sciences and Transcendental Phenomenology* (1936), refined his phenomenological method, sometimes in ways that branched off in quite new directions from his earlier thought.

Husserl believed that philosophy should be a strict science and based on ideas that are absolutely certain. Like Descartes, Husserl found his crucial starting point in our own conscious awareness. Philosophy, he argued, should employ the method of phenomenology. Essentially, this means a careful and precise introspective study of mental phenomena (sensations, concepts, feelings, imagined objects, etc.), without presupposing that any objects of awareness actually exist outside the mind. As Husserl famously put it, for philosophical purposes we should "bracket" the whole issue of whether our minds grasp true reality and focus instead on how reality *appears* to us. This allows philosophy to draw conclusions that are 100 percent certain, even if skeptics are right that what we call reality might be some kind of illusion. Like Brentano, Husserl believed that all thought is "intentional," that is, directed toward some object. We can thus distinguish the object of thought (what Husserl called the *noema*) from the act of consciousness itself (the *noesis*). Both aspects of consciousness can be studied phenomenologically. When we do so we discover "essences" that express necessary features of acts and objects of consciousness. For Husserl, phenomenology is primarily concerned with the study of essences and of the most general features of human thought.

SEE ALSO Intentionality (1874), *Being and Nothingness* (1943), *The Phenomenology of Perception* (1945)

A portrait of Edmund Husserl, by German painter Rudolf Stumpf.

Environmental Preservationism

John Muir (1838–1914)

The beginning of the twentieth century saw the dawn of a new way of thinking about wilderness and the environment. The prophet of that movement was John Muir.

Born in Scotland and raised on a farm in Wisconsin, Muir fell in love with wild nature from an early age. A mostly self-taught naturalist and inventor, Muir moved to California after the American Civil War, where he spent years joyously tramping the Sierra Nevada Mountains before settling down as a prosperous fruit grower and successful writer. In 1892, alarmed by the damage loggers and ranchers were doing to the California wilderness, Muir cofounded the environmental group the Sierra Club. As Muir grew older, his concern for the environment deepened. This was reflected in his 1901 book, *Our National Parks*, where he argued for a radically new approach to wilderness that later came to be called "preservationism."

Preservationists believe that large tracts of wilderness and other areas of scenic natural beauty should be set aside and allowed to remain as much as possible in pristine natural condition. Preservationists see nature as having value for its own sake and not simply as a resource for human use or consumption. This is very different from "conservationism," a view Muir had previously embraced, which seeks to conserve natural resources and manage wild places sustainably in order to maximize long-term human benefit.

Strongly influenced by the American transcendentalists Henry David Thoreau (d. 1862) and Ralph Waldo Emerson (d. 1882), Muir saw nature as a "window opening into heaven, a mirror reflecting the Creator." Majestic natural places, like California's Yosemite Valley, were literally holy "temples," far grander than the feeble constructions of humankind.

Though Muir stressed the intrinsic value of nature, he also believed that humans have an inborn need for wild places and natural beauty. As he wrote in one of his last essays: "Everybody needs beauty as well as bread, places to play in and pray in, where Nature may heal and cheer and give strength to body and soul alike."

SEE ALSO The Birth of Romanticism (c. 1760), American Transcendentalism (1836), *Walden* (1854)

John Muir, c. 1902, photographed in his "temple," nature.

The Varieties of Religious Experience

William James (1842–1910)

William James was not a fan of organized religion, finding all the formal paraphernalia of religion (creeds, theologies, etc.) to be "absurd." Yet he was sympathetic to the religious impulse and believed that our "true end" and "most important function" is to live in harmony with a higher spiritual Reality. In his most popular work, *The Varieties of Religious Experience* (1902)—which he originally delivered as twenty Gifford Lectures (a prestigious annual series of philosophy lectures) in Scotland—James offers a classic psychological analysis of "the divided self," repentance, conversion, regeneration, saintliness, mysticism, and other forms of religious experience.

In writing *Varieties*, James collected an amazing array of firsthand accounts of religious experiences. James's Harvard colleague, George Santayana (1863–1952), complained that James had gone "on a slumming tour" by focusing too much on "sick souls." James's goal, though, was not simply to describe religious experiences but to build what James expert Gerald Myers (1924–2009) calls a "testimonial . . . to the good that religious belief can accomplish in people's lives."

Although the great bulk of *Varieties* is devoted to psychological analysis of religious experiences, James does put on his philosopher's hat at the end of the book to draw some tentative conclusions about what religious experiences might tell us about human nature and the universe. The conclusion that best fits, James argued, is that "the conscious person is continuous with a wider self," a kind of "mother sea" of consciousness, "through which saving experiences come." Given all the pain and evil in the world, James believed that this superhuman consciousness was limited in power, knowledge, or both. This means that God cannot guarantee that all will turn out well in the end, but it does provide a basis for hope. According to James's meliorism, the world can become a better place if we freely cooperate with God in trying to improve it. We might still all go down in flames, but at least we can do so in the spirit of Henry IV of France (quoted by James in "The Will to Believe"): "Hang yourself, brave Crillon. We fought at Arques, and you were not there."

SEE ALSO Mystical Theology (c. 1300), "The Will to Believe" (1897)

This stained glass window in the Basilica of the Sacred Heart of Jesus in Zagreb, Croatia, shows Jesus blessing St. Margaret Mary Alacoque, a seventeenth-century French nun. James discusses her in The Varieties of Religious Experience *as someone whose devotion to the Sacred Heart was so intense that it "[expelled] all human loves and human uses."*

Ethical Intuitionism

George Edward Moore (1873–1958)

English philosopher G. E. Moore is one of the giants of twentieth-century philosophy. Together with Bertrand Russell (d. 1970), he launched a powerful campaign against idealism and in favor of realism. In epistemology, Moore argued vigorously for a "commonsense" approach to questions of knowledge. His method of doing philosophy by means of clear and painstaking conceptual analysis did much to inspire modern analytic philosophy. And in moral philosophy, his 1903 book *Principia Ethica* served as a foundational text for twentieth-century ethics.

Born in Upper Norwood, London, Moore studied classics and philosophy at Trinity College, Cambridge, where he later taught for most of his career. Among his distinguished colleagues at Trinity were Russell and Ludwig Wittgenstein (d. 1951). For over a quarter of a century he edited the prestigious philosophy journal *Mind*. In *Principia Ethica*, Moore claims that the key question of ethics is, What is good? One common answer is to identify goodness with some natural property, such as pleasure or happiness. Moore argues that all naturalistic theories of this sort are false. Any attempt to equate goodness with some natural property is a mistake that Moore famously dubs the "naturalistic fallacy." (Exactly what the mistake is, or even whether it is a mistake, is disputed.) If "good" just means "pleasure," for example, then it would be true by definition to say "What is pleasurable is good," which it clearly is not. All attempts to define goodness in naturalistic terms succumb to "open question argument." No matter what definition is proposed, it will be an open question whether the definition is correct. This shows that the claimed equivalence doesn't hold.

Generalizing these arguments, Moore claims that goodness can't be defined. "Good" denotes a simple, unanalyzable, nonnatural property. So how can we determine what things are intrinsically good? By intuition: We employ a "test of isolation." Imagine if that thing were the sole reality, existing in complete isolation from anything else. Would it still be good? If so, it is intrinsically good. When we employ the test of isolation, Moore argues, we can intuit that the greatest intrinsic goods are those of personal affection and aesthetic experience. This made Moore very popular with the Bloomsbury Group of artists and writers, many of whom were Moore's friends.

SEE ALSO The Moral Sense (1725), Deontological Intuitionism (1930)

Moore believed that one of the greatest intrinsic goods is personal affection, noting in Principia: *"Bears do not love; but the reason is they do not know the sweets of friendship." Here,* Life Was Made for Love and Cheer, *1904, a loving portrait of friends and family by American illustrator Elizabeth Shippen Green.*

The Analytic-Continental Split

George Edward Moore (1873–1958)

Broadly speaking, there are two quite different styles of doing Western philosophy today: analytic philosophy and continental philosophy. Partly, this is a difference in writing styles: analytic philosophers tend to prize argumentative clarity and rigor, whereas continental philosophy is frequently dense and obscure. More substantively, analytic philosophers generally rely more heavily than continental philosophers do on logic and conceptual analysis, are less historically oriented in the way they approach philosophy, are more intellectually aligned with science and mathematics, and tend to focus less on what American philosopher Brian Leiter (b. 1963) calls "actual political and cultural issues and, loosely speaking, the human situation and its 'meaning.'" The analytic-continental split began with the dense philosophical prose of Kant and Hegel, but it has widened since the beginning of the twentieth century. A leading figure in pushing the two traditions further apart was the British philosopher G. E. Moore.

Moore did three things that encouraged the growth of analytic philosophy. First, he tried (not always successfully) to be painstakingly clear in the way he wrote philosophy. Second, he employed the method of "conceptual analysis" in a way that struck many philosophers as quite fruitful. Finally, he launched an attack on idealism (the view, roughly, that all reality is spiritual) that convinced many Anglo-American philosophers to embrace realism rather than any of the idealist systems that were then popular on the continent, especially in Germany and France (hence the name "continental philosophy").

When Moore first began studying philosophy, Hegelian-style absolute idealism was the dominant philosophical approach at most British universities. In 1903, Moore published a landmark paper titled "The Refutation of Idealism." Moore claimed that all arguments for idealism rest explicitly or implicitly on the principle that *esse est percipi* (to be is to be perceived), which Moore tried to refute. Many philosophers, including Moore's friend and colleague Bertrand Russell (d. 1970), found his arguments convincing. The effect, Russell said, was like the breaking of a spell. "It was an intense excitement," Russell wrote, "after having supposed the sensible world unreal, to be able to believe again that there really were such things as tables and chairs."

SEE ALSO To Be Is to Be Perceived (1713), The Rise of British Idealism (c. 1865)

A photocrom of Trinity College, Cambridge, c. 1900, when George Moore was in the fellowship program there working on Principia Ethica.

The Theory of Definite Descriptions

Bertrand Russell (1872–1970)

How can we make sense of sentences that seem to refer to nonexistent things like unicorns and round squares? In his classic 1905 paper "On Denoting," influential British philosopher Bertrand Russell proposed an ingenious solution that was widely seen as a paradigm of twentieth-century analytic philosophy.

Consider the two sentences "The present King of France is bald" and "The present King of France is not bald," both of which contain what philosophers call a "definite description," that is, a phrase of the form "the so-and-so" that seems to pick out just one individual or object. As Russell noted, it seems to follow from a basic principle of logic—the so-called principle of excluded middle—that one of these sentences must be true. Yet how could either be true given that there is no present King of France, bald or otherwise? Russell refused one possible solution he had previously accepted: to say that there are nonexistent beings to which phrases like "the present King of France" refer. Such a solution, he believed, would result in an unnecessarily bloated ontology. His new solution was to rewrite sentences that seem to refer to nonexistent beings in such a way that they can be straightforwardly false. Thus, he suggests, "The present King of France is bald" can be rewritten as "There is somebody or other of whom it is true that (a) he is a present King of France, (b) nobody else is a present King of France, and (c) he is bald." This sentence no longer seems to refer to a nonexistent entity, the present King of France, as its subject. Instead, it asserts the existence of a person who possesses the *attributes* of being the one and only present King of France and being bald. Such a statement is false, as is the supposedly contradictory statement that "The present King of France is not bald." Thus, Russell argued, by utilizing the methods of logical analysis and modern logic, we can preserve the principle of excluded middle, avoid an overcrowded ontology, and hang on to our commonsense judgment that neither "The present King of France is bald" nor "The present King of France is not bald" is true.

SEE ALSO The Analytic-Continental Split (1903), *The Problems of Philosophy* (1912), Logical Atomism (1918)

Bertrand Russell in a classroom at the University of California at Los Angeles, where he taught from 1939 to 1942.

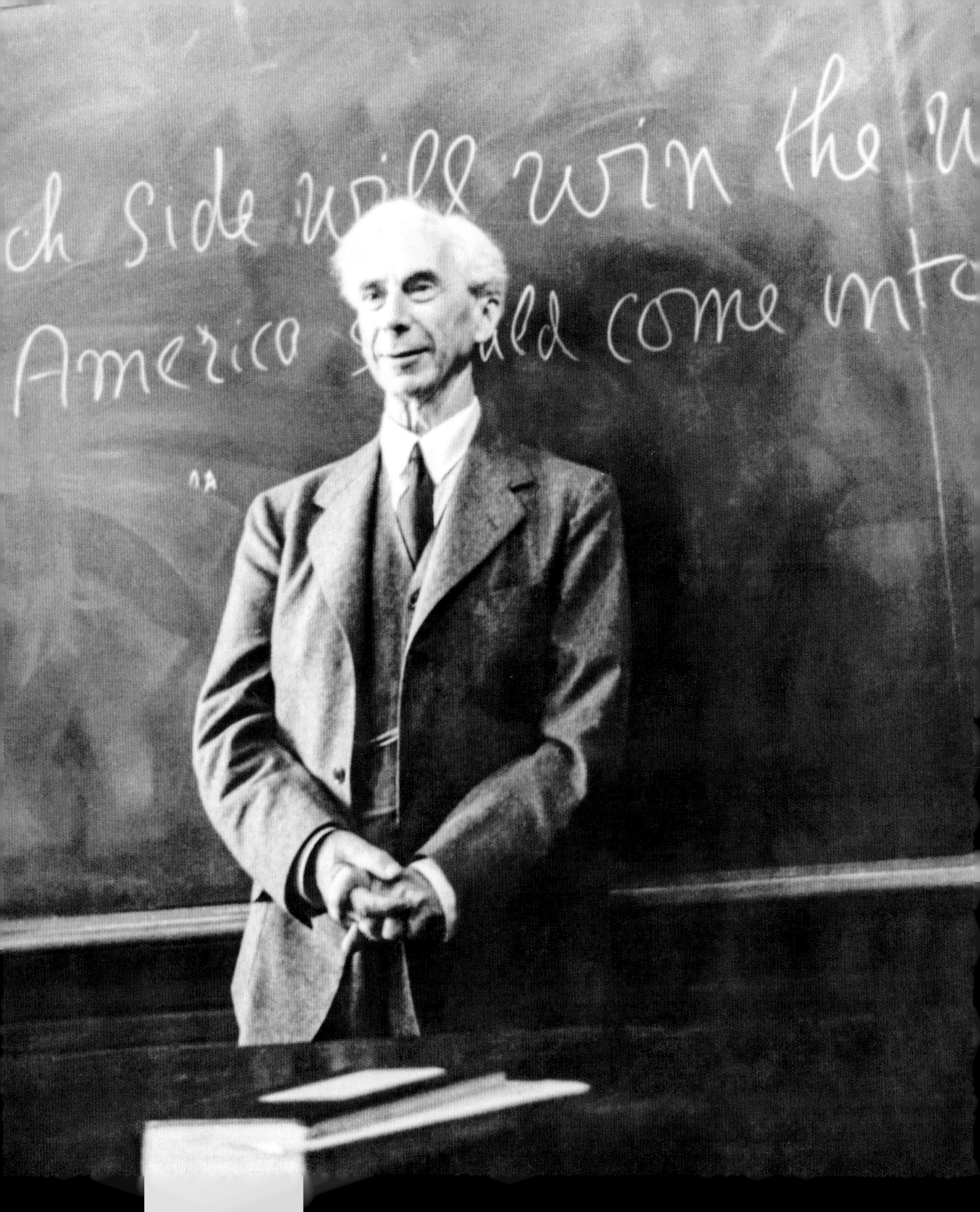
side will win the
America
come

Pragmatism

William James (1842–1910)

Though pragmatism was the brainchild of C. S. Peirce (d. 1914), it was first popularized by William James in his 1907 book *Pragmatism: A New Name for Some Old Ways of Thinking*. Like Peirce, James embraced a pragmatic theory of meaning. He wrote:

> To attain perfect clearness in our thoughts of an object . . . we need only consider what conceivable effects of a practical kind the object may involve. . . . Our conception of these effects, whether immediate or remote, is then for us the whole of our conception of the object, so far as that conception has positive significance at all.

In this sense, pragmatism is a method of clarifying our ideas and also a method of settling philosophical disputes that might otherwise be interminable. Some philosophical disputes can be dismissed as pointless, because nothing of practical significance rides on the outcome, or because on inspection they can be seen to have no practical consequences at all. So far, Peirce would agree, though with one major difference: when James talks about "practical effects" he includes personal reactions and emotional responses, whereas Peirce focuses on general ways that ideas could conceivably influence behavior. There is another important difference between Peirce and James. For James pragmatism is more than a theory of meaning; it is also a theory of truth. He rejects the idea of objective truth. In James's folksy metaphors, an idea is true if it "works," if it has significant "cash-value" in experiential terms. James never succeeded in making altogether clear what he means by such expressions. But it is evident that he is thinking primarily of the way certain parts of our experience can validate others. "True ideas," he writes, "are those that we can assimilate, validate, corroborate and verify." He adds: "Any idea upon which we can ride, so to speak; any idea that will carry us prosperously from any one part of our experience to any other part, linking things satisfactorily . . . is true for just so much, true in so far forth, true instrumentally." Peirce rejected James's pragmatic theory of truth and suggested that his own version of pragmatism be renamed "pragmaticism." Such an ungainly term, he said, "is ugly enough to be safe from kidnappers."

SEE ALSO Origins of Pragmatism (1878), Instrumentalism (1925), The New Pragmatism (1979)

James compared the concept of pragmatism to the optic phenomenon of total reflection: "[Look] through the flat wall of an aquarium. . . . Every ray is totally reflected back into the depths again. Now let the water represent the world of sensible facts, and let the air above it represent the world of abstract ideas. Both worlds are real, of course, and interact; but they interact only at their boundary, and the locus of everything that lives . . . is the water."

Vitalism

Henri Bergson (1859–1941)

Henri Bergson was the most influential French philosopher of the first half of the twentieth century, but few people read him today. His attack on Darwinism, his exaltation of intuition at the expense of scientific intelligence, and his vague and metaphorical style of writing set him at odds with the prevailing currents of late-twentieth-century philosophy. Nevertheless, he remains a notable philosopher, both for his influence on philosophers and writers in his day, and for his protests against mechanistic views of nature and human existence.

Bergson was born in Paris, the second child of a Polish Jewish father and an English Jewish mother. As a high school student, Bergson excelled at math. When he decided to switch to philosophy, his disappointed math teacher exclaimed, "You could have been a mathematician; you will be a mere philosopher." Bergson went on to become the most famous philosopher in France, and perhaps in the entire world. In his greatest work, *Creative Evolution* (1907), Bergson rejected Darwin's view of evolution as a blind materialistic process and argued instead for a goal-directed, spirit-driven conception of evolution. In 1927, he was awarded the Nobel Prize in Literature.

Bergson had important things to say about notions like time and duration, analysis versus intuition, and the sources of morality and religion, but what he is best remembered for is his process-centered view of reality and his vitalist account of evolution. Bergson believed that reflection on our own inner experiences reveals the existence of a vital impetus at the heart of the self's ceaseless process of becoming. A similar impetus—what he called the "élan vital"—is present in all life, and this vital force is what makes evolution a creative process leading to increasingly higher and more complex forms of life. Like contemporary defenders of intelligent design, Bergson denied that materialistic science could ever explain how life could have originated by pure chance or how evolution could work simply by the method Darwin proposed: natural selection operating on random variations of traits. In his final work, *The Two Sources of Morality and Religion* (1932), Bergson links the élan vital with God and argues for a mystical, love-driven view of cosmic evolution.

SEE ALSO Darwin's *Origin of Species* (1859), Process Philosophy (1929)

A portrait of Henri Bergson, 1925, by French photographer Henri Manuel.

Principia Mathematica

Bertrand Russell (1872–1970), Alfred North Whitehead (1861–1947)

Russell and Whitehead's three-volume *Principia Mathematica* (1910–1913) is one of the great achievements of twentieth-century philosophy. To a significant extent, it marked the beginning of modern symbolic logic. Yet the book almost never saw the light of day.

Principia Mathematica seeks to show (probably unsuccessfully) that mathematics can be reduced to logic, and thus is not, as Kant claimed, a kind of "synthetic" knowledge that is "necessary" only in the sense that, given the way the human mind works, it inevitably applies to all possible experience of the phenomenal world (i.e., the world as we experience it). Russell got many of the key ideas he needed to try to show that math is part of logic when he read the works of the Italian mathematician Giuseppe Peano (1858–1932) in the summer of 1900. He worked feverishly that fall with English mathematician and philosopher Alfred North Whitehead, and they completed a five-hundred-page draft of what would be *Principia Mathematica* in only three months.

At that point Russell thought it was clear sailing to complete the monumental project. Then a series of major setbacks occurred. In May 1901, he discovered a contradiction, now called "Russell's paradox," that seemed to short-circuit his proof that math is reducible to logic. Next his marriage fell apart, plunging him into blackest despair. Finally, his collaborator, Whitehead, appeared to be going mad and ran up large bills that Russell paid surreptitiously, sometimes by borrowing. During this difficult period, Russell often contemplated suicide. Then in the spring of 1905 he hit on what he thought was a solution to the contradiction that seemed to derail his attempted proof (his famous "theory of types"). From 1907 to 1910 Russell worked from ten to twelve hours a day laboriously writing out the necessary proofs. The effort left him spent; his intellect, he believed, "never quite recovered from the strain." Finally, in 1910, the first volume of *Principia Mathematica* was published. Believing that the book would incur a large loss, Cambridge University Press insisted that Russell and Whitehead pay part of the publication costs themselves. Thus for ten years of work on one of the landmark books of modern times, Russell and Whitehead earned minus 50 pounds each.

SEE ALSO The New Logic (1879), The Theory of Definite Descriptions (1905), Process Philosophy (1929)

A page from volume I of the original edition of Principia Mathematica, *published in Cambridge in 1910.*

of the type of the argument x in $\chi(x, y, z, \ldots)$, and therefore both ϕx and ψx take arguments of the same type.   Hence, in such a case, if both ϕx and ψx can be asserted, so can $\phi x . \psi x$.

As an example of the use of this proposition, take the proof of *3·47.   We there prove

$$\vdash :. p \supset r . q \supset s . \supset : p . q . \supset . q . r \tag{1}$$

and
$$\vdash :. p \supset r . q \supset s . \supset : q . r . \supset . r . s \tag{2}$$

and what we wish to prove is

$$p \supset r . q \supset s . \supset : p . q . \supset . r . s,$$

which is *3·47.   Now in (1) and (2), p, q, r, s are elementary propositions (as everywhere in Section A); hence by *1·7·71, applied repeatedly, "$p \supset r . q \supset r . \supset : p . q . \supset . q . r$" and "$p \supset r . q \supset s . \supset : q . r . \supset . r . s$" are elementary propositional functions.   Hence by *3·03, we have

$$\vdash :: p \supset r . q \supset s . \supset : p . q . \supset . q . r :. p \supset r . q \supset s . \supset : q . r . \supset . r . s,$$

whence the result follows by *3·43 and *3·33.

The principal propositions of the present number are the following:

*3·2. $\vdash :. p . \supset : q . \supset . p . q$

I.e. "p implies that q implies $p . q$," *i.e.* if each of two propositions is true, so is their logical product.

*3·26. $\vdash : p . q . \supset . p$

*3·27. $\vdash : p . q . \supset . q$

I.e. if the logical product of two propositions is true, then each of the two propositions severally is true.

*3·3. $\vdash :. p . q . \supset . r : \supset : p . \supset . q \supset r$

I.e. if p and q jointly imply r, then p implies that q implies r.   This principle (following Peano) will be called "exportation," because q is "exported" from the hypothesis.   It will be referred to as "Exp."

*3·31. $\vdash :. p . \supset . q \supset r : \supset : p . q . \supset . r$

This is the correlative of the above, and will be called (following Peano) "importation" (referred to as "Imp").

*3·35. $\vdash : p . p \supset q . \supset . q$

I.e. "if p is true, and q follows from it, then q is true."   This will be called the "principle of assertion" (referred to as "Ass").   It differs from *1·1 by the fact that it does not apply only when p really is true, but requires merely the *hypothesis* that p is true.

*3·43. $\vdash :. p \supset q . p \supset r . \supset : p . \supset . q . r$

I.e. if a proposition implies each of two propositions, then it implies their logical product.   This is called by Peano the "principle of composition."   It will be referred to as "Comp."

The Problems of Philosophy

Bertrand Russell (1872–1970)

When British philosopher Bertrand Russell published *The Problems of Philosophy* in 1912, he was already well known in academic circles for his brilliant technical contributions to philosophy, logic, and mathematics. With this book, Russell reached a much larger audience and gained fame as a writer.

The Problems of Philosophy is a gem of clear, sculpted prose, and masterly exposition. In fifteen short chapters, it introduces general readers to a range of classic philosophical problems, focusing mainly (some might say excessively) on questions of knowledge.

Although aimed at general readers, Russell's book also had a significant impact on professional philosophers. Its treatment of sense-data, universals, truth, the problem of induction, and its important distinction between "knowledge by acquaintance" and "knowledge by description" were widely discussed in the philosophical literature of the day. Perhaps even more importantly, Russell's book provided a much-admired model of how philosophy should be done.

What *The Problems of Philosophy* is best remembered for today is its eloquent defense of the value of philosophy in an increasingly practical and hardheaded age. As Russell sees it, philosophy rarely provides clear-cut answers to the questions it addresses. Its real value lies rather in its probing critical spirit and in its very uncertainty. While philosophy usually cannot provide definite answers to the big questions, it can greatly enlarge our sense of what the answers *might* be, thereby enriching our intellectual imaginations. Moreover, philosophy teaches us how little we truly know and frees us from the prejudices, false pieties, and intellectual straightjackets of our culture and our age. Finally, philosophy ennobles the human mind through the greatness of the objects it contemplates. Through the grand vistas of philosophy, we learn to see the self and all human concerns in proper perspective. As our minds expand, so do our loyalties and sympathies. We become free of all narrow hopes and fears and "become capable of that union with the universe which constitutes [our] highest good."

SEE ALSO The Analytic-Continental Split (1903), *Principia Mathematica* (1910), Logical Atomism (1918)

The title page from the first edition of The Problems of Philosophy, *published in London in 1912.*

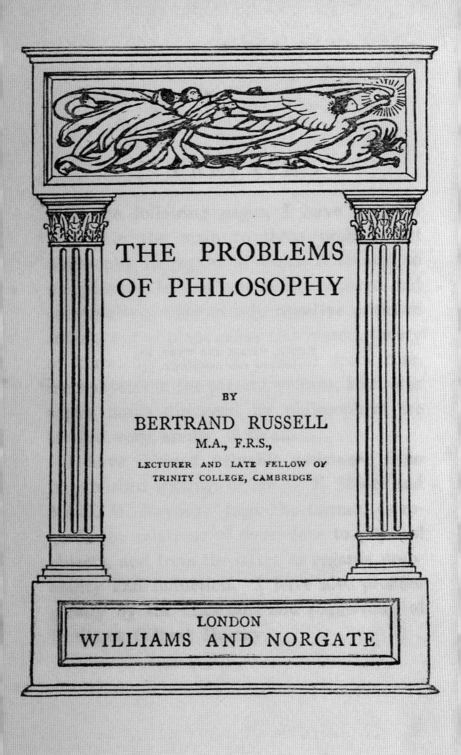

THE PROBLEMS
OF PHILOSOPHY

BY

BERTRAND RUSSELL

M.A., F.R.S.,

LECTURER AND LATE FELLOW OF
TRINITY COLLEGE, CAMBRIDGE

LONDON
WILLIAMS AND NORGATE

Progressive Education

John Dewey (1859–1952)

Schools in nineteenth-century America tended to emphasize rote learning and singsong drill. Children were treated as miniature adults by authoritarian teachers who taught them subjects that often had little connection with their home life, their community, or anything they were interested in outside of school. This began to change during the era of progressive education, which began in the late nineteenth century and reached its heyday in the 1930s and 1940s. The most important exponent of progressive education was John Dewey.

Dewey was born in Burlington, Vermont, in 1859. After receiving his PhD in philosophy from Johns Hopkins in 1884, Dewey taught philosophy and psychology at the University of Michigan, the University of Chicago, and Columbia University. A prolific but often woolly writer, Dewey published more than one thousand books and articles over his sixty-five-year-career. Currently, there is a notable revival of interest in his work as a pragmatist. But Dewey's greatest influence was in the field of education.

Dewey wrote several books on educational theory, but his magnum opus is *Democracy and Education*, published in 1916. There, Dewey criticized traditional methods of education and argued for the creation of schools that were more child-centered and democratic; that stressed critical thinking, problem solving, and active learning by doing rather than rote memorization; that bridged the gap between school and real life; and that recognized the fundamental role education plays in social progress and democratic self-governance. The ultimate aim of education, Dewey argues, is growth. A good education is one that inspires a passion for continued learning and growth, and equips students with the tools they need to achieve it.

Much of this is now part of the educational mainstream, incorporated into the lore of the pedagogical tribe. Critics, such as the "core knowledge" advocate E. D. Hirsch Jr. (b. 1928), charge that Dewey went too far. Hirsch argues that the main reason too many American students cannot read, write, or do basic math is that teachers have bought into a Dewey-inspired "thoughtworld" that emphasizes "critical thinking" and "learning to learn" over facts and essential knowledge. That such debates continue to be central to educational reform is a testament to the enduring influence of John Dewey.

SEE ALSO *Emile* and Natural Education (1762), Instrumentalism (1925)

Children in a classroom in Washington, D.C., c. 1900.

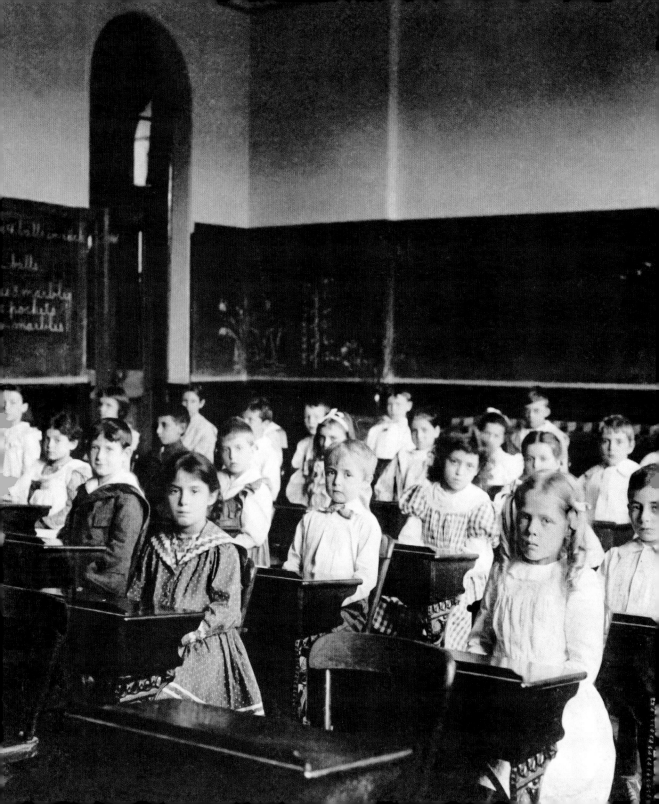

Logical Atomism

Bertrand Russell (1872–1970)

Early in 1918, shortly before he was imprisoned for his vocal opposition to World War I, Bertrand Russell gave a series of lectures in London titled "The Philosophy of Logical Atomism" (first published in the *Monist* journal in 1919 and later included in Russell's 1956 book *Logic and Knowledge*). He chose the term "logical atomism" to describe his general approach to philosophy and logic. In simple terms, what was that approach?

Since Russell's rejection of Hegel-style absolute idealism in 1898, he had embraced commonsense pluralism (the belief that many separate things exist), empiricism (all our knowledge of the world is derived from sense experience), and a commitment to Ockham's razor (entities should not be multiplied without necessity). By 1918 these principles had led Russell to adopt a bare-bones view of what is ultimately real (only simple particulars) and a method, known as "reductive analysis," for translating talk about dubious entities—such as golden mountains, numbers, and even physical objects—into talk about entities that have a more secure empirical and evidential basis. The combination of this spare ontology and the method of reductive analysis is essentially what Russell means by the philosophy of logical atomism.

Russell famously summed up his technique of reductive analysis in the slogan "Wherever possible, logical constructions are to be substituted for inferred entities." By "logical construction" Russell means an object that can be analyzed into some entity, or set of entities, that have a better grounding in direct experience, or what Russell called "knowledge by acquaintance." Consider, by way of example, talk that seems to refer to an enduring "self."

Like Hume, Russell believed that we can have no experience of a self (or soul or ego or mind) as a thing that persists through time. The self is thus what Russell calls an "inferred entity" with a dubious metaphysical status. So in his 1921 book *The Analysis of Mind*, Russell seeks to show that the self is what he calls a "logical fiction." All talk of the self, he claims, can be analyzed in terms of particular mental experiences. Elsewhere, Russell uses a similar principle of ontological parsimony to reduce math to logic, numbers to classes of classes, physical objects to events, and so forth.

SEE ALSO The Analytic-Continental Split (1903), The Theory of Definite Descriptions (1905), *Principia Mathematica* (1910)

An illustration of Bertrand Russell by James Francis Horrabin that appeared in the February 1917 issue of the Ploughshare, *a monthly journal by the Socialist Quaker Society.*

Bertrand Russell

Contemplation vs. Enjoyment

Samuel Alexander (1859–1938)

Samuel Alexander was an important early-twentieth-century metaphysician. In his major work, *Space, Time, and Deity* (1920), Alexander attempts to work out a realist and naturalistic metaphysics that fits with modern science and an empiricist approach to knowledge. In developing his system, Alexander made an important distinction between two sorts of mental acts that he calls "contemplation" and "enjoyment." Several later thinkers picked up on this distinction, including C. S. Lewis (1898–1963), who adapted it in his Christian apologetics by invoking a related distinction between "having an experience" (enjoyment) and "thinking about that experience" (contemplation).

Alexander was born in Sydney, Australia, and educated at Balliol College, Oxford, where he absorbed the reigning neo-Hegelianism of Oxford philosophers such as Thomas Hill Green (d. 1882) and F. H. Bradley (d. 1924). In 1882, he became the first Jew ever elected to an Oxford fellowship. In 1893, Alexander was elected to a chair at the University of Manchester, where he taught for the rest of his career.

According to Alexander, space-time is the ultimate reality and the matrix out of which all things flow. Much influenced by evolutionary theory, Alexander presents a picture of an "emergent universe." Out of space-time and its most general and pervasive features (identity, existence, relation, causality, and so forth) emerge empirical properties of matter, consciousness, and such "tertiary qualities" as truth and goodness. The next highest emergent quality that will arise from cosmic evolution is God, which Alexander speaks of both as a present reality (the universe as containing the seeds, as it were, of divinity) and as a future emergent. The essence of religion, he claims, is the aspiration people naturally feel for this emerging higher reality.

In defending his realist metaphysics against idealist objections, Alexander sharply separates acts of knowing from objects that are known. He marks this distinction by saying we "contemplate" objects outside the mind and "enjoy" our own acts of awareness. In knowing an object outside the mind (e.g., a tree) there is a relation between our minds and an object external to our minds. There is no such cross-border subject-object relationship when we reflect on our own mental acts; then the mind interacts only with itself, creating a different sort of awareness.

SEE ALSO Vitalism (1907)

Contemplating a tree, an object external to our minds; a photomontage by Danish photographer Yuri Arcurs.

Neo-Thomism

Étienne Gilson (1884–1978), **Jacques Maritain** (1882–1973)

In 1879, Pope Leo XIII published an encyclical, *Aeterni Patris* (*Eternal Father*), praising Thomism (the philosophy and theology of St. Thomas Aquinas [d. 1274]) and urging that it have a central role in Catholic education and intellectual life. The encyclical inspired a major revival of medieval Scholasticism in Catholic thought that is known as neo-Thomism, or neo-Scholasticism. The two most prominent neo-Thomists were the French philosophers Étienne Gilson and Jacques Maritain.

Gilson was born in Paris and educated at the Sorbonne. Following World War I, in which he fought with distinction, Gilson taught medieval philosophy at various French universities and cofounded the Institute of Medieval Studies at the University of Toronto. Through his many publications and frequent lecture tours, Gilson achieved fame as a medieval historian and philosopher. For decades he argued tirelessly for the superiority of Thomism over forms of modern thought and for a kind of faith-guided approach to philosophy he called "Christian philosophy."

Jacques Maritain was also born in Paris. Raised as a Protestant, he converted to Catholicism in his mid-twenties under the influence of prominent Catholic writer Léon Bloy (1846–1917). Author of more than sixty books, Maritain applied Thomistic principles to fields ranging from art and education to epistemology and ethics. In politics, Maritain argued for a view he called "integral Christian humanism," which recognizes the spiritual element of human beings and sees natural rights as rooted in natural law. This approach informed his work as one of the drafters of the United Nations' Universal Declaration of Human Rights (1948).

Prior to the Second Vatican Council (1962–1965), Thomism had a powerful influence on Catholic higher education worldwide. It was required curriculum at most American Catholic colleges and universities, and a great majority of philosophy instructors at Catholic universities during this period professed to be Thomists. This prompted Australian philosopher John Passmore (1914–2004) to comment ruefully in 1957 that "neo-Thomism has no serious rival except [Marxist] dialectical materialism." Since the Catholic Church relaxed its official endorsement of Thomism in the 1960s, the number of Thomistic philosophers has declined significantly.

SEE ALSO The Great Medieval Synthesis (c. 1265), The Silver Age of Scholasticism (c. 1525)

Pope Leo XIII—whose encylclical Aeterni Patris (Eternal Father) *advocated Thomism—depicted in a print published in New York in 1878.*

c. 1920

POPE
LEO
XIII.

1878

The Picture Theory of Language

Ludwig Wittgenstein (1889–1951)

Few philosophers can boast that their ideas radically altered the course of philosophy. Yet Wittgenstein did this twice, and in markedly divergent directions. Many contemporary philosophers consider him to be the greatest philosopher of the twentieth century.

Wittgenstein was born in Vienna, where his father owned the largest iron and steel works in Austria. Trained as an engineer, Wittgenstein became interested in the foundations of logic and mathematics after reading the works of Russell (d. 1970) and Frege (d. 1925). After studying with Russell at Cambridge, Wittgenstein served in the Austrian army during World War I. He wrote his great early work, the *Tractatus Logico-Philosophicus* (1921), while serving on active duty. After the war, Wittgenstein worked as a gardener and schoolteacher before returning to Cambridge, where he taught philosophy for the rest of his life. His most important book, *Philosophical Investigations* (1953), was published two years after his death.

The *Tractatus* is a strange and exciting work, written in staccato, numbered propositions, often of oracular obscurity. Its central theme is that language mirrors reality. The world is composed of facts, not things. True propositions are logical pictures of facts. All meaningful propositions must have a precise logical structure. Meaningful propositions are either "atomic" sentences (sequences of simple names) or "molecular" sentences (elementary propositions linked together by logical connectives such as "and" or "or"). Statements of ethics, religion, aesthetics, and philosophy itself are meaningless, because there are no corresponding facts for those statements to picture. It follows that the sentences of the *Tractatus* are themselves nonsensical, as Wittgenstein concedes. Having arrived at a correct view of language and logic, readers of the *Tractatus* could throw away the ladder on which they climbed. Philosophy is thus an attempt to say the unsayable. What is most important in life—values, meanings, "the mystical"—cannot be expressed in language. And "what we cannot speak about we must pass over in silence."

A decade or so after publishing the *Tractatus*, Wittgenstein concluded that most of its main ideas were wrong. Language was much more complex than he had thought. This became the theme of Wittgenstein's later period, which culminated in his second great work, *Philosophical Investigations*.

SEE ALSO *Philosophical Investigations* (1953)

An Austrian stamp from 1989 commemorating the one-hundredth anniversary of the birth of Ludwig Wittgenstein.

I and Thou

Martin Buber (1878–1965)

Martin Buber is one of the most important Jewish philosophers and religious thinkers of the twentieth century. Born in Vienna into an Orthodox Jewish family, Buber was strongly influenced as a youth by Kant (d. 1804) and Nietzsche (d. 1900), as well as by Hasidic Judaism, a branch of Jewish mysticism that arose in Eastern Europe in the eighteenth century. After teaching for many years at Frankfurt am Main, Buber moved to Israel, where he taught at Hebrew University from 1938 to 1951. In 1923, he published his most important book, *I and Thou* (*Ich und Du*), which has become a modern religious classic.

According to Buber, human personhood arises from relation. There are two primary relations: the I-It and the I-Thou. The "self," or the "I," comes into existence and determines itself by the way it engages in these two primary relations. The usual way of relating to things is in the I-It mode. This is the way of using, experiencing, and observing persons and things; it is marked by a subject-object split and is instrumentalist, objectivizing, and lacking in true mutuality. While indispensable, the I-It mode of relationship is not the primary human or spiritual relationship. Real knowledge of another person must be dialogical; it requires openness, participation, empathy, and genuine encounter. This is a unique kind of personal knowledge that can never be adequately expressed by words. It is ineffable, for all speech presupposes a subject-object split, which is transcended in the holistic mutuality of the I-Thou relationship.

According to Buber, we face an existentialist and spiritual crisis today because of the increasing dominance of I-It relations. This makes impossible not only any genuine human community but also any true spiritual life. As a person, the Eternal Thou, God, cannot be known through objectifying I-It modes of relatedness. In fact, God is the one Reality that can never become an It. True openness and mutuality can never be forced. Only when we open ourselves to God and risk commitment can we encounter the Eternal Thou. Such encounters don't require any sacred places or mediating institutions, but occur whenever we embrace the sacredness of the ordinary and everyday; "if you hallow this life you meet the living God."

SEE ALSO Existentialism (1843), Existential Defiance (1942), Atheistic Existentialism (1946)

Martin Buber photographed in 1963 arriving at Amsterdam Airport; he was in the city to receive the Erasmus Prize, a prestigious Dutch award, for his work.

1923

Instrumentalism

John Dewey (1859–1952)

Dewey was a pragmatist in the tradition of Charles Sanders Peirce (d. 1914) and William James (d. 1910), but his version of pragmatism included a few new twists. Dewey called his form of pragmatism "instrumentalism" to highlight his view that ideas and theories are tools to help us make sense of reality and to cope successfully with life's challenges. The practical, instrumental function of thought is a prominent theme in Dewey's most important work, *Experience and Nature* (1925).

Unlike Peirce and James, Dewey was a naturalist who believed that nothing supernatural exists and that every aspect of human existence must be explained in naturalistic (especially biological and evolutionary) terms. Dewey was also an empiricist who refused to recognize the existence of things like objective moral values or Kantian things-in-themselves that lack a clear warrant in experience. For this reason, Dewey rejected the traditional correspondence of truth, the view that a statement or belief is true just in case it "fits the facts" or "matches up with the way reality really is." Dewey agreed with James that the idea of "the way reality really is" is an empty placeholder, because we have no way to compare our beliefs about reality with mind-independent reality itself. Like James, Dewey claimed that the only empirically warranted concept of truth is of that which "works" in human experience. True ideas are those that help us solve problems effectively, lead to higher values and meanings, and have been verified by experience. Late in life, Dewey scrapped talk of "truth" altogether and spoke instead of "warranted assertions." The term "truth," he believed, was too bound up with false metaphysical assumptions to be useful.

If truth, or "warranted assertibility," is what works, then thought has a practical function. Ideas, theories, and methods of inquiry should be seen as tools that may be more or less effective in helping us cope with problems and render our experience of the world richer and more coherent. In this vein, philosophy too should be regarded as a tool. Its main purpose, Dewey contended, was to contribute to the solution of practical problems and to improve the human condition.

SEE ALSO Origins of Pragmatism (1878), *Pragmatism* (1907), Progressive Education (1916)

A photograph of John Dewey, c. 1920.

Being and Time

Martin Heidegger (1889–1976)

In 1927, Martin Heidegger published *Being and Time*, widely recognized as one of the most important philosophical works of the twentieth century. Heidegger's penetrating analyses of such concepts as authenticity, finitude, temporality, guilt, anxiety, and care, have become deeply embedded in contemporary philosophy. For many readers, one of the most thought-provoking parts of Heidegger's philosophy is his discussion of death.

Heidegger was born of peasant stock in the town of Messkirch in southwestern Germany. Educated in Jesuit schools, he trained to become a priest before deciding to leave the Church shortly after the end of World War I. From 1918 to 1923, Heidegger taught at the University of Freiburg, where he was strongly influenced by the phenomenological approach of his senior colleague Edmund Husserl (d. 1938). After publishing *Being and Time*, Heidegger was appointed to succeed Husserl in the chair of philosophy at Freiburg. Following the rise of Hitler, Heidegger joined the Nazi Party; as rector of Freiburg (1933–1934) he gave pro-Nazi speeches and reportedly fired Jewish professors. (The facts are disputed.) Following Germany's defeat in World War II, Heidegger was banned from teaching for several years because of his Nazi sympathies. Much of his later writing is concerned with the thought of earlier thinkers, such as Kant (d. 1804), Nietzsche (d. 1900), and the pre-Socratics. He is buried in the town cemetery of his native Messkirch.

Heidegger notes that humans relate to death differently than do other animals. We know that we will die, and in fact know that we can die at any moment. Finitude, negation, and precariousness is thus built into human existence, and our path through life is inherently a kind of "being-towards-death." For many people, death is a deeply uncomfortable and even taboo subject; our typical response is one of denial, avoidance, and an averted gaze. Moreover, it is easy to objectivize death and regard it as a fact outside ourselves; death is something that happens to "other people." Yet Heidegger argues that accepting death can enhance the human quest for meaning and authenticity. Knowing that our time on earth is limited and that each breath might be our last makes every moment precious and lends depth and "resoluteness" to our lives.

SEE ALSO Phenomenology (1900), *Being and Nothingness* (1943)

Martin Heidegger in a portrait from c. 1927.

Religion as Wish Fulfillment

Sigmund Freud (1856–1939)

Even though Sigmund Freud was a psychiatrist rather than a philosopher, his influence on philosophy has been enormous. His views on the unconscious, psychoanalysis, dream interpretation, the Oedipus complex, repression, sublimation, and the constraints of civilization on humankind's unruly primitive instincts have been extensively discussed by philosophers. Though Freud's reputation has declined dramatically over the past few decades, many of his ideas have more than simply historical interest. One is his claim that religion is an illusion rooted in wishful thinking.

Freud defends this view of religion most fully in his short, hard-hitting book, *The Future of an Illusion* (1927). Earlier thinkers, most notably Feuerbach (d. 1872), had argued that God is a projection of idealized human traits and that religious belief results from human fears and wishes. Freud supplements Feuerbach's critique with a psychological explanation drawn from his own theory of childhood development.

Freud was an atheist who thought that belief in God rested on "feeble grounds" and was "patently infantile." Why is it then that so many intelligent people continue to hold religious beliefs? Freud's answer is that religion survives because it is rooted in something deeper and more primal than reason: human wishes and fears. As Freud sees it, religion gets much of its psychological grip from events in our childhood. "Biologically speaking," Freud writes, "religiousness is to be traced to the small human child's long-drawn-out helplessness and need of help." As children, we're grateful for the protection of our parents, particularly our strong, loving fathers, who can somehow make everything come out all right. As adults, we also confront fears and insecurities. We find ourselves in a cold, implacable world; we hunger for meaning, security, consolation, justice, life beyond the grave. These deep-seated wishes and fears, Freud suggests, explain why so many cling to religion, despite its lack of rational support.

Freud's psychological explanation of religion has drawn many responses. One of the most interesting was offered by C. S. Lewis (d. 1963), the noted Christian apologist. Lewis suggested that even if religion is rooted in wishful thinking (which he denied), God might have implanted in us a deep desire for Himself. In that case, wishful thinking might be one of God's ways of leading us home.

SEE ALSO Idealism Is Turned Upside Down (1841), "God Is Dead" (1882), The New Atheists (2004)

A portrait of Sigmund Freud, in a detail from 50-schilling Austrian banknote.

Process Philosophy

Alfred North Whitehead (1861–1947)

The twentieth century was marked by hostility toward speculative metaphysics in th[e] grand style of, say, Leibniz (d. 1716) or Hegel (d. 1831). But it did produce one nota[ble] exception: the system of process philosophy propounded by the British mathematic[ian] and philosopher Alfred North Whitehead. Whitehead had a long and distinguished career as a mathematician and philosopher of science at Cambridge and the Unive[rsity] of London before moving to Harvard at age sixty-three to teach philosophy. It was th[ere] that Whitehead wrote his most important philosophical works, including his magn[um] opus, *Process and Reality* (1929).

Whitehead believed that the fundamental realities in nature are processes or eve[nts] not substances. His work argues that treating substances as the ultimate constituents o[f] reality leads to skepticism and fails to fit with modern science, especially relativity the[ory.] In Whitehead's process-based philosophy the basic realities are what he calls "actual entities." These are processes of becoming that develop into unities by unconsciously "prehending" (taking account of) actual entities that are in the immediate past. He ca[lls] this unifying process of absorption "concrescence" (literally "growing together"). Wha[t we] call "things" are "societies" of actual entities, bound together in a nexus of prehension[s.] This view reflects his core belief that "connectedness is the essence of all things."

Whitehead's metaphysics also gives an important role to God and to nonphysical entities that he calls "eternal objects." By "eternal objects" Whitehead means qualitie[s] such as redness or roundness. He calls such qualities "possibilities," because they are eternal and can be instantiated in the future even if they are not in the present. (Even [if] nothing is red now, there could be something red tomorrow.) According to Whitehea[d] actual entities become what they are by choosing some particular "eternal object." Eternal objects imprint their character on actual entities, which gives them a definite [set] of properties. Whitehead rejects the traditional notion of God as an all-powerful creat[or.] God operates by love, not coercion. Though God contains within himself all eternal possibilities, he does not impose those possibilities upon actual entities, but rather use[s] them as "lures" to greater harmony and creativity. God is thus "the poet of the world," tenderly "leading it by his vision of truth, beauty, and goodness."

SEE ALSO *Principia Mathematica* (1910)

Whitehead calls qualities such as redness or roundness "possibilities" because they're eternal and can be manifested in the future even if they aren't in the present. Even if nothing is red now (e.g., a poppy bud), th[ere] could be something red tomorrow (a poppy flower.)

An Idealist View of Life

Sarvepalli Radhakrishnan (1888–1975)

Sarvepalli Radhakrishnan is widely recognized as the most important twentieth-century Indian philosopher. Deeply versed in Western philosophy, Radhakrishnan offered a sophisticated defense of a form of Hindu idealism against a variety of Western challenges. Through his magisterial two-volume *Indian Philosophy*, commentaries on sacred Hindu texts, a noted anthology on Indian philosophy coedited with American professor Charles A. Moore (1901–1967), and an active public life as a representative of Hindu thought, Radhakrishnan was a major bridge-builder between East and West. Perhaps the fullest statement of his philosophical views is contained in *An Idealist View of Life* (1929).

Radhakrishnan was born in southern India and educated in Christian schools and at Madras Christian College. After receiving his master's degree in philosophy in 1908, Radhakrishnan taught at a number of universities, including Calcutta and Oxford. After India achieved its independence in 1947, Radhakrishnan entered politics and served as president of India (1962–1967). Like Shankara, the great ninth-century Indian philosopher, Radhakrishnan was an exponent of Advaita Vedanta and believed that there is one Supreme Reality (Brahman, or the Absolute) and that that Reality is spiritual. He was thus what philosophers call a monistic idealist. Yet Radhakrishnan modified some of Shankara's views, holding, for example, that the empirical world is not simply an illusion, and that a personal god is a genuine aspect of the Absolute. God and the physical world are not simply deceptive appearances; "the one reveals itself in the many."

Radhakrishnan offers a number of arguments to support his monistic idealism, but his basic appeal is to a form of direct spiritual perception that he calls "intuition." Quoting extensively from mystical writers in both the East and the West, Radhakrishnan argues that spiritual intuition is a higher and self-validating form of knowing. Through intuition we can directly perceive the unity of all things in Supreme Reality. Achieving such an enlightening and liberating vision is not easy, however; it requires ethical and spiritual discipline. "To know the truth," he says, "we have to deepen ourselves and not merely widen the surface." Toward this end, we must subdue our passions through severe self-discipline and seek a transfigured life through intense aspiration and regular meditation.

SEE ALSO Monism (c. 810), The Beginnings of German Idealism (c. 1795), The Rise of British Idealism (c. 1865)

Sarvepalli Radhakrishnan in New York, 1963, during his term as the second president of India.

Deontological Intuitionism

William David Ross (1877–1971)

In the early decades of the twentieth century, utilitarianism was the dominant ethical theory in Anglo-American philosophy. However, there were powerful critics of utilitarianism. One of the most important was the Oxford classical scholar W. D. Ross. He was the leading Aristotle scholar of his day, but he also made significant contributions to ethics. In his two major works on ethics, *The Right and the Good* (1930) and *Foundations of Ethics* (1939), Ross lays out an attractive form of deontological, or duty-centered, ethics. Unlike Kant's (d. 1804) deontological ethics, which claims there is only one basic moral principle, Ross argues that there are a cluster of fundamental ethical principles. These basic moral principles are "immediately apprehended," or intuited, by all persons of developed moral consciousness. For this reason, Ross's theory is a form of deontological intuitionism.

Ross claims that reflection on moral experience reveals that there are seven basic moral duties: fidelity (telling the truth, keeping promises, etc.); reparation (making up for a harm one has done); gratitude (repaying a kindness); justice (distributing goods fairly and treating people as they deserve); beneficence (doing good); self-improvement (striving to be a better person); and nonmaleficence (not injuring others). Sometimes these duties conflict. For example, by keeping a promise I might wrongly harm someone. No duty is absolute; all have exceptions. All basic moral principles, therefore, state only what Ross calls "prima facie duties." They specify actual moral obligations only if they are not overridden by more weighty duties.

Like Aristotle (d. 322 BCE), Ross denies that there is any simple recipe for making good moral decisions. Ethics is too complicated to be reduced to an algorithm or a catchphrase. Still, many critics have complained that Ross's ethical theory is not terribly helpful. How do we know that there are seven, and only seven, basic moral duties? By intuition. How do we decide which of two conflicting prima facie moral duties is more important? By intuition. This prompted British ethicist G. J. Warnock (1923–1995) to complain that Ross's theory "seems deliberately, almost perversely, to answer no questions, to throw no light on any problem." This may be excessively harsh, but does point to a real weakness in Ross's ethics.

SEE ALSO The Categorical Imperative (1785), Ethical Intuitionism (1903)

The first page of the table of content from Ross's Foundations of Ethics; *the contents of the book were originally delivered as Gifford Lectures at the University of Aberdeen from 1935 to 1936.*

CONTENTS

I. INTRODUCTORY

II. NATURALISTIC DEFINITIONS OF 'RIGHT'

Ordinary Language Philosophy

Gilbert Ryle (1900–1976)

Anglo-American philosophy took a "linguistic turn" in the twentieth century. Thi
took many forms, from Bertrand Russell's method of rewriting problematic senter
in his theory of definite descriptions, to G. E. Moore's practice of conceptual ana
to Wittgenstein's stress on close attention to the complexities of language as a cur
for philosophical confusions, to the microscopic analyses of ordinary-language ter
characteristic of J. L. Austin and other members of the so-called Oxford school of
ordinary language philosophy. Trying to pinpoint an exact date for the beginning:
ordinary language approach that came to dominate postwar Anglo-American phil
is somewhat arbitrary, but Gilbert Ryle's classic paper "Systematically Misleading
Expressions" (1932) is certainly one important early milestone.

Ryle was born in Brighton, the son of a well-to-do doctor. After graduating fron
Oxford in 1924, he taught philosophy there until 1968; he was elected Waynflete P
of Metaphysical Philosophy in 1945. Ryle was an advocate for a modest, stripped-do
view of philosophy, claiming at one point that the "sole and whole function" of phi
is the exposure of bad philosophical theories that result from linguistic confusions.
his important books are *The Concept of Mind* (1949) and *Dilemmas* (1954).

In "Systematically Misleading Expressions," Ryle tries to show how philosophe
have often been misled by careless attention to language. As Russell noted, stateme
like "unicorns do not exist" have led some philosophers to think that such sentence
be about some "entity" such as "the idea of a unicorn" or even about a subsistent be
such as the unactualized essence of a unicorn. One task of philosophy is to get rid c
dubious "entities" by reformulations that make no reference to them. The same tec
can be applied to what Ryle calls "quasi-ontological statements" such as "Mr. Pickw
is a fictional character." This doesn't mean that Mr. Pickwick exists in some mysteri
sense and that he has the property of "being a fictional character." It has to be transl
into some complex statement about Dickens or his novel *The Pickwick Papers*. In th
Ryle was an important forerunner to the Wittgensteinian view that the only job of tl
philosopher is to show the confused philosophical "fly" the "way out of the fly-bottl

SEE ALSO The Analytic-Continental Split (1903), The Theory of Definite Descriptions (1905), *Philosophical Investigations* (1953), Oxford Ordinary Language Philosophy (1962)

What does the statement "unicorns do not exist" really mean? This stone unicorn adorns a fountain at L Palace, a royal residence in Scotland dating back to the twelfth century.

The Rejection of Metaphysics

Rudolf Carnap (1891–1970)

Rudolf Carnap was a major figure in twentieth-century philosophy. In fact, in the highly regarded *Encyclopedia of Philosophy* (1967), the entry on him is longer than those on such important figures as Sartre and Dewey. Most of Carnap's contributions are too technical to discuss in a work such as this, but it is important to note the prominent role he played in shifting interest away from traditional areas of philosophy and toward questions of logic and language.

Carnap was born in Ronsdorf, Germany; attended the University of Jena, where he studied the foundations of mathematics with Frege (d. 1925); and served for three years as a German soldier in World War I. After receiving his PhD in philosophy from Jena in 1921, Carnap taught for several years in Vienna, where he was a leading figure in the Vienna Circle (see page 394). Fleeing the Nazis, Carnap moved to America in 1935, teaching for many decades at Chicago and UCLA, and publishing groundbreaking work in fields such as modal logic, probability theory, semantics, and inductive logic. Today he is best remembered for such early works as *The Logical Syntax of Language* (1934) and *Philosophy and Logical Syntax* (1935), both of which argued for an extremely narrow conception of the proper task of philosophy.

Carnap was a strict empiricist and logical positivist who believed that traditional philosophy was pretty much bankrupt. As he saw it, philosophers should be concerned solely with "logical analysis," by which he meant primarily the clarification of scientific language. All meaningful sentences about reality, he held, are either directly or indirectly verifiable. Since statements in metaphysics and ethics fail this test, Carnap rejects these as legitimate areas of philosophy. Metaphysical statements "are neither true nor false, because they assert nothing." Like music, their function is primarily expressive. This prompted Alvin Plantinga (b. 1932) in a famous lecture to quip, "It isn't known whether [Carnap] expected theology and metaphysics to supplant Bach and Mozart." Certainly it is difficult to imagine Plotinus's *Enneads* or Hegel's *Phenomenology of Spirit* ever being serious competitors to the Beatles, or even Beyoncé.

SEE ALSO Logical Positivism (1936)

Rudolf Carnap, c. 1950.

Logical Positivism

Alfred Jules Ayer (1910–1989)

Many philosophical movements in the twentieth century shared a modest, deflationary view of the proper role of philosophy. One such movement was logical positivism. In Anglo-American philosophy, the chief representative of logical positivism was the English philosopher A. J. Ayer.

Ayer was born in London and educated at Eton and Christ Church, Oxford. From 1932 to 1933, he lived in Vienna, where he studied with members of the Vienna Circle, a group of like-minded philosophers, scientists, and mathematicians who rejected metaphysics and embraced a militant form of empiricism much influenced by David Hume (d. 1776). Members of the Vienna Circle described themselves as logical positivists. The core doctrine of logical positivism was a revolutionary principle known as the "verifiability criterion of meaning." According to this principle, all meaningful statements about reality must in some way be verifiable through observation or experience. The logical positivists wielded the verification principle like a double-sided battle-ax to hew down whole forests of what they saw as metaphysical, theological, and ethical nonsense.

When Ayer returned to London in 1933, he began work on a book that would introduce logical positivism to English-speaking philosophers. The book, titled *Language, Truth and Logic*, was published in January 1936. Brash, hard-hitting, and beautifully written, it remains the classic manifesto of logical positivism.

The book made a splash not only for its complete rejection of metaphysics and theology, but also for its uncompromising defense of an "emotivist" view of ethics. According to Ayer, ethical statements such as "Stealing money is wrong" cannot be literally true or false and in fact are "cognitively meaningless." Their purpose is not to state facts but to express and arouse feelings.

Later in his distinguished career, Ayer conceded that there were serious problems with some aspects of logical positivism. Critics noted, for example, that the verification principle cannot be verified according to its own lights. However, in the heady days following publication of *Language, Truth and Logic*, Ayer was brimming with self-confidence. When asked what he would do next, Ayer mischievously replied, "There's no next. Philosophy has come to an end. Finished."

SEE ALSO Emotivism (1944), Falsifiability in Science (1959)

A photochrom of the University of Vienna, from c. 1900, the stomping ground of the Vienna Circle, whom Ayer studied with from 1932 to 1933.

Nausea

Jean-Paul Sartre (1905–1980)

Jean-Paul Sartre is one of the few philosophers who produced both first-rate work aimed at professional philosophers and literary works such as novels, plays, and essays that enjoy wide popular acclaim. Sartre was the leading representative of existentialism following World War II. One of his most powerful literary presentations of existentialist themes is in his 1938 novel, *Nausea*.

Sartre was born in Paris, where he experienced a lonely and unhappy childhood. After training at the École normale supériere to be a teacher, Sartre taught philosophy at various schools in Le Havre, Laon, and Paris. In 1929, Sartre met Simone de Beauvoir (1908–1986), who became his lifelong partner despite many "contingent loves." Bored with his work as a teacher, Sartre began writing in the mid-1930s and within a decade had become one of the best-known authors in France. His masterwork, *Being and Nothingness* (1943), offers an analysis of consciousness and "Being" (reality, existence) utilizing the phenomenological method of Edmund Husserl (d. 1938). After the war, Sartre became increasingly active in Marxism and radical French politics.

The main character in *Nausea* is Antoine Roquentin, a thirty-year-old writer and intellectual. Friendless and out of touch with his family, Roquentin is living in Bouville (Mud Town) writing a biography of an obscure eighteenth-century nobleman. One day while walking at the waterfront, Roquentin picks up a pebble to throw in the sea. He looks closely at it and feels a wave of disgust at its bare existence. As time passes, he finds himself increasingly overwhelmed by feelings of nausea, vertigo, anxiety, and depression. One day, when staring at the gnarled, slug-like roots of a chestnut tree, he realizes that what is causing these feelings is existence itself. As an atheistic existentialist, Roquentin sees reality as absurd, meaningless, irrational, *de trop* (unwelcome), and radically contingent. As the book closes, Roquentin sits in a café listening to a favorite song. He feels a stab of joy and realizes that in art there is a productive freedom that transcends the contingency of existence and allows one to partially wash away "the sin of existing." He abandons the biography he has been working on and thinks about writing a novel.

SEE ALSO Existential Defiance (1942), *Being and Nothingness* (1943), Atheistic Existentialism (1946)

Jean-Paul Sartre at a café in Paris during the 1960s.

Existential Defiance

Albert Camus (1913–1960)

Albert Camus was a novelist, playwright, essayist, and journalist. Was he also a philosopher? He denied it, saying his work was in some ways an attack on philosophy. Yet he published two nonfiction books—*The Myth of Sisyphus* (1942) and *The Rebel* (1951)—that engage closely with the works of Kierkegaard, Nietzsche, Sartre, and other philosophers, and he expounds at length what Sartre called an "absurdist philosophy" of life. Whatever label one attaches to him, Camus's ideas are worth discussing both for their intrinsic interest and for the impact they had on philosophical discussions in the aftermath of World War II.

Camus was born in Algiers, North Africa, and grew up in poverty after his father was killed in World War I. In 1942, he published a novel, *The Stranger*, which became a classic of existentialist literature. Two other major novels followed: *The Plague* (1947) and *The Fall* (1956). In 1957, he won the Nobel Prize in Literature. He died in a traffic accident in 1960 at age forty-six.

As a philosopher, Camus is best remembered for his passionate and insightful discussions of the meaning of life and "the absurd." As an atheist, Camus believed that human existence is absurd because the universe is indifferent and fails to satisfy unquenchable human desires for hope, justice, meaning, and escape from death. This does not mean, however, that we must yield to despair. Camus referred to the Greek legend of Sisyphus, who was condemned by the gods to spend all eternity rolling a rock up a hill, only to have it roll back to the bottom over and over again. Like Sisyphus, our lives are full of labor and futile strivings that ultimately come to nothing. But we need not accept our fate; we can revolt. In Camus's retelling of the myth, Sisyphus triumphs over the gods by finding joy and meaning in the hopeless labor to which he has been condemned. He scorns the gods, says yes to life, and lives passionately in full consciousness of the futility of all things. In this way, Sisyphus becomes the "absurd hero" and a model of how brave men and women should live and die in a godless universe.

SEE ALSO Existentialism (1843), *Nausea* (1938), *Being and Nothingness* (1943), Atheistic Existentialism (1946)

Sisyphus, c. 1548–1549, by Titian.

Being and Nothingness

Jean-Paul Sartre (1905–1980)

Jean-Paul Sartre's *Being and Nothingness* (1943) is a long and difficult book. Though framed as an examination of the fundamental modes of being, its central theme is human freedom. The passion that simmers beneath Sartre's painstaking philosophical analyses reflects the dark days in which the book was written. Two years before *Being and Nothingness* was published, Sartre had been released from a German POW camp and formed a resistance group in Paris. Daily he faced discovery and death. Later, Sartre remarked to his French readers that "we were never more free than during the German occupation." Then, the true human condition, the inescapability of freedom and responsibility, stared men and women in the face. The upshot of Sartre's dense philosophical prose is this simple message: choose.

In *Being and Nothingness*, Sartre engages in what he calls phenomenological ontology. His purpose, he says, is to use Husserl's (d. 1938) method of phenomenological reduction to "describe in an exhaustive manner the relation of man to being" as it appears in consciousness. Upon analysis, being can be seen to take three chief forms: being-in-itself (nonconscious, objective reality), being-for-itself (human consciousness), and being-for-others (our being considered as an object for others). Pure being, being-in-itself, when stripped of all the categorizations imposed by the human mind, appears as a kind of opaque plenum: simple, undivided, and above all contingent, "without reason for being." It is consciousness, being-for-itself, that divides things into specific objects and invests them with meaning. It is also consciousness that brings nothingness (negation) into the world through awareness of lacks, absences, unrealized possibilities—in short, of what is *not* actual. By means of our power of negation and our ability to confer different meanings on things, we become conscious of our own freedom. In fact, Sartre argues that conscious beings are totally free, undetermined by nature or their own past selves. The dizzying realization of one's unlimited freedom and responsibility gives rise to feelings of anguish, which many try to avoid by means of "bad faith," false excuses cooked up to deny their own freedom. As conscious beings, we are "condemned to be free."

SEE ALSO Phenomenology (1900), Atheistic Existentialism (1946)

According to Sartre, many people lie to themselves about their own realities—they exhibit "bad faith"—to try to avoid the anguish of limitless freedom and responsibility. In Being and Nothingness, *he illustrates this concept with an example of a man "playing at being a waiter in a café . . . a waiter in the mode of being what I am not." Here, a photograph of a waiter taking an order, c. 1906.*

Emotivism

Charles L. Stevenson (1908–1979)

Emotivism is a theory of moral language that emphasizes the way in which ethical terms are used to influence attitudes and to express or evoke emotions. Early versions of emotivism were defended by English semioticians Charles Kay Ogden (1889–1957) and I. A. Richards (1893–1979) in *The Meaning of Meaning* (1923), and by A. J. Ayer (d. 1989) in *Language, Truth and Logic* (1936). A more sophisticated form of emotivism was defended by Charles L. Stevenson in his 1944 classic, *Ethics and Language*.

Stevenson was an American analytic philosopher who studied with G. E. Moore (d. 1958) and Ludwig Wittgenstein (d. 1951) at Cambridge, and later taught for many years at the University of Michigan. Stevenson was sympathetic to Ayer's uncompromising brand of emotivism but believed that it needed refinement. According to Ayer, moral statements like "Stealing is wrong" are "cognitively meaningless." Their function is not to state facts or to express truths but simply to express and evoke feelings. Stevenson believed that this analysis was too crude. He noted, for example, that statements like "Amy is a good neighbor" are intended to, and do, convey some factual information. Moreover, Ayer's theory dubiously implies that there are no genuine moral disagreements, because moral statements aren't assertions that can be true or false. Stevenson proposed a fix for these problems. Typically, he argued, moral claims have both a "descriptive" and an "emotive" meaning. The descriptive meaning might be something as simple as "I approve of this" or something more complex, as when we describe someone as a "good neighbor." The emotive meaning focuses on the way moral talk is used to sway attitudes and evoke emotional responses. Moral language isn't only used to report attitudes ("I approve of this") but to direct or prescribe ("You should as well") so as to evoke favorable or unfavorable reactions to ethical issues. Because moral statements typically have both descriptive and emotive meaning, they do have factual content and can be (in part) true or false. Moreover, even when two people completely agree about the relevant facts in a moral dispute, they can disagree in "attitude" with pro and con stances. Contrary to Ayer, therefore, there can be genuine moral disagreements.

SEE ALSO Logical Positivism (1936), Prescriptivism (1952)

Stevenson believed that statements like "Amy is a good neighbor" are intended to, and do, convey some factual information. Here, a vintage commercial photograph from c. 1920s.

The Phenomenology of Perception

Maurice Merleau-Ponty (1908–1961)

When Maurice Merleau-Ponty died suddenly of a stroke at the age of fifty-three, he was widely regarded as France's leading philosopher. It was Merleau-Ponty who, together with Sartre, introduced phenomenology to French philosophers. He was also the first thinker to offer a detailed "philosophy of the body."

Merleau-Ponty was born on the west coast of France in the fortress town of Rochefort-sur-Mer, where his father served as an artillery officer. After his father's early death in 1913, Merleau-Ponty and his family moved to Paris, where as a teenager he studied philosophy at the famous École normale supériere. In the mid-1930s, Merleau-Ponty abandoned Catholicism and became increasingly interested in Marxism and German philosophy, especially the method of phenomenological "bracketing" practiced by Edmund Husserl (d. 1938), with whom Merleau-Ponty had studied in Paris. Seven years after his major work, *The Phenomenology of Perception* (1945), was published, Merleau-Ponty was appointed to the highly prestigious chair of philosophy at the Collège de France.

Merleau-Ponty rejected both Descartes's (d. 1650) mind-body dualism and a hard-core physicalistic view of human beings as mere machines. Humans are what he calls "body subjects," embodied beings that have both material and irreducibly mental aspects. Merleau-Ponty uses "perception" in a special sense to refer to subconscious, prereflective awareness of either physical objects or our own inner states. His major goal was to burrow below the level of conceptual awareness and shine a light on the most basic level of "dialogue" between mind and world. Strongly influenced by Gestalt psychology, Merleau-Ponty believed that all acts of awareness are shaped by inherent organizing and meaning-conferring structures of the human mind. Even at the most basic, preconceptual level of awareness, Merleau-Ponty claimed, we experience reality as embodied subjects situated in a world; the "lived body" at this level is not an object distinct from the knowing self, but the subject's own point of view on the world. All human experience is thus one of "being-in-the-world." All the higher functions of cognition, such as conscious thought and willing, are rooted in this preconceptual form of active embodied perception.

SEE ALSO Phenomenology (1900), *Being and Nothingness* (1943)

Maurice Merleau-Ponty, 1950.

Atheistic Existentialism

Jean-Paul Sartre (1905–1980)

On October 29, 1945, the French philosopher Jean-Paul Sartre gave a lecture titled "Existentialism Is a Humanism" before a jam-packed audience at Club Maintenant in postwar Paris. Public interest in the talk was so intense that chairs were broken and some people fainted in the overcrowded club. Published as a book in 1946 and in English translation in 1947, the lecture became a foundational text in existentialist literature.

Sartre begins by noting that there are two main camps of existentialists, Christian (e.g., Kierkegaard [d. 1855] and French philosopher Gabriel Marcel [1889–1973]) and atheistic (e.g., Heidegger [d.1976]). Sartre announces that he is firmly in the atheistic camp and fleshes out what his brand of atheistic existentialism entails. First, if God doesn't exist, then humans are "condemned to be free" and can't escape responsibility for their choices by making excuses. If there is no God, then there is no preordained essence to which we must conform; for humans "existence precedes essence." We create our own essence by choosing how to live. Moreover, if God doesn't exist, there can't be any objective values in a heaven of ideas; we must choose our own values to live by. Recognizing these facts makes us "forlorn." We feel abandoned in a world without religious consolations or rules.

We also feel "anguished" because even though we are free and choose our own values, no rational agent can make a purely individual value choice. As Kant (d. 1804) noted, moral judgments are universal in the sense that what is right for person A must also be right for any person who is in A's exact situation. This creates an anguished sense of deep responsibility when we realize that in choosing to be a certain sort of person we are also, in effect, creating an image of how others ought to be.

Finally, Sartre's brand of atheistic existentialism leads to "despair." By this Sartre means a kind of Stoic refusal to depend on anything that one cannot fully control. If people are totally free, then they can change overnight. This negates the possibility of deep human solidarity and trust. "I've got to limit myself to what I see" and (as Descartes [d. 1650] said) seek to "conquer myself" rather than the world.

SEE ALSO Existentialism (1843), *Being and Time* (1927), Existential Defiance (1942), *Being and Nothingness* (1943)

Anxiety, *by Edvard Munch, 1894.*

The Ghost in the Machine

Gilbert Ryle (1900–1976)

The traditional idea that humans possess both a physical body and a nonphysical mind or soul—a view philosophers call "substance dualism"—has fallen on hard times over the past century or so. One book that contributed significantly to this shift was Gilbert Ryle's *The Concept of Mind* (1949).

Ryle's target in *The Concept of Mind* is what he calls the "Official Doctrine" of the mind. By this he means Descartes's (d. 1650) view that humans have both a spiritual soul and a physical body, that in some mysterious way these distinct and radically dissimilar substances interact, that mental events are "private" and play out on our own interior movie screens, and that we have immediate and secure knowledge of our own minds but can only infer what is happening outside our own heads. Ryle offers a barrage of arguments against the Official Doctrine, claiming that it creates insoluble mysteries (e.g., how can mind and matter interact?); leads to skepticism and the so-called problem of other minds (if minds are private and nonphysical, how can one be sure that there are any other minds?); and results in logical problems, such as vicious infinite regresses. Ultimately, Ryle argues, dualism rests on a "category mistake." People assume that because we can talk intelligibly of different mental processes, such as willing, perceiving, and intending, there must be some entity—a spiritual soul—that performs all of these functions. This is like assuming that "the university" is somehow distinct from all its buildings, laboratories, playing fields, and so forth. There is, as Ryle famously says, no "ghost in the machine." In fact, there is no such "thing" as mind at all.

Ryle's proposed alternative to dualism was to try to explain all mental events in behavioral terms. To say, for example, that you *believe* that bears are dangerous is to talk about certain behaviors you exhibit and certain dispositions you possess (e.g., the fact that you always carry bear spray when you go camping in bear country). This view, which is called "logical (or 'analytical') behaviorism," has few fans in contemporary philosophy. The lively debate about how to make sense of mind-talk still continues.

SEE ALSO Mind-Body Dualism (c. 380 BCE), *Meditations on First Philosophy* (1641), Ordinary Language Philosophy (1932)

An illustration from the 1677 French edition of L'Homme *by René Descartes showing the coordination of muscle and visual mechanisms—the concept of a physical body and the nonphysical mind, targeted by Ryle.*

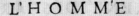

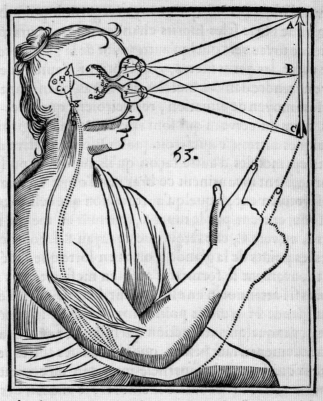

LXXVIII.
Comment
vne idée
peut estre
côposée de
plusieurs; &
d'où vient
qu'alors il
ne paroist
qu'vn seul
objet.

Et de plus, pour entendre icy par occasion, comment,
lors que les deux yeux de cette machine, & les organes de
plusieurs autres de ses sens sont tournez vers vn mesme
objet, il ne s'en forme pas pour cela plusieurs idées dans
son cerveau, mais vne seule, il faut penser que c'est tou-
jours des mesmes points de cette superficie de la glande
H que sortent les Esprits, qui tendant vers divers tuyaux
peuvent tourner divers membres vers les mesmes objets:
Comme icy que c'est du seul point b que sortent les Esprits, qui tendant vers les tuyaux 4, 4, & 8, tournent en
mesme temps les deux yeux & le bras droit vers l'objet B.

The Second Sex

Simone de Beauvoir (1908–1986)

Once widely seen as a mere satellite of her longtime companion, Jean-Paul Sartre, Simone de Beauvoir is now considered a major thinker and a significant philosopher in her own right. Her two-volume 1949 book, *The Second Sex*, has been described by academic feminist Camille Paglia (b. 1947) as "the supreme work of modern feminism."

Beauvoir was born in Paris, the eldest child of middle-class parents, and raised as a devout Catholic. She was an avid reader as a child and became an atheist at age fourteen. For many years she taught philosophy at French secondary schools before becoming a full-time writer during World War II. In 1929, she became romantically involved with Sartre, a close but nonexclusive relationship that continued until Sartre's death. She never married or had children, vowing as a young woman that "whatever happened, I would have to try to preserve what was best in me: my love of personal freedom, my passion for life, my curiosity, my determination to be a writer." Over a long career, Beauvoir published dozens of books, including a highly regarded autobiography, a major work on existentialist ethics, and the novel *The Mandarins*, which won the prestigious Prix Goncourt prize in 1954. Her most influential work, however, is *The Second Sex*, a sprawling eight-hundred-page analysis and deconstruction of the history of women's oppression. In exploring "the pervasiveness and intensity and mysteriousness" of women's subordination, Beauvoir draws upon an amazing variety of insights from biology, sociology, psychoanalysis, history, literature, economics, existentialism, phenomenology, and Marxism. Throughout the work, she argues that gender is a social construction ("one is not born, but rather becomes, woman"). Her defense of abortion, frank discussions of women's sexuality, and uncompromising critique of marriage ("marriage kills love") scandalized conventional readers in her day. In one review, the famous Catholic writer François Mauriac wrote: "We have literally reached the limits of the abject. This is the ipecac they made us swallow as children to induce vomiting."

The Second Sex remains controversial today, even among some feminists. But the book's place as a foundational text of twentieth-century feminism remains secure.

SEE ALSO *A Vindication of the Rights of Woman* (1792), *The Subjection of Women* (1869), Emergence of Feminist Philosophy (c. 1976)

Simone de Beauvoir at her desk in Paris, 1953.

Ecocentrism

Aldo Leopold (1887–1948), **Arne Naess** (1912–2009)

Over the past century or so, human attitudes toward nature and the environment have changed dramatically. Until recently, most people thought about nature in strongly human-centered terms. Nature was not viewed as having value in itself; it was something to be conquered and exploited purely for human benefit. These kinds of attitudes began to change in the 1960s when the modern environmental movement began. People then began to worry about the long-term costs of things like pollution and resource depletion to human welfare. This was an example of what the Norwegian philosopher Arne Naess terms "shallow ecology." Naess himself pleaded for a much more radical form of environmentalism called "deep ecology." Deep ecologists believe that all forms of life have value, and that humans have no right to harm other living things "except to satisfy vital needs." A view that comes somewhere in between shallow ecology and Naess's deep ecology is the ecocentric "land ethic" of Aldo Leopold. According to Leopold, humans should not regard themselves as conquerors of the biotic community on earth, but rather as plain members and citizens of it. Ethical concern should be shown not only to humans but to soils, waters, plants, animals as well—in short, to the land itself.

Leopold was born in Burlington, Iowa, and educated at Yale, where he received a master's degree in forestry. After working for the U.S. Forest Service for many years, Leopold taught game management at the University of Wisconsin. In 1935, he bought an abandoned farm in central Wisconsin and renovated a dilapidated chicken coop ("The Shack") for him and his family to live in on weekends. His great work, *A Sand County Almanac* (1949), is a lyrical expression of the joys Leopold found in the Wisconsin wilderness and in other beautiful parts of America.

Unlike supporters of animal rights, Leopold does not believe that our primary ethical concern should be with the health or welfare of individual plants or animals. Instead, we should be concerned with the good of ecological wholes, what he calls "the integrity, stability, and beauty" of entire ecosystems and species. This holistic approach to nature is now very popular in mainstream environmental theory and policy.

SEE ALSO Environmental Preservationism (1901)

Aldo Leopold sitting outside "The Shack" near the Wisconsin River, c. 1940.

"Two Dogmas of Empiricism"

Willard Van Orman Quine (1908–2000)

Since Leibniz (d. 1716), most modern philosophers have assumed that a fundamental distinction can be drawn between statements that are analytic (roughly, sentences that are true in virtue of their meanings) and those that are synthetic (true in virtue of facts about the world). In his famous paper "Two Dogmas of Empiricism," published in 1951, the American philosopher W. V. O. Quine cast doubt on the analytic-synthetic distinction and argued that no statements are immune from revision.

Quine was born in Akron, Ohio, majored in mathematics at Oberlin College, and received his PhD in philosophy from Harvard, where he studied logic under Alfred North Whitehead (d. 1947) and later taught for many decades. Strongly influenced by the strict empiricism and logical positivism of the Vienna Circle (see page 394), Quine was one of the premier philosophers of the twentieth century, making highly influential contributions to logic, philosophy of language, epistemology, and metaphysics.

The two dogmas Quine attacks in "Two Dogmas of Empiricism" are (1) that a meaningful distinction can be drawn between analytic and synthetic statements and (2) that all meaningful sentences can be translated into statements about immediate experience. What most shocked Quine's contemporaries was his attack on analyticity. Quine admitted that there are logical truths such as "No unmarried man is married." Such statements are true simply in virtue of their logical form. The same can't be said, however, for other supposedly analytic statements like "No bachelor is married." This was thought to be analytic because "bachelor" and "unmarried man" are synonymous, allowing us to reduce the statement to a logical truth of the form "A = A." The problem, Quine maintains, is that the notion of synonymy is just as obscure as the idea of analyticity, and thus can't be used to explain the latter. After puncturing several possible ways of saving the analytic-synthetic distinction, Quine argues that it should be rejected. Instead, he reasons for a view known today as "confirmation holism," wherein statements are not confirmed or disconfirmed by experience individually, but rather as a whole network of interconnected beliefs. It follows that no statements are true "come what may." As long as we are willing to make drastic changes to other parts of our belief systems, even so-called truths of reason can be rejected.

SEE ALSO Logical Positivism (1936), The Indeterminacy of Translation (1960)

Willard Van Orman Quine in academic dress at Harvard University in Cambridge, Massachusetts, where he taught from 1948 until he retired in 1978, the year this photograph was taken.

Prescriptivism

Richard Mervyn Hare (1919–2002)

What do we mean when we use ethical terms like *good* or *wrong*? In the mid-twentieth century, the two most popular answers were those offered by moral realists and emotivists. Moral realists claimed that when we say things like "The death penalty is wrong," we state something that can be true or false and attribute an objective property of wrongness to acts of capital punishment. According to emotivists, such ethical pronouncements do not state anything that can be true or false but merely express the negative feelings of the speaker—rather like saying "The death penalty! Boo!" In 1952, Oxford philosopher R. M. Hare proposed a new way of understanding ethical language. In his book, *The Language of Morals*, Hare argued that moral statements are similar to commands. They are "prescriptive" in the sense that they command and commend courses of action. Since they function much like orders, moral statements cannot be literally true or false. Hare's view, like emotivism, is thus a form of noncognitivism, since it denies the possibility of moral knowledge and the existence of objective moral truths. At the same time, Hare argued that there is a logic of moral discourse. Most important, moral judgments are "universalizable" in the sense that one cannot consistently make different moral judgments about situations where all the relevant facts are the same. This theory of moral language is called "prescriptivism."

Hare was a clear-headed, prolific, and somewhat eccentric philosopher. Born near Bristol in 1919, he was trained as a classical scholar at Rugby School and Balliol College, Oxford, before joining the British army in World War II. In 1942, Hare was captured by the Japanese in Singapore and spent three years in Burma in forced labor on the construction of the notorious Thai-Burma Railway. After the war, Hare turned to philosophy, where while teaching at Oxford and later at the University of Florida he became recognized as one of the twentieth century's most important ethicists. Besides doing influential work on the language of morals, Hare was a pioneer in the field of applied ethics. His 1981 book, *Moral Thinking*, offered a sophisticated defense of a form of utilitarianism by distinguishing different levels of ethical analysis.

SEE ALSO Ethical Intuitionism (1903), Emotivism (1944), Moral Anti-Realism (1977)

In Hare's three-part work The Language of Morals, *he devoted the entire second part to usage of the word "good." In one example, he noted that if you say "The new chamber of the House of Commons is very good Gothic revival," you are actually commending it as "preferable to most other examples of Gothic revival . . . within the class of Gothic revival buildings." Shown here is the Palace of Westminster in London, the meeting place of the House of Commons.*

Philosophical Investigations

Ludwig Wittgenstein (1889–1951)

Wittgenstein's *Philosophical Investigations* (1953) regularly tops lists of the twentieth century's most important and influential philosophy books. Its claims about the connection between meaning and use, the incoherence of the notion of a private language, the notion of rule-following, the "family resemblances" that sometimes characterize various uses of a word, and philosophy as a form of therapy aimed at "dissolving" philosophical problems rather than solving them, all had a huge impact on mid- and late-twentieth-century philosophy. But perhaps Wittgenstein's most influential idea was that of the complexity of language and the importance of what he called "language-games."

In the *Tractatus Logico-Philosophicus* (1921), Wittgenstein had defended a picture theory of meaning that saw language as having just one function: to state facts. In the *Investigations*, Wittgenstein recognized that this picture was far too simple. Language is a social practice, a "form of life," and therefore is as rich and multifaceted as human interaction itself. We use language not only to convey facts but also to pray, sing, tell jokes, give orders, ask questions, write poems, and so forth. Words are not simply name tags that we affix to things; they are more like tools in a toolbox that have a wide variety of purposes. A word like *if*, for example, does not name any object or refer to any fact; its meaning depends on context and use. This is one reason why Wittgenstein compares language to games: to emphasize how meanings are context dependent and arise only within a practice, just as individual rules about when a runner or batter is "out" make sense only within the context of the game of baseball as a whole. A second reason he compares language to games is to stress the rule-governed nature of language. What moves are allowed in chess is determined by rules, which in turn are grounded in social conventions. Likewise, Wittgenstein argues, what "moves" are allowed in language are determined by rules and conventions. Moreover, these rules and conventions vary from context to context. An expression like "stay off the grass" might mean one thing in a lawn-care seminar and quite another in a drug-counseling session. In short, the richness of language should never be forgotten.

SEE ALSO The Picture Theory of Language (1921), Impossibility of a Private Language (1953)

One of the reasons Wittgenstein compares language to games is in order to stress the rule-governed nature of language. In chess, for example, the moves that are allowed are determined by rules and conventions—much like the permissible "moves" in language.

Impossibility of a Private Language

Ludwig Wittgenstein (1889–1951)

One of the most interesting and widely debated themes in Wittgenstein's *Philosophical Investigations* (1953) concerns the impossibility of a purely private language. The topic has generated an enormous subliterature and legions of aroused partisans. But the gist of Wittgenstein's argument can be put very simply.

Wittgenstein sees language as a social, rule-governed activity. Words are context dependent and get their meanings from use, not from personal acts of naming. A private language, in Wittgenstein's sense, is a language that (1) only the speaker understands and (2) only the speaker *could* understand. Imagine trying to create such a language by a kind of mental pointing, or what philosophers call "ostension." You eat a new kind of fruit and have a mild allergic reaction that causes a new kind of butterfly sensation in your gut. Being the whimsical person you are, you call the new sensation "Toby." Wittgenstein denies that you have succeeded in creating a private language. Why?

Because nothing counts as a "language" unless it allows for a certain kind of rule-governed consistency. There must be some reliable way of recognizing recurrence, of deciding whether or not something is "the same." But no such criteria could exist with a purely private language, Wittgenstein claims. Suppose you eat a nut that causes a butterfly sensation similar to the sensation you earlier called Toby. Is it Toby or not? All you could do is try to remember what Toby felt like and compare it to the sensation you are feeling now. But the only criterion of correctness you have is whether the two sensations "seem" to be the same. This collapses the distinction between "seems right" and "is right." And that means, Wittgenstein says, that this is a case where we can't talk about "right."

Whether Wittgenstein is correct or not about the impossibility of a private language, his argument poses a deep challenge to a long tradition of philosophizing, common to both the empiricist and rationalist tradition, which views all knowledge and meaning as grounded in immediate private sensations. This is one of several ways his *Philosophical Investigations* reset the philosophical agenda.

SEE ALSO The Picture Theory of Language (1921), *Philosophical Investigations* (1953)

In Philosophical Investigations, *Wittgenstein wonders how a child could learn the word "toothache" if humans weren't able to physically display outward signs of pain. If the child then coined a name for the painful oral sensation, but no one understood the word, would she "understand the name, without being able to explain its meaning to anyone"?*

The New Riddle of Induction

Nelson Goodman (1906–1998)

The "old" riddle of induction was posed by David Hume in the eighteenth century: how can we rationally justify inductive inferences (i.e., predictions) about the future when any evidence we can offer seems to presuppose the reliability of the very method whose reliability we are trying to demonstrate? In his classic 1954 book, *Fact, Fiction, and Forecast*, the prominent American philosopher Nelson Goodman argues that Hume's riddle is a pseudoproblem. According to Goodman, particular acts of inductive and deductive reasoning are justified in exactly the same way: by showing that they fit general rules that accurately codify the sorts of inferences that, on reflection, we consider to be legitimate. But though Hume's worries were groundless, Goodman argues, there is a genuine problem about inductive reasoning that he dubs "the new riddle of induction."

As Hume pointed out, humans try to predict the future by looking to the past. We draw certain generalizations (all emeralds are green) based on past observations (all emeralds so far observed have been green) that are assumed to "confirm," or validate, the generalizations. These generalizations, in turn, are used to make predictions (the next emerald we observe will be green). But here is the problem Goodman noted: only *some* generalizations are assumed to be confirmed by observed regularities. Consider the made-up word *grue*. Something is grue if it is examined before January 1, 2030, and is green *or* is not examined before January 1, 2030, and is blue. So far every emerald we have observed has been green. We take this to support the general claim that all emeralds are green. But notice that every emerald so far observed has also been grue. In fact, we have exactly the same amount of confirming evidence for the statement "All emeralds are grue" as we do for the statement "All emeralds are green." If we accept that all emeralds are grue, we must predict that the first emerald observed after January 1, 2030, will be blue. Clearly, we would not make such a prediction. But why? Why do we "project" some descriptive terms into the future but not others? This is the new riddle of induction.

SEE ALSO The Problem of Induction (1739)

Is this emerald with a blue reflection green—or grue?

Intention

Gertrude Elizabeth Margaret Anscombe (1919–2001)

Elizabeth Anscombe made a number of important contributions to philosophy. She played a prominent role in the revival of virtue ethics; served as one of Wittgenstein's literary executors, and edited, translated, and commented upon a number of his works; and tangled with C. S. Lewis in a legendary 1948 debate at a meeting of the Oxford Socratic Club. She also made notable contributions to causation theory and in defense of Catholic doctrines such as the principle of double effect and the ban on contraception. Her 1957 book, *Intention*, is widely regarded as a classic of twentieth-century analytic philosophy.

Gertrude Elizabeth Margaret Anscombe was born in Limerick, Ireland, while her father, a British officer, was stationed there. After graduating with first-class honors from St. Hugh's College, Oxford, in 1941, she taught philosophy there from 1946 to 1970, before moving to Cambridge (1970 to 1986). A convert to Roman Catholicism, Anscombe was married to fellow philosopher Peter Geach (1916–2013), with whom she had seven children.

In *Intention*, Anscombe sets out to clarify the notion of intentional action. Most philosophers had assumed that an act is intentional only if it involves a special kind of mental act, "the intention to act in that way." Anscombe denies that intentions are psychological phenomena at all. Intentional acts are those for which a certain kind of "reason why" is appropriate. If I accidentally knock a vase off a table, it makes sense to ask what caused me to knock it off. Perhaps a loud noise startled me. But it makes no sense to ask what reason I had to knock it off, because I did not intend to do so and so had no reason. Anscombe further argues that acts can be intentional under some descriptions but not others. For instance, if I am caught driving 40 miles an hour in a 15-mile-per-hour school zone, I might sincerely plead that I did not know that I was driving that fast. However, I may have known that I was driving faster than 20 miles per hour, so the act of speeding might have been intentional in that sense. Such distinctions have practical application in fields such as ethics and philosophy of law.

SEE ALSO The Revival of Virtue Ethics (1981)

If you get a ticket for going 40 miles an hour in a 15-mile-per-hour zone, you might be sincere when you tell the police officer you didn't know you were going that fast—it was unintentional; yet you also might have known you were intentionally *going over the speed limit.*

Falsifiability in Science

Karl Popper (1902–1994)

How does science work? What is it that distinguishes science from metaphysics and pseudoscience? One popular answer in the middle third of the twentieth century was that scientific claims were verifiable, and metaphysical and pseudoscientific claims were not. This was the answer defended by A. J. Ayer (d. 1989), Rudolf Carnap (d. 1970), and other logical positivists. In 1934, this view was powerfully critiqued by a young Austrian philosopher, Karl Popper, in *Logik der Forschung*. In the book, which Popper himself translated into English in 1959 and updated as *The Logic of Scientific Discovery*, he claimed that falsifiability, not verifiability, is the true mark of science. This view strongly influenced twentieth-century philosophy of science.

Popper was born in Vienna, the son of bookish parents of Jewish descent. After receiving his PhD in philosophy at the University of Vienna, Popper taught at the University of Canterbury in New Zealand before moving to England in 1946. He taught for a quarter of a century at the London School of Economics and the University of London. Popper's 1945 book, *The Open Society and Its Enemies*, was widely hailed for its hard-hitting critique of Marxism, though many British intellectuals thought he was a bit rough on Plato. He was knighted in 1965 for his contributions to philosophy.

Popper denies that verifiability is the touchstone of science, mainly because few scientific theories can be conclusively verified. Scientific generalizations like "Copper conducts electricity" can be corroborated by extensive observational evidence, but it is always conceivable that sometime, somewhere, they will be shown to fail. Scientific knowledge, therefore, is always revisable and uncertain. The true driver of science and scientific progress is falsification, Popper claims. Scientists come up with "conjectures" (tentative hypotheses) that can be tested by observations and experiments. If the conjectures pass the observational tests, well and good; they are corroborated to that degree. The real engine of scientific progress, however, is when some long-accepted theory is disconfirmed by experience and scientists begin scurrying like beavers to plug the leak. That is why, as science-fiction author Isaac Asimov reportedly said, "the most exciting phrase to hear in science, the one that heralds new discoveries, is not 'Eureka!' but 'That's funny.'"

SEE ALSO Logical Positivism (1936)

Karl Popper poses at his home in Croydon, in South London, 1992.

Descriptive Metaphysics

Peter Frederick Strawson (1919–2006)

Metaphysics is a flourishing branch of philosophy today, but in the 1950s it was nearly on life support. One important book that helped turn the tide was P. F. Strawson's *Individuals: An Essay in Descriptive Metaphysics* (1959).

Strawson was born in London and educated at St. John's College, Oxford. After service as a captain in World War II, Strawson was appointed to a fellowship at University College, Oxford. In 1968, he succeeded Gilbert Ryle (d. 1976) as Waynflete Professor of Metaphysical Philosophy at Magdalen College, Oxford. Strawson first achieved international stature in 1950 when he published his famous article "On Referring," which critiqued Bertrand Russell's (d. 1970) iconic theory of definite descriptions. Through his many books and articles, Strawson became one of the leading philosophers in the world, helping to shift philosophy away from a narrow focus on ordinary language to a broader range of concerns. He was knighted in 1977.

In *Individuals*, Strawson distinguishes "descriptive metaphysics," which seeks to describe the basic structure of our thoughts about the world, from "revisionary metaphysics," which attempts to improve that structure. Like most of his contemporaries, Strawson distrusted revisionary metaphysics, but he was sympathetic to the broadly Kantian project of seeking to lay bare the basic concepts and categories we use in thinking about and describing the world as it appears to us. That world consists of enduring material objects that can be identified and reidentified in a unified spatiotemporal field. Strawson argues that material objects are "basic" in this framework, because other sorts of particulars, such as events, processes, and mental experiences, can only be identified by means of material objects. Also basic are persons, which Strawson claims should not be viewed as combinations of mind and body but as irreducible particulars. Persons are embodied, and as such have "material-object predicates" such as "weighs 170 pounds." But they also have "person-predicates" such as "believes that Plato was a greater philosopher than Aristotle." According to Strawson, these two logically primitive concepts—material objects and persons—are the fundamental building blocks we use to structure our experience of reality.

SEE ALSO *Critique of Pure Reason* (1781), The Theory of Definite Descriptions (1905), Oxford Ordinary Language Philosophy (1962)

Strawson claims that material objects and persons are the basic building blocks we use to structure our experience of reality. Because persons are embodied, they have "material-object predicates" such as "weighs 132 pounds." But they also have "person-predicates" such as "believes in veganism."

The Indeterminacy of Translation

Willard Van Orman Quine (1908–2000)

By the 1950s, the Harvard philosopher W. V. O. Quine was one of the greatest philosophers of the era. His 1953 book, *From a Logical Point of View*, had featured two of the most highly discussed philosophy essays of the twentieth century: "On What There Is" and "Two Dogmas of Empiricism." In 1960, Quine published his masterwork, *Word and Object*. There, Quine amplified and defended some of his earlier views, including his attack on the analytic-synthetic distinction, and also advanced some fascinating new claims, such as his celebrated argument for the "indeterminacy" of translation.

Throughout his career, Quine was a consistent naturalist and radical empiricist, with a clear inclination to behaviorism and a minimalist conception of what ultimately exists. His behaviorist side comes out strongly in his views on translation. He asks us to imagine a case of what he calls "radical translation." Suppose an anthropologist encounters a tribe that speaks a completely unknown language and wants to construct an accurate "translation manual" for translating words from their language into English. Obviously, the anthropologist would have to rely heavily on sign language and a variety of verbal and nonverbal behavioral cues, like pointing. Suppose that one day a rabbit hops across the path and a villager points and cries out "*Gavagai!*" The anthropologist would naturally assume that *gavagai* means "rabbit" (or "lo, a rabbit" or something else along those lines). But can this be known for sure? Isn't it possible that *gavagai* actually means "undetached rabbit part" or "rabbit stage" or "rabbit-appearance" or some other such thing that doesn't fit well with our usual ways of compartmentalizing reality? Would there be any definite way of ruling out such hard-to-compute meanings using only the natives' verbal and nonverbal behavioral responses? Quine argues that there wouldn't. For a naturalist like Quine, "there are no meanings, nor likenesses nor distinctions of meaning, beyond what are implicit in people's dispositions to overt behavior." Because no act of pointing or other overt behavior could settle precisely what the natives mean by *gavagai*, no single correct translation manual could be produced. Some meanings would remain indeterminate.

SEE ALSO "Two Dogmas of Empiricism" (1951)

If a hypothetical villager of a remote tribe with an unknown language pointed to this creature and yelled "Gavagai!" would an anthropologist be correct in thinking the villager meant "rabbit"?

Hermeneutics

Hans-Georg Gadamer (1900–2002)

Hermeneutics is the study of interpretive understanding, particularly the task of understanding texts. Important early work in hermeneutics was done by German thinkers such as Friedrich Ast (1778–1841), Friedrich August Wolf (1759–1824), Friedrich Schleiermacher (1768–1834), Wilhelm Dilthey (1833–1911), and Martin Heidegger (d. 1976). But without question the most important figure in contemporary hermeneutics is the German philosopher Hans-Georg Gadamer.

Gadamer was born in Marburg, in central Germany, but he grew up in Breslau (now Wrocław, Poland), where his father was a university professor. After receiving doctorates in both philosophy and classical philology, Gadamer taught at a variety of top German universities, including Marburg, Leipzig (where he served as rector), and Heidelberg. In 1923, Gadamer became a student of Heidegger, who influenced him profoundly. A late bloomer, Gadamer published his most important work, *Truth and Method*, in 1960. Aside from *Truth and Method*, virtually all of his best-known works were written after his official retirement from academic life in 1968.

Gadamer's central focus is on "descriptive" hermeneutics, the study of how interpretation actually takes place. He uses the term *interpretation* broadly to include any attempt to understand texts, works of art, and so forth. Like Heidegger, Gadamer believed that all understanding starts with "pre-understanding," a set of presuppositions and "prejudices" that we may not be explicitly aware of. Gadamer's central claim is that all interpretive understanding is tradition-bound and historically conditioned. To say, as Schleiermacher did, that we interpret a text correctly when we reproduce the mental processes of the text's author is empty, because such an understanding is impossible. We always understand the past through the lenses of the present. Those lenses, moreover, are powerfully shaped by the traditions in which we find ourselves embedded and by the socially created linguistic categories we use to make sense of our experience. All interpretive understanding, therefore, involves a "fusion of horizons" in which past and future coalesce in an active reconstruction of meaning and significance. This is a claim that continues to be front and center in current debates over interpretation.

SEE ALSO *Being and Time* (1927)

Gadamer focused on "descriptive" hermeneutics, the study of how interpretation—the attempt to understand texts, literature, works of art, and so on—takes place. Here, rows of books in the Oberlausitzische Library of Sciences in Görlitz, Germany, built in the eighteenth century.

Functionalism

Hilary Putnam (1926–2016)

As computers have become increasingly powerful, many philosophers have become intrigued with the idea of artificial intelligence. Could machines someday think and have conscious experiences? To show how this is at least conceivable, many philosophers have tried to work out materialist theories of the mind that reject any sharp distinction between mind and body. One popular theory for a while was behaviorism, which tries to explain so-called "mental" events solely in terms of outward behavior. Another widely held early theory was mind-brain identity theory, which claims that mental events are nothing but neurological events in the brain. Both of these theories, however, quickly ran into big problems. This led to a third materialist theory: functionalism. The first person to sketch out a functionalist theory of mind was the Harvard philosopher Hilary Putnam.

Putnam, who was born in Chicago and received his PhD from UCLA, has made important contributions to many areas of philosophy and is widely regarded as one of the world's greatest living philosophers. The gist of the functionalist theory Putnam first proposed in the early 1960s is this: What makes something a mental event is not any special feature of the event itself, but rather certain roles or purposes ("functions") those events serve in us. Pain, for example, might serve the functions of alerting us to bodily injury, motivating us to move to safety, helping us to avoid future injury, and so forth. According to Putnam, it is not the physical composition of a mental event that matters, but rather the functions (especially the causal functions) the event serves within the overall system. Same functions = same event. So, in principle, a Martian with a brain made out of some strange extraterrestrial material or an android with a computer as a "brain" could have exactly the same experiences of pain that we do. In short, they could think and be conscious.

Functionalism is now one of the leading theories of mind, but it faces many problems. The biggest hurdle is whether functionalist theories can account for the "subjectivity" of mental experiences. Could a computer ever really know, for example, what a pineapple tastes like? In short, it is not clear that sameness of function guarantees sameness of experience.

SEE ALSO The Ghost in the Machine (1949), Mind-Brain Identity Theory (1968), Philosophical Zombies (1991)

A contemporary interpretation of a virtual being experiencing pain, by German artist Thorsten Schmitt.

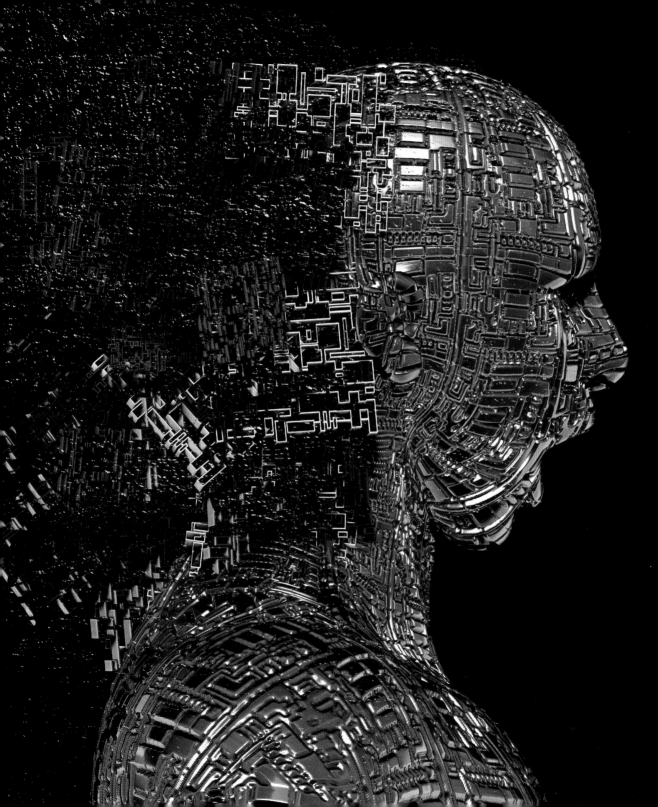

Legal Positivism

Herbert Lionel Adolphus Hart (1907–1992)

For much of the twentieth century, jurisprudence was a dry and intellectually low-wattage area of philosophy. This began to change in the 1950s and 1960s. An important catalyst in this process was H. L. A. Hart's 1961 book, *The Concept of Law*.

Hart was born in Yorkshire, the son of Jewish parents of German and Polish descent. After earning top honors in classical greats at Oxford, he practiced law for many years before returning to Oxford as a tutor in philosophy and later as professor of jurisprudence. With his expertise in both philosophy and law, Hart brought new standards of clarity and analytical rigor to the field of philosophy of law.

Although written primarily for undergraduate students, *The Concept of Law* was hailed by legal scholars as a work of groundbreaking importance. Its aim was to offer a general account of law and to elucidate the conditions under which a legal system exists. Hart also offered powerful criticisms of several influential theories of law, including classical legal positivism. He did agree with classical legal positivists, such as John Austin (d. 1859), that there is no necessary connection between law and morality. As Hart saw it, law is a human creation that may or may not align with correct moral standards. However, Hart disagreed with Austin about the nature of legal obligation. Austin saw legal duties as simply a matter of power. Laws are commands issued by rulers who have the power to punish those who disobey. Hart argued that this fails to distinguish government from a pack of lawless gunmen. Somebody who points a gun at you and says, "Your money or your life," hasn't imposed any kind of "obligation" on you. So if law isn't simply a matter of power, what is it?

Hart's answer is that law is a system of rules. Specifically, law is a union of two kinds of rules: "primary rules" that impose obligations (e.g., criminal laws), and "secondary rules" that empower officials to perform certain tasks and spell out how laws may be identified and changed. Although many critics were unconvinced by Hart's sharp separation of law and morality, *The Concept of Law* is now universally recognized as one of the great classics of twentieth-century legal theory.

SEE ALSO Natural Law (c. 1270), Law and Morality Are Separate (1832), *Taking Rights Seriously* (1977)

The entrance to the Old Bailey, the Central Criminal Court of England and Wales in London. The building's site was previously occupied by the notorious Newgate Prison, where punishment was harsh; it closed in 1902 after eight hundred years of use to make way for the present court structure seen here.

Scientific Revolutions

Thomas Kuhn (1922–1996)

Until recently, it was widely assumed by historians and philosophers of science that science advances slowly through the gradual accumulation of new facts and information. This idea was challenged in Thomas Kuhn's landmark 1962 book, *The Structure of Scientific Revolutions*. According to Kuhn, the biggest scientific advances occur quickly, by means of sweeping scientific "revolutions." After more than half a century, Kuhn's book remains one of the most-cited and influential academic books of our time.

Kuhn was a physicist by training but switched to the history and philosophy of science while teaching at Harvard in the 1950s. Later he taught at Berkeley, Princeton, and the Massachusetts Institute of Technology. When Kuhn studied big scientific changes like the Copernican revolution, he observed a common pattern. For long periods there would be little change, with most scientific work being a kind of puzzle solving within an accepted scientific theory, the reigning scientific "paradigm" as he called it. This is the period of what Kuhn dubbed "normal science." But then problems with the accepted paradigm begin to be noticed. Observations are made that conflict with the paradigm. At first these "anomalies" are swept under the rug or ad hoc modifications are made to the accepted theory to address the conflicts. Eventually, however, the anomalies become too severe and a "crisis" occurs in the scientific community. A new, competing paradigm is proposed. A battle occurs between advocates of the old and new paradigms. Neither side can produce knockdown arguments: the competing theories are "incommensurable," often there are no paradigm-neutral ways of assessing the relevant data, and it is always possible to save one's preferred paradigm by explaining away the apparent anomalies. Over time, the new paradigm prevails, not because of rationally conclusive evidence, but partly for sociological and psychological reasons that have nothing to do with the scientific data. A new period of normal science then begins, but whether the new paradigm is closer to "the truth" than the old one is a question science cannot answer.

Kuhn's book raises a host of troubling questions. Is science an objective way of knowing? Are all claims to scientific knowledge relative? Is science a more reliable way of knowing than (say) art, mysticism, or voodoo? Kuhn's work is at the center of these ongoing debates.

SEE ALSO The Birth of Modern Science (1543)

The Nicolaus Copernicus Monument in Warsaw, 1830, by Danish sculptor Bertel Thorvaldsen.

Oxford Ordinary Language Philosophy

John Langshaw Austin (1911–1960)

In the 1950s and 1960s, Anglo-American philosophy was dominated by a style of philosophizing that originated in postwar Oxford. Some call it "linguistic philosophy," others "ordinary language philosophy." I prefer the label "Oxford ordinary language philosophy" to distinguish it from the significantly different sort of vernacular-focused philosophy that Wittgenstein and his followers practiced at Cambridge in the 1930s and 1940s. The undisputed leader of the Oxford school was J. L. Austin.

Austin was born in Lancaster and was trained primarily as a classicist at Balliol College, Oxford. After serving as a high-ranking intelligence officer in World War II, Austin returned to Oxford, where he became White's Professor of Moral Philosophy in 1952. Austin published relatively little during his lifetime, preferring to devote his time to teaching and discussion. Three volumes of his papers and lectures were published after his death, including his most influential work, *How to Do Things with Words* (1962).

The brand of linguistic philosophy Austin practiced involved a minute parsing of ordinary language. In one famous paper, for example, Austin ransacks dictionaries and thesauruses to clarify the difference between justifications and excuses. (We offer a justification for an alleged wrongdoing when we claim we had good reason to do what we did; we offer an excuse when we say we were not responsible, or not fully responsible, for our act, because it was done "unintentionally," or "unknowingly," or "accidentally," or "unwillingly," or "involuntarily," etc., etc.) Austin did not claim that his method of dissecting ordinary speech is the only legitimate way to do philosophy. Nor did he claim, like Wittgenstein, that close attention to ordinary language will "dissolve" all philosophical problems. He simply believed that it was an interesting and fruitful way to do philosophy, one that can sharpen not only our awareness of words but also our perceptions of reality. Ordinary language, he believed, embodies a wealth of useful concepts and subtle distinctions. For that reason, he urged his fellow philosophers to *start* their inquiries with ordinary language, though they certainly need not end there.

SEE ALSO Ordinary Language Philosophy (1932), *Philosophical Investigations* (1953)

John Langshaw Austin at the University of Birmingham, England, August 1952, while attending the Joint Session, an annual conference of the Aristotelian Society and the Mind Association held at universities across the United Kingdom and Ireland.

The Gettier Problem

Edmund Gettier (b. 1927)

Big perplexities can come in small packages. A perfect example of this is the huge debate stirred up by American philosopher Edmund Gettier's three-page paper titled "Is Justified True Belief Knowledge?" (1963). Prior to Gettier, most philosophers had blithely assumed that they had a good understanding of what counts as "knowledge." Knowledge, they thought, consists in justified true belief. To take a simple example: Most of us would say that we know that Paris is the capital of France. This is not just something we believe; we know it. Why? Because we believe it, it is true, and we have ample justification for believing it. On the traditional account, that is all that is needed for knowledge: true belief backed up by adequate reasons or justification.

Not so fast, Gettier said. He offered two examples in which a person had justified true belief but clearly lacked knowledge. Gettier's examples are a little complicated, so consider a slightly simpler example that makes the same point. Suppose I own a baseball signed by the great Mickey Mantle. I clearly remember Mantle signing the ball for me at a Yankees game when I was a boy, so I am quite confident that I know that I own the ball. Now suppose that my house catches fire while I am on vacation and the ball is completely destroyed. At the same moment, and completely without my knowledge, I win a prize in a sports-memorabilia contest, which turns out to be a baseball signed by Mickey Mantle! At the moment, I know nothing about the fire or the memorabilia prize. What follows? It seems that I have a justified true belief that I own a baseball signed by Mickey Mantle, but I do not *know* that I do, because my belief is true only by an incredibly lucky coincidence.

Gettier's brief paper provoked a flurry of responses. Some attempted to defend the traditional account of knowledge against Gettier's criticisms, but most offered proposed "fixes" of that account. As it turned out, however, all of the fixes seemed to have fatal problems of their own. To this day, there is no agreed definition of "knowledge."

SEE ALSO Reliabilism (1979)

If you are unaware that your prized signed baseball was burnt to a crisp and you simultaneously won a ball signed by the same athlete in a contest . . . is your believing you own a baseball signed by the athlete a justified true belief?

Soul-Making Theodicy

John Hick (1922–2012)

For many people, the biggest obstacle to belief in God is the reality and pervasiveness of evil. If God is all-powerful and all-knowing, it seems that He must have the power and wisdom to prevent evil. And if He is perfectly good, it seems that He must have the desire to prevent evil. So why does evil exist?

For well over a thousand years, the standard Christian response to the problem of evil was rooted in the thought of St. Augustine (d. 430). Augustine argued that all evil is either sin or the justified punishment for sin. God rightly permits sin because of the great value He places on free will. And He justifiably permits other forms of evil, such as natural disasters and the suffering of infants and animals, because these serve as just punishment for sin. Of course, babies and animals cannot themselves sin. But Augustine argues that they still deserve punishment because of the sin of Adam and Eve. Babies inherit the original sinfulness of Adam and Eve, and animals suffer because all of nature is "fallen" as a result of original sin.

In 1966, British philosopher of religion John Hick critiqued this traditional response to the problem of evil in an important book, *Evil and the God of Love*. Hick noted that modern science has shown that animals were suffering and dying long before there were any humans on earth. Thus, it cannot be claimed that all animal pain is due to the sin of Adam and Eve. Hick also argued that a truly loving and just God would not punish innocent babies for sins committed by one of their remote ancestors.

A better response to the problem of evil, Hick argued, is to see evil as a necessary condition for "soul-making." In this view, God allows evil because it provides opportunities for moral and spiritual growth. Only by wrestling with real hardships and challenges can we perfect our characters and become the type of person God wants us to be. Since most of us fall far short of perfection in this life, Hick argues that God must allow further opportunities for soul-making in the afterlife. Ultimately, he claims, everyone will be saved and evil will be just a memory.

SEE ALSO *The City of God* (426), Hume's *Dialogues* (1779)

This dinosaur skeleton fossil with a crushed skull was discovered in a quarry in the province of Trieste, Italy, in 1994, and is approximately 70 million years old.

Deconstruction

Jacques Derrida (1930–2004)

Though Jacques Derrida is unquestionably one of the most influential French philosophers of the latter half of the twentieth century, he continues to be largely ignored by Anglo-American analytic philosophers. Partly this is due to what John Passmore (d. 2004) has described as the "jungle-like obscurity" of Derrida's notoriously dense and unconventional prose. But another reason is that Derrida attacks the very enterprise of philosophy itself, at least as most Western philosophers have conceived of that project. If Derrida is right, philosophy is a good deal like literature and should give up its "logocentric" fixation on logic, rational arguments, and general theories.

Derrida was born near Algiers in French Algeria to a family of Sephardic Jews. After moving to Paris at age nineteen, he studied and later taught at the elite École normale supérieure. In 1967, Derrida rocketed to fame when he published three books that introduced and demonstrated the concept of deconstruction: *L'écriture et la différence* (*Writing and Difference*), *De la grammatologie* (*Of Grammatology*), and *La voix et le phénomène* (*Speech and Phenomena*).

Derrida presents deconstruction as both a method of reading texts and a way of criticizing intellectual systems. As a method of reading texts, deconstruction seeks to tease out internal problems that reveal hidden contradictions and alternative meanings. As a method of conceptual critique it is primarily a technique for "destabilizing" traditional "binary oppositions," such as reason/emotion, male/female, reality/appearance, objective/subjective, truth/fiction, and so forth. One way it does this is by showing that the features that supposedly characterize the "inferior" concept are also found in the "superior" alternative. Derrida's basic critique of traditional philosophy is that it has been too logocentric in its stress on logic, rationality, and the ability of reason to penetrate to a realm of truth that exists independently of human thought and language. Western thought, he claims, has been dominated by a "metaphysics of presence" that stresses direct knowing of eternal and unchanging realities. By contrast, Derrida believes that reality can best be understood in terms of difference, elusiveness, and the "deferment" of meaning (and therefore truth) that results from the dependency of meaning on the vast interconnected web of language.

SEE ALSO Power/Knowledge (1975), Postmodernism (1979)

Jacques Derrida in Berlin, 1994.

The (Re)birth of Applied Ethics

Applied ethics is a flourishing field of philosophy today. Courses in business ethics, medical ethics, environmental ethics, and other areas of applied ethics are standard fare at universities around the world, and well-funded professionally oriented "ethics centers" dot the land. It is easy to forget what a recent development this is. Fifty years ago, ethics was essentially a dry subfield of philosophy of language, dominated by linguistic philosophers who believed that the sole task of a moral philosopher was to clarify value statements and note the many ways that ethical language differs from the gold standard of scientific discourse. All this changed in the late 1960s and early 1970s, with American philosophers leading the way.

Applied ethics is the application of ethical theories and other philosophical tools to the solution or clarification of specific moral problems, such as abortion, corporate responsibility, animal rights, and global warming. So defined, applied ethics is nothing new. Aquinas (d. 1274), for example, wrote hundreds of pages about practical ethical issues such as capital punishment, abortion, premarital sex, suicide, and the morality of war. It was only in the early and middle decades of the twentieth century that most philosophers decided it was not their job to offer advice on real-life moral issues. It did not occur to them that these issues need to be intelligently addressed and that philosophers might have special expertise that they could bring to the discussion.

What sparked the rebirth of applied ethics in the 1960s and 1970s were student demands that colleges should address the burning issues of the day, including racial discrimination, civil disobedience, sexual ethics, the legal enforcement of morality, and the Vietnam War. Notable early contributions to applied ethics include Ronald Dworkin's "On Not Prosecuting Civil Disobedience" (1968), John Rawls's "The Justification of Civil Disobedience" (1969), Judith Jarvis Thomson's "A Defense of Abortion" (1971), and Peter Singer's "Famine, Affluence, and Morality" (1972). In 1971, the journal *Philosophy & Public Affairs* was founded to provide an academic forum for the rigorous discussion of urgent social issues. That same year, James Rachels published the first anthology of applied ethics, *Moral Problems*, and the applied ethics movement was off and running.

SEE ALSO The Rise of Informal Logic (c. 1971), Emergence of Feminist Philosophy (c. 1976)

A student protest of the Vietnam War at Columbia University in New York, 1968; antiwar demonstrations were one of the sociopolitical issues that helped spark the rebirth of applied ethics in the 1960s and 1970s.

Mind-Brain Identity Theory

David Malet Armstrong (1926–2014)

Australia has produced many top-notch philosophers, including Samuel Alexander (1859–1938), J. L. Mackie (1917–1981), Peter Singer (b. 1946), David Chalmers (b. 1966), and the Scottish-born transplant John Anderson (1893–1962). David M. Armstrong certainly belongs in this distinguished company. He made important contributions to many areas of philosophy, including philosophy of mind. His 1968 book, *A Materialist Theory of Mind*, was the first systematic attempt to work out a physicalistic view of the mind that treats all mental events as reducible to physical events.

Armstrong, who was born in Melbourne and taught for many years at the University of Sydney, was a strict physicalist who believed that everything that exists is some form of matter and that everything, in principle, can eventually be explained in terms of a completed physics. A human being, he said, "is nothing but a physicochemical mechanism." In *A Materialist Theory of the Mind*, Armstrong offered a detailed account, compatible with a reductionistic materialism, of a wide range of mental states. Building on the work of British philosopher Ullin Place (1924–2000) and Australian J. C. C. Smart (1920–2012), Armstrong developed a version of what is now called "mind-brain identity theory" or, more simply, the "identity theory." (Armstrong himself preferred to call it the "causal theory" or the "central state theory.") Mental states, he argued, are simply physical states of the brain or of the central nervous system. Like Gilbert Ryle (d. 1976), Armstrong believed that mental phenomena are logically tied to behavior. A belief, for example, can be understood as an inner state that is apt for producing certain ranges of behavior in a person. Later, Armstrong came to admit that particular types of mental experiences, such as pain, cannot be strictly identified with specific types of neurophysiological events (e.g., group C nerve fibers firing). Martians, for example, might be able to feel pain, even though they have no C fibers at all. Nevertheless, Armstrong continued to hold that mental states are identical to brain states, but added that this is a "contingent identity" that can only be discovered scientifically and that may not hold in all "possible worlds." In various permutations, mind-brain identity theory remains a popular option in contemporary philosophy of mind.

SEE ALSO The Ghost in the Machine (1949), Functionalism (1960), Philosophical Zombies (1991)

An artist's rendering of neurons firing in the brain.

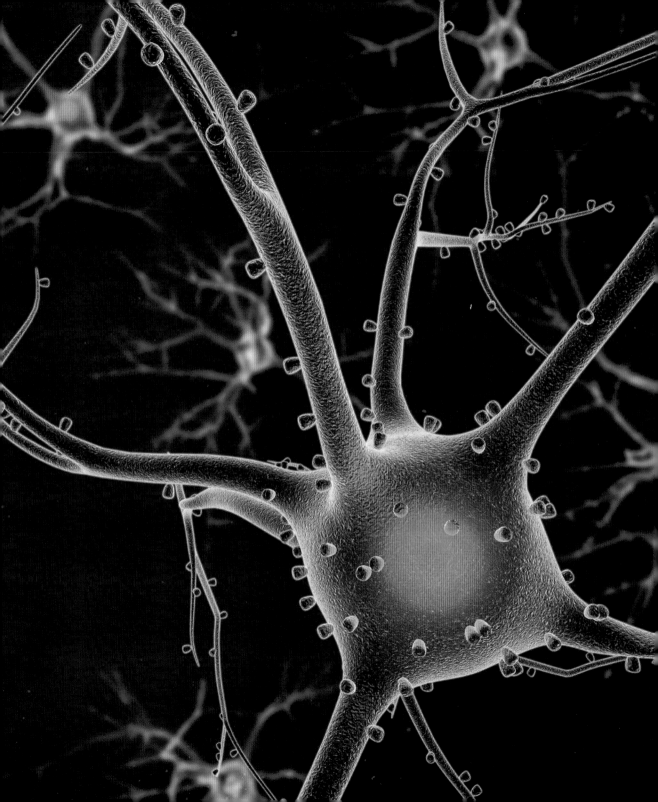

Anomalous Monism

Donald Davidson (1917–2003)

Like his teacher W. V. O. Quine (d. 2000), Donald Davidson was one of the most important analytic philosophers in the second half of the twentieth century. After receiving his PhD at Harvard, Davidson taught at a number of elite universities, including Stanford, Princeton, and Berkeley. Though Davidson did important, cutting-edge work in fields such as action theory, semantics, and philosophy of mind, his influence was somewhat limited until two collections of his papers appeared in the 1980s: *Essays on Actions and Events* (1980) and *Inquiries into Truth and Interpretation* (1984). One of Davidson's best-known claims is contained in his 1970 paper "Mental Events." There he argues that talk of minds cannot be reduced to talk about physical events in the brain.

Davidson was a physicalist who believed that the only things that exist are physical objects and physical events. In "Mental Events," he argues, however, that the same event can be physical under one description and mental under another. This is the basis for Davidson's influential theory of mind that he calls "anomalous monism." Davidson maintains that it is impossible to reduce psychology to physics because there are certain principles of rationality and coherence that are built into our conception of what counts as a "mind." For instance, we tend to interpret people's speech and behavior charitably, so as not to attribute manifestly irrational beliefs to them unless that is the only possible interpretation. This is something that distinguishes the mental from the physical. If mind-brain reductionism were possible, we could completely bypass these rationality constraints and conclude straightaway that whenever a given person is in a particular neural state, they must, say, hold a particular belief. Davidson admits that physical and mental events causally interact. He also believes that there must be strict laws that govern such interactions. There cannot, he assumes, be strict laws between purely mental events. Nor can there be psychophysical laws, because of the rationality constraints he notes. It follows that the relevant laws must be physical. Therefore, he concludes, mental events are identical with physical events, but under different descriptions that serve to insulate mental events from the strict laws that we use to explain and predict physical phenomena.

SEE ALSO Mind-Brain Identity Theory (1968), Philosophical Zombies (1991)

Some events, Davidson claims, can be physical under one description and mental under another. For example, the question "Why is the water boiling?" might be explained in exclusively physical terms (the water is boiling because of physical laws x, y, and z) or in mental terms (the water is boiling because so-and-so wants to drink some tea). Here, a Japanese tea ceremony, c. 1890.

A *Theory of Justice*

John Rawls (1921–2002)

John Rawls's 1971 book *A Theory of Justice* is widely considered the most important work of political philosophy in the twentieth century. Its importance lies not only in the power and sophistication of the theory it defends, but in its effects as well. *A Theory of Justice* revitalized the field of political philosophy, gave new vibrancy to political liberalism, reenergized the social-contract tradition of political theorizing, and dealt a severe blow to utilitarianism, long the most dominant ethical theory.

Rawls was born in Baltimore and received his PhD from Princeton. During World War II, he served as an infantryman and lost his faith in God after witnessing horrific scenes in the Pacific. He taught philosophy at Cornell and MIT for a number of years, publishing a number of important articles in ethics and political philosophy, before moving to Harvard in 1962. Following publication of his magnum opus, *A Theory of Justice*, in 1971, Rawls wrote a number of other important books, including *Political Liberalism* (1993) and *The Law of Peoples* (1999).

In *A Theory of Justice*, Rawls defends a liberal theory of justice he calls "justice as fairness." The basic idea is that a just society should be governed by principles of justice that would be chosen in a discussion format that was fair. Rawls calls such a format the "original position." This is a situation in which the participants know general facts about economics and human nature but otherwise operate under a "veil of ignorance" about the specifics of their own society, social status in that society, and their own life goals. The purpose of this veil of ignorance is to make sure that nobody can skew the discussion to their own advantage. Under these conditions, Rawls argues, social contractors in the original position would choose two basic principles of justice. One ensures equal basic liberties; the other prohibits social and economic inequalities, except when such inequalities benefit everyone in society. The upshot is a liberal regime in which freedom and equality are the two most important political values.

Rawls's theory of justice has been criticized on many fronts. But his work is widely hailed for the power of its central idea and the brilliance and depth of its elaboration.

SEE ALSO Human Rights (1689), *The Social Contract* (1762), Political Libertarianism (1974)

John Rawls in Paris, March 20, 1987, attending an international symposium on A Theory of Justice *held at the École polytechnique.*

The Rise of Informal Logic

Howard Kahane (1928–2001)

Prior to the 1970s, virtually all courses in logic focused mainly on symbolic or formal logic, which might loosely be described as a "mathematical" approach. In formal logic, the focus is on deductive reasoning, and symbols are used to get at the general form or structure of arguments. In the 1970s, a new approach to logic emerged, called "informal logic," or "critical thinking." Informal logic seeks to identify, analyze, and evaluate arguments as they occur in advertising, political speeches, and other sorts of everyday discourse. Early work in the field of informal logic includes Max Black's *Critical Thinking* (1946), Monroe Beardsley's *Practical Logic* (1950), Stephen Toulmin's *The Uses of Argument* (1958), and C. L. Hamblin's *Fallacies* (1970). But the book that really jump-started the movement was Howard Kahane's hugely successful 1971 textbook, *Logic and Contemporary Rhetoric: The Use of Reason in Everyday Life*.

Kahane was a philosophy professor who taught for much of his career at Baruch College in New York City. In 1969, he published a conventional logic text titled *Logic and Philosophy: A Modern Introduction*. But with the Vietnam War raging, Kahane felt the need for a more "relevant" approach to the evaluation of arguments. The result was *Logic and Contemporary Rhetoric*, which gave a whole new impetus to the study of logic and critical reasoning.

Written in a witty and conversational style, Kahane's text devoted less than a chapter to traditional deductive logic. Its central aim was to improve students' ability to think critically about everyday matters in areas such as advertising, the news, textbooks, and political discourse. Kahane's own political leanings were obvious. In a later edition of the text, he urged readers to keep in mind Richard Nixon's "record as a shady liar" in evaluating his credibility on subjects such as Cambodia and Watergate.

Kahane's text (revised after his death by Nancy M. Cavender) became one of the top-selling books in the field and is now in its twelfth edition. Beginning in the early 1970s, the field of informal logic expanded rapidly. Scholars such as Ralph H. Johnson, Richard Paul, and J. Anthony Blair did much to keep the ball rolling.

SEE ALSO The Invention of Logic (c. 330 BCE), *A System of Logic* (1843), The New Logic (1879)

President Richard M. Nixon points to a map of Southeast Asia during a press conference on Vietnam and Cambodia, April 30, 1970.

Political Libertarianism

Robert Nozick (1938–2002)

The twentieth century produced two great classics of analytic political philosophy. One was John Rawls's *A Theory of Justice* (1971). The other was *Anarchy, State, and Utopia*, published three years later by Rawls's Harvard colleague Robert Nozick. The books argued for radically different conclusions. Whereas Rawls defended an egalitarian liberal welfare state, Nozick supported a minimal "night-watchman" government limited to the narrow functions of protection against force, fraud, theft, and other violations of individual rights.

Nozick was born in Brooklyn, the son of Russian immigrant Jews. After graduating from Columbia, he received a PhD in philosophy from Princeton, where he became a convinced libertarian, largely through reading the works of economists Murray Rothbard (1926–1995) and Friedrich Hayek (1899–1992). In 1969, Nozick moved from Rockefeller University to Harvard, where he taught for the rest of his career.

Like Kant (d. 1804), Nozick believed that humans must be treated as autonomous "ends in themselves." In virtue of this inherent dignity, people possess a host of robust natural rights. Among these are a right of self-ownership that, among other things, makes it wrong for government to redistribute income. In *Anarchy, State, and Utopia*, Nozick argues that taxing one person to benefit another is a form of forced labor that wrongly treats persons as mere means to desired ends. A just and morally defensible state would respect individual rights and embrace an "entitlement" approach to wealth distribution that views all holdings as just as long as they arose from a just situation by just steps.

Anarchy, State, and Utopia, which won a National Book Award in 1975, was notable not only for its defense of libertarianism and critique of Rawls, but also for its powerful attacks on utilitarian ethics. In critiquing utilitarianism, Nozick created a famous thought experiment known as the "experience machine." Suppose you could plug into a virtual-reality machine that would give you any experience you desired. Should you plug in for life, knowing that you will thereby be guaranteed a lifetime of pleasurable experiences? According to classical utilitarianism, such experiences are the only things that ultimately matter in life. The fact that most people would choose *not* to plug into the experience machine seems to show that this intuition is not widely shared.

SEE ALSO Human Rights (1689), *A Theory of Justice* (1971)

A 1909 cartoon from Puck *magazine captioned "The Fountain of Taxation: Eventually the Bottom Basin Gets It." The top basin, supported by a crown, is labeled "Millionaire"; the next, "Well-To-Do," rests on a cornucopia; "Middle Class" is held up by an octopus; and the bottom largest basin, "Laboring Class," stands on a platform labeled "Tax System."*

THE FOUNTAIN OF TAXATION.

EVENTUALLY THE BOTTOM BASIN GETS IT.

"What Is It Like to Be a Bat?"

Thomas Nagel (b. 1937)

Thomas Nagel is a leading American philosopher who has made major contributions to many areas of philosophy, including philosophy of mind, ethics, and political philosophy. Throughout his career, Nagel has focused on the contrast between objective and subjective points of view, arguing that objective forms of knowing are not always better for finite creatures like ourselves. Nagel is also well known for his critique of reductionistic theories of mind. His 1974 article "What Is It Like to Be a Bat?" is a classic attack on attempts to treat the mind as a purely physical phenomenon.

Nagel was born in Belgrade, in present-day Serbia. After obtaining a PhD from Harvard in 1963, he taught at Berkeley and Princeton before moving to New York University in 1980. Among his many important books are *The Possibility of Altruism* (1970), *Mortal Questions* (1979), *The View from Nowhere* (1986), and *Mind and Cosmos* (2012).

In "What Is It Like to Be a Bat?" Nagel uses the example of consciousness in bats to criticize purely physicalistic theories of mind. Bats use echolocating sonar to catch flying insects at night. Nagel argues that it is likely that bats, which are mammals, have some form of conscious awareness, but that we have no clue what their inner experiences are like. Science can tell us a great deal about how bats' sonar works, but it cannot give us any real insight into "what it is like to be a bat"—what a bat senses, for example, when it detects a flying moth in its perceptional field. More generally, Nagel claims, theories of mind that try to reduce mental experiences to neurochemical events in the brain miss out on the whole blooming, buzzing *qualitative* dimension of consciousness. The way things feel and seem—the smell of fresh-cut grass, the taste of a strawberry, the redness of a rose—is simply left out of reductionistic accounts of the mind. This is what reduction-minded neuroscientists call the "hard problem of consciousness." It was Nagel who gave canonical expression to the problem.

SEE ALSO The Ghost in the Machine (1949), Mind-Brain Identity Theory (1968), Philosophical Zombies (1991)

A species of fruit bat, which uses a newly discovered type of echolocation via sonar wing clicks.

Essentialism

Alvin Plantinga (b. 1932)

The reigning dogma in the 1960s was that essentialism was confused and that no clear distinction could be drawn between essential and accidental properties. This conflicted with the traditional view, going back to Aristotle, that things like human beings have some attributes that are essential to their being human beings (e.g., having human DNA) and other attributes that a person could lose without affecting his or her humanity (e.g., having long hair or being a Republican). Now a great many philosophers are essentialists. A big reason for the change was the publication of American philosopher Alvin Plantinga's important book *The Nature of Necessity* (1974).

Plantinga, who was born in Michigan and received his PhD from Yale, is best known for his work as a Christian philosopher; many scholars regard him as the most important twentieth-century philosopher of religion. But Plantinga also did groundbreaking work in epistemology, metaphysics, and the philosophy of language, most notably in *The Nature of Necessity*, a full-length study of the concept of necessity. In the book, he spends several chapters defending what he calls necessity *de re* (in Latin, literally "about the thing"): the idea that *objects* (not merely statements) can have "modal" properties such as necessary existence or essential attributes. He also lays out with great clarity an account of "possible worlds," which Plantinga thinks of as immensely complex abstract (that is, nonphysical) "states of affairs." According to him, possible-worlds talk fills out our intuitive notion of "a way things could have been" and helps us make sense of notions like essence, necessary truth, and possible but nonactual objects. Perhaps the most interesting parts of the book are his application of his possible-worlds theory to the theological problem of evil and the ontological argument for the existence of God. Plantinga argues that his modal distinctions can be used to show that there is no logical contradiction between belief in the existence of an infinitely perfect God and the reality of evil, since it is possible that it wasn't within God's power to create a world that contains a better mixture of moral good and moral evil than the actual one contains. He also uses his theory to offer an ingenious and impressively souped-up version of the ontological argument.

SEE ALSO The Ontological Argument (1078), Soul-Making Theodicy (1966), Revival of Christian Philosophy (1984)

God the Father Creating the Heavens, *1760, a print by French engraver Jean-Charles François. According to Plantinga, it's possible that it wasn't within God's power to create a world with a better balance of moral good and moral evil than the balance that exists in reality.*

Animal Liberation

Peter Singer (b. 1946)

During the 1960s and 1970s, many people began to rethink traditional attitudes toward women, minorities, gays, and the environment. As part of this cultural shift, there was a new focus on how humans treat animals. This marked the beginning of what is commonly called the "animal rights movement." At the forefront of this movement was a young Australian philosopher named Peter Singer.

Singer first achieved prominence as a defender of animal welfare when he published a long book review titled "Animal Liberation" in the *New York Review of Books* in April 1973. Two years later, he published a book, also titled *Animal Liberation*, which is often called the "Bible of the animal rights movement."

Describing Singer as an advocate of "animal rights" is misleading, however, because his defense of animals is purely utilitarian. His claim is not that animals have fundamental moral rights but that they have "interests" that must be respected. Like humans, higher animals like cows and pigs have an interest in avoiding pain and suffering. Ethics requires that we treat equal interests equally. Thus, it is wrong to care about human pain but to ignore or discount animal pain. To do so is a form of unjustifiable discrimination that Singer (borrowing a term coined by Richard Ryder [b. 1940]) calls "speciesism." The upshot is that we should stop raising animals for food; abolish hunting, trapping, and zoos; drastically curtail animal experimentation; and become vegetarians.

Singer's book helped to galvanize the nascent animal rights movement. When *Animal Liberation* was first published, very few people in Western societies believed that eating animals was an ethical issue at all. Today roughly 5 percent of Americans are vegetarians, most for moral reasons.

As the animal rights movement has grown, defenders of animal welfare have generally moved away from the types of utilitarian arguments offered by Singer. Today animal rights are more commonly defended by invoking concepts like "intrinsic value," "reverence for life," "equal inherent worth," or other such deontological notions. Such dignity-based arguments are widely thought to provide a firmer grounding for rights than Singer's utilitarianism does.

SEE ALSO Utilitarianism (1789), Refined Utilitarianism (1863), Emergence of Feminist Philosophy (c. 1976)

A contemporary photograph of a cattle feeding trough on a farm in Saskatchewan, Canada.

Power/Knowledge

Michel Foucault (1926–1984)

Many strands of recent French philosophy have denied the possibility of objective knowledge and embraced some version or another of relativism. Various labels are used to describe such schools of thought, including post-structuralism, deconstructionism, and postmodernism. One important French thinker who is often classified as a post-structuralist is Michel Foucault. In a series of important books beginning in the early 1960s, Foucault explored what he termed the "archeology" and "genealogy" of knowledge. Both methods deny the possibility of objective knowledge or universal reason.

Foucault was born in Poitiers and educated in the École normale supérieure, the elite Parisian school that, since its founding in 1794, has produced many leading French philosophers. Early in his career, Foucault embraced Marxism and phenomenological existentialism, but in the 1960s he developed an approach to intellectual history he called the "archeology of knowledge." In works such as *The History of Madness* (1961), *The Order of Things* (1966), and *The Archeology of Knowledge* (1969), Foucault argued that there are no standards of truth or falsity that apply outside "discursive practices," that is, particular culturally conditioned conceptual frameworks of language and thought. These frameworks, he claimed, are governed by rules, some of which are unconscious, that set limits to what is thinkable in a particular system. The task of archeology of knowledge is to show how claims that purport to be based on objective knowledge, scientific fact, and universal truths are really relative and contingent.

Foucault later extended his archeological approach to include a theory of how systems of thought change over time, which he called the "genealogy of knowledge." From 1975 until his AIDS-related death in 1984, Foucault wrote a series of books that sought to show the fundamental connection between power and knowledge. Claims of objective and universal truth, he argued, are used to mask systems of control. By recognizing that what is presented as "human nature" or "self-evident truth" or "scientific fact" is actually a contingent product of historically conditioned forces, individuals are liberated to pursue their own freely chosen experiments in living.

SEE ALSO Deconstruction (1967), Postmodernism (1979)

Michel Foucault, 1979.

Emergence of Feminist Philosophy

Feminist philosophy is important both for what it has done and for what it may yet achieve. Since its emergence in the mid-1970s, feminist philosophy has profoundly affected mainstream philosophical thought about issues of equality, social justice, patriarchy, gender, and identity. It has also posed deep challenges to long-held notions of objectivity, universality, rationality, dualistic thinking, essentialism, the public-private distinction, and the self, which continue to be hotly debated. Only the future will tell how these issues will play out. The history of women in philosophy has not been a happy one. Until recently, women were largely excluded from philosophy because of patriarchal biases and traditional views of gender roles. Moreover, many of the great Western philosophers from ancient Greece to the modern era—including Aristotle, Aquinas, Rousseau, Kant, and Nietzsche—held deeply sexist views about women. Important forerunners of modern feminism such as Mary Wollstonecraft, John Stuart Mill, Harriet Taylor, and Simone de Beauvoir challenged long-held assumptions about women's inferiority and women's roles in society. Feminist philosophy emerged in the 1970s as an outgrowth of the women's movement of the 1960s; among the early pioneers were Alison Jaggar, Marilyn Frye, Jane English, and Sandra Harding. Carol Gould and Marx Wartofsky published the first anthology of feminist philosophy, titled *Women and Philosophy: Toward a Theory of Liberation*, in 1976.

Feminist philosophy is highly diverse; those who practice it may embrace liberalism, socialism, Marxism, pragmatism, postmodernism, or any number of other isms. What unites feminist philosophers is a shared conviction that relations between the sexes are unequal, oppressive, and unjust; that it is important to identify and remedy the sources of women's subordination; and that traditional philosophy has been male-biased in a variety of ways. Many strands of feminist philosophy deny the possibility of objective knowledge or universal truths. Others claim that reason and emotion are coequal sources of knowledge. Some feminists reject all forms of hierarchical thinking, including any human superiority over nature. Still others deny that rules or principles should play a significant role in moral decision making. Such claims pose radical challenges not only to traditional philosophy, but also to science and many aspects of contemporary culture. For this reason, among others, feminist philosophy is one of the most important and exciting movements in contemporary philosophy.

SEE ALSO A *Vindication of the Rights of Woman* (1792), *The Subjection of Women* (1869), *The Second Sex* (1949)

Protesters march with signs in support of the Equal Rights Amendment in Cincinnati, Ohio, August 1973.

Moral Anti-Realism

John Leslie Mackie (1917–1981)

Roughly, moral anti-realism is the view that there are no moral facts or moral values, or at least none that are mind independent. Prominent moral antirealists include Protagoras (d. c. 420 BCE), who defended moral relativism; David Hume (d. 1776), who claimed that moral values are "projected" onto objects that do not in fact possess them; A. J. Ayer (d. 1989), who defended a version of emotivism; and Friedrich Nietzsche (d. 1900), who denied that there are any moral facts and claimed that all ethical truth claims are merely "perspectival." In 1977, the prominent Australian philosopher J. L. Mackie published an influential defense of moral anti-realism in *Ethics: Inventing Right and Wrong.* Unlike moral noncognitivists such as Ayer, who claimed that moral statements are purely emotive and do not even purport to be true, Mackie concedes that when people say things like "Hitler was evil" (my example, not his) they are asserting something that they believe to be true. The problem, he argues, is that there are no moral facts or moral truths, so we must embrace an "error theory" of moral language. In other words, when people say things like "Hitler was evil," they are implicitly asserting that "Hitler was really and objectively evil," which is false, because there are no objective moral facts or objective moral truths. Most moral talk, Mackie claims, is bunk, much as talk about the Loch Ness monster is bunk.

He gives a number of arguments to support this theory. The most important is what he calls the "argument from queerness." If objective moral properties existed, he argues, they'd be very strange and mysterious sorts of entities—nonmaterial entities that somehow "supervene" on material features of the world but aren't reducible to those features. Moreover, how could we be aware of these entities without possessing some special faculty of moral perception or intuition, which fits poorly with a modern scientific worldview? For such reasons, Mackie embraces a view that he calls "moral skepticism": there are no objective moral facts, even though most people mistakenly assume that there are.

Mackie's vigorous, clearly written defense of his error theory of moral talk sparked a renewed interest in moral anti-realism. According to a recent survey, only a slight majority of professional philosophers accept or lean toward moral realism. Mackie's book may well have contributed to this shift away from realist views of ethics.

SEE ALSO Protagoras and Relativism (c. 450 BCE), Morality Is Rooted in Feeling (1751), Logical Positivism (1936), Emotivism (1944)

Adolf Hitler, c. 1935—at the time, chancellor of Germany—greeting a group of Hitler Youth.

Taking Rights Seriously

Ronald Dworkin (1931–2013)

For roughly the past two centuries, there have been two main competing theories of law: Natural law theorists claim that law and morality are necessarily connected, because human laws derive their validity from a "higher law," which emanates from God and is universally binding. Legal positivists, by contrast, claim that law is one thing and morality is another, so that laws can be valid even if they are highly immoral. In 1977, the distinguished American legal philosopher Ronald Dworkin published *Taking Rights Seriously*, defending a third theory of law that offers a compromise of sorts between natural law theory and legal positivism.

Dworkin was born in Providence, Rhode Island, and had a glittering academic career. Educated at Harvard, Oxford, and Harvard Law School, Dworkin taught law at Yale before being appointed to the chair of jurisprudence at Oxford in 1969. His major works, besides *Taking Rights Seriously*, include *A Matter of Principle* (1985), *Law's Empire* (1986), *Sovereign Virtue* (2000), and *Justice for Hedgehogs* (2011).

Dworkin's main target in *Taking Rights Seriously* is the sophisticated form of legal positivism set forth in H. L. A. Hart's *The Concept of Law* (1961). Hart argues that law consists of a system of rules, some of which are vague or "open-ended," leaving law "gappy" and giving judges discretion to (in effect) make law where none previously existed. Dworkin counters that law includes general principles as well as rules, and that legal questions always have right answers, meaning that judges never have discretion in Hart's sense. The reason legal questions always have right answers, Dworkin argues, is that law is interpretive. Law consists not only of settled, uncontroversial law, but also of those general normative principles that best explain and justify the settled law. The right answer in law is whatever follows from the best constructive interpretation under this model. Dworkin claims that this picture of adjudication describes how judges do typically decide hard cases and also how they should do so. If he is right, positivists are correct in thinking that divine higher law is not necessarily part of human legal systems, and natural law theorists are right in thinking that law and morality cannot be sharply separated.

SEE ALSO Natural Law (c. 1270), Law and Morality Are Separate (1832), Legal Positivism (1961)

Ronald Dworkin at Oxford University in the 1970s.

The New Pragmatism

Richard Rorty (1931–2007)

One of the times when philosophy gets very interesting is when philosophers themselves offer deep challenges to long-accepted ways of conceiving or doing philosophy. One recent thinker who has done that is Richard Rorty.

Rorty was born in New York City, the child of reform-minded liberal parents. At age fourteen, he enrolled at the University of Chicago, where he obtained both a BA and an MA in philosophy. After receiving his doctorate in philosophy from Yale, Rorty taught at Princeton, the University of Virginia, and Stanford. Increasingly disillusioned by analytic philosophy, Rorty developed an innovative brand of pragmatism and sought to bridge long-standing differences between analytic and continental approaches to philosophy. His most famous book, *Philosophy and the Mirror of Nature* (1979), criticized foundationalist approaches to knowledge and the idea of the mind as a mirror or accurate copier of a mind-independent reality.

Rorty developed a new version of pragmatism, sometimes dubbed neopragmatism, which views human existence as radically contingent; theories as tools or optional vocabularies that should be adopted or discarded depending on their usefulness and social conventions; and philosophy as a mode of edifying conversation, rather than as a foundational discipline focused on truth.

Politically, Rorty has described himself as a liberal ironist. As a liberal, Rorty rejected radical solutions to political problems, favoring piecemeal reforms aimed at advancing social justice and expanding citizens' freedoms. A central political virtue, he argued, was solidarity—particularly sensitivity to others' suffering and a capacity for putting ourselves in their place. At the same time, Rorty believed, no political convictions should be held as absolutes. They should be viewed ironically, with full recognition of their cultural contingency and lack of grounding in any objective or God's-eye point of view. We should fight for a just and better world, while recognizing that our commitments are transient products of a cultural background that cannot be justified by any universal standards or knockdown arguments. The deep contingency of human existence creates anxiety, but it also opens up opportunities for self-transformation and self-creation. "We create ourselves," Rorty says, "by telling our own story."

SEE ALSO Origins of Pragmatism (1878), *Pragmatism* (1907), Instrumentalism (1925)

Richard Rorty, 1995.

Postmodernism

Jean-François Lyotard (1924–1998)

Postmodernism is notoriously difficult to define. Versions of postmodernist thought are found in film, architecture, literature, the visual arts, and music. As a philosophical movement, postmodernism can be broadly characterized as a family of theories that rejects core elements of Enlightenment "modernism," such as objective knowledge, human progress by means of science and technology, foundational beliefs that are 100 percent certain, language as an accurate "mirror of nature," and faith in our ability to construct general theories that can provide comprehensive explanations of nature and society. Leading thinkers who are often classified as postmodernists include twentieth-century French philosophers Michel Foucault, Jacques Derrida, Jean Baudrillard, Gilles Deleuze, and Jean-François Lyotard. It was Lyotard who first popularized the term "postmodernism" in his important book, *The Postmodern Condition: A Report on Knowledge* (1979).

Lyotard was born outside of Paris to middle-class parents. As a young secondary-school teacher, Lyotard became radicalized and spent fifteen years working for far-left revolutionary causes. After receiving his doctorate in his mid-thirties, he taught at the University of Paris, Vincennes, and at other universities in France and abroad. Publication of *The Postmodern Condition* brought him international prominence.

In *The Postmodern Condition*, Lyotard famously defines postmodernism as "incredulity towards metanarratives." What he means is that educated people today have generally become distrustful of grand, catchall theories like Marxism, or the perfectibility of humanity through scientific progress that appeal to supposed "universal truths" and promise some glorious, not-yet-realized lollapalooza. Such distrust is healthy, Lyotard argues, because grand theories tend to ignore the messy heterogeneity of reality and the importance of individual events, and are often used to prop up some power elite. Like most postmodernists, Lyotard favors replacing big metanarratives with more modest "localized" narratives that recognize a variety of legitimate standpoints. One metanarrative that he criticizes at length is that of science as a privileged form of "objective" knowing that will inevitably lead to human enlightenment and emancipation. Drawing from Wittgenstein's (d. 1951) later philosophy, Lyotard argues that science is simply one "language game" among many, and that no language game can claim that it alone is legitimate.

SEE ALSO Deconstruction (1967), Power/Knowledge (1975)

Jean-François Lyotard in Hannover, Germany, in 1992.

Reliabilism

Alvin Goldman (b. 1938)

In the eyes of many philosophers, Edmund Gettier's (b. 1927) famous 1963 paper "Is Justified True Belief Knowledge?" delivered a knockout blow to the traditional view of knowledge. Massive efforts were then made to rethink concepts such as knowledge, justification, and warrant. One important outcome was the rise of "externalist" accounts of knowledge and justification. Roughly, externalists believe that people can have justified beliefs even if they lack, or cannot provide, reasons for those beliefs. In their view, what makes beliefs rational or justified are factors that may not be available to "internal" inspection, such as whether the beliefs were produced by a reliable cognitive process (e.g., memory or good reasoning). The most prominent externalist theory is called "process reliabilism." Its principal architect and defender is Rutgers University professor Alvin Goldman.

Early versions of process reliabilism date back to the 1930s, but it was Goldman's 1979 paper "What Is Justified Belief?" that kicked things off. Goldman's view is complicated and has evolved over time, but the general idea is that a belief is justified if and only if it is produced by a reliable process or mechanism that produces a high ratio of true beliefs. Process reliabilism has a number of attractions. It provides an easy way to see how direct, noninferential beliefs can be justified. We can readily say, for example, why a small child is justified in trusting her senses that she sees a tree in front of her when one is there, even though she couldn't give a reason to back up her trust. It also provides plausible solutions to many forms of skepticism, such as Hume's (d. 1776) critique of induction or worries about whether we're justified in believing in the existence of other minds.

Process reliabilism also runs into problems, however. How reliable must a cognitive process be to produce a justified belief—60 or 90 percent? Is reliability really necessary for justification? Suppose, as some philosophers have suggested, what we call the "real world" is just a computer simulation. In that case, our senses would not be reliable. But wouldn't a small child still be justified (that is, within her epistemic rights, not at fault) in trusting her senses? The jury remains out on whether a sound version of process reliabilism can be worked out.

SEE ALSO The Problem of Induction (1739), The Gettier Problem (1963)

A photomontage evocative of the streaming data that might be behind the scenes in a computer-simulated reality.

The Chinese Room

John Searle (b. 1932)

One of the most discussed arguments in recent philosophy is John Searle's intriguing thought experiment known as the "Chinese Room." If Searle is right, no matter how sophisticated computers eventually become, no computer could ever actually think.

Searle was born in Denver, studied at the University of Wisconsin-Madison, and received his doctorate from Oxford. He recently retired from the University of California, Berkeley, where he had taught since 1959. Among his many important books are *Speech Acts* (1969), *Intentionality* (1983), and *The Mystery of Consciousness* (1997). Searle is a leading critic of materialistic theories of the mind that deny the existence of nonreducible mental events. He views mind as an emergent nonphysical product of the physical brain. In 1980, Searle published a famous article, "Mind, Brains, and Programs," in the journal *Behavioral and Brain Sciences*. It used the idea of an unwitting question-and-answer process—the "Chinese Room" thought experiment—to challenge mainstream views about whether machines could ever be conscious or think. Here's how it works:

Imagine that you're a native English speaker who speaks no Chinese. You're locked in a room with two slits, a big book of instructions, a pen, and some scratch paper. Slips of paper with mysterious marks on them fall in through one slit. You use the book of instructions to match these marks with other marks that you write down on the scratch paper, and then you push the paper out through the other slit. Later you find out that the slips of paper contained questions written in Chinese, and that what you wrote down on the scratch paper were witty and highly appropriate answers in Chinese. So good, in fact, were your answers, that you fooled everybody into thinking that the answers came from a real Chinese-speaking human being. What does this show about the possibility of artificial intelligence?

According to Searle, it shows that no computer could ever think. What you did is exactly what a digital computer does: use formal rules to manipulate symbols to produce outputs. You had no understanding at all of what the string of marks you received or sent meant. Likewise, he argues, a computer could conceivably mimic human intelligence, but it could never be conscious or engage in genuine thinking.

SEE ALSO Functionalism (1960)

The avatar for the Watson computer system, a technology platform developed by IBM® that competed on the game show Jeopardy!® *in 2011 against the show's top two champions. (Watson won first place; the winnings were donated to charity.)*

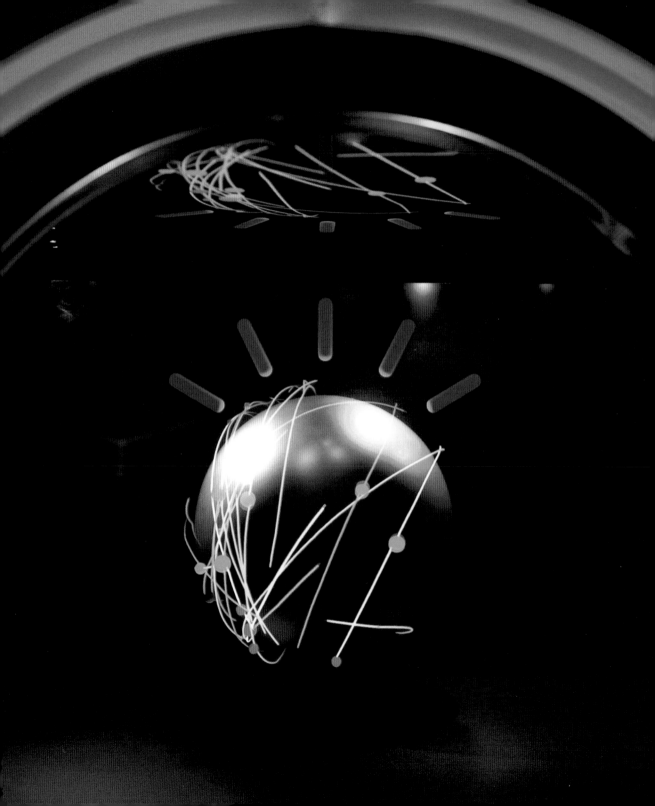

The Causal Theory of Reference

Saul Kripke (b. 1940)

Since at least the time of Kant (d. 1804), it was pretty much universally assumed by philosophers that necessary truths could only be known a priori, not on the basis of observation or experience. In 1980, this view was powerfully challenged in the groundbreaking book *Naming and Necessity*, by noted American philosopher Saul Kripke.

Kripke's main target in *Naming and Necessity* is "descriptivism," a long-held view of how names and other referring expressions get their meaning and reference. Descriptivists believe that the meaning of a proper name, such as "William Shakespeare," is a set of criteria, or descriptions, that speakers use to apply the name, and that these criteria determine who the name refers to. So, for example, the meaning of "William Shakespeare" is given by some definite description (e.g., "the English playwright who wrote *Hamlet*") or by some combination of such descriptions. Kripke pointed out that this would make sentences like "Shakespeare wrote *Hamlet*" trivially true (which it clearly is not), and it would also make it a necessary truth that Shakespeare wrote *Hamlet*. This implies that we could never discover that someone other than Shakespeare wrote *Hamlet*, which also seems to be clearly false.

What Kripke (and others such as Keith Donnellan [1931–2015] and Hilary Putnam [d. 2016]) proposed is that names and general terms for naturally occurring objects such as "tigers" do not get their reference from any set of descriptive criteria, but rather from an initial act of "baptism" that fixes the reference directly. The name is then handed down from speaker to speaker in a kind of causal chain that generally preserves the original reference. This view became known as the causal theory of reference, and is now widely accepted. One important consequence of the theory is that some necessary truths can be learned only through experience. For example, Kripke claims that the statement "Water is H_2O" is a necessary truth ("true in all possible worlds"), but one that became knowable only with the rise of modern science. Kripke's causal theory of reference provoked sweeping changes in many areas of philosophy. As a result, many philosophers consider Kripke to be one of the most important philosophers of the twentieth century.

SEE ALSO The New Logic (1879), The Theory of Definite Descriptions (1905)

An engraved portrait of William Shakespeare, 1860, above a reproduction of what is said to be Shakespeare's signature from the last page of his will.

William Shakespeare

SHAKESPEARE.

The Revival of Virtue Ethics

Elizabeth Anscombe (1919–2001), **Alasdair MacIntyre** (b. 1929)

From Aristotle (d. 322 BCE) until roughly 1600, the dominant approach to ethics in Western civilization was what we today call "virtue ethics." According to virtue ethics, the central focus of moral theory and reflection should be on questions of character, virtue, and wisdom—not on identifying and following correct moral rules or on maximizing good consequences. Broadly, virtue ethicists focus mainly on two questions: (1) What does it mean to be a really good person? and (2) What virtues, or excellences of mind and character, are needed to become such a person? Aristotle was a virtue ethicist in this sense, as were Aquinas (d. 1274) and most other medieval philosophers. In modern philosophy this way of approaching ethics largely broke down. Instead, philosophers such as Kant (d. 1804) and Mill (d. 1873), believed that the central task of ethics was that of working out a good ethical decision procedure—a method for deciding what is morally right or wrong, or good or bad, in pretty much every conceivable situation. It wasn't until the latter half of the twentieth century that thinkers such as Elizabeth Anscombe and Alasdair MacIntyre made a serious case for reviving virtue ethics.

As we saw on page 424, Anscombe was a Catholic philosopher, much influenced by Wittgenstein (d. 1951). In 1958, she published a now-classic article titled "Modern Moral Philosophy." In that paper she argues that modern ethical theory and discourse are rudderless and incoherent, because they employed terms like "obligation" and "ought" that were based on an older, Judeo-Christian way of thinking about ethics that has largely been abandoned. In her opinion, philosophers should stop doing ethics until an adequate psychological basis has been found for doing ethics productively.

An even more influential stimulus for the revival of virtue ethics was Alasdair MacIntyre's 1981 book, *After Virtue*. MacIntyre, a Scottish philosopher, offers a detailed historical account of how modern ethics fell into disarray and proposes a cure that sought to ground ethics in communities and traditions of virtue. In later books, he argues that the tradition of virtue theory rooted in the thoughts of Aristotle and Aquinas—but modernized in certain ways—offers the best available approach to ethics today.

SEE ALSO *Nicomachean Ethics* (c. 330 BCE), Natural Law (c. 1270)

A chromolithograph from 1892 of the Tree of Life filled with apple-like fruits labeled with various virtues; it was designed by one reverend J. A. Hammond.

Critical Theory

Jürgen Habermas (b. 1929)

Critical theory, sometimes known as the Frankfurt School, is a neo-Marxist form of social theory that seeks to promote human freedom and emancipation by critical examination of harmful ideologies and oppressive social structures. Among the leading members of the Frankfurt School are Max Horkheimer (1895–1973), Theodor Adorno (1903–1969), and Herbert Marcuse (1898–1979). Today, the most prominent critical theorist is the German philosopher and sociologist Jürgen Habermas.

Born in Dusseldorf, Habermas received a PhD in philosophy from the University of Bonn and has taught philosophy and sociology at the universities of Marburg, Heidelberg, and Frankfurt. Habermas has also long been active in German public life, weighing in on a variety of hot-button social issues and promoting open and informed discussion. His magnum opus, *The Theory of Communicative Action*, was published in 1981.

Early critical theory took a negative view of reason, emphasizing the ways in which modern notions of efficiency, technological progress, and means-ends rationality contributed to repressive social conditions. Habermas's aim has been to rethink the foundations of critical theory and restore the failed promise of enlightenment ideals of rationality. To do this, he has shifted the focus of critical theory from subject-centered theories of knowledge to communication theory. Drawing on a remarkably wide range of sources in the social sciences, linguistics, and both the analytic and continental philosophical traditions, Habermas puts forth a theory of "communicative action" rooted in a generally positive view of human reason. At the heart of Habermas's theory is a model of an ideal communication community. Such a community, he argues, would be committed to the goals of truth, mutual understanding, and conflict resolution through free, open, and uncoerced public discourse guided only by respect for the force of the better argument. Because such ideal speech situations can take place only within liberal-democratic societies, Habermas's social theory provides an argument for establishing and maintaining such societies. Though he sees the Enlightenment as an "unfinished project," Habermas parts company with leftist social critics who see all appeals to reason as disguised power grabs. As Habermas sees it, true liberation and social progress can come only by fulfilling the promise of the Enlightenment, not by abandoning it.

SEE ALSO *The Communist Manifesto* (1848), Oxford Ordinary Language Philosophy (1962)

Jürgen Habermas in Berlin, June 1998.

In a Different Voice

Carol Gilligan (b. 1936)

A prominent theme in some strands of recent feminist thought has been that women tend to approach ethics differently than men. Women, it is claimed, tend to value relationships and connections—an "ethic of care"—whereas men tend to value rights, autonomy, and impartiality—an "ethic of justice." The origins of this important contemporary debate can largely be traced to the pathbreaking work of Carol Gilligan.

Gilligan, who now teaches at New York University, taught for many years at Harvard, where she received her PhD in Social Psychology. At Harvard, Gilligan worked as a research assistant to Lawrence Kohlberg (1927–1987), creator of a highly influential theory of moral development. She was struck by the fact that women tended to score lower on Kohlberg's moral reasoning scale than men did. Noting that all of his original test subjects were males, Gilligan wondered if Kohlberg's methodology might be male biased. When Gilligan conducted her own interviews with both women and men, she began to hear "a different voice" in the way they tended to wrestle with moral issues. Her resulting book, *In a Different Voice: Psychological Theory and Women's Development* (1982), has generated major discussion in both psychology and ethics.

Building on Gilligan's work, a number of feminist ethicists have defended versions of an ethic of care. Theorists such as Nel Noddings (b. 1929) have argued that traditional ethics has overemphasized values such as objectivity, impartiality, individual rights, autonomy, and rule-driven decision making, while giving short shrift to values such as care, compassion, love, friendship, and relatedness. While acknowledging the importance of rights, rules, and other core notions of traditional ethics, these theorists argue that an ethic of care is generally superior to an ethic of justice and would lead to a more caring and less violent world. Questions abound about Gilligan's work and its implications for ethics and psychology. How strong is the evidence that men and women differ in the way they tend to think about moral issues? Might an ethic of care reinforce stereotypes about caregiving being primarily women's responsibility and lead some women to neglect their own health and happiness? Can a viable ethic of care be defended? These are all important ongoing debates.

SEE ALSO *A Vindication of the Rights of Woman* (1792), *The Second Sex* (1949), Emergence of Feminist Philosophy (c. 1976)

Carol Gilligan is interviewed by the press before the launch of the Global V-Day Campaign for Justice to "Comfort Women" on February 28, 2005, in New York City.

Revival of Christian Philosophy

Alvin Plantinga (b. 1932)

For many centuries, great thinkers in Christian Europe, such as Augustine (d. 430 CE) and Aquinas (d. 1274), practiced a form of what is now called Christian philosophy. In this view, faith and reason were seen as allies, rather than as strangers or enemies. Since all truth flows from God, it was assumed that reason and revelation must harmonize. This did not mean that philosophy collapses into theology; they each have their proper spheres. The idea was that philosophy could be done better if it was guided and illumined by divinely revealed truth.

This way of doing philosophy was widely rejected in the modern era. A complete separation of philosophy and theology was believed to be necessary to avoid theological feuds and to appeal to reasonable people of all creeds, including religious skeptics. In the 1970s and 1980s, a significant revival of Christian philosophy occurred. The central figure in that revival was the distinguished American philosopher Alvin Plantinga, who taught for most of his career at the University of Notre Dame. In 1984, Plantinga published an article titled "Advice to Christian Philosophers," which became something of a manifesto for an unabashed contemporary form of Christian philosophy.

Plantinga argued that Christian philosophers should see themselves as part of the Christian community, with an important role to play in building up that community. Specifically, they should use their talents and specialized training to refute attacks on the Christian faith; to offer reasoned arguments in support of Christian belief; to clarify, systematize, and deepen central Christian teachings; and to explore the implications of Christian theism for the whole range of questions philosophers address. Too often, Plantinga suggested, Christian philosophers kowtow to current fashions in philosophy, most of which are hostile to Christian theism. To serve the Christian community better, they should display more independence, more integrity, and more courage and self-confidence.

Plantinga's call to arms received a hearty response. Hundreds of young Christian intellectuals flocked to universities like Notre Dame and Baylor that offered strong doctoral programs in Christian philosophy. Today Christian philosophy is flourishing in a way that has not been seen for many centuries.

SEE ALSO Neo-Thomism (c. 1920), The New Atheists (2004)

The Word of Life, a mosaic mural by American artist Millard Sheets. The mural adorns the facade of the Hesburgh Library at the University of Notre Dame, a Catholic research university in South Bend, Indiana. The mural, which overlooks the football stadium, is nicknamed Touchdown Jesus.

Reasons and Persons

Derek Parfit (b. 1942)

Reason and Persons is a strange and exciting work. Its strangeness is due mostly to its style. Its sentences are short, spare, and almost machine-like in their precision. Like Aquinas's great thirteenth-century *Summa theologica*, Derek Parfit's book is also remarkably dense with nonstop arguments. It is exciting largely because of the bold and often counterintuitive conclusions Parfit so brilliantly defends. Perhaps the most interesting part of the book deals with "personal identity," the issue of what makes us the same person from one part of our life to the next. His central conclusion—that personal identity is not what we really care about—has been one of the most hotly debated issues in philosophy in recent decades.

Parfit was born in Chengdu, China, the son of two English missionary doctors. After attending Eton, he graduated from Oxford with a degree in modern history. Parfit became interested in philosophy when he received a Harkness Fellowship to study in America. After returning to England, he won a coveted prize fellowship at All Souls College, Oxford, which entitled him to free room and board for seven years, with no teaching responsibilities. He stayed at All Souls as a research fellow from 1967 to 2010. For many years he has served as a visiting professor at Rutgers and New York University. Parfit's personal oddities (for example, he has few memories of his past and cannot remember his wife's face when he is away from her) were profiled in a widely read September 2011 *New Yorker* article. His two landmark books, *Reasons and Persons* (1984) and *On What Matters* (2011), have made him one of the world's most influential living philosophers.

In *Reasons and Persons*, Parfit examines a cluster of ethical and metaphysical issues, including ethical egoism, commonsense morality, rationality and time, personal identity, and effects of acts on future generations. His discussion of personal identity offers a series of ingenious thought experiments to support his claims that there is no "self" in the way most people suppose and that ultimately it is psychological continuity, not personal identity or whether "we" survive death, which really matters.

SEE ALSO No-Self (*Anatta*) (c. 525 BCE), The Triple Theory of Ethics (2011)

Derek Parfit in the Old Library of the Oxford Union (a student debating society affiliated with Oxford University), on June 17, 2015, where he was giving a talk titled "Effective Altruism."

The Moral Limits of the Criminal Law

Joel Feinberg (1926–2004)

What sorts of conduct may the state rightly make criminal? May it prohibit so-called harmless immoralities, like reading really trashy books? May it criminalize conduct that is harmless but causes profound offense, like putting a racist bumper sticker on one's car? May it outlaw conduct that causes harm only to the very person it prohibits from acting, like smoking cigarettes, drinking too many sugary sodas, or swimming on a dangerous beach without a lifeguard?

A standard "liberal" view is that John Stuart Mill (d. 1873) got it pretty much right in *On Liberty* (1859) when he said (roughly) that government may restrict individual liberty only in order in prevent harm to others. But Mill's account left many crucial questions unanswered. What counts as "harm"? How great must the harm be? How likely must it be for the harm to occur? And so on.

In 1984, the distinguished American legal philosopher Joel Feinberg published the first volume of his magisterial series, *The Moral Limits of the Criminal Law*; the fourth and final volume was released in 1988. In this work, Feinberg tries to flesh out, in painstaking detail, what a liberal, broadly Millian penal code would and would not permit. With great clarity and acuity, he seeks to spell out what sorts of "liberty-limiting principles" are consistent with a liberal regime that attaches great value to individual freedom. In the process, he greatly deepens, refines, and complicates Mill's account. He also, in some ways, retreats from Mill's uncompromising liberalism. In particular, he argued that governments may sometimes outlaw harmless but profoundly offensive conduct. And he concedes that in rare instances some types of harmless immoralities and self-harms may be criminalized.

Feinberg was not the type to dance around difficult questions. In a classic passage from volume two of the series, *Offense to Others* (1985), titled "A Ride on the Bus," he describes in excruciating detail a series of thirty-one scenarios involving "harmless" but outrageously vile, shocking, or disgusting behaviors. Despite being a rock-ribbed liberal himself, he argues that some of these types of conduct can rightly be prohibited. In such ways, Feinberg steps back from some of Mill's boldest liberal claims, while greatly strengthening and developing his overall approach.

SEE ALSO *On Liberty* (1859)

In Feinberg's "A Ride on the Bus," one of the scenarios involves having to endure someone next to you taking out a slate blackboard and scratching their nails across it, and refusing to stop when asked.

The Peculiar Institution of Morality

Bernard Williams (1929–2003)

When Bernard Williams died in 2003, he was lauded in a *Guardian* obituary as "arguably the greatest British philosopher of his era." Perhaps his greatest contribution, though, was showing the *limits* of philosophy to answer many of life's most important questions, particularly what he saw as the central question of ethics: How should one live?

Williams, born in Essex, was a standout student of classics and philosophy at Balliol College, Oxford, where he received a rare "congratulatory" first-class honors degree in which his examiners asked no questions but simply stood and applauded. After flying Spitfires in the Royal Air Force for a year in Canada, Williams returned to Oxford to teach philosophy. Despite having no doctorate, Williams served in a series of prestigious academic posts, including provost of King's College, Cambridge, and White's Professor of Moral Philosophy at Oxford. He also taught for many years at UC Berkeley. In his numerous books and articles, Williams contributed to the revival of moral philosophy, became a leading critic of utilitarianism, and probed with great subtlety and complexity the limits of moral theory in helping us navigate the challenges of living a good and satisfying life.

In his most important book, *Ethics and the Limits of Philosophy* (1985), Williams denies the objectivity of ethics and criticizes what he calls the "peculiar institution" of morality as it is conceived in modern ethical theory (particularly Kantian-inspired moral theory). In that view, morality is a neat, tidy, inescapable, and all-encompassing system that overrides all nonethical considerations; is "pure" in the sense of being oblivious to "moral luck" or other sorts of empirical contingencies; and implies that there are no genuine moral dilemmas because moral duties can never conflict. Against this, Williams argues that the morality system, thus conceived, is too bare-boned and monolithic to guide our thinking about how to live. It imposes a simplistic, one-size-fits-all grid that blinds us to both the richness and the messiness of human life and value choice. Some critics complain that such a view is "antiphilosophical." Williams would say that it is an example of how philosophy cautions us to its own limits.

SEE ALSO The Revival of Virtue Ethics (1981), The Capability Approach (2000)

Bernard Williams in his rooms at King's College, Cambridge, in 1978.

Pragmatic Realism

Hilary Putnam (1926–2016)

For many decades, Hilary Putnam has been one of America's most prominent philosophers. In his early work, he was a staunch defender of "metaphysical realism," the view, roughly, that there is a real world that exists independently of how we conceive it. Beginning in the late 1970s, he began to back away from metaphysical realism and defend a kind of compromise view that combines elements of both realism and anti-realism. Originally he called this hybrid view "internal realism," but more recently he has preferred to call it "pragmatic realism." In his 1985 Carus Lectures (an annual series of the American Philosophical Association), later published in expanded form as *The Many Faces of Realism* (1987), Putnam offered a clear and highly readable defense of his "third way" between realism and relativism.

Putnam notes that the great appeal of realism is that it appears to fit with common sense. Realism seems to let us say, "Of course there are tables and chairs!" But Putnam argues that realism promises more than it can deliver. Our commonsense view is that tables are mostly solid matter. Yet science tells us that they are largely empty space, casting doubt on whether there *are* any tables as they are usually conceived. Putnam argues that realism is plagued by other problems as well, including puzzles about how determinate reference to mind-independent objects could be possible. At the opposite end of realism is what Putnam calls "Demon Relativism," which in extreme forms claims that the world is nothing but "texts," or that "truth is what your contemporaries will let you get away with," or other such wild and crazy views. Putnam's proposal is to split the difference. Relativists are right that we can only talk of "truth" in relation to a particular conceptual scheme. We cut the world up into objects when we apply one or another scheme of description. At the same time, realists are right in saying that there are tables and chairs and, more generally, that "facts are there to be discovered and not legislated by us." Thus, as Kant (d. 1804) said, what we call "the world" is empirically real, but it is also in a significant sense mind dependent.

SEE ALSO Protagoras and Relativism (c. 450 BCE), Functionalism (1960), The New Pragmatism (1979)

Do these table and chairs really exist as solid objects? Or are they an illusory collection of molecules and empty space?

Religious Pluralism

John Hick (1922–2012)

Many religious believers today are inclined to accept some form of religious pluralism—the view, roughly, that many religions are true or offer equally effective pathways to salvation. There are several different versions of religious pluralism, ranging from extreme pluralism, the view that all religions are equally true, to inclusive pluralism, the claim that all the great religions of the world provide authentic avenues for experiencing the divine and are more or less equally efficacious in producing salvific moral and spiritual transformation. The most prominent defender of religious pluralism is the distinguished British philosopher of religion John Hick. In his much-discussed 1989 book, *An Interpretation of Religion*, Hick defends a version of inclusive pluralism that owes much to Kant (d. 1804).

Hick believes that there is a divine Ultimate Reality (he calls it the "Real"), but that we can know practically nothing about it. Like Kant's noumenal reality, the Real is "ineffable"—beyond our human powers to describe or to conceptualize. Nevertheless, Hick argues, we can have authentic religious experiences of the Real. The problem is that all such experiences are filtered through different culturally shaped "lenses." Christians and Muslims, for example, experience God as a personal being, whereas Zen Buddhists and Hindu Advaita Vedantists experience it as an impersonal Absolute. Hick suggests that all religious doctrines and language should be seen as faltering human attempts to describe the indescribable. What is important, Hick says, is that all major religions are in touch with the same divine Ultimate Reality (and are "equally true" in that sense), and that all major religions seem to be equally effective in what Hick sees as the basic goal of religion: the "transformation of human existence from self-centeredness to Reality-centeredness."

Hick's view is attractive to many supporters of religious pluralism, but it also raises problems. Mainstream theists of course reject out of hand the notion that statements like "God loves us" and "God is holy" are only "metaphorically true." And is it even possible to *be* (say) a Christian—or to obtain the spiritual fruits of being a Christian—if you believe that statements of core Christian belief like "Jesus saves" or "Jesus loves us" are literally false?

SEE ALSO *Critique of Pure Reason* (1781), Soul-Making Theodicy (1966)

The spiral galaxy Messier 101, photographed by the Hubble telescope in 2006. In An Interpretation of Religion, *Hick explores the physical universe as the "ultimate unexplained reality."*

Philosophical Zombies

Daniel Dennett (b. 1942)

One of the liveliest, most interesting, and most widely read philosophers writing today is Daniel Dennett. As a philosopher, Dennett has done important work on free will, evolution, and the relation between science and religion, but his most notable contributions have been in the field of philosophy of mind. In his important 1991 book, *Consciousness Explained*, Dennett offers a materialistic theory of the mind that tries to break free of a host of traditional views that he believes have impeded a scientific understanding of consciousness. Among these obstructive views is that so-called "philosophical zombies" could exist.

Dennett was born in Boston and educated at Harvard and Oxford University. Since 1971, he has taught at Tufts University, where he codirects the Center for Cognitive Studies. He is the author of over a dozen books and more than four hundred scholarly articles. In *Consciousness Explained*, Dennett seeks to undermine a traditional picture of the mind that he labels the "Cartesian theater." In this scenario, the mind is like a small movie theater where a homunculus, or tiny person, sits in a kind of control room watching sensory information projected on a screen and makes decisions that determine both thoughts and bodily behavior. In opposition to this, Dennett defends a "multiple drafts" view of consciousness, which conceives thoughts on an information-processing model as the product of "parallel, multitrack processes of interpretation and elaboration of sensory inputs"—a view that fits better, he thinks, with contemporary neuroscience and a thoroughly materialistic view of the mind. In defending this view, Dennett weighs in on one of the more interesting thought experiments in contemporary philosophy: whether there could be creatures that are exactly like human beings in all physical respects but totally lack consciousness. These strange fictional creatures are known as "philosophical zombies," or "p-zombies" for short. Dennett claims that such beings are not truly conceivable once we take the effort to imagine specific behaviors in detail. Those who think they can conceive such creatures have not imagined thoroughly enough and "end up imagining something that violates their own definition," either by conceding physical differences or by allowing what amounts to states of consciousness. Happily, the great zombie debate still rages on today.

SEE ALSO The Ghost in the Machine (1949), Functionalism (1960), Mind-Brain Identity Theory (1968)

A contemporary illustration of a group of (non-philosophical) zombies in a field under a full moon.

The Capability Approach

Martha Nussbaum (b. 1947)

How should one measure human welfare and international development? The traditional approach has been to look at purely quantitative measures such as per capita gross domestic product. Yet if a nation's GDP goes up while growing numbers of its citizens struggle to get an education, find work, or be treated with dignity, is the nation really better off? An influential new theory of social justice, well-being, and human development is known as the "capability approach" or the "human development approach." Among its primary architects is the American philosopher and classicist Martha Nussbaum, one of America's best-known public intellectuals.

Born in New York City and raised in what she describes as an "East Coast WASP elite family" (she converted to Judaism in the early 1970s), Nussbaum received her PhD in philosophy from Harvard. Since 1994, Nussbaum has taught at the University of Chicago, where she is Ernst Freund Distinguished Service Professor of Law and Ethics, with joint appointments in the law school and the philosophy department. Her first major book, *The Fragility of Goodness: Luck and Ethics in Greek Tragedy and Philosophy* (1986), won wide acclaim throughout the humanities. A prolific writer, Nussbaum has published widely on topics such as global ethics, feminism, multiculturalism, emotions, civil liberties, and the value of the liberal arts. She is perhaps best known, however, for her work in developing and popularizing the capability approach, which she lays out most fully in *Women and Human Development: The Capabilities Approach* (2000) and *Creating Capabilities: The Human Development Approach* (2011).

First developed by the distinguished Indian philosopher and economist Amartya Sen (b. 1933), the capability approach is a broad theoretical framework for assessing human well-being and international development. The core tenet of the capability approach is that well-being should not be measured simply in terms of aggregate material resources or simple subjective criteria such as happiness, but rather by reference to multidimensional standards of human dignity and human flourishing that focus crucially on questions of what actual opportunities are available to people, of what they can really do and be. This is an approach that is increasingly gaining prominence in international development, scholarship, and policy making.

SEE ALSO *A Theory of Justice* (1971)

Martha Nussbaum at the University of Oviedo in Asturias, Spain, on October 24, 2012. She was there to receive the Prince of Asturias Award for Social Sciences.

The New Atheists

Richard Dawkins (b. 1941), **Sam Harris** (b. 1967), **Christopher Hitchens** (1949–2011), **Daniel Dennett** (b. 1942), **Victor J. Stenger** (1935–2014)

New Atheism is a contemporary antireligious, intellectual movement that erupted in the aftermath of the September 11, 2001, terrorist attacks in the United States. Its best-known defenders are Richard Dawkins, Sam Harris, Christopher Hitchens, Daniel Dennett, and Victor J. Stenger. While many critics claim that New Atheism often lacks the intellectual punching power of notable "old atheists," such as David Hume, John Stuart Mill, Bertrand Russell, and J. L. Mackie, it arguably has had a greater impact on public consciousness. Several books by the New Atheists, including Dawkins's *The God Delusion* (2006), were international best sellers.

As a movement, New Atheism is marked by a number of common themes. Generally, New Atheists reject the existence of the supernatural, are sharply critical of religion in all forms, see "faith" as an inherently irrational intellectual stance, are strongly pro-science, are committed to explaining religious belief in terms of biological evolution, and believe that objective, rationally defensible secular moral standards exist.

New Atheism provoked a number of critical responses from leading theologians and philosophers of religion, including Alister McGrath, Keith Ward, William Lane Craig, and John Haught. Common criticisms were that the New Atheists often attacked traditionalist versions of religion; exaggerated the harms of religion while ignoring the benefits; misunderstood modern understandings of "faith"; knew little of contemporary theology; and relied on a form of "scientism" (the view that science is the only reliable way of knowing) that is indefensible and ultimately self-refuting.

Given the wide readership of the New Atheists, it's clear that they've struck a nerve. Certainly one of the worldwide megatrends of the past century has been the rapid growth of secularism. Religious belief has declined sharply in Europe, China, Canada, Australia, Israel, and other nations. The United States has long bucked this trend, though recent polls show that the number of religiously nonaffiliated "nones" are steadily rising. Certainly philosophers have become an increasingly skeptical bunch in recent decades. A recent survey by the website PhilPapers found that 62 percent of philosophers are atheists. What this bodes for the future is a fascinating question.

SEE ALSO Hume's *Dialogues* (1779), "God Is Dead" (1882), Atheistic Existentialism (1946)

Richard Dawkins speaking about The God Delusion, *his 2006 book, at Barnes & Noble in Tribeca, New York City, on March 14, 2008.*

Cosmopolitanism

Kwame Anthony Appiah (b. 1954)

Like elephants and wolves, humans are social animals. We like to run in packs, and often our strongest bonds and allegiances are to relatively small groups of family, friends, or tribe. Cultivating strong ties and partialities to what sociologists call "in-group" associations can make for strong families, communities, and nations, and also provide individuals with a comforting sense of place and belonging. But as recent history demonstrates, it can also separate us into competing and mutually suspicious enclaves of "us" and "them." What's the right balance here in a globalized and increasingly interconnected world? One ancient but now increasingly popular approach is called "cosmopolitanism," and its best-known advocate is the London-born philosopher Kwame Anthony Appiah.

Appiah grew up in Ghana, the son of a white mother and a black father, both from distinguished political families. After receiving his doctorate from Cambridge University, Appiah taught at a number of leading American universities, including Harvard and Princeton. Recipient of the National Humanities Medal, he is currently a professor of philosophy and law at New York University.

In his 2006 book, *Cosmopolitanism: Ethics in a World of Strangers*, Appiah seeks to revive and refine the ancient Cynic and Stoic idea of being a *kosmopolitês* (citizen of the world). He argues that in a world in which strangers in distant lands can impact each other—for good or ill, in a myriad of ways—traditional views of ethics and politics must be rethought. We must, he claims, move beyond local ties and affiliations and recognize that in important respects all human beings are citizens of a single global community. Some cosmopolitans advocate radical solutions such as a rejection of patriotism or the establishment of a single world state. Appiah argues for a more moderate form of cosmopolitanism that centers on two central values: universal concern and respect for legitimate difference. In brief, he maintains, we need to recognize that we do have obligations to others—even strangers—in virtue of our shared humanity, and we must develop habits of coexistence, mutual respect, and genuine conversation across cultural boundaries.

SEE ALSO Cynicism (c. 400 BCE)

Kwame Anthony Appiah speaking at the John F. Kennedy School of Government at Harvard, on April 20, 2005.

The Triple Theory of Ethics

Derek Parfit (b. 1942)

Derek Parfit's sprawling two-volume work *On What Matters* (2011) has been hailed as the most important work in philosophical ethics since Henry Sidgwick's *The Methods of Ethics* in 1874. Certainly Parfit's book was one of the most eagerly awaited works of philosophy since John Rawls's *A Theory of Justice* (1971). Widely considered one of the world's greatest living philosophers, Parfit worked on *On What Matters* for well over a decade. Drafts of the book circulated on the Internet for years, conferences were held, and a book was published with critical reactions to Parfit's ideas two years before *On What Matters* was even in print.

On What Matters is not an easy book to summarize, not only because of its daunting length (more than 1,400 pages), but also because of the wide range of topics Parfit tackles. At its core the book is a defense of objective moral values against various forms of moral subjectivism and nihilism. He argues powerfully against the currently fashionable view that reason is purely concerned with means, not basic desires or goals. Rejecting all forms of religious ethics, Parfit examines at length what he considers the three most plausible ethical theories: consequentialism, Kantian ethics, and contractualism. Usually these are viewed as sharply contrasting theoretical frameworks. Parfit argues, on the contrary, that the most defensible versions of these theories converge on a relatively simple test of moral conduct. Each view, properly formulated, supports what he calls the "Triple Theory" of ethics: an act is morally wrong if and only if it is disallowed by some principle that (1) makes things go best, (2) is uniquely universally willable, and (3) cannot be reasonably rejected. Thus, he argues, there is far less disagreement in ethics than is often assumed. All along ethicists have been climbing the same mountain, though on different sides.

Whether or not Parfit is right about this surprising claim of ethical convergence, his densely argued and amazingly lucid book is bound to be widely discussed for many years to come.

SEE ALSO The Categorical Imperative (1785), *Reasons and Persons* (1984)

All Souls College, Oxford, where Parfit wrote On What Matters.

Notes and Further Reading

General Reading

Audi, Robert, ed. *The Cambridge Dictionary of Philosophy*. New York: Cambridge University Press, 1995.

Copleston, Frederick. *A History of Philosophy*. 9 vols. New York: Image, 1946–75.

Durant, Will. *The Story of Philosophy*. New York: Pocket Books, 1991. Originally published in 1926.

Edwards, Paul, ed. *Encyclopedia of Philosophy*. 8 vols. New York: Macmillan, 1967.

Internet Encyclopedia of Philosophy, www.iep.utm.edu.

Kenny, Anthony. *A New History of Western Philosophy*. Oxford, UK: Clarendon Press, 2010.

Lavine, T. Z. *From Socrates to Sartre*. New York: Bantam, 1985.

Magee, Bryan. *The Story of Philosophy*. London: DK, 1998.

Parkinson, G. H. R., and Stuart Shanker, eds. *Routledge History of Philosophy*. 10 vols. New York: Routledge, 1993–2003.

Russell, Bertrand. *A History of Western Philosophy*. New York: Simon & Schuster, 1945.

Soccio, Douglas J. *Archetypes of Wisdom: An Introduction to Philosophy*. 9th ed. Belmont, CA: Wadsworth, 2015.

Stanford Encyclopedia of Philosophy, plato.stanford.edu.

c. 1500 BCE, The Vedas

Radhakrishnan, Sarvepalli, and Charles A. Moore, eds. *A Sourcebook in Indian Philosophy*. Princeton, NJ: Princeton University Press, 1957.

c. 585 BCE, Birth of Western Philosophy

Guthrie, W. K. C. *A History of Greek Philosophy*. Vol. 1, *The Earlier Presocratics and the Pythagoreans*. Cambridge, UK: Cambridge University Press, 1962.

c. 550 BCE, The Dao

Chan, Alan. "Laoxi." *Stanford Encyclopedia of Philosophy*, http://plato.stanford.edu/entries/laozi/.

c. 540 BCE, Reincarnation

Barnes, Jonathan. *The Presocratic Philosophers*. Rev. ed. London: Routledge & Kegan Paul, 1983.

c. 540 BCE, Ahimsa

Webb, Mark Owen. "Jain Philosophy." *Internet Encyclopedia of Philosophy*, http://www.iep.utm.edu/jain/.

c. 530 BCE, Anthropomorphization

Robinson, John Mansley. *An Introduction to Early Greek Philosophy*. Boston: Houghton Mifflin, 1968.

c. 525 BCE, The Four Noble Truths

Hanh, Thich Nhat. *The Heart of the Buddha's Teaching*. New York: Broadway Books, 1999.

c. 525 BCE, No-Self (*Anatta*)

Siderits, Mark. "Buddha." *Stanford Encyclopedia of Philosophy*, http://plato.stanford.edu/entries/buddha/.

c. 500 BCE, Confucian Ethics

Huang, Chichung, trans. *The Analects of Confucius*. Oxford, UK: Oxford University Press, 1997.

c. 500 BCE, Reciprocity

Yutang, Lin, ed. and trans. *The Wisdom of Confucius*. New York: Modern Library, 1938.

c. 500 BCE, Change Is Constant

Graham, Daniel. "Heraclitus." *Stanford Encyclopedia of Philosophy*, http://plato.stanford.edu/entries/heraclitus/.

c. 500 BCE, The Book of Job

Habel, Norman. *The Book of Job*. Cambridge, UK: Cambridge University Press, 1975.

c. 470 BCE, Change Is Illusory

Graham, Daniel. *Explaining the Cosmos: The Ionian Tradition of Scientific Philosophy*. Princeton, NJ: Princeton University Press, 2006.

c. 460 BCE, Mind Organizes Nature

Patzia, Michael. "Anaxagoras." *Internet Encyclopedia of Philosophy*, http://www.iep.utm.edu/anaxagor/.

c. 460 BCE, The Paradoxes of Motion

Salmon, Wesley C., ed. *Zeno's Paradoxes*. Indianapolis, IN: Hackett, 2001.

c. 450 BCE, Survival of the Fittest

Inwood, Brad. *The Poem of Empedocles*. Rev. ed. Toronto: University of Toronto Press, 2001.

c. 450 BCE, Protagoras and Relativism

Poster, Carol. "Protagoras." *Internet Encyclopedia of Philosophy*, http://www.iep.utm.edu/protagor/.

c. 450 BCE, The Sophists

Kerferd, G. B., *The Sophistic Movement*. Cambridge, UK: Cambridge University Press, 1981.

c. 450 BCE, Ladder of Love

Waithe, Mary Ellen, ed. *A History of Women Philosophers*. Dordrecht, Netherlands: Klewer, 1987.

c. 430 BCE, Know Thyself

Guthrie, W. K. C. *Socrates*. Cambridge, UK: Cambridge University Press, 1969.

c. 420 BCE, Atoms and the Void

Bailey, Cyril. *The Greek Atomists and Epicurus*. New York: Russell and Russell, 1964.

c. 420 BCE, Universal Love

Loy, Hu-chieh. "Mozi." *Internet Encyclopedia of Philosophy*, http://www.iep.utm.edu/mozi/.

c. 400 BCE, Cynicism

Guthrie, W. K. C. *The Sophists*. Cambridge, UK: Cambridge University Press, 1969.

c. 400 BCE, Cyrenaic Hedonism
O'Keefe, Tim. "Aristippus." *Internet Encyclopedia of Philosophy*, http://www.iep.utm.edu/aristip/.

c. 400 BCE, The Bhagavad Gita
Radhakrishnan, Sarvepalli. *The Bhagavadgita*. New York: Harper & Row, 1973.

399 BCE, The Trial and Death of Socrates
Stone, I. F. *The Trial of Socrates*. New York: Doubleday, 1988.

c. 399 BCE, Socratic Dialogues
Vlastos, Gregory. *Socrates: Ironist and Moral Philosopher*. Ithaca, NY: Cornell University Press, 1991.

c. 386 BCE, Plato Founds the Academy
Guthrie, W. K. C. *A History of Greek Philosophy*. Vol. 4, *Plato: The Man and His Dialogues: Earlier Period*. Cambridge, UK: Cambridge University Press, 1975.

c. 380 BCE, The World of the Forms
Hare, R. M. *Plato*. Oxford, UK: Oxford University Press, 1982.

c. 380 BCE, Plato's *Republic*
Annas, Julia. *An Introduction to Plato's Republic*. New York: Oxford University Press, 1981.

c. 380 BCE, Mind-Body Dualism
Grube, G. M. A. *Plato's Thought*. 2nd ed. Indianapolis, IN: Hackett, 1980.

c. 367 BCE, Aristotle Enrolls in the Academy
Guthrie, W. K. C. *A History of Greek Philosophy*. Vol. 6, *Aristotle: An Encounter*. Cambridge, UK: Cambridge University Press, 1981.

334 BCE, Hellenization Begins
Algra, Keimpe, Jonathan Barnes, Jaap Mansfield, and Malcolm Schofield, eds. *The Cambridge History of Hellenistic Philosophy*. Cambridge, UK: Cambridge University Press, 1999.

c. 330 BCE, The Invention of Logic
Kneale, William, and Martha Kneale. *The Development of Logic*. Oxford, UK: Clarendon Press, 1962.

c. 330 BCE, The Earth-Centered Universe
Ross, W. D., *Aristotle*. Cleveland, OH: Meridian Books, 1959.

c. 330 BCE, Matter and Form
Lloyd, G. E. R. *Aristotle: The Growth and Structure of His Thought*. Cambridge, UK: Cambridge University Press, 1968.

c. 330 BCE, The Four Causes
Adler, Mortimer J. *Aristotle for Everybody*. New York: Bantam, 1978.

c. 330 BCE, *Nicomachean Ethics*
Urmson, J. O. *Aristotle's Ethics*. Oxford, UK: Blackwell, 1988.

c. 320 BCE, Maybe Life Is a Dream
Hansen, Chad. "Zhuangzi." *Stanford Encyclopedia of Philosophy*, http://plato.stanford.edu/entries/zhuangzi/.

c. 300 BCE, Ecclesiastes
Kusher, Harold. *When All You've Ever Wanted Isn't Enough: The Search for a Life That Matters*. New York: Fireside, 1986.

c. 300 BCE, Epicureanism
Rist, John M. *Epicurus: An Introduction*. Cambridge, UK: Cambridge University Press, 1972.

c. 300 BCE, Stoicism
Sandbach, F. H. *The Stoics*. 2nd ed. Indianapolis, IN: Hackett, 1994.

c. 300 BCE, Innate Goodness
Yu-Lan, Fung, *A History of Chinese Philosophy*. Translated by Derk Bodde. Princeton, NJ: Princeton University Press, 1953.

155 BCE, Carneades on Justice
Burnyeat, Myles. *The Skeptical Tradition*. Berkeley, CA: University of California Press, 1983.

c. 55 BCE, *On the Nature of Things*
Sedley, David. *Lucretius and the Transformation of Greek Wisdom*. Cambridge, UK: Cambridge University Press, 1998.

51 BCE, Universal Moral Law
Nicgorski, Walter, ed. *Cicero's Practical Philosophy*. Notre Dame, IN: University of Notre Dame Press, 2012.

c. 30 CE, The Christian Era Begins
Dodd, C. H. *The Founder of Christianity*. New York: Macmillan, 1970.

c. 65, Buddhism Comes to China
Ch'en, Kenneth. *Buddhism in China: A Historical Survey*. Princeton, NJ: Princeton University Press, 1972.

65, The Death of Seneca
Morris, Tom. *The Stoic Art of Living*. Chicago: Open Court, 2004.

c. 125, Epictetian Stoicism
Rist, J. M. *Stoic Philosophy*. Cambridge, UK: Cambridge University Press, 1969.

c. 150, Platonism and Christianity
Copleston, Frederick. *A History of Medieval Philosophy*. Vol. 2, *Medieval Philosophy: Augustine to Duns Scotus*. New York: Harper & Row, 1972.

180, The Philosopher-King
Hadot, Pierre. *The Inner Citadel: The Meditations of Marcus Aurelius*. Translated by Michael Chase. Cambridge, MA: Harvard University Press, 1998.

c. 200, *Outlines of Pyrrhonism*
Annas, Julia, and Jonathan Barnes. *The Modes of Skepticism*. Cambridge, UK: Cambridge University Press, 1985.

c. 250, Neoplatonism
O'Meara, Dominic J. *Plotinus: An Introduction to the Enneads*. Oxford, UK: Clarendon Press, 1993.

c. 285, The Problem of Universals
Emillson, Eyjólfur. "Porphyry." *Stanford Encyclopedia of Philosophy*, http://plato.stanford.edu/entries/porphyry/.

386, Augustine's Conversion
Brown, Peter. *Augustine of Hippo: A Biography*. Berkeley: University of California Press, 2000.

415, Death of Hypatia
Deakin, Michael A. B. *Hypatia of Alexandria: Martyr and Mathematician*. Amherst, NY: Prometheus Books, 2007.

426, *The City of God*
Stump, Eleonore, and Norman Kretzmann, eds. *The Cambridge Companion to Augustine*. Cambridge, UK: Cambridge University Press, 2001.

c. 460, The Last Great Greek Philosopher
Helmig, Christoph, and Carlos Steel. "Proclus." *Stanford Encyclopedia of Philosophy*, http://plato.stanford.edu/entries/proclus/.

476, The Dark Ages Begin
Durant, Will. *The Age of Faith*. New York: Simon & Schuster, 1950.

c. 500, The Way of Negation
Rorem, Paul, trans. *Pseudo-Dionysius*. Oxford, UK: Oxford University Press, 1993.

c. 520, Origins of Chan/Zen Buddhism
Watts, Alan. *The Way of Zen*. New York: Pantheon, 1957.

524, *The Consolations of Philosophy*
Marenbon, John. *Boethius*. Oxford, UK: Oxford University Press, 2003.

529, Justinian Closes the Academy
Blumenthal, Henry J. "529 and Its Sequel: What Happened to the Academy?" *Byzantion* 48 (1978): 369–85.

c. 630, The Rise and Spread of Islam
Brown, Jonathan A. C. *Muhammad: A Very Short Introduction*. Oxford, UK: Oxford University Press, 2011.

c. 700, Huineng and the *Platform Sutra*
Thompson, John M. "Huineng." *Internet Encyclopedia of Philosophy*, http://www.iep.utm.edu/huineng/.

c. 810, Monism
Radhakrishnan, Sarvepalli. *Indian Philosophy*. Vol. 1. London: George Allen & Unwin, 1923.

c. 840, Islamic Philosophy Begins
Adamson, Peter. *Al-Kindī*. Oxford, UK: Oxford University Press, 2006.
Netton, Ian Richard. *Al-Fārābī and His School*. Surrey, UK: Curzon Press, 1999.

c. 865, Eriugena's Christian Neoplatonism
Carabine, Dierdre. *John Scottus Eriugena*. Oxford, UK: Oxford University Press, 2000.

c. 1015, Ibn Sīnā's Islamic Aristotelianism
Goodman, Lenn E. *Avicenna*. London: Routledge, 1992.

1078, The Ontological Argument
Davies, Brian, and Brian Leftow, eds. *The Cambridge Companion to Anselm*. New York: Cambridge University Press, 2005.

c. 1093, *The Incoherence of the Philosophers*
Griffel, Frank. *Al-Ghazālī's Philosophical Theology*. Oxford, UK: Oxford University Press, 2009.

1121, The Birth of Scholasticism
Marenbon, John. *The Philosophy of Peter Abelard*. Cambridge, UK: Cambridge University Press, 1999.

c. 1130, Aristotelian Revival in the West
Copleston, Frederick, *A History of Philosophy*. Vol. 2, *Medieval Philosophy: Augustine to Duns Scotus*. Westminster, MD: Newman Press, 1950.

c. 1135, Qualified Dualism
Bartley, Christopher. *The Theology of Ramanuja*. London: RoutledgeCurzon, 2002.

c. 1180, Revival of Confucianism
Thompson, Kirill O. "Zhu Xi." *Internet Encyclopedia of Philosophy*, http://www.iep.utm.edu/zhu-xi/.

c. 1185, The Commentator
Leaman, Oliver. *Averroes and His Philosophy*. Surrey, UK: Curzon Press, 1988.

c. 1190, *The Guide for the Perplexed*
Leaman, Oliver. *Moses Maimonides*. New York: Routledge, 1990.

c. 1220, Philosophers Join Academia
Rashdall, Hastings. *The Universities of Europe in the Middle Ages*. 1895. Reprint, New York: Cambridge University Press, 2010.

c. 1250, The Universal Doctor
Führer, Markus. "Albert the Great." *Stanford Encyclopedia of Philosophy*, http://plato.stanford.edu/entries/albert-great/.

1259, A Franciscan Approach to Philosophy
Cullen, Christopher M. *Bonaventure*. Oxford, UK: Oxford University Press, 2006.

c. 1265, The Great Medieval Synthesis
Davies, Brian. *The Thought of Thomas Aquinas*. Oxford, UK: Oxford University Press, 1993.
Stump, Eleonore. *Aquinas*. New York: Routledge, 2005.

c. 1265, The Five Ways
Kenny, Anthony. *The Five Ways*. New York: Routledge, 2008.

c. 1270, Natural Law
Murphy, Mark. "The Natural Law Tradition in Ethics." *Stanford Encyclopedia of Philosophy*, http://plato.stanford.edu/entries/natural-law-ethics/.

c. 1300, Attack on the Medieval Synthesis
Williams, Thomas, ed. *The Cambridge Companion to Duns Scotus*. New York: Cambridge University Press, 1993.

c. 1300, Mystical Theology
McGinn, Bernard. *The Mystical Thought of Meister Eckhart*. New York: Crossroad Pub. Co., 2003.

c. 1320, Ockham's Razor
Spade, Paul Vincent. "William of Ockham." *Stanford Encyclopedia of Philosophy*, http://plato.stanford.edu/entries/ockham/.

c. 1320, Conceptualism
Adams, Marilyn McCord. *William Ockham*. 2 vols. Notre Dame, IN: University of Notre Dame Press, 1990.

1324, *The Defender of Peace*
Garnet, George. *Marsilius of Padua and 'the Truth of History.'* Oxford, UK: Oxford University Press, 2006.

c. 1350, The Renaissance Begins
Durant, Will. *The Renaissance*. New York: Simon & Schuster, 1953.

1440, The Synthesis of Opposites
Hopkins, Jasper. *A Concise Introduction to the Philosophy of Nicholas of Cusa*. 2nd ed. Minneapolis: University of Minnesota Press, 1980.

1468, The Recovery of Platonism
Celenza, Christopher S. "Marsilio Ficino." *Stanford Encyclopedia of Philosophy*, http://plato.stanford.edu/entries/ficino/.

1516, *Utopia*
Baker-Smith, Dominic. *More's Utopia*. Toronto: University of Toronto Press, 2000.

1517, The Reformation Begins
Durant, Will. *The Reformation*. New York: Simon & Schuster, 1957.

c. 1520, The Humanist Ideal
Nauert, Charles. "Desiderius Erasmus." *Stanford Encyclopedia of Philosophy*, http://plato.stanford.edu/entries/erasmus/.

c. 1525, The Silver Age of Scholasticism
Copleston, Frederick. *A History of Philosophy*. Vol. 3, *Late Medieval and Renaissance Philosophy: The Revival of Platonism to Suárez*. Westminster, MD: Newman Press, 1953.

1532, *The Prince*
Pocock, J. G.A. *The Machiavellian Moment: Florentine Political Thought and the Atlantic Republican Tradition*. Princeton, NJ: Princeton University Press, 1975.

1539, The Rights of Native Peoples
Kretzmann, Norman, Anthony Kenny, and Jan Pinborg, eds. *The Cambridge History of Later Medieval Philosophy*. Cambridge, UK: Cambridge University Press, 1982.

1543, The Birth of Modern Science
Butterfield, Herbert. *The Origins of Modern Science*. Rev. ed. New York: Free Press, 1997.

1580, Revival of Classical Skepticism
Popkin, Richard H. *The History of Skepticism from Erasmus to Spinoza*. Leiden, Netherlands: Gorcum van Assen, 1979.

1605, *The Advancement of Learning*
Bowen, Catherine Drinker. *Francis Bacon: The Temper of a Man*. 2nd ed. New York: Fordham University Press, 1993.

1620, The Enlightenment Begins
Durant, Will, and Ariel Durant. *The Age of Reason Begins*. New York: Simon & Schuster, 1961.

1625, *On the Law of War and Peace*
Tuck, Richard. *The Rights of War and Peace: Political Thought and the International Order from Grotius to Kant*. Oxford, UK: Oxford University Press, 1999.

1637, The Father of Modern Philosophy
Kenny, Anthony. *Descartes: A Study of His Philosophy*. New York: Random House, 1968.

1641, *Meditations on First Philosophy*
Cottingham, John, ed. *The Cambridge Companion to Descartes*. New York: Cambridge University Press, 1992.

1651, *Leviathan*
Sorell, Tom, ed. *The Cambridge Companion to Hobbes*. Cambridge, UK: Cambridge University Press, 1996.

1651, Free Will and Determinism Are Compatible
McKenna, Michael, and D. Justin Coates. "Compatibilism." *Stanford Encyclopedia of Philosophy*, http://plato.stanford.edu/entries/compatibilism/.

1670, Pascal's Wager
Morris, Thomas V. *Making Sense of It All: Pascal and the Meaning of Life*. Grand Rapids, MI: Wm. B. Eerdmans, 1992.

1674, Occasionalism
Jordan, Jason. "Occasionalism." *The Internet Encyclopedia of Philosophy*, http://www.iep.utm.edu/occasion/.

1677, *Ethics*
Bennett, Jonathan. *A Study of Spinoza's Ethics*. Indianapolis, IN: Hackett, 1984.

1689, Human Rights
Simmons, A. John. *The Lockean Theory of Rights*. Princeton, NJ: Princeton University Press, 1992.

1689, Religious Liberty
Tuckness, Alex. "Locke's Political Philosophy." *Stanford Encyclopedia of Philosophy*, http://plato.stanford.edu/entries/locke-political/.

1689, Empiricism
Ayers, Michael. *Locke: Epistemology and Ontology*. London: Routledge, 1991.

c. 1700, Preestablished Harmony
Jolley, Nicholas, ed. *The Cambridge Companion to Leibniz*. New York: Cambridge University Press, 1994.

1713, To Be Is to Be Perceived
Pitcher, George. *Berkeley*. London: Routledge, 1999. First published 1977 by Routledge & Kegan Paul.

1725, The Moral Sense
Kauppinen, Antti. "Moral Sentimentalism." *Stanford Encyclopedia of Philosophy*, http://plato.stanford.edu/entries/moral-sentimentalism/.

1730, Deism
Stephen, Leslie. *History of English Thought in the Eighteenth Century*. 2 vols. 1876. Reprint, London: Forgotten Books, 2012.

1736, *The Analogy of Religion*
Penelhum, Terence. *Butler*. London: Routledge, 2008. First published 1985 by Routledge & Kegan Paul.

1739, *A Treatise of Human Nature*
Stroud, Barry. *Hume*. New York: Routledge & Kegan Paul, 1977.

1739, The Problem of Induction
Salmon, Wesley C., *The Foundations of Scientific Inference*. Pittsburgh, PA: University of Pittsburgh Press, 1967.

1748, An Attack on Miracles
Norton, David Fate, and Jacqueline Taylor, eds. *The Cambridge Companion to Hume*. New York: Cambridge University Press, 1993.

1748, *The Spirit of the Laws*
Pangle, Thomas L. *Montesquieu's Philosophy of Liberalism: A Commentary on* The Spirit of the Laws. Chicago: University of Chicago Press, 1973.

1751, Morality Is Rooted in Feeling
Norton, David Fate. *David Hume: Common-Sense Moralist, Sceptical Metaphysician*. Princeton, NJ: Princeton University Press, 1982.

1754, America's First Major Philosopher
Flower, Elizabeth, and Murray G. Murphey. *A History of Philosophy in America*. Vol. 1. Indianapolis, IN: Hackett, 1977.

1759, *Candide*
Durant, Will, and Ariel Durant. *The Age of Voltaire*. New York: Simon & Schuster, 1965.

c. 1760, The Birth of Romanticism
Berlin, Isaiah. *The Roots of Romanticism*. Princeton, NJ: Princeton University Press, 1999.

1762, *The Social Contract*
Bertram, Christopher. *Rousseau and* The Social Contract. London: Routledge, 2004.

1762, *Emile* and Natural Education
Rorty, Amélie Oksenberg, ed. *Philosophers on Education*. New York: Routledge, 1998.

1764, The Philosophy of Common Sense
Lehrer, Keith. *Thomas Reid*. London: Routledge, 2008.

1770, A Godless, Mechanistic Universe
Copleston, Frederick. *A History of Philosophy*. Vol. 6, *Modern Philosophy: The French Enlightenment to Kant*. Westminster, MD: Newman Press, 1960.

1779, Hume's *Dialogues*
Gaskin, J. C. A. *Hume's Philosophy of Religion*. London: Macmillan, 1987.

1781, *Critique of Pure Reason*
Guyer, Paul, ed. *The Cambridge Companion to Kant*. New York: Cambridge University Press, 1992.

1785, The Categorical Imperative
Aune, Bruce. *Kant's Theory of Morals*. Princeton, NJ: Princeton University Press, 1979.

1787, *The Federalist*
Wills, Garry. *Explaining America:* The Federalist. New York: Doubleday, 1981.

1789, Utilitarianism
Harrison, Ross. *Bentham*. London: Routledge, 1999.

1790, *Critique of Judgment*
Copleston, Frederick. *A History of Philosophy*. Vol. 6, *Modern Philosophy: The French Enlightenment to Kant*. Westminster, MD: Newman Press, 1960.

1790, Forefather of Conservatism
Harris, Ian. "Edmund Burke." *Stanford Encyclopedia of Philosophy*, http://plato.stanford.edu/entries/burke/.

1792, *A Vindication of the Rights of Woman*
Tomaselli, Sylvana. "Mary Wollstonecraft." *Stanford Encyclopedia of Philosophy*, http://plato.stanford.edu/entries/wollstonecraft/.

c. 1795, The Beginnings of German Idealism
Copleston, Frederick. *A History of Philosophy*. Vol. 7, *Modern Philosophy: Fichte to Nietzsche*. Westminster, MD: Newman Press, 1963.

1807, *The Phenomenology of Spirit*
Copleston, Frederick. *A History of Philosophy*. Vol. 7, *Modern Philosophy: Fichte to Nietzsche*. Westminster, MD: Newman Press, 1963.

1819, The Philosophy of Pessimism
Magee, Bryan. *The Philosophy of Schopenhauer*. Rev. ed. Oxford, UK: Clarendon Press, 1997.

1821, The Real Is the Rational
Singer, Peter. *Hegel: A Very Short Introduction*. New York: Oxford University Press, 2001.

1830, Positivism
Bourdeau, Michel. "Auguste Comte." *Stanford Encyclopedia of Philosophy*, http://plato.stanford.edu/entries/comte/.

1832, Law and Morality Are Separate
Bix, Brian. "John Austin." *Stanford Encyclopedia of Philosophy*, http://plato. stanford.edu/entries/austin-john/.

1836, American Transcendentalism
Gura, Philip F. *American Transcendentalism: A History*. New York: Hill & Wang, 2008.

1841, Idealism Is Turned Upside Down
Küng, Hans. *Does God Exist? An Answer for Today*. Translated by Edward Quinn. New York: Doubleday, 1980.

1843, Existentialism
Hannay, Alistair. *Kierkegaard*. New York: Routledge, 1999.

1843, *A System of Logic*
Skorupski, John, ed. *The Cambridge Companion to Mill*. Cambridge, UK: Cambridge University Press, 1998.

1846, Truth Is Subjectivity
Barrett, William. *Irrational Man: A Study in Existential Philosophy*. Garden City, NY: Doubleday, 1962.

1848, *The Communist Manifesto*
Berlin, Isaiah. *Karl Marx: His Life and Environment*. 4th ed. Oxford, UK: Oxford University Press, 1978.

1854, *Walden*
Richardson, Robert D., Jr. *Henry Thoreau: A Life of the Mind*. Berkeley: University of California Press, 1986.

1859, *On Liberty*
Ten, C. L. *Mill's* On Liberty. Oxford, UK: Clarendon Press, 1980.

1859, Darwin's *Origin of Species*
Ruse, Michael. *Taking Darwin Seriously: A Naturalistic Approach to Philosophy*. Oxford, UK: Oxford University Press, 1986.

1862, Social Darwinism
Hofstadter, Richard. *Social Darwinism in American Thought*. Boston: Beacon Press, 1990.

1863, Refined Utilitarianism
Skorupski, John, ed. *The Cambridge Companion to John Stuart Mill*. Cambridge, UK: Cambridge University Press, 1998.

c. 1865, The Rise of British Idealism
Mander, W. J. *British Idealism: A History*. Oxford, UK: Oxford University Press, 2011.

1867, *Capital*
Singer, Peter. *Marx: A Very Short Introduction*. New York: Oxford University Press, 2001.

1869, *The Subjection of Women*
Morales, Maria H., ed. *Mill's* The Subjection of Women: *Critical Essays*. Lanham, MD: Rowman & Littlefied, 2005.

1874, *The Methods of Ethics*
Schneewind, J. B. *Sidgwick's Ethics and Victorian Moral Philosophy*. Oxford, UK: Clarendon Press, 1977.

1874, Intentionality
Huemer, Wolfgang. "Franz Brentano." *Stanford Encyclopedia of Philosophy*, http://plato.stanford.edu/entries/brentano/.

1878, Origins of Pragmatism
Hookway, Christopher. *Peirce*. London: Routledge, 1985.

1879, The New Logic
Munitz, Milton Karl. *Contemporary Analytic Philosophy*. New York: Macmillan, 1981.

1882, "God Is Dead"
Kaufmann, Walter. *Nietzsche: Philosopher, Psychologist, Antichrist*. 3rd ed. New York: Random House, 1968.

1882, Perspectivism
Hollingdale, R. J. *Nietzsche: The Man and His Philosophy*. Rev. ed. Cambridge, UK: Cambridge University Press, 1999.

1887, The Revaluation of Values
Leiter, Brian. "Nietzsche's Moral and Political Philosophy." *Stanford Encyclopedia of Philosophy*, http://plato.stanford.edu/entries/nietzsche-moral-political/.

1890, *The Principles of Psychology*
Myers, Gerald E. *William James: His Life and Thought*. New Haven, CT: Yale University Press, 1986.

1897, "The Will to Believe"
Gale, Richard M. *The Philosophy of William James: An Introduction*. Cambridge, UK: Cambridge University Press, 2005.

1900, Phenomenology
Smith, Barry, and David Woodruff Smith, eds. *The Cambridge Companion to Husserl*. Cambridge, UK: Cambridge University Press, 1995.

1901, Environmental Preservationism
Worster, Donald. *A Passion for Nature: The Life of John Muir*. New York: Oxford University Press, 2008.

1902, *The Varieties of Religious Experience*
Gale, Richard M. *The Philosophy of William James: An Introduction*. Cambridge, UK: Cambridge University Press, 2005.

1903, Ethical Intuitionism
Baldwin, Tom. "George Edward Moore." *Stanford Encyclopedia of Philosophy*, http://plato.stanford.edu/entries/moore/.

1903, The Analytic-Continental Split
Soames, Scott. *Philosophical Analysis in the Twentieth Century*. Vol. 1, *The Dawn of Analysis*. Princeton, NJ: Princeton University Press, 2003.

1905, The Theory of Definite Descriptions
Munitz, Milton K. *Contemporary Analytic Philosophy*. New York: Macmillan, 1981.

1907, *Pragmatism*
Flower, Elizabeth, and Murray G. Murphey. *A History of American Philosophy*. Vol. 2. Indianapolis, IN: Hackett, 1977.

1907, Vitalism
Lacey, A. R. *Bergson*. New York: Routledge, 1989.

1910, *Principia Mathematica*
Irvine, Andrew David. "Principia Mathematica." *Stanford Encyclopedia of Philosophy*, http://plato.stanford.edu/entries/principia-mathematica/.

1912, *The Problems of Philosophy*
Ayer, A. J. *Bertrand Russell*. Chicago: University of Chicago Press, 1972.

1916, Progressive Education
Dykhuizen, George. *The Life and Mind of John Dewey*. Carbondale: Southern Illinois University Press, 1973.

1918, Logical Atomism
Munitz, Milton K. *Contemporary Analytic Philosophy*. New York: Macmillan, 1981.

1920, Contemplation vs. Enjoyment
Thomas, Emily A. E. "Samuel Alexander." *Stanford Encyclopedia of Philosophy*, http://plato.stanford.edu/entries/alexander/.

c. 1920, Neo-Thomism
Cantor, Norman F. *Inventing the Middle Ages*. New York: William Morrow, 1991.

1921, The Picture Theory of Language
Kenny, Anthony. *Wittgenstein*. Oxford, UK: Blackwell, 2006.

1923, *I and Thou*
Schilpp, Paul Arthur, and Maurice S. Friedman, eds. *The Philosophy of Martin Buber*. LaSalle, IL: Open Court, 1967.

1925, Instrumentalism
Tiles, J. E. *Dewey*. London: Routledge, 1988.

1927, *Being and Time*
Dreyfus, H. L. *Being-in-the-World: A Commentary of Heidegger's* Being and Time. Cambridge, MA: MIT Press, 1991.

1927, Religion as Wish Fulfillment
Küng, Hans. *Freud and the Problem of God*. Rev. ed. Translated by Edward Quinn. New Haven, CT: Yale University Press, 1990.

1929, Process Philosophy
Sherburne, Donald. *A Key to Whitehead's Process and Reality*. Chicago: University of Chicago Press, 1981.

1929, *An Idealist View of Life*
Schilpp, Paul Arthur, ed. *The Philosophy of Sarvepalli Radhakrishnan*. LaSalle, IL: Open Court, 1952.

1930, Deontological Intuitionism
Feldman, Fred. *Introductory Ethics*. Englewood Cliffs, NJ: Prentice Hall, 1978.

1932, Ordinary Language Philosophy
Urmson, J. O. *Philosophical Analysis: Its Development between the Two World Wars*. Oxford, UK: Clarendon Press, 1956.

1934, The Rejection of Metaphysics
Uebel, Thomas. "Vienna Circle." *Stanford Encyclopedia of Philosophy*, http://plato.stanford.edu/entries/vienna-circle/.

1936, Logical Positivism
Foster, John. *Ayer*. London: Routledge, 2009.

1938, *Nausea*
Lavine, T. Z. *From Socrates to Sartre: The Philosophic Quest*. New York: Bantam, 1985.

1942, Existential Defiance
Aronson, Ronald. "Albert Camus." *Stanford Encyclopedia of Philosophy*, http://plato.stanford.edu/entries/camus/.

1943, *Being and Nothingness*
Caws, Peter. *Sartre*. London: Routledge, 1984.
Warnock, Mary. *The Philosophy of Sartre*. London: Hutchinson, 1965.

1944, Emotivism
Urmson, James Opie. *The Emotive Theory of Ethics*. London: Hutchinson University Library, 1968.

1945, *The Phenomenology of Perception*
Copleston, Frederick. *A History of Philosophy*. Vol. 9, *Modern Philosophy: From the French Revolution to Sartre, Camus, and Levi-Strauss*. New York: Image Books, 1994.

1946, Atheistic Existentialism
Howells, Christina, ed. *The Cambridge Companion to Sartre*. Cambridge, UK: Cambridge University Press, 1992.

1949, The Ghost in the Machine
Urmson, James Opie. "Gilbert Ryle." In *Encyclopedia of Philosophy*, vol. 7, edited by Paul Edwards. New York: Macmillan, Free Press, and London: Collier Macmillan, 1967.

1949, *The Second Sex*
Mussett, Shannon. "Simone de Beauvoir." *Internet Encyclopedia of Philosophy*, http://www.iep.utm.edu/beauvoir/.

1949, Ecocentrism
DesJardins, Joseph R. *Environmental Ethics*. 5th ed. Boston: Wadsworth, 2013.

1951, "Two Dogmas of Empiricism"
Hahn, Lewis Edwin, and Paul Arthur Schilpp, eds. *The Philosophy of W. V. Quine*. 2nd ed. Chicago: Open Court, 1999.

1952, Prescriptivism
Warnock, G. J. *Contemporary Moral Philosophy*. London: Palgrave Macmillan, 1967.

1953, *Philosophical Investigations*
Grayling, A. C. *Wittgenstein: A Very Short Introduction*. Oxford, UK: Oxford University Press, 2001.

1953, Impossibility of a Private Language

Fogelin, Robert J. *Wittgenstein.* 2nd ed. New York: Routledge, 1995.

1954, The New Riddle of Induction

Vickers, John. "The Problem of Induction." *Stanford Encyclopedia of Philosophy,* http://plato.stanford.edu/entries/induction-problem/.

1957, *Intention*

Teichmann, Roger. *The Philosophy of Elizabeth Anscombe.* Oxford, UK: Oxford University Press, 2008.

1959, Falsifiability in Science

O'Hear, Anthony. *Popper.* London: Routledge, 1999.

1959, Descriptive Metaphysics

Hahn, Lewis Edwin, ed. *The Philosophy of P. F. Strawson.* Chicago: Open Court, 1998.

1960, The Indeterminacy of Translation

Hylton, Peter. *Quine.* New York: Routledge, 2007.

1960, Hermeneutics

Hahn, Lewis Edwin, ed. *The Philosophy of Hans-Georg Gadamer.* Chicago: Open Court, 1996.

1960, Functionalism

Rachels, James, and Stuart Rachels. *Problems from Philosophy.* 3rd ed. New York: McGraw-Hill, 2011.

1961, Legal Positivism

Lacey, Nicola. *A Life of H.L.A. Hart.* Oxford, UK: Oxford University Press, 2004.

1962, Scientific Revolutions

Nickles, Thomas, ed. *Thomas Kuhn.* Cambridge, UK: University of Cambridge Press, 2003.

1962, Oxford Ordinary Language Philosophy

Warnock, Geoffrey. *J. L. Austin.* London: Routledge, 2009.

1963, The Gettier Problem

Feldman, Richard. *Epistemology.* Upper Saddle River, NJ: Prentice Hall, 2003.

1966, Soul-Making Theodicy

Tooley, Michael. "The Problem of Evil." *Stanford Encyclopedia of Philosophy,* http://plato.stanford.edu/entries/evil/.

1967, Deconstruction

Norris, Christopher. *Derrida.* London: Routledge, 1987.

c. 1968, The (Re)birth of Applied Ethics

Singer, Peter. *Practical Ethics.* 3rd ed. Cambridge, UK: Cambridge University Press, 2011.

1968, Mind-Brain Identity Theory

Kim, Jaegwon. *Philosophy of Mind.* 3rd ed. Boulder, CO: Westview Press, 2011.

1970, Anomalous Monism

Hahn, Lewis Edwin, ed. *The Philosophy of Donald Davidson.* Chicago: Open Court, 1999.

1971, *A Theory of Justice*

Daniels, Norman, ed. *Reading Rawls.* Stanford, CA: Stanford University Press, 1989.

c. 1971, The Rise of Informal Logic

Groarke, Leo. "Informal Logic." *Stanford Encyclopedia of Philosophy,* http://plato.stanford.edu/entries/logic-informal/.

1974, Political Libertarianism

Paul, Jeffrey, ed. *Reading Nozick.* Totowa, NJ: Rowman & Littlefield, 1981.

1974, "What Is It Like to Be a Bat?"

Kim, Jaegwon. *Philosophy of Mind.* 3rd ed. Boulder, CO: Westview Press, 2011.

1974, Essentialism

Tomberlin, James E., and Peter van Inwagen, eds. *Alvin Plantinga.* Dordrecht, Netherlands: D. Reidel Publishing Co., 1985.

1975, *Animal Liberation*

Sunstein, Cass R., and Martha C. Nussbaum, eds. *Animal Rights: Current Debates and New Directions.* New York: Oxford University Press, 2004.

1975, Power/Knowledge

Gutting, Gary, ed. *The Cambridge Companion to Foucault.* 2nd ed. New York: Cambridge University Press, 2005.

c. 1976, Emergence of Feminist Philosophy

Stone, Alison. *An Introduction to Feminist Philosophy.* Cambridge, UK: Polity Press, 2007.

1977, Moral Anti-Realism

Joyce, Richard. "Moral Anti-Realism." *Stanford Encyclopedia of Philosophy,* http://plato.stanford.edu/entries/moral-anti-realism/.

1977, *Taking Rights Seriously*

Guest, Stephen. *Ronald Dworkin.* 3rd ed. Palo Alto, CA: Stanford University Press, 2012.

1979, The New Pragmatism

Brandom, Robert, ed. *Rorty and His Critics.* London: Blackwell, 2001.

1979, Postmodernism

Woodward, Ashley. "Jean-François Lyotard." *Internet Encyclopedia of Philosophy,* http://www.iep.utm.edu/lyotard/.

1979, Reliabilism

Goldman, Alvin. "Reliabilism." *Stanford Encyclopedia of Philosophy,* http://plato.stanford.edu/entries/reliabilism/.

1980, The Chinese Room

Cole, David. "The Chinese Room Argument." *Stanford Encyclopedia of Philosophy,* http://plato.stanford.edu/entries/chinese-room/.

1980, The Causal Theory of Reference

Devitt, Michael, and Kim Sterelny. *Language and Reality.* 2nd ed. Cambridge, MA: MIT Press, 1999.

1981, The Revival of Virtue Ethics

Hursthouse, Rosalind. *On Virtue Ethics.* Oxford, UK: Oxford University Press, 1999.

1981, Critical Theory

White, Stephen K., ed. *The Cambridge Companion to Habermas.* Cambridge, UK: Cambridge University Press, 1995.

1982, *In a Different Voice*

Sander-Staudt, Maureen. "Care Ethics." *Internet Encyclopedia of Philosophy,* http://www.iep.utm.edu/care-eth/.

1984, Revival of Christian Philosophy

Sennett, James F., ed. *The Analytic Theist: An Alvin Plantinga Reader.* Grand Rapids, MI: Eerdmans, 1998.

1984, *Reasons and Persons*

Dancy, Jonathan, ed. *Reading Parfit.* Malden, MA: Blackwell, 1997.

1984, *The Moral Limits of the Criminal Law*

Stanton-Ife, John. "The Limits of Law." *Stanford Encyclopedia of Philosophy,* http://plato.stanford.edu/entries/law-limits/.

1985, The Peculiar Institution of Morality

Chappell, Sophie Grace. "Bernard Williams." *Stanford Encyclopedia of Philosophy,* http://plato.stanford.edu/entries/williams-bernard/.

1987, Pragmatic Realism

Auxier, Randall, Douglas Anderson, and Lewis Edwin Hahn, eds. *The Philosophy of Hilary Putnam.* Chicago: Open Court, 2015.

1989, Religious Pluralism

Quinn, Philip L., and Kevin Meeker, eds. *The Challenge of Religious Diversity.* New York: Oxford University Press, 1999.

1991, Philosophical Zombies

Searle, John R. *The Mystery of Consciousness.* New York: New York Review of Books, 1997.

2000, The Capability Approach

Robeyns, Ingrid. "The Capability Approach." *Stanford Encyclopedia of Philosophy,* http://plato.stanford.edu/entries/capability-approach/.

2004, The New Atheists

Haught, John F. *God and the New Atheism.* Louisville, KY: Westminster John Knox Press, 2008.

2006, Cosmopolitanism

Kleingeld, Pauline, and Eric Brown. "Cosmopolitanism." *Stanford Encyclopedia of Philosophy,* http://plato.stanford.edu/entries/cosmopolitanism/.

2011, The Triple Theory of Ethics

Schroeder, Mark. Review of *On What Matters,* Volumes 1 and 2, by Derek Parfit. *Notre Dame Philosophical Reviews,* https://ndpr.nd.edu/news/25393-on-what-matters-volumes-1-and-2/.

Image Credits

Index